Taxation

Incorporating the Finance Act 2012

31st edition 2012

Taxation

Incorporating the Finance Act 2012

Alan Combs BA, MSc, FCCA
Stephanie Dixon LLB, LLM, DipLP, ACA, CTA
Peter Rowes BSc(Econ), FCA, ATII

FISCAL
PUBLICATIONS

Taxation: incorporating the 2012 Finance Act – 31st Edition 2012/2013

British Library Cataloguing-in-Publication Data
A catalogue record for this book is available from the British Library

Lecturer supplement and other materials are available from the Rowes 2012 website – see http://www.fiscalpublications.com/rowes/2012

ISBN 978-1906201180

Thirty first edition 2012

Cover design by FD Design Ltd
Printed in Great Britain by Antony Rowe Ltd., Chippenham, Wiltshire

Typesetting and production by

 P. K. McBride, Southampton

Contents

Acknowledgements

The authors would like to express thanks to the following for giving permission to reproduce past examination questions and forms:

Association of Chartered Certified Accountants (ACCA)
Chartered Institute of Management Accountants (CIMA)
Chartered Institute of Taxation (CIOT)
Controller of Her Majesty's Stationery Office

Many of the questions and answers in the 31st edition are from a bank of materials compiled by Jill Webb of Leeds Metropolitan University and Dora Hancock of Birmingham City University. The use of these questions and answers is gratefully acknowledged. Richard Andrews of the University of Hull shared authorship of the 25th to 28th editions, and the authors gratefully acknowledge his contribution.

Preface

Aims of the book

1.   The main aim of this book is to provide a thorough basic knowledge of UK taxation, covering Income Tax, Corporation Tax, Taxation of Chargeable Gains, Inheritance Tax, and Value Added Tax.

It has been written for students of the following:

Association of Chartered Certified Accountants
Paper F6 (UK) Taxation

Certified Accounting Technicians
Paper 9 Preparing Taxation Computations

Association of Accounting Technicians
Unit 18 Preparing Business Taxation Computations
Unit 19 Preparing Personal Taxation Computations

Association of Taxation Technicians
All papers (introductory text)

Association of International Accountants
Professional 2 Paper 16 Taxation and Tax Planning

Universities and colleges
Accounting and Business Studies Degrees – Taxation Modules

Approach

2. a)   This book should provide the student with:

i) A knowledge of the basic relevant statutory law

ii) A knowledge of some of the case law developed to interpret statutory law.

It should enable the student to apply these legal principles to practical problems and prepare the necessary computations, and to understand the importance of tax planning.

b)   Each of the areas of taxation is introduced by a general principles chapter which outlines the main features of each tax. Subsequent chapters develop the principles in detail with examples.

c)   Illustrative examples form an important feature of this text. At the end of each chapter and each section (except the introductory text) there are questions with answers for student self-testing. Also provided are further questions, the answers to which are contained in a separate supplement which can be obtained direct from the publishers by lecturers recommending the manual as a course text.

3. Students should be aware the terminology being used in taxation examinations of professional bodies is changing. As a result what was previously called a balance sheet may be a statement of financial position, with fixed assets called non current assets; a profit and loss account may be called an income statement; stock, debtors and creditors may be inventory, receivables and payables.

This edition incorporates the provisions of the Finance Act 2012 in so far as they relate to the year 2012/13.

Alan Combs, Stephanie Dixon, Peter Rowes, 2012.

Abbreviations and statutes

Abbreviations

All.ER	All England Law Reports	ITA	Income Tax Act 2007
BSI	Building society interest	ITEPA	Income tax (Earnings & Pensions) Act 2003
CAA	Capital Allowances Act 2001		
CFC	Controlled foreign company	ITTOIA	Income Tax (Trading and Other Income) Act 2005
CGT	Capital gains tax		
CIHC	Close Investment Holding Company	ORI	Official rate of interest
		PAYE	Pay as you earn
CRC	Commissioners for Revenue and Customs	PRT	Petroleum revenue tax
		RPI	Retail prices index
CT	Corporation tax	Sch.	Schedule
CTA2009	Corporation Tax Act 2009	STC	Simon's Tax cases
CTA2010	Corporation Tax Act 2010	STI	Simon's Tax Intelligence
CTAP	Corporation tax accounting period	TA 1988	Income and Corporation Taxes Act 1988
DTR	Double taxation relief	TIOPA	Taxation (International and Other Provisions) Act 2010
E U	European Union		
GAAP	Generally Accepted Accounting Practice	TC	Tax Cases
		TCGA	Taxation of Chargeable Gains Act 1992
FA 2012	Finance Act 2012		
HMRC	HM Revenue and Customs	TMA	Taxes Management Act 1970
IAS	International Accounting Standards		
		VAT	Value added tax
IHT	Inheritance tax	VATA	Value Added Tax Act 1994

Statutes

Income Tax	Income Tax Act 2007
Income Tax	Income Tax (Trading and Other Income) Act 2005
Income Tax	Income Tax (Earnings & Pensions) Act 2003
Income Tax	Finance Act 2012
Corporation Tax	Corporation Tax Act 2009, Corporation Tax Act 2010, Taxation (International and Other Provisions) Act 2010
Corporation Tax	Finance Act 2012
Capital Gains Tax	Taxation of Chargeable Gains Act 1992
Inheritance Tax	Inheritance Tax Act 1984
Value Added Tax	Value Added Tax Act 1994
Capital Allowances	Capital Allowances Act 2001

Summary of main changes 2012/13

Part II. Income tax

1.	Personal reliefs	2012/13 £	2011/12 £
	a) Personal allowance	8,105	7,475
	Abatement of allowance where income exceeds	100,000	100,000
	Blind person's allowance	2,100	1,980
	Allowances: Aged 65–74		
	Personal allowance	10,500	9,940
	Abatement of relief where income exceeds	25,400	24,000
	Allowances: Aged 75+		
	Personal allowance	10,660	10,090
	Married couple's allowance	* 7,705	* 7,265
	Minimum married couple's allowance	* 2,960	* 2,800
	Abatement of relief where income exceeds	25,400	24,000

b) The allowances marked with an asterisk (*) allowed at the 10% rate are given as a deduction in computing the tax liability.

2.	Income tax rates	2012/13	2011/12
	Starting rate - savings	10%	10%
	- where savings income comprises taxable income up to	£2,710	£2,560
	Remaining rates are unchanged i.e.		
	Basic rate		
	- savings income	20%	20%
	- non-savings income	20%	20%
	- dividends	10%	10%
	Higher rate – savings and non-savings	40%	40%
	- dividends	32.5%	32.5%
	Additional rate – savings and non-savings	50%	50%
	- dividends	42.5%	42.5%

3. Taxable bands

Taxable income	Band	2012/13 Rate	Tax payable on band
£	£	%	£
0 – 34,370	34,370	20	6,874
34,371 – 150,000	115,630	40	46,252
150,001+		50	

Taxable income	Band	2011/12 Rate	Tax payable on band
£	£	%	£
0 – 35,000	35,000	20	7,000
35,001 – 150,000	115,000	40	46,000
150,001+		50	

4. Class 4 National Insurance

	2012/13	2011/12
Taxable band (£)	7,605-42,475	7,225 – 42,475
Rate of tax	9%	9%
Taxable band (£)	above 42,475	above 42,475
Rate of tax	2%	2%

5. Seed Enterprise Investment Scheme (SEIS)

A new scheme will give tax relief to individual investors who subscribe for equity shares in a qualifying SEIS company and have a stake of less than 30% in the company. The individual investor limit for SEIS is £100,000 per year. SEIS investment will offer income tax relief of 50%. No capital gains tax is payable on gains on the disposal of SEIS shares held for more than three years.

6. Enterprise Investment Scheme

The enterprise investment scheme annual investment limit for individuals is increased to £1 million from 6 April 2012.

7. Company car benefit

Car benefit is based on a pecentage of the list price of the car when new, graduated according to CO_2 emissions. The percentage charge is from 10% to 35% of the list price. For 2012/13 the lowest, 10%, benefit is only available for cars with CO_2 emissions up to 99 grams per km (formerly 120g/km). Cars with emissions of 100g and above incur an additional 1% benefit for 5g emissions. Thus for emissions of 100-014g the benefit is 11%, for 105-109g the benefit is 12%, and so on. See Chapter 7, section 16 for the full table and a shorter formula. The maximum annual benefit is still 35% of the list price, including a 3% surcharge for diesel. Cars which cannot produce CO_2 emissions have a zero percentage and thus no benefit.

8. Car fuel benefit

	2012/13	2011/12
Car fuel petrol/diesel	CO_2 emissions % x £20,200	CO_2 emissions % x £18,800

9. Company van benefit   £3,000 (unchanged).

10. Company van fuel benefit   £550 (increased from £500 in 2011/12).

11. Authorised mileage rates

The statutory tax- and NIC-free approved mileage rates for mileage done in an employee's own car are unchanged at April 2012:

	2012/13	2011/12
Car and Vans		
First 10,000 miles	45p per mile	45p per mile
Over 10,000 miles	25p per mile	25p per mile
Motorcycles	24p per mile	24p per mile
Bicycles	20p per mile	20p per mile
Additional passenger	5p per mile	5p per mile

12. Class 1 National Insurance Thresholds – non-contracted out

	2012/13	2011/12
Weekly pay	£	£
Upper earnings limit	817	817
Upper accruals limit	770	770
Earnings threshold (employee)	146	139
Earnings threshold (employer)	144	136
Lower earnings limit	107	102

The rates of Class I NI are unchanged from 2011/12. However the option for transferring 1.6% of a worker's "main band" NIC payments into a contracted-out money purchase pension scheme (COMP) is abolished from 6 April 2012. Savers in COMP schemes are thus, without exception, contracted in to the State Second Pension from 6 April 2012, with no NIC rebate going to their COMP pension provider.

The Government has also announced, as part of reforms to State pensions, that the possibility of contracting out of the State Second Pension will also cease for approved salary-related schemes (COSR schemes) - but not until circa 2015/16.

13. Official rate of interest

At 6 April 2012   4%

14. Capital allowances from 6 April 2012 (1 April 2012 for companies)

a) Annual investment allowance £25,000 per year (2011/12 £100,000).

b) Plant and Machinery main pool expenditure writing down allowance - 18% per year (2011/12 - 20%);

c) Plant and Machinery special rate expenditure writing down allowance 8% per year (2011/12 - 10%);

15. Pensions

A lifetime limit for the value of pension savings will be reduced to £1.5 million from 2012/13 (£1.8 million 2011/12).

16. Individual Savings Accounts ISAs

a) The annual ISA allowance for 2012/13 is increased to £11,280 (2011/12 £10,680), with a limit of £5,640 (2011/12 £5,340) in the cash ISA element.

b) The annual Junior ISA allowance, for children not currently holding a Child Trust Fund, is £3,600.

c) Individuals aged 16 or 17 may take out a cash ISA (but not a shares ISA) in 2012/13, up to the cash ISA limit of £5,640 (2011/12 £5,340).

Part III. Corporation tax

1. Rates

	FY 2012 y/e 31.3.2013	FY 2011 y/e 31.3.2012
Full rate	24%	26%
Small profits rate	20%	20%
Marginal profits band	£300,000 - £1,500,000	

2. Research and Development Tax Credit

SME rate will increase from 200% to 225% from April 2012.

3. Capital allowances

Legislation will be introduced to provide 100% First Year Allowance for companies investing in plant and machinery between 1 April 2012 and 31 March 2017 for use primarily in designated areas within enterprise zones.

Part IV. Capital gains tax

1. Annual exempt amount

The personal annual exemption is £10,600 for 2012/13 (unchanged from 2011/12).

Part V. Inheritance tax

Rates

For 2012/13, the IHT rates are unchanged, but a new death relief is noted below. For chargeable transfers:

On or after 6th April 2012

£	%	
0 - 325,000	0	
325,001 -	40	(lifetime rate 20%)

For deaths on or after 6 April 2012, a lower rate of Inheritance Tax of 36% can be claimed on the rest of the chargeable estate, if 10% or more of the deceased person's net assets was left to charity.

Part VI. Value added tax

1. **Registration**

    Registration levels applicable from 1 April 2012.

	£
Taxable turnover in previous 12 months	77,000
Taxable turnover in next 30 days	77,000

2. **Deregistration**

    The annual limit for deregistration is £75,000 from 1 April 2012.

3. **VAT fuel rates 2012/13**

    Scale charges for supply of private use fuel by a VAT-registered business to its proprietors or employees are calculated on the basis of CO_2 emissions. New rates are applicable from 1 May 2012.

2012/13 CO_2 emissions	1 Month period VAT-incl. scale charge	1 Month period VAT due per car	3 Month period VAT-incl. scale charge	3 Month period VAT due per car
	£	£	£	£
120g/km or less	55	9.17	166	27.67
increasing in bands of 5g/km to				
225g/km or more	194	32.33	583	97.17

2011/12 CO_2 emissions	1 Month period VAT-incl. scale charge	1 Month period VAT due per car	3 Month period VAT-incl. scale charge	3 Month period VAT due per car
	£	£	£	£
120g/km or less	52	8.67	157	26.17
increasing in bands of 5g/km to				
225g/km or more	183	33.50	551	91.83

    See Chapter 36, section 16 for the full 2012/13 table of fuel charges.

Part I

Introduction

1 Principles of taxation

Definition of tax

1.   Taxes are contributions levied on persons, property or business, for the support of national or local government[1].

Reasons for tax

2.   Organised societies are said to exist because they provide greater benefits to members than living individually or in small groups[2]. Highly developed societies who use money for exchange fund the benefits by public expenditure. Some of the oldest records in history are of wealth used as a basis for raising the money for public expenditure by taxation.

3.   Tax is justified by the benefits it provides. In a society that tolerates free speech public spending is subject to intense scrutiny. One reason for this may be that if benefits are not being provided to the members of society, the reason for collecting tax is lost. Adverse comments, and civil disobedience, can also result where taxation is seen as unfair.

A balanced budget

4.   The amount of money raised by taxation and the amount of public expenditure will not necessarily equal each other in a particular year. A 'budget deficit' arises in a year where public expenditure is more than the amount raised by taxation. The government can fund the extra expenditure by inviting people to lend it money, in the form of government securities or investments in National Savings. Years of 'budget surplus' where taxation exceeds public expenditure would give the opportunity for government borrowings to be repaid.

Early in the history of modern Western economics 'classical' economists, such as Adam Smith, formed a view that market forces would produce the most efficient allocation of resources of labour and financial capital[3]. If there was unemployment, for example, market forces would cause wages to fall, until lower wages encouraged employers to take on more workers. It was believed the wages received by the newly employed workers would stimulate demand for more goods and services, and a virtuous circle of growth would continue until equilibrium was reached when everyone was employed. The belief in efficient markets implied it was best for governments to intervene as little as possible in the economic choices made by people and businesses. This 'fiscal neutrality' would include running a 'balanced budget' where necessary public expenditure was financed by an equal amount of taxation.

'Keynesian' economists formed the view that equilibrium in the economy could be reached at points below full employment[4]. In times when market demand was low it would be beneficial for the government to use reflationary policies to stimulate demand, and start the cycle of growth. These policies might include[5]:

- increasing government expenditure;

- cutting direct or indirect taxation to encourage spending;

- cutting interest rates to discourage saving and encourage spending;

- allowing money supply growth.

The first two techniques are 'fiscal' policies which directly affect public expenditure and tax revenue. Applying these policies could cause a budget deficit. Keynesian economics accepts a budget deficit in years when the market economy is in recession, providing it is matched by a budget surplus in years of high growth in the market economy. The deflationary policies available to achieve budget surpluses and restrain demand would be the opposite of the reflationary policies above. Budgets should still be balanced over the long term. Applying Keynesian economics to the government's budget would involve using changes in public expenditure and taxation to affect demand for goods and services[6], and so counteract the effects of the 'boom and bust' cycles in the market economy: 'counter-cyclical demand management policies'.

The UK Treasury predicted[7] total government receipts for 2011/2012 of £589bn and total managed expenditure of £710bn. This is a budget deficit of £121bn, with expenditure 20% more than receipts. In 2010/2011 the government planned for a budget deficit with an excess of 27% expenditure compared to receipts, and 35% in 2009/10.

For each of the 6 preceding years from 2003/04 onwards the budget deficit of excess of expenditure compared to receipts varied between 6.1% and 7.5%.

Desirable characteristics of taxation

5.   Adam Smith[8] proposed 'Canons of Taxation' which listed desirable features for a system of taxation. These may be restated in contemporary terms as equity, certainty, convenience and efficiency.

Equity means taxes should be fair. Horizontal equity would require justice and equality of treatment, so taxpayers having similar circumstances would be treated in a similar way by the tax authorities and have similar tax liabilities. Vertical equity would mean the burden of tax fell fairly across taxpayers with different circumstances. This requires a subjective value judgement about what is fair. Adam Smith believed fairness would link tax liabilities with the taxpayer's ability to pay, so taxpayers with high income and wealth would pay more tax than those with low income and little wealth. Another possible approach to fairness would be linking the amount of a taxpayer's liability with the value of benefits from public expenditure they receive.

Certainty means taxpayers should be able to establish how taxes will result from their economic decisions such as whether to work in return for income, save or spend their wealth, or deal in assets. This would mean the tax law and regulations would need to be clearly written, and not applied retrospectively.

Convenience would minimise the taxpayer's costs in complying with tax laws and regulations. A tax requiring only simple calculations by a taxpayer would satisfy the 'Canons of taxation' better than a tax requiring complex calculations based on records kept over many years.

Efficiency has two elements:

Administrative efficiency means that the costs of collecting tax should be as low as possible in comparison with the revenue raised.

Economic efficiency means that tax does not distort taxpayers' economic decisions, such as whether to work or take leisure, and whether to save or spend their income and wealth.

In working through this book it will be seen there are limits to which taxes in the UK achieve the ideals set out as the Canons of Taxation. Indeed some features of UK taxes are intended to influence taxpayers and have distorting effects on economic decisions. There is a current theme of encouraging spending on assets which help minimise environmental damage, and discouraging spending on vehicles with high levels of carbon dioxide emissions. Taxes with an intentional distorting effect are called 'corrective'.

Tax bases

6.   What to tax? The most basic form of tax is a poll tax, where every taxpayer has an equal liability. Such a tax is widely regarded as inequitable, because it is not related to ability to pay, or to benefits consumed. A form of poll tax was used for local taxation in the UK during the 1980s and 1990s. The tax was administratively inefficient because of widespread non-payment through lack of public acceptance and the impossibility of collecting tax from people without the ability to pay. The 'community charge' caused riots and the prime minister of the time was removed from office.

Major tax bases in modern economies are income, expenditure and wealth. Taxing income or expenditure recognises transactions are taking place, and so it has some relationship to ability to pay. Wealth may not be in the form of cash and so does not necessarily show an ability to pay. In the UK wealth taxes at the national level are linked to wealth being transferred by sale, gift or inheritance. The existence of a transaction increases the likelihood of cash being available to pay tax.

Direct and indirect taxes

7.   Direct taxes are related to a taxpayer's circumstances, for example income or wealth. The taxpayer in principle is personally responsible for making payments of tax directly to the tax authorities. However, for some types of income, including bank and building society interest and earnings from employment, an estimated (not the final) amount of income tax is deducted by the savings institution or employer before the taxpayer receives the income. The institution or employer pays this tax over to HM Revenue and Customs, and notifies the taxpayer. This is still direct tax, as the tax liability (which may require an adjustment at the end of the tax year) is directly related to the taxpayer's personal circumstances.

8.   Indirect taxes are charged on a taxpayer, but with the effect that the cost of the tax is suffered by another person or organisation. For example, retailers are responsible for paying Value Added Tax (VAT) to HM Revenue and Customs, but the tax is collected by the retailer from customers, who actually bear all the cost.

Incidence of tax

9.   The 'incidence' of tax may simply be described as the person or organisation obliged to pay the tax. Indirect taxes have a different 'formal incidence', the taxpayer legally responsible for making tax payments to the tax authorities, and 'effective incidence', the person or organisation whose wealth is actually reduced by the tax. Direct taxes are more likely to have the same formal and effective incidence.

Hypothecated taxes

10.   Hypothecated taxes are taxes collected to fund a particular service. Although in the UK hypothecation is rare, some government charges can be seen as akin to hypothecated taxes. For example, money collected from the UK television licence is used to pay for the television programmes of the BBC. In the same way, money collected from National Insurance contributions was originally matched against spending on State pensions and benefits, but Treasury accounts no longer reconcile income and outgoings. Thus UK National Insurance is now in effect a direct tax, although class 1, 2 and 3 NI contributions still earn entitlement to State pension, and certain other social security benefits (see chapter 17).

Excise duties

11.   Excise duties are indirect expenditure taxes on goods such as alcohol, tobacco and fuel oil. They are unit taxes based on the quantity of the product. This distinguishes them from indirect taxes based on value, such as value added tax and insurance premium tax.

Withholding taxes

12.   Withholding taxes are deducted from certain types of income before a taxpayer receives it. Withholding taxes are in general used as a safeguard against certain types of income escaping tax. In states with developed self-assessment tax systems, they survive mainly as deductions imposed on certain payments of "passive income" (i.e. interest, dividends, royalties and rents) which might otherwise escape tax, especially if paid to persons not resident in the state where the income source is located.

Another form of withholding tax is the UK income tax at basic rate deducted by banks and building societies paying interest to individuals on deposit and savings accounts. Also, currently UK individuals must deduct 20% tax at source from patent royalty payments made, and account for it to HMRC on behalf of the royalty recipient.   This is a classic domestic (as opposed to cross-border) withholding tax. The person who deducted the tax pays it over to the tax authorities on behalf of the patent owner, who can later claim it back if they do not in fact owe any tax (e.g. because they had tax losses to set off).

Double taxation

13. If a taxpayer receives interest, royalty, rent or dividend income from foreign individuals, firms or companies, withholding tax may have been deducted in the foreign country. If domestic tax is also charged in the taxpayer's home country the same income has been taxed twice. Double taxation treaties between countries will arrange for some relief to be available against double taxation. There are various possibilities for the practical workings of double taxation relief, any of which may be specified in a tax treaty:

- income taxed in one country may be exempted from tax in another;

- withholding tax deducted, or other direct tax paid, in a foreign country may be credited against the taxpayer's tax liability in the home country;

- the proportion of the 'underlying tax' on a foreign company's profits that relates to dividend income distributed to the home country may be deducted from the taxpayer's liability in their home country;

- the net income, after any foreign tax, may be taken as the amount of income to be taxed in the home country.

The UK has an extensive network of double tax treaties. If a UK taxpayer has income from a source country with which no treaty exists, unilateral (non-treaty) double tax relief may be claimed by the "credit method" (the second type above), but only up to a maximum of the UK tax due on the same income.

Imputation system of Corporation Tax

14. A problem of double taxation arises when a company distributes dividends to shareholders. The company pays corporation tax on its profits and gains. When dividends are received by a shareholder the profits being distributed may well be taxed a second time, as investment income. In the UK this is avoided for companies by excluding all dividends received from their total of taxable income. Individuals are taxed on dividend income but at a lower rate, and can claim a tax credit on the dividends received, as though some income tax has already been paid. This credit is for the tax the individual is 'imputed' to have paid when the company paid corporation tax on its profits. However, the imputation tax credit only covers the personal income tax liability on dividends at basic rate (10%). As UK companies in Financial Year 2012 pay tax on profits at between 20% and 24%, a higher rate income tax payer's claim to tax credits at 10% is only partial imputation, and some element of double taxation remains. For a non-taxpayer, the imputed income tax credit on dividend income is not refundable.

Evasion and avoidance

15. Tax evasion involves breaking the law to reduce tax paid. Examples could include failing to record income, falsifying accounting records, or failing to make any returns of income, gains, or taxes collected. Tax avoidance involves a taxpayer arranging their affairs so as to minimise the tax they legally have to pay. It has been an established principle for many years that a taxpayer should not be expected to pay more tax than they legally must. Indeed some features of the tax system depend on a taxpayer making choices in order to reduce tax liabilities, for example encouraging taxpayers to buy a car with low levels of exhaust emissions. However, a view has started to be put forward from the Treasury and HM Revenue and Customs that tax avoidance can be either 'acceptable' or 'unacceptable'. Tax avoidance schemes which are considered unacceptable tend to be complex transactions which do not reflect the economic substance of the taxpayer's activities, but have a reduction in tax liability as a leading motive, or the main motive, for the transactions undertaken. In recent years the UK and other governments have legislated against identified tax avoidance schemes, so that even where the arrangements are legally effective, they will not be effective in saving tax.

In the 2012 Budget speech the Chancellor indicated that a "general anti-abuse rule" would be proposed as part of future legislation to counter tax avoidance. Consultation on its wording is now in progress. The proposal follows a 2011 Report by Graham Aaronson QC, commissioned by the Treasury, which can be accessed at: http://www.hm-treasury.gov.uk/d/gaar_final_report_111111.pdf .

Tax gap

16. The 'tax gap' is a term used to describe the shortage of actual tax collected, compared to the total tax which should be collected if there was no non-payment through tax evasion, fraud and error. It is a necessarily hypothetical figure. The main focus of concern in recent Government reports tends to be on whether it is reducing due to efficiency measures, rather than on proving how much it is.

'Stealth taxes'

17. Increases in taxation which are not the result of explicit changes in rates, allowances or methods of calculating tax, have come to be called 'stealth taxes' by the media.

As prices inflate the practice until recent years had been for the allowances for income which could be earned tax-free, and the bands of income taxed at the various rates of income tax, to rise in line with general price inflation. This meant income tax remained at a similar proportion of most people's income, provided the inflation in their wages was at a similar level to general price inflation.

Some prices have increased at a much greater rate of inflation than general prices. This can unexpectedly increase the tax revenue generated by a transaction. In the UK increased tax revenue has been generated for value added tax (VAT) from increases in the cost of fuel, and for stamp duty land tax and inheritance tax from the increases in house prices. Until recently, the government would face a problem in reducing tax on transactions experiencing rapid inflation, as a reduction in tax could cause even more severe inflation in the prices of the goods. Recessionary price falls allowed the UK government the opportunity of temporarily increasing exemptions from stamp duty land tax.

Some UK tax limits have not been linked to inflation and the result is that over the years their real value has diminished. Greater tax liabilities are incurred from benefits in kind received by employees earning more than £8,500 a year, than on benefits received by their 'lower paid' colleagues. This limit has remained unchanged over many years, to a point where all full-time employees earning the minimum wage for 18-year-olds are subject to the rules for those who were once called 'higher-paid employees' (a term changed in 2005 to 'P11D employees').

Timing of tax changes may have the effect of increasing tax revenues generated for a year. For the Financial Year 2007 the rate of corporation tax paid by small companies was increased from 19% to 20%. The rate of corporation tax for large companies was reduced from 30% to 28%, but not until the Financial Year 2008.

18. Recently (in the 2011 and 2012 Finance Acts), the income tax personal allowance has been increased by more than the rate of inflation, to help people with low incomes. However, to prevent this increase benefiting higher rate taxpayers, there was a fall in the top limit of the basic rate band, so that the overall income level at which higher rate tax is charged stayed roughly the same.

Questions without answers

1. What 'corrective' taxes, if any, might you introduce in the UK at present?

2. Discuss the extent to which taxes on income create disincentive effects.

3. What are the advantages of an indirect tax such as VAT compared with an income tax?

References

1   Sykes, J.B. ed., *Concise Oxford Dictionary of Current English*, Oxford University Press, 1976.
2   Hobbes, Thomas (1651), *Leviathan*, Penguin, Harmondsworth, 1968.
3   http://www.bized.co.uk/virtual/economy/library/theory/classical
4   Keynes, John Maynard, (1936), *General Theory of Employment Interest and Money*, Prometheus Books, Amherst, New York, 1997.
5   http://www.bized.co.uk/virtual/economy/library/theory/keynesian
6   Sheehan, Brendan, *Understanding Keynes' General Theory*, Palgrave Macmillan, Basingstoke, 2009.
7   http://budget.treasury.gov.uk
8   Smith, Adam, (1776), *The Wealth of Nations*, Penguin, Harmondsworth, 1999.

Part II

Income Tax

2 General principles

Introduction

1.   Income tax is a direct tax. Tax on some types of income is paid directly by the taxpayer to HM Revenue and Customs. For other types of income, including bank and building society interest and earnings from employment, the savings institution or employer deducts income tax before the taxpayer receives the income. The institution or employer then pays the tax over to HMRC. However, this tax payment is only an estimate. The taxpayer is still responsible for settling the final position with HMRC, if the tax already paid is not the final liability on the income.

In this chapter the main features of the income tax system are outlined, all of which are developed in detail in later chapters. It begins with some basic expressions. A summary of taxable income, its classification and basis of assessment is then provided. The remainder of the chapter deals with savings income, and non-taxable income. A summary of tax rates for tax year 2012/13 is given at the end of the chapter, and in the full reference tax tables at the end of the book.

Under the UK Tax Law Rewrite Project (which lasted from 1998 to 2011), the previous technical language of UK income tax, which dated from the nineteenth century, was rewritten in 'plain English'. Income tax law is now contained in the Income Tax (Employment and Pensions) Act 2003 (ITEPA), the Income Tax (Trading and Other Income) Act 2005 (ITTOIA) and the Income Tax Act 2007 (ITA), as amended by later Finance Acts.

Basic expressions

2.   **Tax Year 2012/13**

This runs from the 6th April 2012 to the 5th April 2013. The Income Tax Act 2007 uses the term 'Tax Year' but the period from 6 to 5 April is still referred to elsewhere in law as the 'fiscal year'. Personal Self-assessment Tax Returns are submitted for complete tax years.

Tax rates and the annual Finance Act Rates of income tax for a tax year are determined annually in the Finance Act. It is a constitutional principle in the UK that income tax is an annual tax, requiring a new approval by Parliament for each tax year. Currently, the legislation continuing the existing tax and setting out any changes is published as a Finance Bill in March or April, and then is debated in Parliament, before being enacted by the end of July. The Provisional Collection of Taxes Act 1968 (PCTA) allows temporary Parliamentary resolutions to be passed to permit HM Revenue and Customs to act on the assumption that the Finance Bill for a tax year will pass into law but was effective only where the Act was passed by 5 August. The effective duration of the PCTA 1968 was extended to 5 October by Finance Act 2011. However, at time of writing, the authors expect Finance Act 2012 to be law by the end of July 2012.

Taxable persons Income tax is charged on the income of individuals and trusts resident in the UK. Non-residents deriving any income from a UK source are also in principle liable to UK income tax, though this liability may be varied or removed by the terms of a Double Tax Treaty.

Taxable income Income on which income tax is payable is known as taxable income. This consists of the sum of income from all taxable sources, as defined, less deductions for allowable payments, less personal allowances and reliefs (other than allowances and reliefs given 'in terms of tax', that is as a deduction from tax liability rather than from income).

Order of taxing income The ITA 2007 requires income to be classified into three types: non-savings income (also called 'other income'), savings income and dividend income.

Allowable deductions and personal reliefs and allowances reduce total income in the following order: non-savings income first, then savings income, finally dividend income. This order is prescribed because dividend income is treated as the highest part of total income and savings income as the next highest part (section 16, ITA 2007).

The order in which the various sources of income are combined and the reliefs and allowances against total income are deducted is shown in the following Summary of taxable income for 2012/13:

Summary of Taxable Income 2012/13

		£
Non-savings income:		
Income from employment	– salaries, wages, pensions etc	–
	– benefits in kind treated as earnings	–
Social security income	– State retirement pensions etc.	–
Income from trade profits	– business income less capital allowances	–
Income from property		–
Foreign non–savings income		–
Miscellaneous income not savings or dividends in nature (e.g. patent income received by someone who was not the original inventor)		–
Savings income:	– UK bank/building society interest	–
	– interest on Government stocks	–
	– other UK savings income, eg gains on life assurance policies taxed as income	–
Foreign savings income		–
Dividend income:	– dividends from UK companies	–
	– dividends from foreign companies	–

Total income   —
LESS:
Allowable payments   —
Loss Reliefs against total income   —

Net income   —
LESS:
Personal allowances   —

Taxable income   —

Note: Under ITA 2007, allowable payments, loss reliefs and personal allowances reduce total income in the following order: non-savings income, then savings income, then dividend income.

Tax calculation on taxable income

(see section 4 or the introductory Summary for tax rate bands in 2012/13)   £

Starting rate – tax at 10% (applies to savings income only)   —

Basic rate – at 20% on non-savings and savings income (10% on dividends)   —

Higher rate – at 40% on non-savings and savings income (32.5% on dividends)   —

Additional – at 50% on non-savings and savings income (42.5% on dividends)

Subtotal   - tax on taxable income at full rates   —
LESS: Allowances and reliefs given in terms of tax:

     Age-related Married Couple's Allowance – 10% relief   —

     New Enterprise Investment Scheme investments – 30% relief   —

     New Venture Capital Trust investments – 30% relief   —

     Double tax relief on foreign income (relief at maximum of

         UK tax on same income)   —
ADD: Child Benefit income tax charge (new in 2012/13)   —

UK Tax borne on taxable income   —

Add: UK tax retained on rent paid to overseas resident landlords and/or patent royalties   —

UK income tax liability 2012/13   —

Less:

Tax suffered at source (PAYE and CIS deductions, tax on savings income, etc.)   –

Tax credits on dividend income   –

Tax payable by self-assessment   –

The following points should be noted at this stage:

a) The Married Couple's Allowance is only available where one or both spouses reached the age of 75 before 6th April 2010; relief is given at a 10% tax rate. See Chapter 4.

b) The Personal Allowance is available to most UK taxpayers but there are exceptions, and for the tax year 2012/13 it is gradually withdrawn for incomes over £100,000. See Chapter 4.

c) Income from employment is after the deduction of any expenses specifically allowable against employment income, and includes taxable benefits in kind from employment. See Chapters 7 and 8.

d) Income from self-employment is the taxable profits of a trading business for the tax year, less capital allowances, and is measured using 'basis period' rules which mean the profit measurement period does not always match the tax year. See Chapters 10 to 15.

e) Savings income paid by banks and building societies to individuals is, in general, subject to deduction at source of income tax at the basic rate of 20%. Savings income derived by UK residents from UK Government sources is generally received gross. See Chapter 6.

The nature of income

3. Income for a tax year is measured by rules set out in the Income Tax (Earnings and Pensions) Act 2003 and the Income Tax (Trading and Other Income) Act 2005.

Nature of Income	Source
Employment income, pensions income, social security	ITEPA 2003
Income taxed as trade profits	ITTOIA 2005
Savings income	
Dividend income	
Property business income (Income from UK land and property)	
Foreign income	
Miscellaneous income	

Details of the rules for measuring each type of income are contained in later chapters.

Tax rate bands 2012/13

4. In 2012/13, taxable income is taxed at the basic rate up to £34,370. Up to this limit the rate of income tax is 20% for non-savings and savings income (with a lower starting rate for savings income – see below), and 10% for dividend income.

The higher tax rate of 40% (32.5% for dividends) applies to taxable income in excess of £34,370 and up to £150,000.

The basic rate band limit of £34,370, and the higher rate band limit of £150,000, are extended on an individual basis to give relief at the difference between the basic and the higher or additional rate of tax on qualifying charitable donations or personal pension plan contributions (payments which receive basic rate income tax relief when paid). See Chapters 5 and 16.

The additional rate of 50% (42.5% for dividends) applies to taxable income in excess of £150,000.

The initial savings rate of 10% instead of 20% applies to savings income that makes up any part of the first £2,710 of income falling to be taxed at basic rate.

As already noted, ITA 2007 prescribes that dividend income is the highest 'slice' of total income, and savings income is the next highest. It follows that if taxable non-savings income exceeds £2,710, the starting rate is not available on any savings income, because the first £2,710 of taxable income is not classed as savings income.

If under the matching rules in ITA2007 any of the first £2,710 of taxable income is classed as dividend income, then the basic tax rate on this is only 10% in any case.

Basis of assessment and doctrine of the source

5. In order to ascertain an individual's assessable income for a tax year, it is necessary to identify all sources of income that existed in the year, and then measure the income under the statutory rules (ITEPA 2003 or ITTOIA 2005) for that income.

Since the introduction of income tax self-assessment in 1997, income from all sources is measured on a current year basis for income tax purposes.

PAYE system

6. A substantial proportion of all income tax due on employment and pension income is collected under the Pay As You Earn (PAYE) system. The main features of this are described in Chapter 8.

Due dates for payment – 2012/13 Tax Year

7.   Under the system for self-assessment introduced in 1997, a taxpayer whose tax liability is not substantially collected at source, and whose self-assessment tax payments exceeded set levels the year before, is required to make two payments on account of income tax before the self-assessment return goes in.

A third 'balancing' payment meets remaining liability for the year, and is due on the same date by which the self-assessment return must ultimately be with HMRC. The payment dates for 2012/13 income tax, under the payments on account system, are:

First payment on account	31 January 2013
Second payment on account	31 July 2013
Balancing payment	31 January 2014

Taxpayers whose income is largely or wholly received net of tax deducted at source do not have to make any income tax payments on account. The date for them to pay any balance of income tax due for a year is 31 January following the tax year end (ie 31 January 2014 for tax year 2012/13). For an employee who pays tax by PAYE, there is an optional alternative of having any remaining 2012/13 income tax liability not exceeding £2,000 collected from employment income during the following year, by including the tax underpayment in the 2013/14 PAYE code.

Further details of the income tax payments on account system are in Chapter 3.

Non-taxable income

8.   The following types of income are exempt from UK income tax:

a)   Certain NSI (Government-backed) savings products: Index-Linked Savings Certificates, Fixed Interest Savings Certificates, and Children's Bonus Bonds.

b)   Interest and bonuses on certified Save As You Earn (SAYE) contractual savings schemes.

c)   NSI Premium Bond prizes.

d)   Interest on certain UK government securities held by non-residents.

e)   Ex gratia compensation for loss of office/employment, up to £30,000, so long as not paid for services, and not contractually promised (which is what 'ex gratia' means). See Chapter 7.

f)   Redundancy payments, statutory or contractual, within the same £30,000 limit.

g)   Job release allowances, if paid within one year of normal retirement age.

h)   War widows' pensions.

i)   Interest payable on damages for personal injury or death.

j)   Gambling winnings (including the National Lottery) and competition prizes.

k)   Scholarship awards and other educational grants.

l)   Payments for service in the armed forces relating to:

   i)   wound and disability pensions

   ii)   service grants, bounties and gratuities

   iii) annuities and additional pensions paid to holders of the Victoria Cross, George Cross and other gallantry awards.

m)   Long service awards to employees, subject to certain limitations (see Chapter 7).

n)   Certain social security income: Working Tax Credit, Child Tax Credit, Pension Credit, housing benefit, Maternity Allowance, attendance allowance, mobility allowance, disability living allowance, Guardian's Allowance, means-tested Employment Support Allowance, the first 28 weeks of Incapacity benefit, Industrial Injuries Benefit, Severe Disablement Allowance, winter fuel payment.

   Note that Job Seeker's Allowance, statutory sick pay, and contributions-based Employment Support Allowance are taxable. Incapacity Benefit becomes taxable after the first 28 weeks of payment.

o)   Child Benefit is a tax-free social security payment until 6 January 2013. The rules proposed for changing this from that date are quite complicated. The present proposals at time of writing are set out in Chapter 17 section 9, but it is possible that further changes will be made to the new rules before implementation from January 2013.

p)   Lump sum Bereavement Payment (currently £2,000) paid to the spouse of a deceased person who has paid NI contributions. Bereavement Allowance paid weekly thereafter (formerly called Widow's Pension) is taxed as pension income.

q)   Free TV licences for those aged over 75.

r)   Up to £4,250 p.a. of gross rent received on furnished lettings in the taxpayer's only or main residence ('Rent-a-Room relief' - see Chapter 9).

s)   Outplacement counselling paid for by a third party or an employer.

9.   **Income Tax Personal allowances 2012/13** (for more details see Chapter 4)

Deducted from net income   Relief at 10% rate

	£
Personal allowance	8,105*
Abatement income level for * above	100,000
Blind person's allowance	2,100
Allowances aged 65–74:	
Personal age-related allowance	10,500**

Allowances aged 75–:

Personal age-related allowance	10,660**	
Married couple's age-related allowance		7,705**
Abatement income level for ** above	25,400	
Minimum married couple's age-related allowance		2,960

Note

Married couple's age-related allowance is only available where one or both spouses reached the age of 75 before 6th April 2010. It is also available to civil partnerships which meet the age condition– see Chapter 4.

Student self-testing questions

1. In 2012/13 Jules had the following income: £

Income from employment (salary) - amount before tax   35,100

Building society interest - net of 20% tax   7,200

Jules' personal allowance is £8,105 and there were no payments to be treated as allowable deductions from income.

Required: How much income tax is due in total and, if £5,400 was deducted under PAYE, what is the tax remaining payable?

Solution:

		Non-savings	Savings	£
Income		£	£	
Salary/ bonus		35,100		35,100
Taxed interest B Soc. 7,200 x 100/80			9,000	9,000
Total income		35,100	9,000	44,100
Less Personal allowance		(8,105)		(8,105)
Taxable income		26,995	9,000	35,995
Tax on this income:	£		£	£
At starting rate	n/a	x 10%		0
At basic rate - on non-savings	26,995	x 20%		5,399
- on savings	7,375	x 20%		1,475

Basic rate income limit	34,370		
At higher rate – on savings	1,625	x 40%	650
	35,995		
			7,524
Income tax borne on taxable income			
(= also Income tax liability)			
Less: PAYE already paid		5,400	
Tax already suffered on interest		1,800	
			(7,200)
Remaining income tax, due			324

Note: The 10% savings tax rate band is not available to Jules, because his first £2,710 of taxable income is not classed as savings income. For more examples of taxed interest being 'grossed up' by adding back the 20% tax deducted, please see Chapter 6.

2. During 2012/13 Jamie has income from employment of £86,000 gross, from which PAYE of £34,400 has been deducted. He also received bank deposit interest of £11,200 net, and dividends from UK companies of £54,000.

Required: Show the income tax liability and tax remaining payable by Jamie in respect of 2012/13.

Solution

		Non-savings £	Savings £	Dividends £
Employment		86,000		
Interest	£11,200 x 100/80		14,000	
Dividends	£54,000 x 100/90			60,000
Total/net income		£160,000	86,000	14,000	60,000
Personal allowance maximum	£8,105			
Restricted for high net income: (160,000 – 100,000) x 1/2				
[No PA left]	(30,000)		(0)	
Taxable income		£160,000	86,000	14,000	60,000

Tax:		£		£
Basic rate	Non-savings	34,370	@ 20%	6,874
Higher rate	Non-savings	51,630	@ 40%	20,652
		86,000		
	Savings	14,000	@ 40%	5,600
	Dividends	50,000	@32.5%	16,250
		150,000		
Additional rate	Dividends	10,000	@42.5%	4,250
		£160,000		

Income tax borne/ income tax liability			£	53,626
Less:				
Tax suffered	PAYE		34,400	
	Interest		2,800	
Tax credit	Dividends		6,000	(43,200)
Tax payable by self-assessment				£10,426

3 The following concerns the tax payable by Adam for two successive tax years:

	2011/12	2012/13
	£	£
Total income tax payable	20,000	24,000
Tax deducted under PAYE	12,000	13,000

The income tax payable has been computed by self-assessment and is not disputed by HMRC.

Requirement: Show how Adam's income tax for 2012/13, to the extent not deducted at source, is required to be paid.

Solution:

Adam – total tax paid by self-assessment 2011/12:

	£
Tax liability	20,000
Less PAYE	(12,000)
Payable under self-assessment for 2011/12	8,000

(this may have been met partly by payments on account, or met by a single payment if no payments on account were needed in 2011/12)

Adam - Tax payable by self-assessment for 2012/13:

	£
Tax liability	24,000
Less PAYE	(13,000)
Payable under self-assessment for 2012/13	11,000

Payments to be made under self-assessment for 2012/13:

	£	£
Total payable		11,000
Interim payments (based on prior tax year's figures)		
31 January 2013 : £8,000 x 1/2	4,000	
31 July 2013 : £8,000 x 1/2	4,000	
		(8,000)
Balancing payment due on 31 January 2014		3,000

3 Administration

1.   This chapter outlines the administrative features of the income tax system. More detailed information can be found on the HM Revenue and Customs website (www.hmrc.gov.uk).

2.   Income tax is administered by the Commissioners for Revenue and Customs, who are responsible to HM Treasury and the Chancellor of the Exchequer, through the Financial Secretary to the Treasury.

HMRC is an executive agency of the UK Government and was formed by a merger in 2005 of the Inland Revenue and Her Majesty's Customs and Excise.

The merged HMRC operates through Revenue Officers (formerly called Inspectors of Taxes or Customs and Excise Officers).

HMRC Area and District offices are responsible for the issue and receipt of tax returns for income tax payers handled from that office. However, as income tax returns are now increasingly submitted online, and enquiries are handled by central telephone call centres, the link to a particular tax district is not very significant for most people who complete income tax returns.

HMRC Accounts Offices are concerned with the collection of the assessed (usually, this means **self**-assessed) amounts of tax, and matching these to the liabilities shown by taxpayers' self-assessment returns.

HMRC Enquiry Centres give an initial point of contact for taxpayers with queries of any kind. It is possible for anyone to visit any Enquiry Centre in person, though an increasing number of enquiries are handled by telephone and email.

HMRC also has dedicated telephone numbers and email addresses for the use of professional tax agents, such as accountants and chartered tax advisers acting for their taxpaying clients.

HMRC Specialist Offices and Agencies exist to handle particular administrative areas. Examples of these in the income tax field are the Charities Office, three Enterprise Investment Scheme (EIS) offices, the Employee Shares and Securities Unit (ESSU), the Pension Schemes Office (PSO), and the Financial Intermediaries and Claims Office (FICO). The High Net Worth Unit, established in 2009, deals exclusively with the wealthiest income tax payers.

Legal appeals in all tax disputes are handled by a common tax tribunals system, which took over all new and existing cases on 1 April 2009 from the judicial bodies that formerly existed to hear appeals relating to different taxes (the General Commissioners, Special Commissioners, and VAT and Duties Tribunals).

Criminal prosecutions in income tax matters are now handled by the Crown Prosecution Service in England, Wales and Northern Ireland, and by the Crown Office and the Procurator Fiscal Service in Scotland.

Tax returns due in 2012/13 for tax year 2011/12

3. A paper Short Self-Assessment Tax Return was issued immediately after the end of the tax year 2011/12 to all taxpayers who either had submitted a paper return for 2010/11 or had since registered for self-assessment. The return issued in April 2012 covers the Tax Year 2011/12.

Taxpayers who filed their self-assessment return online for 2010/11 were not sent a paper self-assessment return for 2011/12 in the post in April 2012. They were instead simply sent a Notice to Complete a Tax Return (Form SA316). A paper return can still be requested by these taxpayers, or downloaded from HMRC's website, but the assumption is that these taxpayers will file online for 2012/13.

Taxpayers receiving a paper return for 2011/12 were initially sent a tax return headed 'Short Tax Return 2012 for the Tax Year 6 April 2011 to 5 April 2012', together with any extra pages that they were previously known to need (e.g. for reporting income from property). Further extra pages can be requested, or downloaded from HMRC's website, as can the full Tax Return Guide and Helpsheets for 2011/12.

For taxpayers who did not have a registered tax agent, any paper return issued in April 2012 was accompanied by the Tax Return Guide 2011/12 and the Tax Calculation Guide 2011/12. For taxpayers whose tax agent filed a paper return for 2010/11, only the paper Tax Return itself was issued to the taxpayer in April 2012, as the tax agent was assumed to have obtained the rest.

Self-assessment

4. The following are the main administrative features of self-assessment.

   a)   The Tax Return consists of a main return and varying supplementary pages.

   b)   The separate Tax Return Guide explains how income for each page of the tax return, and capital gains where relevant, are computed. The Tax Calculation Guide provides instructions for the self-calculation of income tax, CGT and Class 4 National Insurance due, or income tax repayable. Helpsheets are also available explaining how to deal with specific types of income, and allowable deductions and reliefs including loss claims.

   c)   There are two key dates for the filing of tax returns.

   i)   For taxpayers still filing a paper return, by 31st October following the end of the tax year;

   ii)   For taxpayers filing online, by 31st January following the end of the tax year.

   d)   Thus for 2012/13 the two filing dates are 31st October 2013 and 31st January 2014.

   e)   Failure to file a tax return for any year by the due date incurs an automatic fixed penalty of £100. If the return is filed more than 3 months late, additional penalties of £10 per day up to a maximum of £900 can be charged. If the return is still outstanding 6 months after the filing date a further penalty applies of 5% of tax unpaid at the original filing date, or £300, whichever is the greater. From 2011/12 onwards, late filing penalties still apply even if there was no tax actually unpaid at the original due filing date. For returns filed 12 months late there are further penalties, which are the greater of 5% of the tax unpaid or £300, or in cases of deliberate concealment, up to 100% of the tax due.

f) Under self-assessment, the obligation to pay tax is not linked to the issue of an estimated assessment by HMRC. All taxpayers are obliged to calculate and make the necessary tax payments based on his or her self-assessment. The taxpayer is liable to interest, and eventually surcharges, on any part of the tax liability that is not paid on time. For payment more than 30 days late the penalty is 5% of the tax unpaid, 6 months late a further penalty of 5%, 12 months late a further penalty of 5%. Interest and penalties for late payment of tax are not expenses deductible from business profits or other assessable income.

g) For taxpayers whose tax is not largely collected by deduction at source, two payments on account are required with a balancing payment to meet any tax outstanding at 31 January following the tax year-end.

h) Based on the latest information submitted to them, the expected payments on account for the next tax year are notified by HMRC in regular Self-Assessment Statements of Account, addressed to the taxpayer. These statements can be checked online if the taxpayer has registered for online filing. Paper Statements also contain a bank payslip for the next payment on account, but it can alternatively be paid online.

Self-assessment payments on account (POAs)

5. For self–employed taxpayers, PoAs also operate for Class 4 National Insurance (see Chapter 17). The following points should be noted:

i) A taxpayer does not need to make POAs if either:

a) the self-assessment income tax (and class 4 NIC) due for last year was £1,000 or less; or

b) the amount payable by self-assessment for the preceding year was 20% or less of the total income tax and Class 4 NIC liability for the preceding year.

In other words, no PoAs are required if more than 80% of the total income tax (and Class 4 NIC) liability last year was met either by deduction of tax at source, or by tax credits on dividends..

ii) The ways in which income tax is deducted at source include Pay As You Earn (PAYE), the construction industry sub-contractors' (CIS) scheme (not examined in this book), and or tax deducted from interest paid by banks and building societies. Other income paid to individuals, such as patent royalties, or some self-employment income, may also be received net of basic rate income tax.

iii) It should be clear that income tax and Class 4 NIC liability (net of tax deducted at source and tax credits) for the preceding year will determine whether payments on account are needed. If they are due, they are set at half the total income tax and Class 4 NIC payable for the preceding year, net of last year's tax deducted at source and dividend tax credits.

iv) Where payments on account do not meet the entire tax (and Class 4 NIC) liability – net of tax deducted at source and tax credits – for this tax year, a final payment will be due by 31st January after the end of the tax year. If payments on account are found to exceed the total tax payable, a repayment arises.

v) If the taxpayer considers that expected payments on account for the current year are excessive (because tax payable by self-assessment for the current year is reasonably expected to be less than for the prior year), the taxpayer can make a formal application to reduce one or both payments on account. HMRC will revise the Self-Assessment Statement of Account to reflect the reduction(s). However, interest will be charged in due course from the original PoA due dates, if reductions were applied for but later shown (per the next year's tax return) to have been unjustified.

Interim payments on account for 2012/13

6. To summarise the above, payments on account are due in the following circumstances:

Assessment to income tax –	Income tax deducted	= 'Relevant amount'
& Class 4 NIC 2011/12	at source 2011/12	for 2012/13
Relevant amount	$\geq$ £1,000	$\rightarrow$ POA required 2012/13
Relevant amount	$\geq$ 20% of tax liability 2011/12	$\rightarrow$ POA required 2012/13

Notes

i) Income tax deducted at source includes tax on savings income such as bank or building society interest, PAYE and CIS deductions.

ii) Capital gains tax for a tax year is also payable on the final tax payment date of 31 January. No payments on account are necessary for CGT.

Example

For 2011/12 X's self-assessment return showed the following:

	£
Gross income tax liability	10,000
Class 4 NIC (see Chapter 17 for more on this tax)	1,030
PAYE deducted at source (relating to 2011/12)	2,570
Tax deducted at source from bank interest	430

Calculate the interim payments on account which X must make for 2012/13.

Solution

Relevant amount	Income tax liability 2011/12		10,000
Less income tax at source	PAYE	2,570	
	Tax on Interest	430	(3,000)
			7,000
Class 4 NIC			1,030
Paid by self-assessment 2011/12			8,030
2012/13 Payments on Account	31st January 2013		4,015
	31st July 2013		4,015

Example

Mrs J has the following data shown on her self-assessment tax return for 2011/12

	£
Gross income tax liability	7,500
PAYE deducted at source	6,900
Tax suffered at source on savings income	150

Calculate the interim payments to be made on account for 2012/13.

Solution

Relevant amount	Income tax liability		7,500
Less	PAYE	6,900	
	Tax on savings	150	(7,050)
			450

As this is less than £1,000, no POA for 2012/13 is required.

Final payment (repayment) of tax

A final payment (or repayment) of income tax occurs in the following circumstances:

2012/13 self-assessment tax return

(Income tax liability + Class 4 NIC liability + Capital gains tax liability)

less PoAs = Final payment or repayment due

Example

P has the following income tax and capital gains tax liabilities for the year ended 5th April 2013, based on his self-assessment tax return.

	£
Trade profits (income tax & class 4 NIC)	25,000
Capital gains tax	1,000

The relevant amount for 2011/12 was £18,000, all attributable to income tax on trade profits and NIC.

Show the payments to be made in respect of the tax year to 5th April 2013, and the due dates.

Solution: P's tax and Class 4 NIC liability for 2012/13   £

31st January 2013	50% × Relevant amount 2011/12 = 50% × 18,000	9,000
31st July 2013	50% × Relevant amount 2011/12 = 50% × 18,000	9,000
31st January 2014	Balance of tax and NIC due	8,000
		26,000

Note

The total tax due for 2012/13 is

Income tax and Class 4 NIC	25,000
Capital gains tax	1,000
	26,000
Less Payment on account (same as 2011/12 relevant amount)	(18,000)
Balance due	8,000

Surcharges on income tax

7.   In addition to the interest charged on any tax paid late, there is a scheme of tax surcharges to encourage prompt payment. (Refer to section 4 above.)

Interest on under and overpayments

8.   A charge to interest will automatically arise on any tax paid late whether in respect of income tax, NIC or capital gains tax and can apply to:

   i)   any payment on account;

   ii)   any balancing payment;

   iii) any tax payable following an amendment to self-assessment, whether made by the taxpayer or by HMRC;

   iv)   any tax payable following a 'discovery assessment' by HMRC. (See section 9 for more on discovery assessments.)

Interest runs from the due date for payment to the date on which payment is finally made for payments on account and balancing payments.

For amendments to original self-assessments, the interest charge runs from the annual filing date for the income tax year, i.e. the 31st January following the end of the income tax year. Interest on any overpayments of tax is added automatically when the repayment is made.

HM Revenue and Customs enquiries

9. A Revenue Officer may carry out an 'enquiry' into any taxpayer's self-assessment tax return. Such returns may be selected on a sample basis, or because the Officer has concerns about some of the information returned. The enquiry system includes both powers for the Revenue Officer and rights for the taxpayer. For example, the Officer may request a meeting with the taxpayer, but the taxpayer has a right to representation, and to decline to attend. The enquiry should be restricted to a specified area of investigation, and concluded within a regulated time limit.

The normal 'enquiry window' period is twelve months from the date of submitting the return. Formerly, it was twelve months from the latest date for filing (31 January) regardless of the actual filing date, but this was altered to encourage early filing.

The enquiry window is re-opened if the taxpayer submits an amendment to a submitted return. This includes the lodging of a further claim or withdrawal of a claim made on the original return. HMRC has up to twelve months to enquire into the amendment, or any related matter on the return.

After the enquiry window period has closed, HMRC can only reopen the return if there is a discovery of 'incomplete disclosure'. This means that HMRC finds out (sometimes by reviewing information from a third party) that something was omitted or concealed from the submitted return, causing a loss of tax to the Crown. A discovery assessment can only be made if HMRC could not reasonably have been able to tell the true tax liability from the self-assessment return and any supporting information as originally submitted.

Incomplete disclosure that was not the result of fraudulent or negligent conduct by the taxpayer allows a discovery assessment by HMRC in the period up to five years after the original last filing date for the return (i.e. nearly five years and ten months after the end of the tax year to which the incomplete return relates).

Incomplete disclosure that was the result of fraudulent or negligent conduct by the taxpayer allows a discovery assessment at any time up to twenty years from the original last filing date. In addition to the additional tax due, and interest at normal rates, 'tax-geared' penalties can be imposed that depend on the taxpayer's behaviour (see section 13).

Challenging the decisions of HM Revenue and Customs

10. Letters informing taxpayers of HMRC decisions will include information on the right of appeal. Appeals should be sent to HMRC in writing, within 30 days of the disputed decision. Some appeals may be settled by agreement with HMRC.

When agreement is not reached, HMRC may offer an internal review of the decision by another officer. The taxpayer may ask for an internal review if HMRC does not offer one. Whether or not a review takes place, a taxpayer may then appeal to the Tribunal Service.

Tribunal service

11. The tax appeals system is a two-tier tribunal system:

Most cases are heard by the First Tier Tribunal (Tax Chamber);

The Upper Tribunal (Finance and Chancery Chamber) hears complex cases, and also all appeals from the First Tier Tribunal. The Upper Tribunal is a court of record, whose decisions create binding precedents for the First Tier.

Appeals from the Upper Tribunal are to the Court of Appeal (Inner House in Scotland), and finally to the Supreme Court of the UK.

Penalties

12. Taxpayers are expected to take 'reasonable care' in making and keeping accurate records to enable them to provide a complete and accurate tax return. This principle applies to all income tax and national insurance contributions information in the self-assessment income tax return, along with return documents for other taxes (principally CGT for individuals).

Taxpayers can demonstrate they have taken reasonable care by: keeping accurate records, confirming the correct position when they do not understand tax issues, answering any enquiry questions raised by HMRC, and telling HMRC promptly about any errors discovered in tax returns after they have been sent.

Where taxpayers do not pay enough tax, and have not taken reasonable care, they may have to pay a penalty in addition to the tax due and any interest on late payment. The penalties can be reduced if the taxpayer makes an 'unprompted' disclosure of the underpayment, rather than one forced by the result of investigations by the tax authorities:

Taxpayer's approach to disclosure of underpayment	Minimum penalty	Maximum penalty
Reasonable care	No penalty	No penalty
Careless unprompted	0%	30%
Careless prompted	15%	30%
Deliberate unprompted	20%	70%
Deliberate prompted	35%	70%
Deliberate and concealed unprompted	30%	100%
Deliberate and concealed prompted	50%	100%

Error or mistake relief

13.   The relief formerly called error or mistake relief under Taxes Management Act 1970 section 33 was replaced from 1 April 2010 by Overpayment Relief under new Schedule 1AB of the same Act.

The taxpayer can claim relief in writing against any over-payment of tax made due to an error or mistake (including an omission) in any return or statement. The relief must be claimed within 4 years of the end of the tax year.

The claim in writing must be separate from a submitted self-assessment return and must provide the following information (Source HMRC Brief 22 / 2010):

- State that the person is making a claim for overpayment relief under Schedule 1AB TMA 1970
- Identify the tax year for which the overpayment or excessive assessment has been made.
- State the grounds on which the person considers that the overpayment or excessive assessment has occurred.
- State whether the person has previously made an appeal in connection with the payment or the assessment.
- If the claim is for repayment of tax, include documentary proof of the tax deducted or the tax being suffered in some other way.
- Include a declaration signed by the claimant, stating that the particulars given in the claim are correct and complete to the best of their knowledge and belief.

Student self-testing question

A has the following data relating to 2011/12 and 2012/13.

	2011/12	2012/13
Total income tax liability	18,500	22,000
Capital gains tax liability	1,500	3,000
Tax credit on dividend income	(1,000)	(1,500)
Total tax due by self -assessment	19,000	23,500

Calculate the tax payments in respect of 2012/13 and show the due dates for payments.

Solution:

	2012/13 Payments		
	Interim Payments		**Final Payment**
	31. 1. 13	**31. 7. 13**	**31. 1. 14**
1st Interim payment 50% × (18,500 – 1,000)	8,750		
2nd Interim payment 50% (18,500 – 1,000)		8,750	
Final payment (23,500 – 17,500)	_____	_____	6,000
	8,750	8,750	6,000

Notes

i) The interim payments are computed by reference to the tax liability for 2011/12, i.e. (18,500 – 1,000) = 17,500 excluding any capital gains tax.

ii) The final payment for 2012/13 includes the capital gains tax liability for that year, i.e. £3,000:

(22,000 + 3,000 – 1,500) = 23,500 – POA,

i.e. 23,500 – 17,500 = £6,000.

(For CGT generally see Chapter 26 onwards.)

4 Personal allowances and reliefs

Introduction

1.   This chapter is concerned with the main features of the system of taxation in relation to the personal allowances and reliefs for individuals, blind persons, and married couples.

List of topic headings

2.

> Personal allowance
>
> Personal age allowance
>
> Husbands and wives /civil partners
>
> Married couple's allowance
>
> Blind person's allowance
>
> Death of husband or wife
>
> Year of permanent separation and divorce
>
> Non-residents

Personal allowance (PA) 2012/13 £8,105   (2011/12 £7,475)

3.   This allowance is given automatically to all individuals, male or female, single or married, and set against UK net income, except for:

(a) non-domiciled UK residents who have elected to file on the remittance basis (who are in general outside the scope of this book); and

(b) taxpayers whose 'adjusted net income' exceeds £100,000, for whom the personal allowance is   subject to gradual withdrawal ('abatement') above that level.

There are higher rates of personal allowance for people over the age of 65, discussed in Section 5 below.

For 2012/13, the normal PA is reduced by £1 for every £2 excess of an individual's 'adjusted net income' over £100,000. This means that it is removed completely once adjusted net income exceeds £116,210.

Unless withdrawn, the PA is deducted from net income in arriving at taxable income, and thus receives relief at the taxpayer's highest marginal rate of tax.

Net income is defined as total income less any trading losses (see Chapter 14) and allowable payments (see Chapter 5). 'Adjusted net income' is the taxpayer's net income, less the gross amount of any Gift Aid donations (see Chapter 5) or personal pension contributions (see Chapter 16) which have received tax relief at source. Any relief given against employment income for subscriptions to trade unions or police organisations is added back in calculating adjusted net income.

The personal allowance is not transferable.

Example

A is single, has a salary income from employment for 2012/13 of £105,000 and no other income.

Compute his income tax liability for 2012/13

Solution: A's Income tax computation 2012/13

	£	£
Income from employment		105,000
Personal allowance	8,105	
Restricted (105,000 – 100,000) x ½	(2,500)	
Remaining PA		(5,605)
Taxable income		99,395
Tax liability	n/a @ 10% (no savings income)	0
	34,370 @ 20%	6,874
	65,025 @ 40%	26,010
	99,395	32,884

Note

Given high income from employment, most of this tax would already have been collected by PAYE (See Chapter 8), with any balance due after the end of the year.

The personal age-related allowance (PAA)

4.   **2012/13**

Age 65–74	£10,500
Age 75–	£10,660

For taxpayers over the age of 65 at any time during the tax year, a higher personal allowance is available, and there is a further additional amount for those aged 75 and over. This increased level of allowances is available even if the taxpayer dies before the age of 65, if he or she would have reached that age during the tax year.

The full amount of the PAA may be claimed where adjusted net income is not greater than £25,400.

Where adjusted net income is greater than £25,400, the PAA is reduced by half the excess (£1 withdrawn for every £2), until the basic personal allowance becomes more beneficial.

For a taxpayer aged over 65, unless adjusted net income exceeds £100,000, the personal allowance can never be reduced below the basic personal allowance for a person under 65, i.e. £8,105 for 2012/13.

The basic personal allowance is subject to the further restriction /withdrawal if a person over 65 has an adjusted net income exceeding £100,000.

Income limits for Age Allowance

	PAA starts being restricted at	Normal PA
Age 65–74	£25,401	£30,190 – £100,000
Age 75–	£25,401	£30,510 – £100,000

Age 65–74	10,500 – ½ (30,190 – 25,400) = £8,105
Age 75	10,660 – ½ (30,510 – 25,400) = £8,105

Phasing out of PAA

In the March 2012 Budget Announcements, , advance notice was given that the qualifying age for PAA will be 'frozen' from 5 April 2013, so that taxpayers born on or after 6 April 1948 will never receive PAA. In addition, PAA will not increase from the 2012/13 level in 2013/14. All taxpayers who qualified for the PAA before 6 April 2013 will still receive it in 2013/14. The stated intention is however for the ordinary PA to 'catch up to' the PAA in time, so that older taxpayers will receive the same income tax personal allowances as other taxpayers.

Example

Kiran, who is 66 and single, has income from employment in 2012/13 of £24,000 and a state retirement pension of £5,400.

Compute Kiran's income tax liability for 2012/13.

Solution: Kiran's Income tax computation 2012/13

	£	£
Income from employment		24,000
State Pension		5,400
Total income (all non-savings)		29,400
PAA	10,500	
Less abatement ½ (29,400–25,400)	(2,000)	(8,500)
Taxable income		20,900
Tax liability:		
Non-savings: n/a @ 10%		0
Basic Rate 20,900 @ 20%		4,180
20,900		
Tax		4,180

Note: For Kiran, the partly-restricted PAA of £8,500 is still greater than the normal personal allowance of £8,105. If the PAA abatement calculation results in a lower figure than the normal PA, the normal PA is given instead.

Husbands and wives /civil partners

5. Since the legalisation of same-sex civil partnerships in the UK from December 2005, all references to 'spouses' in tax legislation apply equally to registered civil partners from the tax year 2005/06. The following should therefore be read as applying also to registered civil partners, even where not mentioned.

For income tax purposes, in order to count as 'a couple' at a given date, a couple must be both legally married/in a civil partnership, **and** living together. Living together means 'not separated in circumstances where the separation is likely to be permanent'. A mid-tax-year permanent separation terminates the relationship for income tax. (The position is different for capital gains tax and inheritance tax; see Chapters 27 and 35 respectively).

a) Husband and wife / civil partners are treated as separate taxpayers, each completing his/her own tax return and responsible for his/her own tax liabilities.

b) Each spouse receives a personal allowance, which is non-transferable to the other spouse even if the first spouse has not enough net income to use it all. As noted above, the allowance is increased for persons over 65, and again for those over 75. As already noted, the personal allowance in tax year 2012/13 is withdrawn progressively for incomes over £100,000 and disappears at income of £116,210. These limits operate separately for married couples.

c) The married couple's age-related allowance (MCA) was phased out from 6 April 2000 but is still available (at a 10% effective tax rate only) for couples where one spouse or civil partner reached the age of 65 before 6 April 2000. Further details are in section 6.

d) Each person entitled to the personal age allowance is subject to the annual income limit of £25,400 for 2012/13 above which the PAA is withdrawn or abated. There is no sharing of this limit between spouses or civil partners.

e) Joint property giving rise to income is treated for income tax as belonging to spouses and civil partners in equal shares for income tax purposes, regardless of the true or beneficial ownership split. This applies for example to rent from a let property, or to a joint bank deposit, or shares held jointly. The income for income tax purposes is therefore allocated 50:50, even if the ownership is different for other legal purposes.

It is possible for spouses/partners to elect for a different split of the income arising from joint property, but they must when doing so declare that the proportions being specified reflect the true beneficial ownership of the underlying asset. The same shares would then apply for CGT or inheritance tax calculations relating to the same asset.

The married couple's age-related allowance (MCA) – 10% rate relief

6.   **2012/13**

Age 65–75	n/a
Age 76–	£7,705
Minimum amount	£2,960

a) The MCA is now quite a minor relief. It is only available where one or both spouses reached the age of 75 before the 6th April 2010.

b) A claim for the higher level of married couple's allowance is made by the husband for marriages before 6 December 2005, and by the partner with the higher taxable income (which may vary year on year) for marriages or civil partnerships entered into since 6 December 2005. In the rest of this section, to save space, the husband is assumed the one claiming the MCA.

c) MCA is given relief at the 10% rate. So if the MCA due after partial abatement (see below) is £4,500, then this allowance is given by an amount of £450 (10% of £4,500) being deducted from the tax liability of the husband.

d) If the husband cannot use all the MCA, the unused amount can be transferred to his wife. Note that for marriages before 6 December 2005, the wife's income, even if higher than the husband's, has no effect on the MCA available.

e) The full amount of MCA is reduced by 1/2 of the excess where the husband's adjusted net income exceeds £25,400.

f) Where the husband's MCA is reduced because his net income exceeds £25,400, it can never be reduced below a minimum of £2,960 (which at 10% is a relief of £296 deducted from the tax liability on taxable income).

g) In applying the reduction in the MCA for higher income, the following rules should be used to apply abatement first to the normal age-related personal allowance, and only then to the MCA:

> First – reduce the PAA by £1 for every £2 of excess income, until it reaches the level of the PA for people under the age of 65.

> Second – reduce the MCA by £1 for every £2 of excess income, until it reaches the level of the MCA for people under 65.

The above has the effect of preserving as late as possible any MCA that can be transferred to the wife.

Example

In 2012/13, Mr Z is aged 72 and his wife is aged 80. They have been married for 40 years. In the year 2012/13 Mr Z has employment and pension income of £26,000 and Mrs Z has employment and pension income of £27,000.

Compute the tax payable by Mr and Mrs Z for 2012/13.

Solution: Mr Z's Income tax computation 2012/13

	£	£
Employment and pension income		26,000
Reduction in total allowances		
½ (26,000 – 25,400) = 300		
PAA	10,500	
Less reduction	(300)	(10,200)
Taxable income (non-savings)		15,800
Tax liability:		
n/a @ 10%		0
15,800 @ 20%		3,160
15,800		
Less deduction for MCA 7,705 @ 10%		(770)
Tax payable		2,390

Mrs Z's income tax computation 2012/13

	£	£
Employment and pension income		27,000
PAA	10,660	
Less ½ (27,000 – 25,400)	(800)	
		(9,860)
Taxable income (non-savings)		17,140
Tax liability: n/a @ 10%		0
17,140 @ 20%		3,428
17,140		
Tax payable		3,428

Notes

i)   The PAA of £10,660 for Mrs Z is reduced to £9,860.

ii)   The level of Mrs Z's income has no effect on the MCA claimed by her husband.

iii)   The MCA due to Mr Z is not abated at all because abatement for high incomes applies first to the PAA, and would only reduce his MCA after his PAA had been fully reduced to the basic personal allowance.

Blind person's allowance 2012/13 £2,100

7.   This allowance is available to any person who is on the local authority blind person's register. Where both husband and wife are blind, each can claim the allowance. If either the husband or the wife (or one civil partner) cannot fully use the amount of their blind allowance then the balance can be transferred to the other spouse. This rule applies whether or not the spouse receiving the transferred

allowance is a registered blind person. A notice to transfer any unused allowance must be made in writing to HMRC within four years of the end of the tax year.

This allowance is deducted from net income to arrive at taxable income, and is thus given relief at the taxpayer's marginal rate of tax. There is no income limit. It is given in addition to the PA or PAA, and the MCA if applicable.

Example

Kathy, who is a widow aged 55, is a registered blind person. Kathy's income for the year 2012/13 consists of the following.

	£
Widow's pension	6,000
Wages for part-time employment (gross)	14,505
(PAYE deducted £1,406)	

Compute K's income tax liability for 2012/13.

Solution: K income tax computation 2012/13

	£	£
Income from employment		14,505
Widow's pension		6,000
Net income (also total income)		20,505
Personal allowance	8,105	
Blind person's allowance	2,100	(10,205)
Taxable income (all non-savings income)		10,300
Tax liability: n/a @ 10%		0
10,300 @ 20%		2,060
10,300		
Tax liability		2,060
Less PAYE already paid		(1,406)
Tax payable		654

Year of death of either spouse

8.   The following points should be noted under this heading:

Death of either spouse /civil partner

a)   A full personal allowance for the deceased, and a full MCA to either partner, is available in the tax year of death.

b)   Net income up to the date of death, less allowances and reliefs for the whole year, is ascertained and any remaining income tax due is payable by the personal representatives, out of the deceased's estate.

c) The balance of any MCA not used against the husband's (or higher earning partner's, for marriages/partnerships after 5 December 2005) tax liability on income up to the date of death is available for set-off against the surviving partner's own tax liability for the whole year.

Personal allowances for non-residents

9. A 'qualifying' non-resident can claim full personal allowances against his or her UK income, to the extent that the income is within the charge to UK tax.

Qualifying non-residents means:

a) residents of the European Union or the European Economic Area;

b) residents of the UK Commonwealth;

c) residents of any other Taxing State, where UK personal allowances are given on UK source income as part of double tax treaty arrangements.

Student self-testing question

Barney aged 68, a widower, looks after his mother aged 92. For the year to 5th April 2013 Barney has salary and pension income of £28,000

Calculate the tax payable by Barney for 2012/13.

Solution: Barney income tax computation 2012/13

	£	£
Income from employment and pension		28,000
PAA	10,500	
less 1/2 ×(28,000 − 25,400)	(1,300)	9,200
Taxable income		18,800
Tax liability n/a @ 10%		0
18,800 @ 20%		3,760
18,800		
Tax payable		3,760

Notes. PAA after abatement is £9,200, which exceeds the basic PA of £8,105.

No specific tax deduction is available for living with and looking after a parent.

5 Allowable payments and Gift Aid

Introduction

1. Allowable payments reduce total income, but are not referable to any particular source of income – unlike for example the specific reliefs that are deductible only against income from employment (see Chapter 7).

Total income is reduced by allowable payments to give net income (see Chapter 2).

The concept of allowable payments remains that these costs have the character of 'annual payments'. Before the Income Tax Act 2007, 'charges on income' was the term used to describe all annual payments.

Until the Finance Act 2000, personal charitable donations (other than payroll giving) had to be over £250 if they were to obtain tax relief as 'Gift Aid', and were deducted from total income. However since 2000, personal Gift Aid payments can be small payments, and under ITA 2007 they are not dealt with as allowable payments, but by the 'extended basic rate band' method of tax relief. The stated reason for this change was to make Gift Aid easier to understand for basic rate taxpayers.

Annual payments

2. These are payments which possess the quality of annual recurrence, are not voluntary transactions, and are usually supported by a legal obligation.

Annual payments are not allowable payments unless they fall within the following categories:

a) payments of interest;

b) payments of patent royalties;

c) other annual payments made for bone fide commercial reasons in connection with the payer's trade, profession or vocation.

Qualifying interest payments

3. Interest due in the UK on a loan used for any of the under-mentioned purposes is payable without deduction of income tax, and is an allowable payment against total income.

a) To purchase plant or machinery (but not a car) for use in a partnership or necessary for an employment.

b) To purchase an interest in or make a loan to a partnership, where the taxpayer is a partner, but not a limited partner.

c) Loans made in acquiring an interest in a co-operative enterprise as defined in section 2 of the Industrial Common Ownership Act 1976.

d) To pay inheritance tax. Relief is available for one year only.

e) To acquire ordinary shares or make loans to a close company, but not a close investment company. (See Chapter 18 for what these are.) The borrower must, with his or her associates:

  i) have a material interest in the company, i.e. more than 5% of the ordinary share capital or be entitled to more than 5% of the assets on a notional winding up; or

  ii) if having less than a 5% interest, work for the greater part of his or her time in the management of the company.

Business loan interest

4. Interest paid on loans taken out wholly for business purposes by traders is charged as an expense of trading, and not as a separate allowable payment. This applies to business bank loan or overdraft interest, providing the loan is used wholly and exclusively for the purposes of trade. Similarly, interest on a loan taken by an individual to buy property for letting is allowable for income tax as an expense of the letting, and not as an allowable payment against total income.

Annual payments for business purposes – patent royalties

5. Patent royalties paid by an individual for bona fide commercial reasons in connection with his or her trade, profession or vocation are still eligible to be treated as allowable payments. However, where an individual is trading, a patent (or copyright) royalty related to the trade may alternatively be treated as a trading expense and deducted against business profits, rather than against total income. The trade expense treatment is normally simpler and to be preferred, unless the business is making a trading loss before any royalty costs.

Whether treated as a trade expense or an allowable payment, patent royalty payments made by an individual must be paid to the patent owner after deduction of basic rate income tax at source. The gross amount of the royalty is the deductible trading expense or allowable payment for the royalty payer. The tax withheld is added to the paying individual's own tax borne, to give a total liability for the tax year that in effect includes 20% basic rate tax on the royalty income, paid on behalf of the patent owner.

The Budget Announcements of 22 June 2010 included a commitment by the new Government to review the system of collecting UK tax on patent royalties, which was stated to be little known, old fashioned and open to unintentional law breaking.

Copyright royalties

6. Copyright royalties differ from patent royalties because they may be paid gross without any deduction of tax. They are still trading expenses if related to trading income, and only have to be treated as an allowable payment if paid for some other purpose (e.g. in connection with an investment asset).

Present system of giving income tax relief for Gift Aid donations

7.   As already noted, Gift Aid donations to Charities or Community Amateur Sports Clubs (CASCs) are no longer classed as an allowable payment for income tax, though they were dealt with as such before 2004.

The present Gift Aid income tax system works as follows:

a)   The donor must give the charity/CASC a Gift Aid declaration, either at the time of the donation, or at an earlier time (to cover future donations). This must state that the donor wishes Gift Aid tax relief to apply to the donation, and that the donor pays tax each year of at least as much as the tax withheld from all Gift Aid donations.

b)   The declaration may be given in writing, over the phone or over the Internet, and the charity or CASC must keep a record of the date of the declaration and the donor's full name and address.

c)   The amount donated is treated for all tax purposes as paid net of 20% basic rate tax withheld by the donor. The charity/CASC can reclaim the tax on a quarterly or six-monthly basis but must preserve records of all Gift Aid donations received.

d)   The form of declaration charities and CASCs have to obtain was amended by HMRC in March 2012. The new approved wording includes a statement that the donor is aware that the only taxes taken into account for Gift Aid are income tax and CGT, not council tax or VAT.

e)   Donors who pay income tax at higher or additional rate may claim further higher or additional rate income tax relief for the gross donation. This is done on the self-assessment tax return by entering the amount of gift-aided donations. It can be done by letter if the taxpayer is not within self-assessment.

f)   Relief at the higher rate is given by extending the basic rate income band by the gross amount of Gift Aid payments. Relief at the additional rate is given by extending the higher rate band by the same figure.

g)   Gift Aid payments made after the end of a tax year but before submission of the self-assessment return may, if the taxpayer wishes, be related back to the tax year of that return. If this is done, the same payment(s) cannot be claimed again in the tax year when actually paid.

h)   Charities claim back basic rate tax withheld on their total Gift Aid income from HMRC Charities using Form R68. The names of all Gift Aid donors must be stated on the form or included in an attachment.

i)   If a taxpayer does not pay enough income tax and CGT for a tax year (including tax credits on dividend income) to cover the total tax reclaimed by charities on his or her donations, then he or she must pay HMRC the difference, under section 424 ITA 2007. This situation could arise where trading losses of a later year are carried back against total income, so that an earlier year's tax liability is totally eliminated – see Chapter 14.

Computational rules for extending the basic rate band for Gift Aid payments

a) **Higher rate taxpayer:** Gross the gift aid payment up by the basic rate of income tax (ie multiply by 100/80), and extend the taxpayer's personal basic rate band by that gross amount.

b) **Additional rate taxpayer:** Extend the basic rate band by the grossed up amount of the gift aid payment as above, and extend the top limit of the higher rate band by the same amount. This ensures that higher rate tax is paid in total on the same amount of income.

c) **Basic rate taxpayer:** Ignore Gift Aid altogether in the income tax computation, as full relief for the gross payment was given at source by the fact the payment was made net.

The gross amount of Gift Aid payments must also be considered for either a basic or a higher rate taxpayer, when computing the 'adjusted net income' for applying the Personal Allowance and Age Allowance income limits (see Chapter 4).

Example

Terry, who is married, has employment income of £49,000 for 2012/13. His wife Gloria has salary income of £15,000. They have no other income in 2012/13. Terry makes payments of £800 net (£1,000 gross) to a registered charity under Gift Aid. Gloria makes Gift Aid payments of £240 net (£300 gross) to the same charity.

Compute the income tax liability for 2012/13 for Terry and Gloria, who are both aged less than 65.

Solution: Income tax computation 2012/13

				Terry £	Gloria £
Income from employment (= net income)				49,000	15,000
Personal allowance				(8,105)	(8,105)
Taxable income				40,895	6,895
Tax liability:				£	£
Income tax		n/a	@ 10%	0	0
BR	34,370 / 6,895		@ 20%	6,874	1,379
Extend band 1,000			@ 20%	200	0
	35,370				
HR	5,525 / 0		@ 40%	2,210	0
	40,895 6,895			9,284	1,379

Notes:

Terry can claim higher rate relief at (40-20) % on his Gift Aid donation. This is given by extending the amount of income on which he pays basic rate tax by £1,000, the gross amount of his total donations (£800 x 100/80 = £1,000).

Therefore Terry's basic rate band in 2012/13 becomes £ (34,370 + 1,000) = £35,370.

For Gloria, only basic rate tax relief is due on her donations: she has not enough income to pay tax at higher rate. Her tax saving has been received by her making the payment net, so there is no need to show the Gift Aid in her tax computation.

The charity meanwhile receives £1,300 in total: £800 from Terry, £240 from Gloria, and the other £260 on application to HMRC using Form R68.

Payroll giving scheme for charitable donations

8.   Individual taxpayers who pay tax under PAYE (on employment or pension income) can give to charity with tax relief at their highest marginal rate via the 'payroll giving' scheme. The donations are deductible from employment income and relief is available up to the total of the money earnings from the employment. The employer or pension provider is responsible for making the payments to the charity, and adjusts the employee's or pensioner's PAYE liability using the 'net pay arrangements' (see Chapter 8).

This relief has become less used since Gift Aid was extended in 2000 to single payments under £250, and since Gift Aid declarations were permitted to be made orally and by internet. There is more on payroll giving in Chapter 8.

Student self-testing question

Junaid and Sunita, who are married, and both aged 55, have the following income for 2012/13.

	£
Employment earnings Junaid	48,000
Employment earnings Sunita	28,000

On 1st February 2013 J paid £960 (net) by way of a Gift Aid payment to a recognised charity.

Compute the income tax liability of both of them for 2012/13.

Solution: Income tax computation 2012/13

	Junaid	Sunita
	£	£
Income from employment (net income)	48,000	28,000
Personal allowance	(8,105)	(8,105)
Taxable income (all non-savings)	39,895	19,895
Taxation liability		
n/a / n/a @ 10%	0	0
35,570* / 19,895 @ 20%	7,114	3,979
4,325 @ 40%	1,730	
39,895 19,895		
Tax liability	8,844	3,979

Note *

As the gift aid payment by Junaid is allowed at the higher rate, his basic rate income tax band is extended i.e. £34,370 + £1,200 = £35,570.

 (Gross up donation: £960 x 100/80 = £1,200)

As both of them are employed, most or all of the tax liability would have been paid under PAYE before the end of the tax year.

6 Savings and investment income

Introduction

1.   This chapter is mainly concerned with the taxation of savings and dividend income. It also covers the income tax relief available for investment in EIS shares, SEIS shares (new in 2012/13), and Venture Capital Trusts (VCTs). At the end of the chapter are brief notes about two kind of investment income which are classed as non-savings income under the ITA2007, namely income from patents or copyrights, and the charge on notional income from 'pre-owned assets'.

'Savings income' is basically interest income. It is often (but not always) received after deduction of income tax at source by the payer. The tax treatment of dividend income is dealt with in sections 4 and 5.

Bank/building society interest etc – 20% rate deducted at source

2. a) The deduction of 20% income tax at source applies to the following types of savings income, when paid in the UK to individuals and trusts:

      –   interest from banks and building societies

      –   interest from some government securities (see section 3 below for those which currently pay interest gross)

      –   interest on corporate loan stocks and debentures

      –   purchased life annuities (non-capital element)

      –   interest distributions from authorised unit trusts.

b)   The 10% starting rate band applies to savings income that falls within the first £2,710 of taxable income. However, savings income is treated as the 'second slice' of an individual's taxable income, and is only taxed after all non-savings income has been taxed first as the 'lowest slice'.

c)   If the taxpayer is ultimately taxable on savings income at the starting rate of 10% or at the basic rate of 20%, then the tax deducted at source will meet all income tax liability.

d)   A repayment can be claimed after the end of the tax year if tax was deducted at 20% from savings income that is ultimately taxable at 10%. It is not possible to ask a savings institution to deduct tax at only 10%.

e)   For a higher rate or additional rate taxpayer, the 40% or 50% rate applies to the gross savings income (after adding back tax deducted at source). Credit is given against the full liability for the basic rate tax already paid.

f)   Non-taxpayers who receive taxed interest can claim a refund of the 20% tax deducted, but only after the end of the tax year.

g) Alternatively, for bank and building society interest, an individual can register with the bank or building society to receive interest gross without any tax deducted, if he or she can reasonably show that no tax will be payable on the income. However, individuals cannot register to receive bank and building society gross merely because they expect to pay only the 10% rate on savings income.

h) In general, savings income of individuals arises on the date of payment (receipts basis). There is an exception made by certain anti-avoidance legislation, not considered further here (the 'accrued income scheme').

Interest received gross

3. The following forms of investment pay interest gross:

a) certificates of deposit and sterling or foreign currency time deposits, provided that the loan is not less than £50,000 and is repayable within five years;

b) National Savings and Investments (NSI) interest is paid gross on the following taxable National Savings products: Easy Access Account, Investment Account, Pensioners' Income Bonds, Fixed Rate Savings Bonds, Capital Bonds;

c) general client accounts with banks and building societies, operated by solicitors or estate agents;

d) accounts held at overseas branches of United Kingdom banks and building societies;

e) bank and building society accounts where the owner is not ordinarily resident in the United Kingdom and has made a declaration to that effect;

f) bank and building society accounts in the names of companies, clubs, societies and charities;

g) loans to unincorporated borrowers;

h) all holdings of UK government securities (gilts) acquired after 5th April 1998, and other gilts acquired before then, if since then the holder has elected to receive the interest gross.

Example

Alan has the following income for the tax year ended 5th April 2013.

Income from property	£16,000
Bank interest (net)	£8,000

(For this example, it is simply necessary to know that income from property is non-savings income.)

Compute Alan's income tax liability and income tax payable for 2012/13.

Solution: Alan's income tax computation 2012/13

	£
Income from property	16,000
Bank interest income (8,000 x 100/80)	10,000
Total income / net income	26,000
Less PA	(8,105)
Taxable income (analysed as £10,000 savings and £7,895 non-savings)	17,895
Tax liability	
n/a @ 10% (see note)	0
on Non savings income 7,895 @ 20%	1,579
On Savings income 10,000 @ 20%	2,000
Tax borne/ tax liability	3,579
Less tax suffered at source	(2,000)
Tax payable by self-assessment	1,579

Notes:

i) Tax of 20% was paid on the savings income at source. No further liability arises on this income, as Alan is not a higher-rate taxpayer.

ii) None of Alan's savings income can benefit from the 10% starting tax rate, as his taxable non-savings income exceeds £2,710.

iii) The tax payable by self-assessment all relates to property income, but this is not all taxed, because PA is set first against non-savings income.

Example

Bill has the following income for the tax year ended 5th April 2013.

Income from property	£44,000
Bank interest (net)	£ 8,000

Compute Bill's income tax liability and income tax payable for 2012/13.

Solution: Bill's income tax computation 2012/13

	£
Income from property	44,000
Bank interest (8,000 x 100/80)	10,000
Total income/net income	54,000
Less PA	(8,105)
Taxable income(analysed as £10,000 savings and £35,895 non-savings)	45,895
Tax liability : n/a @ 10%	0
Non-savings 34,370 @ 20%	6,874
34,370	

Non-savings <u> 1,525</u> @ 40%   610
    35,895
Savings   <u>10,000</u> @ 40%   <u>4,000</u>
    <u>45,895</u>   11,484
Less tax suffered at source   (2,000)
Tax payable   9,484

Note

Savings income is treated as the top slice of taxable income in this example.

Dividend income from UK and foreign companies

4. Dividend income received from companies, other than from UK real estate investment trusts (REITs - see section 5 below), is not 'savings income' for individuals. It is taxed by separate rules in the Income Tax Act 2007, as follows:

a) The date when dividend income arises is the date when the dividend is received by the taxpayer.

b) To reflect the profits tax already paid by a company on pre-dividend profits (see Chapter 1 section 14), a notional 'tax credit' attaches to each dividend when received by an individual shareholder. In 2012/13, the same notional tax credit applies to dividends from companies resident outside the UK.

c) In 2012/13, the tax credit is one-ninth of the dividend. This is equivalent to a tax credit of 10% of the sum of the dividend plus the tax credit.

              £

e.g. Dividend received   900
  Tax credit 10/90 × 900   <u>100</u> (10% × 1,000)
  Gross dividend assessable as dividend income   <u>1,000</u>

d) Dividend income is treated as the top slice of income, above savings income, when applying the UK income tax rate bands. However, the tax rate on dividend income is lower within every band than the rate on savings income.

e) Dividend income falling in the basic rate income band is taxed on the gross dividends at the 'ordinary dividend rate', which is 10%.

f) Dividend income falling in the higher rate income band is taxed on the gross dividends at the 'dividend upper rate', which is 32.5%.

g) Dividend income falling in the additional rate income band is taxed on the gross dividends at the 'dividend additional rate', which is 42.5%.

h) In all the above cases the 10% tax credit on gross dividend income can be deducted from the final tax liability, thus meeting some or all of the tax d

i) Non-taxpayers do not have the right to repayment of any dividend tax credits, even if this exceeds their final tax liability on the dividend income.

Example

Rosie, aged 50, has the following income for the tax year ended 5th April 2013.

Income from property	£24,000
Dividend income received	£1,800

Compute Rosie's income tax liability for 2012/13.

Solution: Rosie's income tax computation, 2012/13

	£	£
Income from property		24,000
Dividends received	1,800	
Tax credits (10/90 × 1,800)	200	
Gross dividend income		2,000
Total / net income		26,000
PA		(8,105)
Taxable income (£15,895 is non-savings)		17,895
Tax payable :		
n/a @ 10%		0
(i) 15,895 @ 20% on non-savings		3,179
(ii) 2,000 @ 10% on gross dividends		200
17,895		3,379
Less dividend tax credits		(200)
Tax payable by self-assessment		3,179

Notes

i)   Dividends have a tax credit of 10/90 attached to each payment.

ii)   The basic rate of tax on dividends is fully met by the tax credit on them. The self-assessment tax is all on the property income.

iii) Dividend income is treated as the top slice of taxable income, but is then taxed at the dividend rate of 10% within the basic rate band.

iv)   The dividend tax credit would not be repayable even if Rosie were a non-taxpayer – e.g. if her only assessable income were from dividends.

Example

Angus, aged 50, has the following income for the year ended 5th April 2013.

Income from property	£25,000
Dividend income received	£18,000

Compute Angus's income tax liability for 2012/13 and the tax payable by self-assessment.

Solution: Angus, tax computation 2012/13

	£
Income from property	25,000
Dividends gross (18,000 x 100/90)	20,000
Total income/net income	45,000
PA	(8,105)
Taxable income (non-savings £16,895)	36,895
Tax liability	
n/a @ 10%	0
16,895 @ 20% (non-savings)	3,379
17,475 @ 10% (dividends)	1,747
34,370	5,126
2,525 @ 32.5% (dividends)	820
36,895	5,946
less dividend tax credits (20,000 x 10%)	(2,000)
Tax payable by self-assessment	3,946

Note

(i) Angus's dividend income is taxed partly at 10% (on £17,475) and partly at 32.5% (on £2,525).

(ii) The 22.5% additional tax on dividends of £2,525 makes up £568 of the tax payable by self-assessment. The rest of the final tax payable arises at basic rate on non-savings (property) income, net of the PA.

Dividends from Real Estate Investment Trusts (REITs)

5. REITS are a special kind of corporate investment vehicle, which invests solely in property for letting. They have existed in the UK since 2007. Individuals can buy shares in REITS and receive 'dividends' on them. However, 'dividends' from REITS have not been subjected to any tax in the REIT before being distributed. Therefore, they do not carry a dividend tax credit. They are not taxed on the individual as dividend income, but as property income. (See Chapter 9.)

Individual savings accounts (ISAs)

6. The main features of these tax-free investments are summarised as follows:

a) ISAs can only be held by UK resident individuals over the age of 16. All income received from an ISA, whether interest or dividends, is exempt from income tax. (However, see final point (k) below, regarding dividends.)

b) Trustees cannot hold ISAs for other people.

c) ISAs are classified into two investment categories, 'cash', and 'stocks and shares'.

d) Annual limits set the maximum amount which each individual can invest into 'mini' ISAs, or one 'maxi' ISA, in each tax year. In 2012/13, an individual can invest money in up to two 'mini-ISAs', but only one of each category; or one single 'maxi-ISA', which can contain both types of investment, with cash deposits being limited to 50% maximum, while 100% if desired can be in stocks and shares.

e) Money may be withdrawn from an ISA, but when withdrawn it loses its ISA character. If it is subsequently reinvested that counts as a fresh ISA investment and counts towards the annual maximum for that tax year. So ISAs are not suitable for fluctuating savings or short term deposits. They are intended for long-term saving.

f) The annual ISA subscription limit for 2012/13 is £11,280, of which not more than £5,640 may be in cash. (Up to the full maximum of £11,280 can be invested in shares, using one 'maxi-ISA'.)

g) From 6 April 2011 onwards, individuals of 16 or 17 can invest in a cash mini-ISA, but not a shares mini-ISA, so their total annual limit is £5,640.

h) From 2011/12, a junior cash mini-ISA, in which up to £3,600 a year may be deposited, may be set up for any child not holding a Child Trust Fund.

(A CTF is a special investment account which had to be started in early life for a child born in the UK between 1 September 2002 and 2 January 2011. A CTF must currently remain invested until the child is 18.)

i) As ISAs with an annual subscription limit of several thousand pounds have existed since 1999, some individuals could by 2012/13 have large holdings built up in ISAs, and generating tax-free capital gains (for shares), interest or dividends. There is no overall lifetime limit on ISA holdings, but ISA status is lost on all investments held if the individual ceases permanently to be a UK resident.

j) ISA income does not have to be recorded in the self-assessment tax return. It is not included as income for the purposes of the calculations causing restriction (abatement) of the Personal Age Allowance and the Married Couple's Allowance for higher incomes.

k) The 1/9 tax credit on dividends received from a stocks and shares ISA is not repayable to the investor, despite the 'tax-free' description, but there is no further tax liability on ISA dividends. But dividend income from an ISA is exempt from inclusion in total income, and also from tax at the higher and additional rates. In addition, the shares held in an ISA are exempt from any CGT on gains realised on their sale.

Other exempt savings income, apart from ISAs

7. Interest on some NSI savings products is exempt from tax: Index-Linked Savings Certificates, Fixed Interest Savings Certificates, Children's Bonus Bonds, and Premium Bond prizes.

Enterprise investment scheme (EIS) shareholdings

8.   Investments in EIS company shares attract UK income tax relief and other tax exemptions for the individual investor.

An EIS company must be an unquoted trading company (or an unquoted company that is preparing to trade), and other detailed conditions apply as to its maximum size and its permitted activities. Broadly, no activities that are 'asset-backed', such as leasing or agriculture, can qualify under current rules, and nor can activities that involve investing in other companies. EIS status is granted to a company by HMRC, and then notified to potential and existing investors by the company.

According to HMRC announcements made in 2012, about 2,000 companies raise EIS capital each year, and about 10,000 individuals invested through EIS in the last year for which figures were available.

Finance Act 2012 substantially raised the maximum number of employees which an EIS company can have (previously 49, now 249) and the maximum amount of gross assets which it can have before the EIS share issue occurs (previously £7 million, now £15 million). By 2011/12, EIS companies had acquired a reputation as very high-risk investments. The latest increases in the permitted size were to allow more companies access to EIS funding.

Cash subscribed for new EIS shares attracts income tax relief at 30% on the amount subscribed, if further qualifying conditions are met by the shareholder. Any income from EIS shares is taxable as dividend income. However, if EIS shares on which income tax relief has been claimed are held for more than three years, capital gains on disposal will be tax-free. (See Part IV, Chargeable Gains.)

EIS relief for income tax works as follows.

a)   An individual can subscribe for up to £1 million of EIS company shares in 2012/13 (£500,000 in 2011/12) and obtain tax relief at the 30% rate. The relief is given 'in terms of tax', so 30% of the qualifying subscription cost is deducted from the tax liability of the individual. EIS relief cannot be used to reclaim tax credits on dividend income, as these are not repayable.

b)   To qualify for income tax relief,

   i)   the eligible shares must be held for at least three years from the date the company's trade started, or the date of the share subscription, if later;

   ii) the individual and his or her associates (this includes family, business partners etc.) must not be connected with the company as an employee, a lender or a shareholder of more than 30% of the share capital at any time in the two years before the EIS subscription or the three years after it;

   iii) the individual must not receive any value from the company, for example a loan or a benefit in kind, during the qualifying 3-year shareholding period.

c) The company must retain its EIS status throughout the qualifying 3-year shareholding period.

d) Any part of the total amount invested by an individual in EIS shares in a tax year can be treated by election as if subscribed for EIS shares in the previous tax year, up to the maximum of EIS relief which could be claimed for that earlier year. So in 2012/13, the maximum amount of EIS subscription that can be related back to tax year 2011/12 is equal to the 2011/12 EIS subscription limit, which was £500,000. This limit would then be reduced by any actual EIS subscriptions made by the same taxpayer in 2011/12, for which relief had already been taken in 2011/12.

(As EIS income tax relief for shares issued before 6 April 2011 was given at the lower rate of 20%, it is unlikely that many taxpayers will have elected to carry back 2011/12 EIS share subscriptions to 2010/11.)

e) If EIS shares are sold at a loss, the taxpayer can elect to claim that loss against total income of that or the preceding tax year, instead of as a capital loss. If this is done, they must deduct from the loss claimed the value of EIS relief already given against income tax.

The Seed Enterprise Investment Scheme (SEIS)

9. The SEIS is new in 2012/13, enacted in Finance Act 2012. It is designed to assist small or early-stage enterprises to obtain equity finance, and offers a higher rate of tax relief than EIS investment, but otherwise complements the EIS.

The rules about qualifying trades mirror those for EIS, and it is envisaged that a company that starts up with the assistance of SEIS tax relief may well use EIS for later equity share issues. A SEIS company must have spent at least 70% of the finance raised under SEIS, before it can make an EIS-qualifying share issue.

UK income taxpayers who subscribe on or after 6 April 2012 for equity shares in a SEIS company can claim income tax relief for 50% of the amount subscribed, by deduction from their UK tax liability. The annual limit for SEIS investment is £100,000 per year, giving a UK tax offset of £50,000. As for EIS, the offset cannot be effective against a liability that was met by the tax credit on dividend income. No capital gains tax is payable on SEIS shares held for more than 3 years.

In principle SEIS share subscriptions can be carried back one year just like EIS subscriptions. This gives greater flexibility for taxpayers to invest only once they know their final income tax position and tax relief capacity for a tax year. However, as no SEIS limit existed in 2011/12, no SEIS carry-back is possible from 2012/13 to 2011/12.

Qualifying companies must obtain confirmation of their SEIS status from HMRC. They must:

a) be undertaking or planning a new business (if already trading, the trade must be less than 2 years old);

b) have 25 or fewer employees;

c) have gross assets of less than £200,000;

d) raise not more than £150,000 in total over three years from SEIS share issues.

Directors, but not other employees, may invest under SEIS in the company for which they work. This allows 'business angels' to take a paid director's role in a company to which they have provided SEIS finance.

Venture capital trusts

10. The main features of this type of investment are as follow.

a) The VCT scheme is designed to stimulate individual investment in a spread of unquoted trading companies, through the mechanism of quoted 'venture capital trust' companies. The type of companies that VCTs invest in is the same as under EIS (see section 8), but by using a VCT the investor is able to choose a broader range of EIS-type investments while still obtaining income tax relief for the investment.

b) Individuals can invest up to a maximum of £200,000 per tax year in VCT shares, attracting income tax relief at 30%, providing the shares are then held for five years. If the shares are not held for five years, the tax relief must be repaid.

c) Dividends received from VCT shares are tax-free.

d) VCT status is awarded to the VCT company by HMRC.

e) There are also capital gains tax reliefs (see Chapter 32)

Miscellaneous income

11. a) **Patent royalties received.** These are normally received by individuals under deduction of basic rate income tax at source. The gross amount is treated as non-savings income under section 579 ITTOIA 2005. It is classed as 'miscellaneous income' for a third party investor, and as trading income if the royalty recipient invented the patented process.

b) **Copyright royalties received**. Copyright royalties are paid to authors or artists gross without deduction of income tax at source. Like patent royalties, they are taxable under section 579 as non-savings income (miscellaneous income for an investor in the copyright, and trading income if the recipient is the original creator of the work).

Pre-owned assets charge

12. As a result of inheritance tax anti-avoidance legislation, an income tax charge may arise in respect of a deemed benefit which a UK resident receives by having free or low-cost enjoyment of an asset or assets which he or she formerly owned, but has given to another person, or has provided another person with the funds to purchase. The charge applies to both tangible (typically land and chattels) and intangible assets formerly owned by, and still enjoyed by, the taxpayer.

However the pre-owned assets charge does not apply to the extent that:

i)   the property in question ceased to be owned before 18 March 1986;

ii)   property formerly owned by a taxpayer is now owned by their spouse;

iii)   the asset in question still counts within the taxpayer's estate for inheritance tax purposes, under the 'gift with reservation' rules (see Chapters 35-36);

iv)   the property was sold by the taxpayer at an arm's length price, and paid for in cash that was not not indirectly supplied by the taxpayer;

v)   the taxpayer was formerly the owner of an asset only by virtue of a will or intestacy, which has subsequently been varied by agreement between the beneficiaries; or

vi)   any enjoyment of the property is no more than incidental, including cases where an outright gift to a family member comes to benefit the donor following an unforeseen change in circumstances. This exception was introduced to cover the situation where an individual contributes ass a gift to the purchase price of accommodation for a family member, but later moves in to live there because of age or infirmity. The exception would not apply if the donor expected eventually to live in the accommodation at the time when the gift of money was made.

The pre-owned assets charge is calculated, broadly, for a house or a flat, as the rental income that could reasonably be expected from the property.

It is calculated on chattels and intangibles as notional income at a 'prescribed rate' of interest, applied to the market value of the 'pre-owned asset', which is re-valued for this purpose every five years.

The prescribed rate of interest currently matches the official rate of interest used for valuing certain employment benefits (see Chapter 7). The official rate was 4% per year on 6 April 2012, but has been set higher in the past.

As no one is really paying this interest or rent, there is no matching deduction for any other taxpayer to match the notional income assumed to be received by the person who formerly owned the asset and is still 'enjoying' it.

The pre-owned assets charge is not a common item to see on real income tax returns or tax computations, because the main purpose of the 'pre-owned assets' income tax regime is deterrent, rather than to raise tax revenue.

If a taxpayer is caught by the pre-owned assets charge, he or she can escape it by electing instead to have the asset included in their estate for inheritance tax purposes, even if the exact circumstances of disposal were not caught by the normal 'gift with reservation' IHT rules (see Part VI for these).

Student self-testing questions

1.   The following information relates to the self-assessment tax return of Abigail.

	Year ended 5th April 2013
	£
Salary (gross before PAYE deducted of £8,284)	46,000
Taxed dividends (net)	540
Bank interest (net)	400
Gift Aid to Oxfam (net)	1,600

Calculate the income tax liability and remaining tax payable by or repayable to Abigail for 2012/13.

Solution: Abigail, Income tax computation 2012/13

	Non-savings income £	Savings income £	Dividend income £	Total £
Salary	46,000			46,000
Bank interest 400 x 100/80		500		500
Dividends 540 x 100/90			600	600
Total income				47,100
Personal allowance	(8,105)			(8,105)
Taxable income	37,895	500	600	38,995

Tax liability:

		n/a @ 10%		0
On non-savings:	Basic rate	34,370 @ 20%		6,874
	Extend for gift aid	2,000 @ 20%		400
		36,370		
	Higher rate	1,525 @ 40%		610
		37,895		
On savings:	Higher rate	500 @ 40%		200
On dividends	Higher rate	600 @ 32.5%		195
		38,995		

Tax liability	8,279
Less tax paid under PAYE	(8,284)
Tax deducted on savings income	(100)
Tax credit on dividends	(60)
Tax repayable	(165)

Notes

i)   Tax credit on dividends 10/90 × 540 = £60 + tax on bank interest 20/80 × 400
      = £100.

ii)   The basic rate is extended by (1,600 x 100/80) £2,000 to £36,370 to give relief
      for the Gift Aid at the higher rate.

2.   Emma, a 25 year-old, has business trading profits of £22,500 for the year
ended 5 April 2013. She also receives building society interest of £6,400 (net).

What is her income after tax for 2012/13, ignoring National Insurance?

Solution

	Non-savings £	Savings £	Total £
Income:			
Trading income	22,500		22,500
Taxed investment income BSI gross		8,000	8,000
Net Income	22,500	8,000	30,500
Personal allowance	(8,105)		(8,105)
Taxable income	14,395	8,000	22,395
Tax:			
At savings rate	n/a x 10%		0
At basic rate	22,395 x 20%		4,479
	22,395		

Income tax borne on taxable income	4,479
(= Income tax liability)	
Tax suffered on building society interest	(1,600)
Final income tax due 31.1.2014	2,879
Calculation of income after tax but before NIC:	
Profits of trading	22,500
Net Building society interest	6,400
	28,900
Balance of tax payable	2,879
Net income after tax	26,021

Note: for self-employed NIC see Chapter 17

3. Chris, aged 35, has the following income and outgoings for the year ended 5 April 2013

Business trading profits	7,840
Salary	22,975
Bank interest received net	416
Building society interest received net	712
Rent receivable from let property (not in Chris's own home)	1,890
Allowable expenses of employment	95

Requirement: Calculate Chris's tax liability for 2012/13

Solution

	Non savings	Savings	Total
	£	£	£
Income from employment			
(22,975 – 95)	22,880		22,880
Income from trading	7,840		7,840
Income from property	1,890		1,890
Bank & building society interest			
(712+416) x 100/80		1,410	1,410
Total income/ Net income	32,610	1,410	34,020
Personal allowance	(8,105)		(8,105)
Taxable income	24,505	1,410	25,915
Non savings			
n/a x 10%	0		
24,505 x 20%	4,901		
Savings			
1,410 x 20%	282		
Tax borne = Tax liability	5,183		

Note: The question asked for tax liability, not tax payable, so the calculation can stop here.

4. Pat has the following income for 2012/13

	£
Income from his business	19,450
Dividends	1,944
Income from property	1,000

Pat claims the personal allowance of £8,105

Requirement:

(a) Calculate Pat's income tax payable by self-assessment for 2012/13

(b) How would your answer differ if Pat had £144,450 income from his business?

Solution

Pat : Income tax computation for 2012/13

Income	Non-savings £	Dividends £	Total £
Income from property	1,000		1,000
Income from trading	19,450		19,450
Dividends gross (1,944 x 10/9)		2,160	2,160
Net income	20,450	2,160	22,610
Less: personal allowances	(8,105)		(8,105)
Taxable income	12,345	2,160	14,505

Income tax

n/a	x 10%	0
12,345	x 20%	2,469
2,160	x 10%	216
14,505		
Tax borne		2,685

Less: tax credits on dividends

2,160 x 10%	(216)
Tax payable by self-assessment	2,469

Part b Income tax computation for 2012/13

Income	Non-savings	Dividends	
Income from property	1,000		1,000
Income from trading	144,450		144,450
Dividends gross (as before)		2,160	2,160
Net income	145,450	2,160	147,610

Personal allowance	8,105			
Restricted				
(147,610 – 100,000) x ½				
	(23,805)	0		0
Taxable income		145,450	2,160	147,610
Income tax				
n/a	x 10%	0		
34,370	x 20%	6,874		
111,080	x 40%	44,432		
2,160	x 32.5%	702		
147,610				
Tax liability		52,008		
Less: tax credits on dividends				
2,160 x 10%		(216)		
Tax payable by self-assessment		51,792		

Questions without answers

1. Jacqui, aged 35, has the following income for 2012/13

Salary (PAYE £5,200)	26,000
Building society interest (net)	4,800
Dividends (net)	11,700
Gift aid donation (net)	700

Requirement: Calculate Jacqui's income tax payable.

2. Jackie is aged 42.

Requirement: Calculate Jackie's tax position in 2012/13 if her income was:

a) trading profits of £148,500 and building society interest of £6,800 net.

b) trading profits of £2,500 and building society interest of £6,800 net.

7 Income from employment I – general aspects

Introduction

1. This chapter is concerned with the taxation of income from employment.

The major part deals with the taxation of earnings from employment and benefits treated as earnings. A summary of the benefits treated as earnings within the 'benefits code' is provided, showing the taxation effects on 'Non P11D employees' (employees earning less than £8,500 p.a.), and 'P11D employees' (i.e. company directors, and employees earning more than £8,500 p.a.).

The legislation is contained in the Income Tax (Earnings and Pensions) Act 2003.

Summary of taxable income

2. Tax under the ITEPA 2003 is charged in respect of the following income.

Employment income.

Pension income.

Social security income.

Employment

3. a) Employment includes in particular:
   i) any employment under a contract of service;
   ii) any employment under a contract of apprenticeship;
   iii) any employment in the service of the Crown; and
   iv) any office, which includes in particular any position that has an existence independent of the person who holds it and may be filled by successive holders.

   b) Employment is usually evidenced by a written contract of employment, or in older legal language, a 'contract of service'. UK employment law now provides that anyone employed for longer than a minimal period is legally entitled to a written statement of the terms of their employment.

   However, under income tax law, even if a written contract exists (and even if it states that the engagement is not an employment), the factual details of the worker's involvement, rather than the words of the contract, determine whether the engagement is an employment.

   In contrast to a 'contract of service', a contract for particular 'services rendered' is associated with self-employment, the rewards of which are assessable as trading profits. For a leading case, see Hall v Lorimer 1992 CA STC 23.

   c) An office can be thought of as a position with duties attached to it which do not change with the holder, and which in a sense still exists between holders, even while the next holder is being chosen. It is the income of the office that is taxable as employment income. Examples of office holders are: a judge; a town clerk; a company director or company secretary.

Employment income

4. a) The legislation provides that earnings, in relation to employment, means:

    i)   any salary, wages or fee;

    ii)   any gratuity or other profit or incidental benefit of any kind obtained by the employee if it is money or money's worth; or

    iii) anything else that constitutes either general earnings or specific income of the employment.

(Before ITEPA 2003, the term 'emoluments' covered all the chargeable earnings of an employment. This word is still found in case-law, but no longer appears in the statute.)

  b) For the purposes of (ii) above, 'money's worth' means something that is:

    i)   of direct monetary value to the employee; or

    ii)   capable of being converted into money or into something of direct monetary value to the employee.

Receipt of money earnings

5. a) Employment income is assessable in the tax year when it is received. General earnings consisting of money are to be treated as received at the earliest of the following times:

Rule 1

The time when payment is made of or on account of the earnings.

Rule 2

The time when a person becomes entitled to payment of or on account of the earnings.

Rule 3

If the employee is a director of a company and the earnings are from employment with the company (whether or not as a director), whichever is the earliest:

    i)   the time when sums on account of the earnings are credited in the company's accounts or records (whether or not there is any restriction on the right to draw the sums);

    ii)   if the amount of the earnings for a period is determined by the end of the period, the time when the period ends, and

    iii) if the amount of the earnings for a period is not determined until after the period has ended, the time when the amount is determined.

b) Rule 3 applies if the employee is a director of the company at any time in the tax year in which the time mentioned falls.

c) In this section director means:

   i) in relation to a company whose affairs are managed by a board of directors or similar body, a member of that body;

   ii) in relation to a company whose affairs are managed by a single director or similar person, that director or person, and

   iii) in relation to a company whose affairs are managed by the members themselves, a member of the company,

   and includes any person in accordance with whose directions or instructions the directors of the company (as defined above) are accustomed to act.

d) For the purposes of subsection (c) a person is not to be regarded as a person in accordance with whose directions or instructions the directors of the company are accustomed to act merely because the directors act on advice given by that person in a professional capacity.

Gifts and voluntary payments

6. In principle, gifts and voluntary payments unconnected with an employment are not taxable, but there is a presumption that payments from an employer to an employee are in return for service. A key test here is whether the employee would have reasonably expected the additional payment when they were originally carrying out the services to which the payment potentially refers. Case-law and HMRC practice have established the following exceptions where the presumption that a payment was in return for employment services can be successfully defeated (rebutted) by factual evidence.

a) Reasonable gifts made by an employer in connection with an employee's marriage or retirement are not taxable.

b) Long-service awards in the form of gifts of objects or non-cash vouchers are not taxed, providing that: the award is in respect of not less than 20 years' service; no similar payment has been made during the previous 10 years; and the cost to the employer does not exceed £50 (previously £20) for each year of service. A cash award would be taxable.

c) The proceeds of a 'benefit' match for a sportsman were held not to be taxable as emoluments ('employment income' since 2003), so long as they were not part of the employment contract. However, transfer signing fees received personally by footballers are taxable employment income.

d) A cash award of £130 (at the time a significant amount) to a bank clerk for passing his professional examinations was held to be a non-taxable gift. (However, if such exam awards are included in the contract of employment, they will be taxable.)

e)   £1,000 paid by the English Football Association to each of the members of the 1966 England World Cup team for winning the football tournament (not promised in advance) was held to be a gift, and not taxable employment income.

f)   Tips of an employed taxi driver were held to be taxable in Calvert v Wainwright 1947 27 TC 475. ITEPA section 62 now confirms specifically that tips and gratuities received directly from customers by employed taxi drivers, postmen, hairdressers, waiters, etc, in respect of services provided to the employer's customers, are in principle part of earnings.

g)   The Easter offerings that a vicar received, being donations from his congregation following an appeal by his Bishop, were held to be emoluments (now employment income).

h)   Gifts from third parties made to an employee in the course of employment costing not more than £100 in any tax year are not taxable, by concession.

i)   A payment to a footballer by his old club to join a new club was held to be taxable as emoluments i.e. as a 'farewell' payment on retirement or removal from an office. The 'signing-on fee' paid by the new club on another footballer's transfer was held to be taxable as emoluments from the new employment.

Benefits treated as earnings – Benefits Code

7.   As a general rule, all benefits provided by an employer are treated as earnings and valued under the Benefits Code. However, some benefits are specifically exempted.

The Benefits Code is now found in ITEPA 2003. It contains general rules for taxing any non-cash benefits for which no special rules exist, and particular rules dealing with specific types of benefit, e.g.,

Cars, vans and related benefits	Loans
Living accommodation	Cash equivalent benefits

Lower-paid employment ('Non-P11D employment' - ITEPA 2003)

8.   a)   The Benefits Code does not apply to an employment in relation to a tax year if:

i)   it is lower-paid employment in relation to that year, and

ii)   condition A or B is met.

An employment is lower-paid employment in relation to a tax year if the earnings rate for the employment for the year is less than £8,500.

b)   Condition A is that the employee is not employed as a director of a company.

c)   Condition B is that the employee is employed as a director of a company but has no material interest (broadly defined as a 5% shareholding) in the company and either:

i) the employment is as a full-time working director, or

ii) the company is non-profit-making or is established for charitable purposes only.

Non-profit-making means that the company does not carry on a trade and its functions do not consist wholly or mainly in the holding of investments or other property.

The taxation of benefits as earnings

9. The taxation of benefits in kind as earnings depends upon placing a value on the goods and services that are provided at less than full cost, for an employee. This is achieved as follows.

a) In respect of non-P11D employees, unless provided otherwise by ITEPA, benefits are only taxable if they can be converted into money's worth, at their second-hand value.

Benefits which cannot be converted into money's worth are therefore in principle not taxable, e.g. interest free loans, or the private use of a company car.

b) For directors and employees earning £8,500 or more (called 'P11D employees' in ITEPA), benefits are taxable whether or not they can be converted into money's worth. The P11D employee rules state that benefits are to be valued at the cost to the employer, unless another prescribed method is laid down (eg. as it is for private cars).

c) Following the decision in Pepper v Hart HL 1992 STC 898 (which related to the taxable value of a private school place provided to the child of a school-teacher), benefits provided 'in-house' in the form of the employer's own goods or services are valued at 'cost to the employer' on the marginal cost basis, not on an average cost basis including a share of overheads.

In Pepper v Hart, it was held that as long as there were still places unfilled at the school, the taxable value of the benefit of a free school place for a teacher's child was only the marginal cost of extra books, meals and laundry, less any such costs reimbursed by the employee.

Directors and employees earning £8,500 or more p.a. (P11D Employees)

10. The rules of the benefit code apply to P11D employees. These are defined as:

a) Any employee whose total earnings, plus reimbursed expenses and benefits treated as earnings, are greater than £8,500 p.a. (this means 'at a rate of £8,500 pa', so if the employee was only employed for 3 months in a tax year the applicable limit is £2,125)

b) Any director who has a material interest in the company i.e. is either the owner of or able to control more than 5% of the ordinary share capital of the company.

c) A full-time working director with a material interest of 5% or less in the company, if his or her total earnings and benefits treated as earnings is greater than £8,500 p.a.

Employers must complete a return (form P11D) of all expenses reimbursed and all benefits in kind provided each year in respect of each P11D employee, unless a dispensation is obtained (see 11 below).

Any benefits provided for the members of the family or household of an employee are treated as if they were provided for the employee personally. The term family or household covers the employee's spouse, children and their spouses, his or her parents, servants, dependants and guests.

Dispensations

11. Where the company is able to explain to HMRC its arrangements for paying expenses and providing benefits, and satisfy HMRC that these would be fully matched by a 'necessary expenses of employment' in the personal tax computation of the employee, then it is possible for the employer to obtain a 'P11D dispensation' in respect of named types of expense reimbursements and benefits.

The nature of the expenses covered by a dispensation depends to some extent on the particular circumstances, but they can cover:

> travelling and subsistence
>
> cost of entertaining incurred wholly and exclusively for business
>
> subscriptions to professional bodies related to employment
>
> telephone rentals to employees on call outside normal hours
>
> overnight incidental cost allowances within the permitted tax-free limits.

Benchmark rates for day subsistence

12. HMRC has introduced advisory benchmark scale rates for day subsistence, which will not give rise to taxable benefits. Employers may alternatively use dispensations agreed with HMRC. The benchmark rates are:

> Five-hour rate – Up to £5 may be paid where the worker has been away from his or her home or normal place of work for at least five hours, and incurred cost for a meal.
>
> Ten-hour rate - Up to £10 may be paid where the worker has been away from his or her home or normal place of work for at least ten hours, and incurred cost for a meal, or meals.
>
> Breakfast rate (irregular early starters only) – Up to £5 may be paid where a worker leaves home earlier than usual and before 6.00 a.m. and incurs a cost on breakfast taken away from home.
>
> Late evening meal rate (irregular late finishers only) – Up to £15 may be paid where the employee finishes work late after 8.00 p.m. and buys a meal which he or she would usually eat at home.

Summary of benefits treated as earnings 2012/13

13 The Benefit Code	P11D employees
Private use of employer's car	Car and fuel benefits (see below)
Private use of employer's van	Van and fuel benefits (see below)
Accommodation (see below).	Accommodation can be wholly or partly exempt, otherwise taxed on rent paid, or annual value if owned, plus expenses paid, plus an additional charge for accommodation costing more than £75,000. (see below)
Board and lodging	Taxed on cost to the employer
Suits and clothing	Taxed on cost to employer
Medical insurance	Premiums paid by employer taxable
Beneficial loans (see below)	Generally taxable at the deemed interest saving, with some exceptions
Cash vouchers, saving certificates	Full value taxable (even if employer pays less)
Assets loaned	20% of market value when first provided is taxable for each complete tax year
Assets transferred	Taxed on value increase enjoyed (see section 24 below for details)
Season tickets and transport vouchers.	Taxed on cost to the employer
Sick pay	Taxed on amount received (as it is cash, NIC on cash earnings will also apply, see Chapter 17)
Scholarships provided by reason of employment	Taxed on cost to employer
Employer-subsidised nursery facilities	Taxed on cost to employer (unless the nursery is at the workplace itself, in which case it is a tax-free benefit)
Loan written off	Taxed on full value (and as it becomes cash remuneration at that point it is also liable to NIC on cash earnings – see Chapter 17)

14. Benefits with exemptions from Income Tax — All Employees

'Green commuting' benefits, including: loan of cycling equipment, works buses, subsidised fares on public buses.	Tax-free
Mobile telephones with private use	One phone provided to employee personally is exempt; any further phones are taxed at cost to the employer
Job-related living accommodation (see below).	Either wholly or partly exempt (see section 21 onwards)
Non-job-related living accommodation	Taxed on rental cost or annual value , plus any furniture loaned and expenses paid (see section 21 onwards)
Industrial clothing	Tax-free (does not cover 'ordinary' clothing)
Approved share option schemes (See section 21 onwards)	If the scheme is HMRC-approved, there is no income tax on the grant of share options and no income tax on later exercise, if the exercise price is not less than the shares' market value when the option was granted. The employee is also liable to CGT and not income tax on gains on disposal of shares acquired via options.
Savings related approved share options	Not subject to income tax, CGT applies on final disposal
Free or subsidised meals in staff canteen	Tax-free if generally available to all employees
In-house sports facilities	Not taxable, if not available to the public
Overnight expenses	Up to £5 per night UK, and £10 overseas, exempt
Workplace nurseries	Not taxable
Child-care vouchers which can be used to pay for childcare from various approved providers	Up to £55 per week per employee is exempt. The relief is limited, for new joiners in 2011/12 or later, to basic rate tax only.

Private use of employer-provided motor cars 2012/13 – benefit valuation rules

15.

The benefit is calculated as follows:	£	£
List price of car and optional accessories when first provided	X	
Less capital contribution (if any) by employee	(X)	
= **Net Value**		X
Value of benefit = Percentage of net value based on		
CO_2 emissions (per table)		X
Less reduction for unavailability		(X)
Less payment by employee (if any) for private use		(X)
Car **Benefit treated as earnings**		X

Notes

i)   The percentage to be applied to the net value of the car is determined from the CO_2 emission table, reproduced below.

ii) List price is the manufacturer's published price for that model when first registered, plus the list price of any optional accessories. HMRC obtains data on list prices from car manufacturers to check to Form P11D submitted information. Any purchasing discount received by the employer from list price is irrelevant for this purpose.

iii) In 2012/13 there is no maximum for the list price taken into account. (Formerly an £80,000 maximum applied to the list price to be used.)

iv) Where the car is more than 15 years old at the end of the income tax year then its original list price, if more than £15,000, is taken as £15,000.

v)   The benefit for private use is reduced proportionally if the car is not available for any period of 30 days or more in the year. Periods of less than 30 days of unavailability are ignored. The benefit is also pro-rated in a tax year when the benefit started to be given for the first time, or ceased to be given.

vi) Where the employee makes a capital contribution to the cost of the car, then, subject to a maximum of £5,000, the amount is deducted from the list price.

vii) Where an employee is required to make a revenue contribution to the employer for private use of the car, the annual amount of this is deducted in arriving at the assessable benefit.

16. CO_2 emission table 2012/13:

CO_2 emissions, grams per km	% of list price
2012/13	**Petrol cars**
99 or less	10%
100	11%
105	12%
110	13%
115	14%
120	15%
125	16%
130	17%
135	18%
140	19%
145	20%
150	21%
155	22%
160	23%
165	24%
170	25%
175	26%
180	27%
185	28%
190	29%
195	30%
200	31%
205	32%
210	33%
215	34%
220	35%

Notes

i)   The exact CO_2 figure is always rounded down to the nearest 5 grams per kilometre. For example, CO_2 emissions of 188g/km are treated as 185g/km.

ii)   The maximum charge is 35% of the list price.

iii)   The rates in the above table are increased for cars using diesel fuel by 3% (but not so as to increase the maximum percentage above 35%):

iv)   For cars with no approved CO_2 emissions figure, the percentage of the car's list price to be taxed is determined using the car's engine size. One scale is for all cars registered before 1998; and another for the small number of cars registered from 1998 onwards which do not have approved CO_2 emissions.

Engine size (cc)	Pre-1998 car	1998 or later car
0 – 1,400	15%	15%
1,401 – 2,000	22%	25%
2,001 and over	32%	35%

Once determined, the same car benefit is used for Class 1A National Insurance contributions (see Chapter 17).

Example

Alex drives a Ford petrol company car in 2012/13 with a list price of £16,000. CO_2 emissions are 182g/km.

Compute the assessable car benefit for 2012/13.

Solution: Cash equivalent benefit 2012/13

List price × 27% = 16,000 × 27%   £4,320

Notes

i) CO_2 emissions of 182g/km are rounded down to 180g/km.

ii)   The benefit percentage for 2012/13 (per table) for 180g/km is 27%;

iii)   Alternatively the percentage may be calculated from the base level:

180g – 100g = 80g

80g/5g = 16 graduations of 5g, at 1% each, above the 11% level for 100g/km

11% +16% = 27%.

Private motor cars 2012/13 £20,200 – fuel benefit CO_2%

17. Fuel scale charges for employees receiving free fuel for private mileage in company cars are based on the same percentage as was calculated for the car benefit (linked with the car's CO_2 emissions) which is applied to a scale charge of £20,200 (2011/12 £18,800).

Once determined, the same fuel benefit is used for employer's Class 1A National Insurance contributions (see Chapter 17).

The fuel benefit charge is proportionally reduced where an employee permanently stops receiving free fuel partway through the tax year. However, an employee opting out and then back into a free fuel benefit within the same year will result in a full year's charge with no reduction for non-availability.

(This rule was presumably designed to encourage employees to agree permanently to give up the benefit of employer-provided private fuel.)

Notes

i)   The fuel benefit is reduced to nil if all private fuel is paid for or reimbursed (at approved rates) by the employee/director.

ii) The charge is not reduced at all if the employee/director reimburses only a partial amount of private journeys fuel provided by the employer.

iii) Employers (not employees) are also required to pay NI at 13.8% on the assessable benefit value of cars /fuel provided for private use of P11D employees. This NI is paid annually - see Chapter 17.

iv) Where one car is used jointly by two or more employees, a separate assessable benefit can arise in respect of each user.

Example

Ali is employed by Beta Ltd and is provided with a car (CO_2 emissions 240g/km) which cost £22,000 on 1st January 2010. Ali used the car during 2012/13 and Beta Ltd paid for all fuel, business and private. Ali pays £300 to the company each year for the private use of the car.

Calculate the value of any car benefit for 2012/13.

Solution: Ali – Value of car benefits 2012/13

	£
Motor car benefit 35% × £22,000	7,700
Less contribution	300
	7,400
Motor fuel benefit	7,070
Total (included in Ali's assessable employment income)	14,470

Notes: i) The 2012/13 percentage for for 240g/km CO_2 emissions is 35%.

ii) The fuel benefit is 35% × £20,200 i.e. £7,070

Vans – benefit of permitted private use of vans 2012/13

18. Private use of a van with a vehicle weight up to 3,500kg is taxed at a fixed benefit value of £3,000 for a full tax year (proportionately reduced for part-year).

There is no taxable benefit where the employee is required to take an employer's van home overnight for reasons of either security or work efficiency, so long as there is no other personal use of the van. This is different from the rule for cars, where a private use benefit arises even if the only use of the car is for home to work commuting.

Vans – private fuel benefit 2012/13

19. If an employee makes no reimbursement for fuel used during private use of a company van, there is a flat-rate fuel benefit of £550 (2011/12 £500).

Authorised mileage allowance payments

20. Where an employee uses his or her own vehicle to complete business journeys, mileage allowances are allowed by HMRC to be paid tax-free up to rates deemed not to involve a profit element for the employee. There are separate rates for cars and vans, motorbikes, bicycles and for carrying passengers.

An authorised mileage allowance payment must be:-

a) paid to the employee, not to someone else for the employee's advantage

b) specifically for business mileage

The April 2012/13 maximum rates are as follows: 2012/13

Cars and vans	
- First 10,000 miles	45p per mile
- Over 10,000 miles	25p per mile
Motorcycles	24p per mile
Bicycles	20p per mile
Carrying a passenger	5p per passenger

These permitted maximum rates may be varied at any time during a tax year by Statutory Instrument.

Where an employer has paid business mileage expenses of less than the statutory rate, the employee can claim an expense deduction against employment income for the difference. Payments in excess of statutory rates are liable to income tax.

Living accommodation

21. Cash-equivalent value of benefits (directors and all employees)

Where any employee (whether P11D or non-P11D category) is provided with living accommodation by an employer, then, subject to certain exemptions noted below, he or she is liable to tax on the 'cash equivalent value' of the benefit. This is defined as

[Annual value + Cost of ancillary services – Employee's contribution – business use]

Annual value is the gross rateable value of the property, whether rented or owned by the employer. (Gross rateable values can still be obtained from Government sources, although domestic rates are no longer based on them.)

For a property rented by the employer, the annual value benefit is the greater of the annual value itself or the actual rent paid by the employer.

Cost of ancillary services is the total of any expenses incurred in providing services such as heating, lighting, rates, domestic services or gardening, and the loan value of any furniture provided by the employer.

Employee's contribution means any rent paid by an employee. Any payment by the employee towards expenses may also be deducted from the value of the taxable benefit.

Business use means the proportion of any benefit attributable to business use.

Total exemption from annual value charge - job-related accommodation

An individual is not taxed on the annual value of the accommodation if it is:

a)   necessary for the proper performance of his or her duties, or

b)   customary for the better performance of his or her duties, and in general provided for others in the same employment, or

c)   required for security reasons.

A full-time working director with less than 5% interest in a company is eligible to claim exemption under (a) and (b), but not under (c). All other directors, whether or not they control the company, are ineligible for accommodation exemptions.

Partial exemption from the 'ancillary costs' benefit

If an individual is exempted from the annual value charge as noted above, then the taxable value of all ancillary services is limited to a maximum of an extra 10% of their net assessable earnings for the year.

Net assessable earnings for this purpose are computed as all income from the employment (ignoring the ancillary costs benefit), less allowable employment expenses, approved pension scheme payments and capital allowances.

Example

Quentin is an employee of T plc, occupying a house with an annual value of £1,000, which is exempt accommodation. The employer pays the following expenses in 2012/13:

	£
Heating and lighting (electricity bills)	1,200
Gardening	800
Domestic help's wages	500
New furniture costing	10,000

Quentin's salary for the year 2012/13 is £45,000. He pays T plc £300 towards running costs of the house and pays £5,000 of occupational pension contributions.

Calculate the value of the benefit for 2012/13.

Solution: Quentin, Cash equivalent value accommodation benefit 2012/13

		£
i) Annual value of property (exempted as job-related)		–
Ancillary services:		
Heating and lighting cost	1,200	
Domestic help cost	500	
Gardening cost	800	2,500
Use of furniture 20% × 10,000		2,000
		4,500
less employee contribution		(300)
Ancillary use benefit on normal terms		4,200

Compare:	£
Quentin – Net assessable earnings £(45,000 – 5,000)	40,000
× 10% =	4,000
Less employee contribution	(300)
Maximum assessable cash-equivalent benefit	3,700

Notes

i)   The restriction applies in this case so the assessable benefit is £3,700.

ii)   The furniture is valued as an asset loaned to an employee, at 20% of its market value when first provided, i.e. £10,000. (This assumes that there was no existing loaned furniture in the house at the start of the tax year.)

iii)   If Q's occupation was non-exempt, the value of his total accommodation benefits would be the annual value, plus the other benefits, i.e. £1,000 plus £4,500, less the contribution of £300, giving £5,200.

Living accommodation costing more than £75,000 ('expensive accommodation')

22.   An extra taxable accommodation benefit arises if an employer owns rather than rents the accommodation and it is 'expensive accommodation' as defined.

This rule was added to the Benefits Code to deal with arrangements that had been adopted in cities such as London where the official 'annual value' of properties had diverged below the market rents. Without this additional 'deemed loan' benefit an employer could reduce the taxable benefit significantly by buying property rather than renting it.

It applies only to P11D employees (but in practice that means nearly all employees, given that there has been no rise in the P11D earnings threshold for many years).

The extra benefit applies if :

a)   living accommodation is provided by reason of an office or employment, and

b)   the cost of providing the accommodation was greater than £75,000, and

c)   the occupier is liable to a taxable benefit in respect of the provision of the living accommodation. So, if the employee is exempt from the 'annual value' charge as noted above, he or she is also exempted from the expensive accommodation charge.

d)   The additional value is determined as:

ORI % × [cost or deemed cost – £75,000] less employee 'contribution', where:

ORI percentage= the official rate of interest in force on the 6th April of the tax year. For 2012/13 it is 4%.

Cost   = capital cost of acquisition of the property, + cost of any capital improvements completed before the beginning of the current tax year. If the property was acquired more than six tax years before its first occupation by the employee, then the market value on first occupation is taken as the 'cost of providing' the accommodation.

'Contribution'   = the amount by which any rent paid by tenant exceeds the annual value of the accommodation.

The £75,000 definition above which accommodation is classed as 'expensive' has not been increased since this legislation was first introduced. As a result the charge now applies to a lot of employer-owned accommodation.

Example

J plc acquired a property in October 2009 for £265,000 which had an annual value of £10,000. In May 2013 improvements costing £25,000 were incurred. On 7th April 2012, Zack, the marketing director, occupied the property paying J plc a rent of £5,000 p.a. He paid £15,000 towards the original cost.

Calculate the value of the accommodation benefit in kind for 2012/13.

Solution: Cash equivalent value of benefit 2012/13

	£	£
2012/13 value of accommodation benefit:		
Annual value of property	10,000	
Less rent paid by director	(5,000)	5,000
Additional value charge for accommodation:		
Cost of accommodation	265,000	
Part of cost paid by director	(15,000)	
= deemed loan to director	250,000	
Less exempt amount	(75,000)	
	175,000	
Less 'contribution'	0	
	175,000	
4% × 175,000 =		7,000
		12,000

Notes

i)   £12,000 is Zack's benefit chargeable to income tax for 2012/13. This will be reported on his Form P11D by his employer (see Chapter 8).

ii) The improvement expenditure of £25,000 will not count in the additional value 'cost' until 2013/14.

iii) As the rent paid by Z is less than the annual value, there is no further deduction for this rent in the computation of the additional value.

iv) The official rate of interest on 6 April 2012 was 4%.

v) Additional value charge, within the total benefit, is $175,000 \times 4\% = \pounds7,000$.

vi) If a property is not occupied throughout the year the charge is pro-rated.

Assets other than cars – private use

23. Where assets are made available for use by P11D employees, then the annual benefit is calculated as follows.

a) Land and property (other than accommodation) is valued at a market rent.

b) Other assets e.g. a company motor cycle, are valued at 20% of the original market value when provided, or if higher, the rental paid by the employer.

Assets transferred to an employee

24. If an asset made available on loan to a P11D employee is subsequently acquired by that person, then the assessable benefit on the acquisition is the greater of:

a) the excess of the current market price over the price paid by the employee and,

b) the excess of the market value when first provided for use by the employee, less any amounts assessed as annual benefits (at 20%) over the price paid by the employee.

When an employee buys, from his or her employer, a previously loaned computer or bicycle for its full market value, no tax charge arises on the transfer of ownership.

Beneficial loans

25. Where an individual is provided with an interest-free or cheap loan, the financial benefit derived from such an arrangement is taxable. There is an exemption for a loan that at no time in the tax year exceeded £5,000. This exemptions allows employers to offer 'season ticket loans' or other convenience loans of a relatively small amount to employees without income tax consequences.

Non-P11D employees are not taxed on cheap loan benefits, since the interest saving is not convertible into cash. The following are the benefit valuation rules for P11D employees:

a) A loan to an employee, or to his or her relative, giving rise to an interest saving is a benefit in kind if obtained due to an employment.

b) The assessable amount is calculated by two methods, (see below) in both cases using the **official rate of interest** less any interest actually paid by the employee.

(ORI at the start of 2012/13   = 4%)

c)   No benefit arises where the interest on the loan would normally qualify for tax relief, such as a loan for the purchase of plant or machinery (apart from cars) for use in the employment.

d)   If the value of all the loans outstanding at any time during the year does not exceed £5,000, there will be no charge.

Methods of calculation

26. I. **Average method**

a)   This method averages the amount of the loan for the whole tax year by reference to the opening and closing balances at the beginning of the year (or the date of first advance if later) and at the end of the year, and applies the official rate to this amount.

b)   Any actual interest paid is deducted from the amount computed in (a), to determine the benefit to be taxed.

c)   This method is applied automatically, unless an election is made by either the taxpayer or HMRC, to apply the second (precise) method.

Example

Z Ltd makes an interest-free loan to R, a P11D employee, on the 1st October 2012 of £24,000. It is repayable by eight quarterly instalments of £3,000, payable on the 1st January, April, July and October. The first repayment is made on the 1st January 2013.

Calculate the assessable benefit for 2012/13. The official rate is 4%.

Solution: Computation of interest benefit 2012/13

		£
1.10.2012	Loan granted	24,000
5.4.2013	Balance of loan outstanding	
	(24,000 – (2 x 3,000))	<u>18,000</u>
		<u>42,000</u>
	Average loan outstanding	
	$\dfrac{42,000}{2}$	<u>21,000</u>

Period of loan

1.10.2012–5.4.2013 = 6 months. (i.e. complete tax months)

Notional Interest $4\% \times \dfrac{6}{12} \times 21,000 =$ 420

Actual interest	<u>Nil</u>
Assessable benefit 2012/13	<u>420</u>

27. II. **Alternative method**

a)   Under this method, the interest is calculated on the balance outstanding on a daily basis, at the official rate of interest.

b)   Any interest actually paid is deducted from the amount calculated.

Example

Using the data relating to Z Ltd in the previous example, calculate the assessable benefit under the alternative method.

Solution: Computation of interest benefit – 2012/13

		£	£
1.10.2012	Loan granted	24,000	
1.1.2013	Loan repayment	3,000	
		21,000	
	Number of days from 1.10.2012 to 1.1.2013 = 92		
	Interest 92/365 × 4% × 24,000		242
1.1.2013	Balance outstanding	21,000	
1.4.2013	Loan repayment	3,000	
5.4.2013	Balance outstanding	18,000	
No. of days from 1.1.2013 to 1.4.2013 = 90			
do. 1.4.2013 to 5.4.2013 = 5			
Interest 90/365 ×4% × 21,000			207
5/365 × 4% × 18,000			10
Assessable benefit 2012/13			459

Given these figures the taxpayer will not elect for the precise method.

Deductions from earnings

28. The following may be deducted as expense of the employment under ITEPA. None of these expenses can be set against total income, as allowable payments.

a)   Expenses falling within the general rule of Section 336. This states that a deduction from earnings is allowed for an amount if:

i)   the employee is obliged to incur and pay it as holder of the employment, and

ii)   the amount is incurred wholly and exclusively and necessary for the performance of the duties of the office or employment; for example, industrial clothing; tools of trade.

Travelling expenses from the employee's home to the employer's place of business are not permitted expenses of the employment, see Ricketts v Colquhoun 1926 10 TC 118.

b)   Travel and subsistence costs incurred on the employer's business. Current rules can be checked on the HMRC website but in summary are as follows:

i)   Site-based employees are employees whose duties require them to report for duty at a succession of workplaces, with no one 'normal place of work'. They can receive tax relief for expenses incurred on travelling from home to the site and for reasonable subsistence costs incurred (eg lunches) while working at a temporary site. The tax relief need not be claimed if the employer reimburses the expenses and has obtained a P11D dispensation in respect of the expenses. If no P11D dispensation is held, the expense reimbursement is taxable earnings but is separately covered by the deduction claimed.

ii) employees who do have a normal place of work cannot normally treat home-to work travel as an expense of employment. However, they can receive tax relief (or can be reimbursed without any net taxable earnings being identified) for the cost of business journeys which start from home, if these are no longer than the equivalent business journey starting from work.

iii) employees who are seconded by their employer to a temporary place of work can receive tax relief for subsistence and travel to the temporary workplace, providing there is the intention to return to the normal place of work within two years.

c) ITEPA also permits specific deductions for fees and subscriptions to professional bodies, and contributions to exempt approved pension schemes.

d) Capital allowances on plant or machinery necessarily provided by the employee in order to perform his duties may be deducted as an allowable payment , - e.g. on the cost of office equipment, but not a private car.

e) Payroll giving to an approved charity or charitable agency is an allowable expense of employment (see section 33 below).

Employee liabilities and indemnity insurance

29. Income tax relief is available to employees and directors for payments they make to obtain indemnity insurance against liability claims arising from their job or to meet uninsured work-related liabilities. Relief is also extended to situations where the employer or a third party pays the insurance, which will not give rise to any benefit in kind. The cost of the insurance, if paid by the employee, is deductible as an expense from the earnings of the year in which the payment is made. Relief is extended to payments made by ex-employees for periods of up to six years after the year in which employment ceases.

Employees' incidental expenses paid by employer

30. Payments by employers of certain miscellaneous personal expenses incurred by employees are exempt from income tax and NIC.

The exemption covers round sum allowances paid by employers for incidental expenses such as newspapers, telephone calls home and laundry bills incurred by employees when they stay away from home overnight on business.

Payments of up to £5 a night in the UK (£10 outside the UK) are tax-free. However, if the employer pays round sum allowances (without requiring receipts) which exceed these limits, the whole amount paid becomes taxable.

Removal expenses and benefits

31. The amount that can be paid tax-free to an employee as qualifying removal expenses has been greatly restricted since the 1990s and now stands at £8,000. This figure has not been increased for many years. The low limit means that in 2012/13 relocating employees who are at all adequately reimbursed for genuine removal costs will find that part of the payment is liable to tax and NIC.

Within this limit, any of the following removal expenses may be paid tax-free in connection with moving his or her home (for work reasons).

a) sums paid to an employee, or to a third party on behalf of an employee in respect of qualifying removal expenses, and

b) any qualifying removal benefit provided for the employee or to members of his or her family or household (including sons and daughters in law, servants, dependants and guests).

I) Qualifying removal expenses comprise the following.

1) Expenses of disposal, i.e. legal expenses, loan redemption penalties, estate agents' or auctioneers' fees, advertising costs, disconnection charges, and rent and maintenance, etc. costs during an unoccupied period in the employee's former residence.

2) Expenses of acquisition i.e. legal expenses, procurement fees, survey fees, etc. relating to the acquisition by the employee of an interest in his or her new residence.

3) Expenses of abortive acquisition.

4) Expenses of transporting belongings, i.e. expenses, including insurance, temporary storage and disconnection and reconnection of appliances, connected with transporting domestic belongings of the employee and of members of his or her family or household from the former to the new residence.

5) Travelling and subsistence expenses during the travelling journey (subsistence meaning food, drink and temporary accommodation).

6) Bridging loan expenses, i.e. interest payable by the employee on a loan raised at least partly because there is a time gap between paying for the new residence and the receipt of the proceeds of the old residence.

7) Duplicate expenses, i.e. net expenses incurred as a result of the change in the replacement of domestic goods used at the former residence but unsuitable for use at the new residence.

II) Qualifying removal benefits consist of benefits or services corresponding to the seven headings noted above, with the restriction that the provision of a car or van for general private use is excluded from category 5 above.

Payroll giving to charities

32. An employee can obtain income tax relief on donations to a charity to any value. The main features of the scheme are as follows:

a) Schemes are operated through charity agencies that must be approved by HMRC.

b) Employers are legally bound to pay donations over to the agency or charity and they may not be refunded to the employee.

c) The employer will deduct the specified donation from pay before PAYE is applied, in the same way as occupational pension contributions. These are called 'net pay' arrangements.

d) National Insurance contributions (Chapter 17) are due on the gross pay, ie the amount before payroll giving.

e) Pensioners can be incorporated into the scheme if they are subject to PAYE.

Gift aid

33. Gift Aid has no special connection with employment income, but is mentioned here for comparison, because it has taken over from payroll giving as the main way for UK employees to make tax-relieved charity donations.

An individual can make a single gift of any amount to a qualifying charity. The gift is treated as if the donor had made a payment to a charity equal to the grossed up amount of the gift.

For example, a payment of £800 to a charity is treated as a gross gift of

$$800 \text{ x } 100/(100\text{-}20) = 800 \text{ x } 100/80 = £1,000.$$

The charity recovers the 20% tax paid by the donor directly from HMRC. Higher and additional rate taxpayers also obtain income tax relief later at the higher or additional rate on the gross donation – see Chapter 5.

Payments on termination of employment

34. The provisions on taxation of payments for loss of office or employment are now in Part 6 of ITEPA, and they include the following rules:

a) The first £30,000 is exempt, so long as it is compensation for the fact of being redundant, or for the stress of losing office. If the latter it is only tax-free if paid 'ex gratia' and not if paid under the employment contract.

Any excess 'compensation for loss of office' over £30,000 is taxed by statute as employment income, even if it is awarded for the pain and distress of losing the job, and not as payment for past services.

b) Complete or partial exemption is available for termination payments which relate to foreign service, ie employment duties performed wholly outside the UK.

c) A general exemption applies to payments made:
  i) on the death or permanent disability of an employee;
  ii) as benefits due under a pension scheme;
  iii) as terminal payments to members of the armed forces.

d) Termination payments and benefits are taxed as income in the year in which they are actually received rather than the year of termination.

e) A loss-of-office payment made to an employee who is at or near to retirement age may be rejected by HMRC as not genuinely paid to compensate for the pain and distress of becoming unemployed: HMRC have been known to argue that such payment is in reality a unapproved lump-sum 'pension', and taxable in full when received.

Example

Nina is dismissed as a director of T Limited on the 1st October 2012 and receives the sum of £35,000 by way of compensation. No loss-of-office compensation was provided for in Nina's service agreement.

Nina's other income for 2012/13 is a salary of £38,000, and debenture interest of £3,200 (net).

Calculate Nina's taxable income.

Solution: Nina's taxable income 2012/13

	£	£
Income from employment		38,000
Terminal payment - employment	35,000	
Less exempt amount	(30,000)	5,000
Bank interest gross 3,200 x 100/80		4,000
Net income (£4,000 savings, £43,000 non-savings)		47,000
Less Personal allowance		(8,105)
Taxable income		38,895

Outplacement counselling

35. This involves services paid for by the employer, for employees who are or become redundant, to help them find new work. Expenditure on this is exempt from tax and does not count towards the £30,000 limit for redundancy payments.

Pension income

36. Any pension paid to a former employee is taxable as earned income on the recipient. This includes payments from company operated schemes, from schemes operated by assurance companies, and voluntary payments where there is no formal pension scheme.

If an occupational pension scheme is approved by and registered with HMRC then any contributions made by the employee into the pension scheme are deductible from taxable earnings. The employer's contributions to an approved scheme are tax-free benefits of employment (as well as being allowed as an remuneration expense for the employer - see Chapter 10).

Pensions paid by the state are taxable as social security income of the recipient. Other pensions are taxed as employment income

Social security pensions

37. The following social security pensions are taxed as social security income of the recipient.

State pension	Graduated retirement pension
State Second Pension	Widowed Parent's Allowance

Social security benefits

38. The following benefits are taxable under this heading. Statutory Maternity Pay (SMP) and Statutory Sick Pay (SSP)s are normally paid by the employer.

Job seeker's allowance (contributions-based)

Carer's allowance

Bereavement allowance; but not bereavement lump sum payment of £2,000

Incapacity benefit (contributions-based)

Company share options schemes (CSOP)

39. The UK government's policy is to encourage limited participation by employees as shareholders in the employing group or company. To obtain HMRC approval a CSOP must be open to all permanent employees on similar terms.

Under these schemes an employee is given the option to buy shares at a fixed price in future. Any discount which the option exercise price represents on the future market value will not be subject to income tax as a benefit in kind if certain conditions are met by the option contract. The main conditions are:

i) The option must be held for a minimum to maximum period (3 to 10 years) before it can be exercised,

ii) The exercise price of the share option is fixed at not less than the market value, at the time the employee gets his or her option.

iii) The share option must relate to part of the ordinary share capital of the company.

iv) Employee participants in the scheme must work at least 20 hours a week for the company, and full-time working directors must work at least 25 hours a week.

If the conditions are met then there is no income tax liability on the grant of the option or on any increase in the value of the shares up to the date of exercise.

On an eventual disposal of the shares by the employee the normal rules of capital gains tax apply, and the cost for CGT is the price the employee actually paid for the shares, which is normally the exercise price of the options (but could include any cost paid for the options).

Approved schemes are not limited to quoted shares but include shares in any company which is not controlled by other companies. If the shares are not quoted the relevant market values must be agreed with HMRC's Valuation Office Agency.

Enterprise management incentive share schemes (EMI)

40. The main features of these schemes are:

a)   unlike CSOPs, they can be restricted to key employees and still get approval;

b)   employees can hold options over shares which at the time of grant of the option(s) had a market value of up to £120,000 – share options acquired on different occasions over 3 years are all combined to apply this limit ;

c)   to be eligible, employees must work for the employing company for at least 25 hours per week or, if less, for 75% of their working time;

d)   only trading companies with gross assets equal to or less than £30m can participate in the EMI scheme;

e)   there is no income tax liability on the grant of the option or on any increase in the value of the shares between grant and exercise, providing that the option is only exercisable, and actually exercised, at least three years and no more than ten years after the grant;

f)   on the eventual disposal of the shares, normal CGT rules apply.

Share incentive plans (SIPs)

41. The rules for these Plans enable a company to give an employee free SIP shares worth up to £3,000 per tax year (for which performance targets may be set) and also enable an employee to buy further SIP shares worth up to £1,500 per tax year (called 'partnership shares') by deduction of the cost from salary.

SIP shares are allocated by trustees of the SIP to funds on behalf of named employees. The company may also give the employee up to two additional free SIP shares for each partnership share he or she has purchased. The terms on which free shares match partnership shares must be the same for all employees.

The employee in the SIP leaves all shares for a specified period after purchase if the value awarded by the employer is to be free of tax and national insurance. The amount of dividends on SIP shares that can be reinvested in the plan tax-free on a participant's behalf are £1,500 per year.

8 Income from employment II – PAYE

Introduction

1.   The Pay As You Earn system of deducting income tax at source applies to monetary employment income (see Chapter 7) from offices or employments such as wages, salaries, bonuses, taxable expenses and pensions. The system is operated by employers who collect the income tax on behalf of HMRC.

National Insurance contributions payable be employees on money earnings (see Chapter 17) are also collected under the PAYE system.

The PAYE system does not apply to self-employed individuals. However there is a system of deducting tax from payments to subcontractors in the construction industry, known as CIS (the Construction Industry Scheme), which for the principal contractor has some similarities to PAYE including the payment dates for the tax.

From 2012/13, PAYE is being reformed to a new 'real time information' (RTI) system. All employers should be operating PAYE on the new system by 2014/15.

Under the new system PAYE will be reported to HMRC on an individual employee basis every time an employee is paid, not simply after the end of the tax year as at present. This should allow more in-year adjustments of PAYE codings to keep the cumulative tax collected more accurate even when a worker's circumstances change through the year.

In addition, one aim of RTI is to reduce the time for which some taxpayers have PAYE 'emergency codes', due to accidental or deliberate failure to submit information relating to a mid-year change of employment.

Taxable pay

2.   For the purposes of tax deduction, pay includes the following:

   a)   salaries, wages, fees, bonuses, overtime, commissions, pensions, honoraria, etc. whether paid weekly, monthly or irregularly

   b)   holiday pay

   c)   Christmas boxes or other seasonal bonuses paid as cash

   d)   termination payments, to the extent not exempt (see Chapter 7)

   e)   statutory sick pay and statutory maternity/paternity pay.

The income tax liability on non-cash benefits in kind is, as far as practicable, taken into account by adjustment of the employees' PAYE code for either that year or the following year (see below), rather than HMRC expecting significant tax to be paid on benefits by self-assessment.

Net pay arrangements

3. In calculating taxable pay, the employer deducts any contribution to a pension scheme on which the employee is entitled to relief from tax as an expense. The agreement applies only to pension schemes which have been approved by the HMRC Pension Schemes Office. The net pay scheme also applies to the payroll giving scheme for gifts to charities (see also Chapter 7).

Code numbers

4. a) All employees, including Directors and private pensioners, are allocated a PAYE code number for each relevant employment. This code number is based on the personal allowances, other income, and reliefs available to individuals, as evidenced by the information contained in their last Tax Return or by the PAYE information submitted by the employer . In appropriate cases the code number also takes into consideration other factors such as tax underpaid or overpaid in previous years.

The PAYE code number is equal to the sum of expected tax allowances and reliefs, less expected non-cash benefits for the year, divided by 10, rounded down.

Other non-employment income such as casual profits, property income, interest and untaxed State pensions may be recognised in the tax code number, if the employee consents.

The resulting tax code tells the employer the periodic (weekly or monthly) amount of tax-free income an employee may earn and therefore the level of salary or wages at which income tax must start to be deducted in the current employment.

b) Some of the letters used at present after a code number are as follows:

L   Basic personal allowance

P   Personal allowance for those aged 65 – 74

V   Personal allowance for those aged 65 – 74 plus the MCAA

Y   Personal allowance for those aged 75 or over

K   see section 6

T   This is used if the taxpayer notifies the tax office that for reasons of confidentiality they do not wish to use one of the other letters.

c)   The following special codes are also used:

BR   This means that income tax is to be deducted from all pay at the basic rate. It is also called the 'emergency code', because employers use it temporarily while waiting for evidence of the correct code to be received from the employee or from HMRC.

F   This code, followed by a number, means that the tax due on a social security benefit, e.g. retirement pension, or widow's pension or allowance, is to be collected from the taxpayer's earnings from an employment.

NT   This means that no tax is to be deducted when making payments.

D   This code followed by a number means that the pension/benefit is more than the allowances.

OT   This means that no allowances are allocated against earnings from this employment. (Usually because there is another pension or employment, against which all allowances have been provisionally set.)

Deductions from allowances in code numbers

5.   The following items may be deducted in arriving at the code number:

a)   State benefits or pension

b)   Income from property

c)   Unemployment benefit

d)   Untaxed interest

e)   Taxable expense allowances and benefits in kind

f)   'Excessive basic rate' adjustment where too much tax is paid at the basic rate and not enough at the higher rate

g)   Savings or dividend income taxed at the higher rate

h)   Allowance restriction. This is to compensate for allowances and reliefs that are due in terms of tax, at a lower rate than the marginal rate, e.g. MCA.

i)   Tax underpaid in earlier years: under self-assessment the balancing amount due for last year by a PAYE taxpayer may be 'coded out' up to £2,000. (See Chapter 3)

K Codes

6.   'K' codes arise where there is a negative coding allowance, which usually occurs where the non-PAYE income, e.g. accommodation benefits in kind, are greater than the total allowances due.

The excess number shown is added to the taxable pay and taxed accordingly.

Statutory sick pay (SSP) and private sick pay

7.   Where private or statutory sick pay is paid by the employer when an employee is unfit for work, this is part of gross pay for the purposes of both income tax and National Insurance.

An employer can recover some of the SSP paid if the SSP payments for an income tax month exceed 13% of the Employer's Class 1 contributions for that month. See Chapter 17 section 8 for more on Statutory Sick Pay and National Insurance generally.

Forms for use with PAYE

Forms formerly submitted as paper returns from employers to HMRC have moved to online submission since 2010. For example P11D forms are now submitted to HMRC by employers online by the deadline in July each year.

8. P2   Notice of coding – sent by HMRC to the employee: tells an employee the PAYE code and shows how it is calculated

P9   Coding Notice sent by HMRC to the employer (does not show how the code is calculated)

P9D   Return of expenses payments, fees, bonuses etc. sent to HMRC by an employer for a 'non-P11D employee'.

P11D   Return for the tax year of reimbursed expense payments, and the value of all benefits provided, to or for each 'P11D employee'. A copy of the form P11D must be given to the employee.

P11D (b)   Employer's form sent to HMRC showing the Class IA National Insurance due on P11D non-cash benefits to employees (see Chapter 17)

P14   End of year return of pay, tax and National Insurance contributions for each employee.

P35   Employer's annual statement, declaration and certificate of the total of P14

P45   Particulars on leaving an employment: current PAYE tax code of the employee, cumulative pay and tax and NIC deducted so far this tax year.

Part 1. Front page - sent to HMRC by old employer.

Part 2. Copy retained by old employer.

Part 3. Copy given by employee to new employer, who sends it to HMRC

Part 4. Copy retained by employee.

P46   Notice to HMRC of details regarding a new employee without a P45.

P46 (expat)   Notice to HMRC of a new employee who is on secondment from abroad

P60   Employer's certificate of total pay and tax deducted, given to the employee at the end of the year (may be sent electronically).

Payment of tax

9. Income tax and National Insurance contributions (employer's and employee's) are due for payment not later than the 19th day of each month. Thus the tax and NIC due for period 8, 2012, which covers the period from 6th November to 5th December, is payable on or before the 19th December 2012.

Employers whose average monthly payments of PAYE and NIC are less than £1,500 in total are allowed to pay the tax quarterly. Payments are due on the following dates: 19th July, 19th October, 19th January and 19th April. Similar arrangements apply to contractors in the construction industry.

Interest on late payment of tax

10. Late payments by employers of PAYE (income tax, Class 1 and 1A NIC contributions) are charged interest at the prescribed rate.

Bonus and commission payments - timing

11. As a general principle, taxable pay is assessed in the year in which it is paid under the rules of the ITEPA, as outlined in Chapter 7.

Thus, for example, where J has a salary of £20,000 for 2011/12 and earns a commission of an additional £5,000 for that year which is only ascertained and paid in July 2012, then the commission is assessable in the tax year 2012/13.

Directors' remuneration

12. The rules of taxation under ITEPA apply to directors and all other employees or office-holders. (See Chapter 7)

PAYE regulations

13. Regulations for the operation of PAYE are provided under Part II of the ITEPA and embodied in The Income Tax (PAYE) Regulations 2003 (S.1 2003/2682). Where failure to operate PAYE takes place it is the employer who is primarily responsible for making good any deficit, and an assessment subject to appeal may be issued for recovery of PAYE not paid over.

If the determined amount is not paid within 90 days then the tax may be recovered from an employee/director. This can arise where the employee/director received his or her employment income from the employer, knowing that the employer had wilfully failed to deduct tax. In general wilful failure means 'with intention or deliberate' – see R v IRC Chisholm 1981 STC 253.

In R v CIR ex parte Keys and Cook 1987 QB. DT. 25.5.87 the controlling directors of a company which failed to deduct income tax under the PAYE system from their own remuneration were held to be liable for that tax.

PAYE investigations

14. The regulations enabling HMRC to undertake a PAYE control visit are contained in The Income Tax (PAYE) Regulations 2003.

These provide that, wherever called upon to do so by any authorised officer of HMRC, the employer must produce at his or her premises for inspection, all wages sheets, deduction working sheets and other documents and records whatsoever, relating to the calculation or payment of PAYE income of his employees, or to the deduction of tax from such income, or to the amount of earnings-related NI contributions payable.

End of year returns

15. At the end of the tax year the employer must complete and return to the tax office the following forms:

Form P35 (P35SC for sub-contractors within the CIS)

Form P14.

The P35 is the employer's Annual Statement, Declaration and Certificate, which is signed by the employer and returned to the tax office by 19th May following the end of the income tax year.

The back of Form P35 contains a summary of the deduction card totals for the year, while the front contains a list of questions concerning payments for casual employment, expenses and Forms P11D etc.

Form P14 is an end of year summary made out in respect of each employee for whom a tax deduction card (P11) has been used.

The P14 is in effect a summary of all the P60 information for all employees on the staff at the end of the year, plus all P45 information for those who have left during the year.

An automatic penalty will arise if end of year returns are late. The statutory deadline for the P14 and P35 is the 19th May. There is a penalty of £100 per month (or part) per unit of 50 employees. Employees must be given their individual P60 information by 1st June.

Where forms P11D are required then these must be returned to the tax office before 6th July following the end of the tax year, with an initial penalty of up to £300 per 50 employees.

Online PAYE filing

Online filing increases the efficiency of the PAYE system. Forms P35 and P14 are now filed online except by the smallest employers.

Student self-testing question

Tabitha's P60 from X plc for the year 2012/13 shows total gross pay of £31,500. She is employed as a sales manager with a salary of £22,000 p.a. for 2012/13. In addition, she receives commission paid by reference to the profits shown by the company's accounts, amounting to:

Year ended 31st December 2011 £9,500 – confirmed and paid June 2012

Year ended 31st December 2012 £13,000 – confirmed and paid June 2013

Tax deducted under PAYE for the year 2012/13, according to her P60, amounted to £4,600. Tabitha has no other income.

Compute Tabitha's Income Tax liability for 2012/13.

Solution: Tabitha, Income tax computation 2012/13.

			£
Income from employment	- salary		22,000
	- commission paid June 2012		9,500
			31,500
Less Personal allowance			(8,105)
Tax liability:			23,395
	n/a	@ 10%	0
	23,395	@ 20%	4,679
Tax liability	23,395		4,679
Less paid by PAYE			(4,600)
Amount still payable			79

Note: It is likely this small liability will be collected via next year's PAYE coding - provided HMRC knows in time to adjust the 2013/14 PAYE code.

9 Income from UK land and property

Introduction

1. This chapter deals with the rules applicable to UK Property income, together with computational examples.

Basis of charge

2. a) The definition of 'property business income' is: 'the annual profits or gains arising from any business carried on for the exploitation, as a source of rents or other receipts, of any estate interest, or rights in or over land in the UK'.

Receipts in relation to land include:

i) any payment in respect of any licence to occupy or otherwise use any land, or in respect of the exercise of any further right over land.

ii) rent charges, ground annuals and any other annual payments derived from land.

b) The following are not taxed as property income, but as trade profits:

i) Profits or gains from the occupation of any woodland managed on a commercial basis;

ii) Farming and agriculture;

iii) Mines, quarries and similar concerns;

iv) Hotels, serviced apartments, or bed-and-breakfast businesses.

c) The letting of furnished accommodation without meals or additional services is taxed as property income, with no separate assessment for the furniture hire; but there are special rules for furnished holiday lettings, which can be treated as a kind of a trading business for limited purposes (see section 11).

d) The letting of caravans on fixed sites and houseboats on fixed moorings is chargeable as property income, while the hire or leasing of mobile caravans and boats is a trade.

Basis of assessment

3 The basis of assessment is the annual profits or gains arising in the income tax year. It is not possible to use an 'accounts basis' of taxation for property income tax. Therefore, the income tax basis period runs from 6 April to 5 April even if the letting business draws up its balance sheet at some other date for business reasons.

Computation of taxable profits of a 'property business'

4. a) All profits or gains are computed in accordance with the rules applicable to a trading business (i.e. normal commercial accounting principles).

b)   All property situated in the UK is to be treated as one letting business regardless of the type of lease or whether or not it is furnished accommodation.

c)   Any business expenditure incurred in earning the profits from letting is to be deducted from the total pooled income, and is subject to the same rules for allowable expenditure as apply to trading income.

d)   Capital allowances available (see (e) are given as an expense chargeable against property income, so that the assessable property profits are after capital allowances. A landlord need not claim the capital allowances available.

e)   Capital allowances are not generally available for plant and machinery (e.g. furniture) located in a let dwelling house. Instead, tax relief on the renewals basis, or alternatively a fixed wear and tear allowance (10% of annual rents less council tax), applies for replacements of furniture and moveable items included in a lease. Except for furnished holiday lettings (see section 11), capital allowances are only available for plant and machinery used for estate management or for property maintenance (e.g. office equipment, or a garden lawnmower).

f)   Interest payable on a loan to acquire assets for a property business is allowed as a deduction in calculating the profits of the business, under the same rules as apply to other expenses incurred for business purposes. This allows all the interest on a 'buy to let' mortgage to be set against rental income.

Rental business losses must in general be carried forward and set against future profits from the same rental business. Where there are capital allowances due in respect of the rental business, that part of the loss attributable to capital allowances may be set against total income of the year as an allowable payment. The rest of the loss, if any, must still be carried forward.

Expenses of properties let on uncommercial terms (for example, at a nominal rent to a relative) can only be deducted up to the amount of the rent or other receipts generated by the uncommercially let property. The excess of the expenses over the receipts from an uncommercially let property cannot be deducted in the rental business, and therefore cannot create a loss. These expenses can, however, be set against future rentals received from the same tenant, should the lease be renegotiated.

Example

Z purchased a freehold factory site on the 6th April 2012, which he lets for an annual rental of £15,000 payable quarterly in advance. First payment due 6th April 2012 covered the period to 5th July 2012. Property expenses paid by Z for the year to 5th April 2013 amounted to £2,500 and interest paid on a loan to purchase the factory was £3,500.

Landlord's capital allowances for the 12 months to 5th April 2013 have been agreed at £2,000.

Compute Z's property business income for 2012/13.

Solution: Z's property business income 2012/13

	£	£
Rents receivable - let for 12 months for £15,000		15,000
Less expenses:-		
Property expenses	2,500	
Loan interest	3,500	6,000
Adjusted profit		9,000
Less capital allowances		(2,000)
Taxable profits		7,000

Notes

i) Rental income is always computed on an accruals basis.

ii) Property business income is not 'trading income'.

Lease premiums

5.   A lease premium is a capital payment paid to the landlord by the tenant at the inception of a lease.   Historically, UK law viewed it as a different type of payment from rent. Until special income tax rules were passed in the 1950s lease premiums were not liable to tax as income of the landlord, even though they could often be seen as a capitalised substitute for all or part of the future rent payments.   The special capital-revenue splitting rules enacted for lease premiums in 1956 still remain in force, even though the accounting treatment of premiums has become less variable.

The income tax system treats lease premiums paid by the tenant for a lease for up to 50 years as partly a payment of rental income and partly a capital payment. The capital/revenue split for income tax depends on the length of the lease in whole years.   A lease premium includes any sum whether payable to the immediate or a superior landlord, arising in connection with the granting of a lease, but not arising from an assignment to a new tenant of an existing lease, with consent of the landlord.

Under an assignment, the new tenant takes the position of the original tenant, with the same terms and conditions.

Where a lease is granted (but not assigned) at a premium, for a period not exceeding 50 years, then the landlord is deemed to be in receipt of a rental income equal to the premium, less an allowance of 2% of the premium for each complete year of the lease remaining, excluding the first 12 month period. This deduction recognises what tax law treats as the 'capital element' of the premium.

Example

B granted a lease for 24 years of his warehouse to a trader on the following terms:

A lease premium of £12,000 to be paid on 1 May 2012 and an annual rent of £7,200 payable monthly in advance from 1 May 2012.

B's allowable letting expenditure for the year 2012/13 was £5,800.

Solution: B Property business income 2012/13

	£
Year ended 5 April 2013:	
Lease premium received – 24 year lease	12,000
Less capital element 2% × 12,000 × (24 – 1)	
i.e. 1/50 × 12,000 × 23	(5,520)
= rental income received in premium	6,480
Add rent receivable (11 months) 7,200 × 11/12	6,600
	13,080
Less allowable expenses	(5,800)
Assessable property business income	7,280

In effect the lease premium is discounted by reference to its duration, and the longer the unexpired portion, the greater the discount. Thus if a lease had 49 years to run, the discount would be:

$(49 - 1) \times 2\%$ i.e. 96%.

A premium on a lease for a period greater than 51 years would not be taxed as property income at all. If the lease premium is paid by instalments, the full amount, less the discount, is taxable in the usual way. However, if hardship can be proved, the landlord's income tax on a premium received may be paid over a period not exceeding 8 years.

Lease premiums and the lessee

6. Where the lessee pays a lease premium on the granting of a lease, a proportion of that premium may be set against the following:

a) any trading income, if the leased premises are used for business purposes;

The amount of the premium assessed as income on the lessor can be claimed as a deemed rental expense of trading by the lessee, but the tax deduction is spread evenly over the remaining lease, as illustrated below in section 7.

b) any rental income or lease premium received from any sub-lease granted by the lessee, as illustrated below in section 8 .

Example of notional rental claimed by the lessee

7. S is granted a lease of premises to be used for trading purposes, for a period of 20 years, at an annual rent of £600 p.a. and an initial lease premium of £32,000.

Computation of income element of total premium:	£
Lease premium	32,000
Less capital element: 2% × 32,000 × (20 – 1) i.e. 38% × 32,000	(12,160)
= Lease premium charged on lessor as rental income	19,840

Additional rental relief available to S can be claimed over 20 years

So the notional rental to include in S's trade expenses is $\dfrac{19840}{20}$ i.e. £992 p.a.

This expense claim is in addition to S's actual rental expense, of £600 per year.

Sub-leases and assignments

8. The creation of a sub-lease out of a head-lease for a premium can give rise to an immediate income tax liability on part of the premium for the intermediate lessee; but complete assignment of the existing lease could not as any proceeds received for an assignment for that are capital proceeds potentially liable to CGT.

Where a charge to income tax has already arisen when a head-landlord granted a lease at a premium, and this is followed by the intermediate tenant granting a sub-lease at a premium, then any liability arising on the intermediate landlord can be reduced, as shown in the example below.

Example

J granted a lease for 20 years to M for a premium of £10,000. After occupying the premises for five years (not for business), M granted a sub-lease to R for a period of 10 years, at a premium of £6,000.

Show the computation of J's and M's assessable lease premium income.

Solution: Computation of J's liability (5 years ago)

	£
Lease premium (20 year lease)	10,000
Less 2% × 10,000 × (20 − 1) i.e. 38% × 10,000	(3,800)
	6,200

Computation of M's liability (now)

	£
Lease premium received (10 year lease)	6,000
Less 2% × 6,000 × (10 − 1) i.e. 18% × 6,000	(1,080)
Income element of premium received	4,920

M can then deduct from this deemed rental income 10 years' worth of the amount assessed on J as deemed rental income when M signed the 20-years head-lease.

$$\text{M's assessable premium income} = 4,920 - \frac{\text{Duration of sub lease}}{\text{Duration of head lease}} \times (\text{premium assessed on J})$$

$$= 4,920 - [10/20 \times 6,200] = 1,820$$

The amount of the new lease premium assessed on M is therefore £1,820. M has been able to claim tax relief for half of the amount of the premium taxed on J.

The above calculations are independent of any periodic rental also receivable under the new sub-lease garnet by M. That rent would be true (not deemed) property income of M, and measured on the accruals basis.

Furnished accommodation

9.   Rents from furnished accommodation are assessed as property income.

Relief for depreciation of original capital invested in furniture and fittings is not given, but relief for gradual replacement of furniture and kitchen equipment etc. may be given either on the 'renewals basis', or as an annual fixed 10% deduction from 'net rent', known as the wear and tear allowance.

Net rent is gross rent receivable, less charges and services normally borne by a tenant, but under some inclusive leases borne by the landlord, such as council tax and water rates.

See section 11 for special rules on Furnished Holiday Lettings.

It is possible for furnished letting income to be taxed as trade profits where the taxpayer provides substantial services in connection with the letting e.g. meals, cleaning, laundry, and other services of a similar nature. This is deemed to be carrying on a trade.

Rent-a-room: tax-free letting income

10.   For 2012/13 the income tax exemption continues which allows any householder (including those who do not own their home) to let a room or rooms in their own home for up to £4,250 p.a. tax-free, provided it is let as furnished accommodation, and does not have its own entrance. The rules work as follows:

a)   Gross rents up to £4,250 p.a. are exempt.

b)   Gross rents greater than £4,250 are taxable as follows:

  i)   either pay tax on excess rent i.e. (rent – £4,250);

  ii)   or pay tax on gross rents less expenses.

A claim must be made in writing for the Rent a Room exemption within one year of the end of the tax year to which it is to apply. The self-assessment tax return includes a tick-box to claim the exemption. If joint householders let a room or rooms in the same home, the exemption limit is split equally between them.

Real Estate Investment Trusts (REITS)

11.   As already noted in Chapter 6 (section 5), dividends from REITS are treated on the self-assessment return and in the tax computation as property rental income of the period in which they are received.

Furnished Holiday Lettings

12.   The property income from a special class of letting called 'furnished holiday letting' is subject to additional rules giving semi- 'trading' treatments such as the ability to treat FHL property as a business asset for capital taxes purposes (see Parts IV and V), and to treat FHL income as net relevant earnings for pension contributions (see Chapter 16).

Losses from FHL businesses used to be claimable as trade losses but this has been abolished. Now FHL losses have to be carried forward and set against future profits from FHLs. They cannot be combined with profits from non-FHL lettings.

It is possible to claim plant and machinery capital allowances (see Chapter 10) on the furniture and kitchen appliances etc installed in a FHL property. This is in contrast to the treatment of furniture in other furnished lettings, which is not eligible for capital allowances, though plant used to maintain, but not located in, the let property is so eligible.

Full details of the qualifying conditions for FHL treatment in 2012/13 are available at:

http://www.hmrc.gov.uk/manuals/pimmanual/PIM4105.htm

In summary, to be a FHL source of income, the property must be available for short lets (under thirty days to different tenants) for at least 20 weeks of the year and actually let for at least 10. It can however be let 'out of season' (ie during the rest of the year that it is not on short letting) for a longer let and will not thereby lose its status as a FHL property.

To the extent that the taxpayer uses a FHL property sometimes for private use, all general expenses of the year and any capital allowances must be time apportioned to remove the private use period(s). Private use incudes use by family or friends who do not pay a market rent for the property. However, specific expenses related only to the holiday letting business (e.g. advertising) need not be apportioned.

Rent paid to non-residents

13. Where UK rental profits are paid to a non-resident landlord, basic rate income tax must be deducted at source from the rent payments and accounted for to HMRC, unless a registered UK letting agent handles the collection.

Student self-testing questions

1. (a) Geta rents out a room in her house. In 2012/13 she received rent of £4,900 and paid expenses of £2,000.

Requirement: Calculate the amount of Geta's assessable income from property for 2012/13 assuming any necessary election is made. (2 marks)

1. (b) Raj owns three flats which he lets out.

Flat 1. The flat was purchased on 6 September 2012 and let unfurnished from 29 September 2012. The new seven-year lease was at an annual rental of £3,500 payable on the usual quarter days. The incoming tenant was required to pay a premium of £5,000.

Flat 2. The flat was let unfurnished at an annual rental of £4,000 on a lease which expired on 23 June 2012, the rent having been paid on the usual quarter days. The property was re-let on 30 September 2012 on the same conditions at an annual rent of £6,000.

Flat 3. The flat was let furnished for the full year on a weekly rental of £120.

The usual quarter days are 25 March, 24 June, 29 September and 25 December.

Details of expenditure in the year ended 5 April 2013 were:

	Flat 1	Flat 2	Flat 3
	£	£	£
Insurance	400	200	600
Repairs	4,500	600	350
Water rates	-	-	400
Council tax	-	-	800

Notes

1. The amount of £400 insurance for Flat 1 was an annual premium for 12 months insurance commencing on 6 September 2012.

2. £4,000 was spent on UPVC double glazing on 10 September 2012 replacing leaking wooden window frames. To replace with wooden frames would have cost £1,200. The windows needed to be repaired to make Flat 1 habitable.

Requirement: Calculate Raj's profit from property for 2012/13. (8 marks)
NB Calculations may be made to the nearest month.

(c)   **State how loss relief is given where the loss is in respect of property let unfurnished.**   **(1 mark)**
                                                       (Total: 11 marks)

Solutions

(a) Geta

(i)	Ordinary basis		£
	Rent		4,900
	Expenses		(2,000)
			2,900
(ii)	Alternative basis		£
	Rent		4,900
	'Rent a room' limit		(4,250)
			650

Assessment of income from property (lower figure) £650

(b) Raj: Income from property 2012-13

		£	£	
Rent receivable	- Flat 1		1,750	(W1)
	- Flat 2		4,000	(W2)
	- Flat 3		6,240	
Premium on lease	- Flat 1		4,400	(W3)
			16,390	
Insurance	- Flat 1	233 (W4)		
	- Flats 2&3	800		
Repairs	- Flat 1	500 (W5)		
	- Flats 2&3	950		
Wear and Tear Allowance	- Flat 3	504 (W6)		
Water rates and council tax	- Flat 3	1,200	(4,187)	
Property business income			12,203	

Working 1

6/12 x £3,500	£1,750

Working 2

3/12 x £4,000	£1,000
6/12 x £6,000	£3,000
	£4.000

Working 3

Premium	£5,000
less (7-1) x 2%	600
	£4.400

Working 4

7/12 x £400	£233

Working 5

As the replacement of the window frames was necessary before Flat 1 could be let, the expenditure is deemed to be capital and not, therefore, allowable as an expense.

Working 6

The 'wear and tear' allowance is 10% of the rent, less the items that are the tenant's responsibility, i.e. water rates and council tax.

£6,240 – (400 + 800) = £5,040; 10% - £504

(c) If the expenses of letting property in a tax year exceed the income from property, the excess is carried forward to be set against the first available income from letting property in the future.

Question without answer

1. Arthur has two shops for unfurnished letting.

Shop 1. The annual rent was £3,000 on a lease which expired on 30 June 2012. Arthur took advantage of the shop being empty to carry out repairs and decorating. The shop was let to another tenant on a five-year lease at £4,000 per annum from 1 October 2012.

Shop 2. The shop was purchased on 10 April 2012 and required treatment to wood damaged by dry-rot before it could be let out. Arthur also undertook some normal re-decorating work before the shop was let on 1 October 2012 on a seven-year lease at an annual rental of £6,000. A premium of £2,000 was received from the incoming tenant upon signing the lease 1 October 2012.

The rent for both shops was due quarterly in advance on the usual calendar quarter days (25 March, 24 June, 29 September and 25 December).

The following expenditure was incurred for 2012/13:

	Shop 1	Shop 2
	£	£
Insurance	190	300
Ground rent	10	40
Repairs and decorating	3,900 (1)	5,000 (2)
Accountancy	250	250
Advertising for tenant	100	100

Notes:

(1) Includes £2,500 for re-roofing the shop following gale damage in February 2013. Because the roof had been badly maintained the insurance company refused to pay for the repair work.

(2) Includes £3,000 for remedial treatment to dry-rot damaged wood flooring discovered when the shop was bought. The floor needed to be repaired before the shop could be let out.

Requirement: Calculate the income assessable on Arthur for 2012/13 from the shops, and show how any losses would be dealt with.

(ACCA updated)

10 Income taxed as trade profits: I - general principles

Introduction

1. This chapter covers the measurement of the tax-assessable trading profits of an unincorporated business. The legislation and some of the case-law and concessionary practice on this area has been rewritten in ITTOIA 2005. A list of the main topic headings in this chapter is followed by an analysis of the main principles of tax law and practice coming under each heading. Questions and answers illustrating the adjustment of profit for tax purposes appear at the end of the chapter.

The 'basis period' rules for matching unincorporated trade profits to tax years are dealt with in the next two chapters. These basis period rules apply only to unincorporated traders, as companies have their own rules (see part III).

However most of the principles discussed in *this* chapter, on determining trade profits, apply to both unincorporated and incorporated trades. If a rule differs when the trader is a company, the company rule is briefly noted here, then given more detailed coverage in Chapter 19 on corporation tax. In other cases, the trade profits rules may be assumed the same for sole traders, partnerships and companies. This chapter is therefore also relevant to answering exam questions on the trading profits of companies (see Part III for corporation tax in general).

List of topic headings

2. Charge to tax on trade profits

The concept of trading

Capital receipts

General rules restricting deductions

Allowable expenditure

Non-allowable expenditure

Asset values for tax purposes

Other adjustment of profits

Charge to tax on trade profits

3. Income derived from a trade in the form of profits is chargeable to income tax where the trade is conducted by an individual, either as a sole trader or in partnership with someone else. Where the trade is undertaken by an incorporated person, typically a company, trade profits form part of the total taxable profit charged to corporation tax, not income tax.

> **Tax** under this heading is charged on the full amount of the profits or gains arising or accruing to any person residing in the UK from any trade, profession or vocation, whether carried on in the UK or elsewhere.

Trade is defined to include any 'manufacture, adventure, or concern in the nature of trade'. All farming and market gardening in the UK are treated as carrying on a trade.

The concept of trading

4. As Lord Wilberforce pointed out in the case of Ransome v Higgs 1974 STC 539 'everyone is supposed to know what trade means so Parliament, which wrote this into the law in 1799, has wisely abstained from defining it'.

The Royal Commission on the Taxation of Profits and Income in 1955 looked at all the case law up to that time and listed 'six badges of trade' that are still used by the courts and HMRC in determining what is a trade, or an 'adventure in the nature of trade'. These are:

    a)   the subject matter of the realisation

    b)   the length of the period of ownership

    c)   the frequency or number of similar transactions by the same person

    d)   supplementary work on or in connection with the property realised

    e)   the circumstances that were responsible for the realisation

    f)   motive.

5. The present day meaning of 'trade' must therefore be deduced from a mixture of previous and subsequent legal decisions, accepted practice and the 'badges of trade'. The following is a summary of some general points.

    a)   Betting and gambling are not regarded as trading unless carried on by an authorised bookmaker. This is in HMRC's interest as statistically more losses than profits are made by gamblers.

    b)   The fact that a trade is illegal does not mean that it is not taxable.

    c)   Even where transactions are concluded within a year they may nevertheless be regarded as 'annual profits or gains'. See Martin v Lowry 1926 11 TC 297.

    d)   Isolated transactions can amount to trading if they are of a commercial nature. See Wisdom v Chamberlain 1968 45 TC 92 (buying gold bars short-term for profitable resale, using borrowed money, was a trade); and Rutledge v CIR 1929 14 TC 490 (buying far more toilet rolls than could possibly be needed for personal use suggested a commercial intention to resell them at a profit).

    e)   All farming and market gardening carried on in the UK is treated as a trade.

    f)   Changes in the activities or customer sector of a trade may amount to the establishment of a separate and different trade for tax purposes.

Capital receipts

6. Profits arising from 'capital transactions' are in principle not trade profits, although they may be taxable under some other tax, typically capital gains tax. A profit on the disposal of a fixed asset by an unincorporated business is not therefore subject to income tax, and conversely, the loss is not allowed as a business expense. Companies are treated differently from unincorporated businesses in respect of some such capital receipts – e.g. on sale of a trade intangible asset, the net profit or loss is a revenue item for corporation tax.

Where a person receives a sum of money which is paid under a legal obligation, in return for goods or services provided in the normal course of trade, this is clearly a trading transaction. However, where the receipt does not arise from any contractual obligation, and the person has given nothing in return, then it may be accepted as a non-taxable receipt. Some such transactions are considered below.

Foreign exchange profits and losses

For individuals, exchange profits arising from trading transactions are potentially chargeable to income tax, whereas those relating to capital or non-trading transactions will not be chargeable.

For companies all foreign currency exchange gains and losses fall under the corporation tax loan relationships rules and are thus part of the companies' total taxable profits for corporation tax. For a company, it is a trading loan relationship if the foreign currency was held for trading, and a non-trade loan relationship (but still not 'capital') if the foreign currency was held for investment.

Insurance claims

Insurance compensation received in connection with damage or loss to a fixed asset is not taxable as a trading receipt; it may be subject to CGT treatment instead. Claims for loss of profits under personal accident insurance, and claims relating to any loss suffered on a current asset, such as destroyed inventory, are taxable as trading receipts.

Damage compensation and voluntary payments

If these transactions arise in the ordinary course of a trade then they are taxable on the recipient. If they are voluntary ex gratia payments, arising outside the domain of trading, then they are generally not taxable for the recipient or deductible by the payer.

General rules restricting deductions in computing profits of a trade (ITTOIA)

7. a) **First rule** : In calculating the profits of a trade, no deduction is allowed for items of a capital nature.

The concept of materiality applied by accounting standards is not formally incorporated into tax law and this causes differences in particular when the question arises of whether to capitalise or expense certain regular purchases which may individually last the business for more than one year.

While an acceptable division between capital and revenue can normally be drawn on accounting principles, it does not follow that the accounting treatment is always conclusive for tax purposes as to what is definitely 'capital' and what is not. Case law has supplied most of the guidance on this matter, and the words of Viscount Cave in Atherton v British Insulated and Helsby Cables Ltd 1925 10 TC 155, are the most frequently quoted:

> 'when an expenditure is made not only once and for all but with a view to bringing into existence an asset, or an advantage for the enduring benefit of a trade, I think that there is a very good reason for treating such expenditure as properly attributable not to revenue, but to capital'.

b) **Second rule**

1) In calculating the profits of a trade no deduction is allowed for –

   a) expenses not incurred wholly and exclusively for the purposes of the trade, or

   b) losses not connected with or arising out of the trade.

2) If an expense is incurred for more than one purpose, subsection (1) does not prohibit a deduction for the identifiable part or proportion of the expense which is incurred wholly and exclusively for the purposes of trade.

The following Court decisions provide some idea of the importance and range of the two important statutory rules noted above.

1. Associated Portland Cement Mfs Ltd v Kerr 1946 27 TC 103. Payments to retiring directors in consideration of covenants not to carry on a similar business in competition with the company were held to be capital, because they affected the longer term future.

2. The Law Shipping Co. Ltd v IRC 1924 12 TC 103. 'Repair' expenditure required after purchase of a ship, necessary to enable it to be used as a profit-earning asset, was held to be capital expenditure and not 'repairs' for tax purposes.

3. Odeon Associated Theatres Ltd v Jones 1972 48 TC 257. Repair expenditure incurred some time after the purchase of a cinema was held to be an allowable repairs expense for tax. A significant point was that the cinema had been successfully used for trading whilst in a state of disrepair during wartime conditions.

4. Strong & Co (Romsey) Ltd v Woodfield 1906 5 TC 215. Damages and costs of injuries to a guest, caused by a falling chimney were held to be non-revenue expenditure. This case would be unlikely to be decided in the same way today, due to occupier's liability laws, but it still contains judicial comments about the extent of a trading activity.

5. Morgan v Tate & Lyle Ltd 1954 35 TC 367. Expenses incurred to prevent the nationalisation of the sugar industry were held to be allowable

deductions for a sugar refiner. This case is the exception to the rule that donations to political parties or campaigns are generally not accepted as allowable or trade-related.

6.   Copeman v Flood (William) & Sons Ltd 1941 24 TC 53. Sums paid as director's remuneration are not necessarily expended wholly and exclusively for the purposes of trade, if the director is carrying out non-trade duties.

7.   ECC Quarries Ltd v Watkins 1975 STC 578. Abortive expenditure on planning permission was held to be capital expenditure hence not deductible against profits. (Moreover, it was not deductible as a cost for capital gains tax, because the planning permission was never obtained.)

8.   Tucker v Granada Motorway Services Ltd 1979 STC 393. A sum paid to a landlord to secure a favourable change in the formula for determining profit-related rents for the lease of a service station was held to be capital, because it affected many future years of the service station business, and also the lease was viewed by the court as a capital interest in the property.

9.   C.S. Robinson v Scott Bader Co. Ltd 1980 STC 241. The salary, expenses and social costs of an employee, seconded to a foreign subsidiary, were held to be allowable trading expenses of the parent company.

10. Dollar v Lyons 1981 STC 333. Payments made to a farmer's children for working on the farm were held to be pocket money, and not an allowable trading expense. It was significant that the children were too young to be legal employees of the farm.

Allowable expenditure – a summary

8.   Subject to the general principles noted above, the following is a list of the most common items of expenditure that are allowed as an expense in computing taxable trading income. Except where noted otherwise, accruals accounting under UK or International GAAP applies. Some of these items are open, in the case of an individual trader or partnership, to proportionate disallowance for 'private use' under the 'wholly and exclusively' rule.

1.   Cost of materials, components and goods purchased for resale.

2.   Gross wages and salaries, and employer's NI.

3.   Redundancy payments.

4.   Ex gratia payments and compensation for loss of office.

5.   Pension scheme contributions to approved schemes – not deductible on an accounts basis, but based on what was actually paid in the year (see also section 21).

6.   Rent business rates and telecommunication expenses.

7.   Fuel and power.

8.   Printing and stationery.

9.   Vehicle and aircraft running and maintenance expenses.

10. Repairs and renewals, see below.

11. Bad and doubtful debts expenses, see below.

12. Travelling and accommodation expenses for business purposes, e.g. sales representatives, trade fairs and conferences.

13. Advertising and promotional expenditure.

14. Bank/loan interest, so long as the loan is wholly for trading purposes.

15. Leasing payments (except leasing high emissions cars, see Chapter 13 section 20).

16. Hire purchase interest.

17. Patent renewal fees and expenses, see below.

18. Insurance of assets, employees, goods etc.

19. Legal expenses arising from trading, such as debt collection, see below.

20. Professional charges such as audit fees and consultancy charges, but not those ancillary to the acquisition of a non-current (fixed) asset.

21. Training expenditure incurred by an employer for staff. Where the trader is self-employed and incurs training expenditure for himself or herself, further questions must be asked about duality of purpose.

22. Welfare expenditure for employees.

23. Subscriptions and donations, see below.

24. Losses and defalcations of employees, see below.

25. Penalty payments for late delivery of goods.

26. Pre-trading expenditure of a revenue nature, incurred up to seven years before trading.

27. Incidental costs of obtaining loan finance, see below.

28. Expenditure on waste disposal.

29. Gifts to educational establishments.

30. Interest on late paid tax and VAT is deductible for companies, but not for sole traders or partnerships.

31. R&D expenditure (companies only) obtains special deductions: small or medium sized companies 225% of qualifying costs (200% in 2011/12); - large companies 130% of qualifying costs. See Chapter 19.

Non-allowable expenditure – a summary

9.   The following is a list of the most common items of expenditure that are not generally allowed as an expense in computing trading income.

1. Depreciation of fixed assets, and losses on disposals of fixed assets. (Companies may deduct amortisation of some post-2002 intangible fixed assets, see Chapter 19).

2. Professional charges concerned with a taxation appeal.

3. General provisions against future expenditure such as those for doubtful debts, pension schemes, furnace relining, or for preventive maintenance. These costs are however potentially allowable once actually paid, i.e. when the provision set up in the accounts is applied.

4. Legal expenses on the acquisition of a capital asset.

5. Entertainment, except staff functions.

6. Losses and defalcations by directors.

7. Repairs which involve any improvement, or amount to a complete or substantial renewal.

8. Fines for illegal acts (except parking fines of employees in junior positions when on business, eg van delivery drivers: these fines may be reimbursed to the employees and claimed as an allowable business expense. The same rule does not apply to parking fines of business proprietors or directors).

9. Political donations, (see exception in Tate and Lyle case above, section 7).

10. Non-trading losses or non-trade costs of any kind.

11. Tax penalties for tax defaults (distinguish this from interest on late-paid tax, which is allowable for companies but not for sole traders or partnerships)

12. Surcharges arising from VAT late payments or returns (see part V).

13. Unpaid staff remuneration paid more than 9 months after an accounting date may only be deducted against profits once actually paid.

14. Council tax of proprietors or partners and other personal expenses of the same.

15. Crime-related payments – blackmail or extortion.

16. Criminal bribes paid either in the UK or overseas.

Business entertainment and gifts

10. Entertaining expenses are not allowed unless they are incurred for the entertainment of one's own staff, and this must be the main purpose of the function and not merely incidental to the provision of hospitality to others (e.g. clients). Where an employer bears the cost of an annual Christmas party, or similar function such as a staff dinner and dance, which is open to the staff generally, then HMRC will not tax the staff on the benefit in kind, until it exceeds £150 per annum for each employee. Entertaining within this permitted limit need not be included on the employee's form P11D (see Chapter 8). In theory there is no limit to the amount of staff entertaining allowed to the employer as a business expense, but it will be taxed on the staff as earnings if it exceeds the annual exempt benefit limit.

Gifts of any kind given by way of entertainment are also disallowed, except small business gifts which:

a) carry a prominent advertisement;

b)   are not food, drink or tobacco;

c)   do not amount in value to more than £50 per person per year.

Modest donations or gifts to local charities or recreational associations are allowed, if they are incurred 'wholly and exclusively for the purposes of trade'. This suggests that they must not be anonymous but must promote the business name or product.

Repairs and renewals

11. Improvements to premises are not allowed, but repairs occasioned by normal wear and tear would be deductible. Repair is not defined but has been held to amount to 'restoration or replacement of subsidiary parts', whereas a renewal is the reconstruction of the entirety, meaning not the whole but substantially the whole. A renewal would therefore be regarded as capital expenditure and not allowed as a trading expense. As noted in the Odeon Theatre case above, repairs to newly acquired premises, necessary to make them usable, would also be disallowed.

Patent fees and expenses

12. Deduction as an expense is allowed for any fees paid or expense incurred in obtaining for the purposes of a trade:

a)   the grant of a patent or extension of a patent period

b)   the registration of a design or trade mark.

Expenditure on any abandoned or rejected application for a patent is also allowable.

Bad and doubtful debts

13. Bad debts already proved to be irrecoverable are allowed as a deduction, and doubtful debts are also allowed, in so far as they are specifically and reasonably expected to go bad. Thus a provision for specific bad debts is allowable, but a general provision based on some overall percentage of outstanding debtors, without any detailed consideration of the particular balances, is not allowable for tax purposes, as it is too general.

Where a debt is incurred outside the trading activities of the business, e.g. loans to employees written off, then any loss arising will not be allowable. This would also apply to any bad debts arising from the sale of any fixed assets.

Any bad debts recovered are treated as trading receipts in the period when received.

Pension scheme contributions

14. Sums paid to an approved retirement benefits (pension) scheme by an employer are allowed as a deduction. Approved in this sense means by the HMRC Office which deals with the approval of all schemes. The sums must be actually paid and not just accrued or set aside for future payment.

Redundancy payments/outplacement counselling

15. Payments made to employees under the Employment Rights Act 1996 are permitted deductions, and any rebates received are taxable as trading income. Payments made outside the provisions of the Act are also in general, allowed.

Training costs

16. Expenditure on staff training related to the trade is allowable as a business expense. Expenditure by employers on training for new skills for employees who are about to leave, or those who have already left, is also allowed as a trading expense, if not already so treated. (This complements the outplacement counselling allowance.)

Legal expenses

17. Legal charges incurred in maintaining existing trading rights are allowable, and this would include costs of debt recovery, settling disputes, preparation of service agreements, and defence of title to business property, and damages and costs arising from the normal course of trade.

As already noted, legal costs incurred in contesting an income tax appeal were held to be not allowable. However, accounting and legal expenses incurred in seeking taxation advice on matters relating to trading activities would normally be allowed.

Expenses concerned with the acquisition of an asset would not be allowed, but those arising in connection with the renewal (not acquisition) of a short lease (i.e. less than 50 years) are permitted.

The legal and professional costs of raising or altering any share capital of a company are disallowed, but costs relating to issuing loan capital are permitted as 'incidental costs of obtaining loan finance'.

Losses and defalcations

18. Any loss not arising from the trade, or not incurred wholly and exclusively for the purposes of trade, will not be allowable as a deduction in computing taxable profits. Two categories give substance to this principle and indicate types of loss which are not deductible:

a) Any loss not connected with or arising out of the trade, profession or vocation.

b) Any sum recoverable under an insurance or contract of indemnity.

With regard to losses arising from the sorts of risks that are usually insured against such as fire, burglary, accident or loss of profits, then the loss sustained is allowable if arising from the trade, e.g. loss of stocks, and any compensation received must be treated as a trading receipt.

Where assets are involved then any loss arising would be of a capital nature and not allowable as a deductible expense.

Losses arising from defalcations or embezzlement by an employee would normally be allowable, but defalcations by a person having control over the business would not. See Curtis v Oldfield J & G Ltd 1925 9 TC 319.

Post-cessation expenditure

19. For payments made in connection with a trade that has been permanently discontinued, relief is available for payments made wholly and exclusively

    a)   in remedying defective work done, goods supplied or services rendered

    b)   in meeting legal and professional charges.

The relief is available within seven years of the discontinuance for self-employed individuals.

Relief is given primarily against an individual's total income for the year but where this is insufficient it may be set against any chargeable gains for that year.

Miscellaneous items

20. Unpaid remuneration

In calculating the profits of a trade, no deduction is allowed for employees' remuneration paid more than 9 months after the end of the period of account. A deduction is given instead in the period when the remuneration is paid.

Apart from this, all bona fide salaries to employees and directors, including commissions and bonuses, and including amounts paid after the period-end but accrued for at the period-end, are allowable if they are incurred for the purposes of trade. See Copeman v Flood 1941 24 TC 53.

Unpaid pension contributions

However, pension schemes contributions by employers are not allowed against trade profits as a deduction on an accruals basis. These may only be claimed as an expense once the cash has actually been paid to the scheme. There is a logical reason for this rule: the technicalities of accounting for employers pension contributions may be seen from a tax point of view as akin to 'general provisions'; also, the funds once paid to an approved pension scheme are in a tax-free growth vehicle (see Chapter 16), so HMRC will not give tax relief on the expense until funds have actually been transferred.

Subscriptions and donations

Subscriptions to trade associations or other bodies for the purposes of trade are allowable, but not those unconnected with trade, or involving entertainment.

Where the payment is for the benefit or welfare of employees it will usually be allowed, e.g. a donation to a hospital or convalescent home which is used by employees of the firm. Gifts to registered charities are allowed if made for the purposes of trade.

Where a donation is structured as a Gift Aid payment then it is not recognised as a business expense, and the taxpayer receives relief through another method (see Chapter 5 sections 3 and 4, and Chapter 21 section 4).

Employees seconded to charities

When an employer seconds an employee temporarily to a charity, then any expenditure attributable to that employment by the employer is deductible as a business expense.

Costs of obtaining loan finance (rules for companies)

Incidental costs of obtaining loan finance (including convertible loan stock) are allowed as a deduction in computing trading income of a company, and this includes fees, commissions, advertising, printing and stationery (eg a debenture prospectus). This is a statutory deduction. By contrast any incidental costs of raising new equity finance for a company (even under EIS – see Chapter 6) are disallowable as capital costs.

Pre-trading expenses

Expenses incurred within seven years prior to the actual commencement of a trade is allowed as a trading expense of the first period of trading, if the expenditure would have been allowed as a trading expense had trading already been going on during that period. See also Chapter 14.

Gifts to educational establishments

Where a person carrying on a trade, profession or vocation makes a gift of business plant and machinery to an educational establishment, the proceeds of sale can be treated as zero. Thus there is no loss of capital allowances .

Capital allowances

Capital allowances are claimed and deducted from the adjusted trade profits for the purposes of computing the net trade profits. See Chapter 13.

Mileage rates – self-employed

Self-employed persons can use the authorised mileage rates applicable to employees (see Chapter 7) instead of claiming actual motor expenses and capital allowances. To be eligible the taxpayer's turnover must not exceed the current VAT registration threshold (£77,000 in 2012/13).

Asset values for tax purposes

21. Tangible fixed assets

Fixed assets such as land and buildings or plant and machinery, fixtures and fittings etc., do not usually affect the determination of taxable trading income, except where the cost of an asset is charged against income, or in so far as there is a charge for depreciation. In the former case, the cost would be disallowed as capital, whether or not capital allowances are available. With regard to the charge for depreciation, then this is not allowed as a business expense, however computed.

Where a short lease of property is acquired by the taxpayer on payment of a premium, and the property is used for purposes of the trade, then an extra allowance based on the notional rental element of the premium is available, but must be spread over the lease term. See Chapter 8.

Intangible fixed assets

Under this heading are included goodwill, patents and trademarks, licences of intellectual property, copyrights and know how. In the hands of an unincorporated trader these are viewed as capital assets, and may give rise to a claim for capital allowances, see Chapter 13.

Different rules for the tax treatment of Intangible Fixed Assets (other than leases of premises) apply to companies, as explained in Chapter 19. Amortisation of patents, licences, purchased goodwill etc. may be deductible for a company on certain conditions.

Long-term investments

Long-term investments held as a fixed asset do not give rise to any particular problems as they are normally non-trading assets, and any surpluses or deficits arising from annual revaluations are not brought into the computation of taxable income. Realisations would require capital gains tax consideration, however. For companies the 'loan relationships' regime, and not the chargeable gains regime applies to any fixed or current assets defined as a loan relationship. See Chapter 19.

Where the investments are trading assets then they will be valued on the same basis as other current assets.

Current assets

Current assets held by a business for the purposes of its trade would normally be valued for accounts purposes at the lower of cost or net realisable value. The same principles are applied for taxation purposes, but there are some special factors relating to stock and work in progress.

Inventory and work in progress

The following is a summary of the valuation of inventory and WIP in a tax context.

1. In the absence of statutory authority stocks should be valued at the lower of cost or market value. Market value means selling price less selling expenses, and not replacement value. See CIR v Cock Russell & Co. Ltd 1949 29 TC 287: BSC Footwear Ltd v Ridgway 1971 47 TC 495.

   Under the International Accounting Standard 2 (IAS 2), mandatory for UK listed companies from 1 January 2005, inventory value needs to be shown in accounts at the lower of cost and net realisable value (NRV). The same is true for unlisted companies under UK Accounting SSAP 9.

2. Consistency of method of valuation does not of itself guarantee that a correct method of valuation has been used. See BSC Footwear v Ridgway case noted above.

3. Overhead expenditure does not have to be included in the valuation of work in progress or finished stocks for tax purposes, even if this is done for accounting purposes. See Duple Motor Bodies v Ostime 1961 39 TC 537.

4. Standard cost values may be used but due allowance for variances from the standard must be made where they are material.

5. In general neither the base stock method nor the LIFO method of stock valuation is an acceptable method of inventory valuation for tax purposes. See Patrick v Broadstone Mills Ltd 1953 35 TC 44; Minister of National Revenue v Anaconda American Brass Ltd 1956 AC.

   From 1st January 2005 the LIFO method of valuation is also not permitted for accounts of listed companies under IAS 2.

6. Where there is a change in the method of inventory valuation from one valid basis to another, then the opening and closing stocks in the current period must both be valued on the same basis. A valid basis of valuation is one which does not violate the tax statutes as interpreted by the Courts, and which is recognised by the accounting profession.

7. Where a trade is discontinued, its stock must be valued at an open market price, or if sold to another trader, at realised selling price.

   Where the trade is discontinued, stock that is sold must be valued on an 'arm's length basis' if the purchaser and the vendor are connected persons.

8. Professional work in progress (e.g. solicitors' or accountants' professional work already completed, but unbilled) must be valued at recoverable selling price in the closing balance sheet, unless the receipt of fees is uncertain at the year-end. This recognises profit on the accruals principle.

Trading stock appropriated by traders for personal use

Where a trader takes goods from the business trading stock for personal consumption or consumption by his or her household, then it must be valued at its open market realistic value, and not at cost. Effectively the trader must sell himself the goods at selling price. This rule was established in the tax case of Sharkey v Wernher but has now been incorporated into ITTOIA. This is so even though accounting standards say that the cost price should be used – otherwise the proprietor is recognising a non-existent business profit from trading with himself.

Tax and accounting principles

22. United Kingdom tax law requires that tax computations are prepared in accordance with generally accepted accounting practice subject to any adjustment required by law. Generally accepted accounting practice is defined as being the accounting practice that is used in preparing accounts which are intended to give a 'true and fair' view. The various financial reporting standards issued by the

United Kingdom Accounting Standards Board generally require that the relevant Financial Reporting Standard needs to be applied to all transactions of a reporting entity whose financial statements are intended to give a true and fair view. Since 1 January 2005 listed companies apply International Financial Reporting Standards, and these are acceptable for tax purposes under CTA 2009 subject to the adjustments required by corporation tax law.

In Budget 2012 the Government proposed, provisionally from tax year 2013/14, the introduction of an optional 'cash' or 'receipts and payments' basis of accounting for profit of UK 'microbusinesses' (the smallest sole traders). The exact definition of a micro business is still under consultation. Flat rate deductions for certain expenses have also been proposed for these small businesses. The proposals follow a report of the Mirrlees Review in 2011 and discussions led by the Office For Tax Simplification.

Student self-testing questions

1. Hilary has been in business many years as a tile maker. Her profit and loss account for the year ended 31 March was as follows:

	Notes	£	£
Sales			900,000
Cost of sales			(553,795)
Gross profit			346,205
Less: Expenses			
Salaries and wages	1	55,000	
Rent & rates		8,500	
Motor expenses	2	12,000	
Legal expenses	3	13,000	
Advertising		5,500	
Loss on sale of fixed asset		150	
Depreciation		9,095	
Donation to Oxfam made with Gift Aid declaration (net amount paid)		50	
Employees' Christmas party		1,450	
			(104,745)
Net profit			241,460

1. Salaries and wages include Hilary's drawings of 'salary' of £24,000.

2. Motor expenses include Hilary's private use of the car amounting to 25%.

3.   Legal expenses comprise the following:

Costs associated with a tax appeal	3,000
Costs associated with the renewal of a short term lease	5,000
Defending a litigation case with a customer	5,000

Requirement: Calculate Hilary's income from trading for the year.

Solution: Adjusted trading profits calculation

	£	£
Profit per financial statements		241,460
Add: disallowable expenditure:		
Hilary salary	24,000	
Hilary motor expenses	3,000	
Legal costs : tax appeal	3,000	
Loss on sale of fixed asset	150	
Depreciation	9,095	
Donation to Oxfam - Gift Aid scheme applies	50	
		39,295
Income from trading		280,755

2. Mr S Eason has the following business accounting results:

	£
Profit and loss account for the year to 31st Dec 2012:	
Gross operating profit	171,000
Taxed interest received	900
	171,900

Wages and salaries	48,000
Rent & rates	2,500
Depreciation	1800
Bad debts written off	120
Provision* for future building repair costs	5500
Entertainment expenses	800
Patent royalties	1250
Bank interest	350
Legal expenses on acquisition of factory	300

	(60,620)
Net profit	£111,280

Notes:

(i) Salaries include £22,000 paid to Mrs R Eason who worked as an employee in the business

(ii) No staff were entertained

(iii) The provision * is charged because of an anticipated expense for future building repair costs

(iv) Patent royalties were paid net, as required by law, but are shown gross

Requirement: Compute the assessable profit from trading for the year to 31 December 2012.

Solution

Profit per accounts		111,280
Add		
Depreciation	1,800	
Provision for future building repair costs (not GAAP)	5,500	
Entertainment expenses	800	
Legal expenses (relating to non-current asset)	300	
	8,400	
		119,680
less interest received (non-trading savings income)		(900)
Adjusted trading profit		118,780

Notes:

(i) Patent royalties are allowable gross as an expense in calculating income from trading, if wholly and exclusively for business purposes; otherwise treat as an allowable payment deducted from total income in the main income tax computation. The fact they were paid net means that the income tax withheld is added to Mr Eason's own tax borne on income, in his tax computation to give a personal liability that includes the income tax withheld on royalties paid. The liability calculation is not part of the answer above.

(ii) The adjustment for interest received is based on the figure actually included in the business income statement However, Mr Eason's self-assessment tax return should include the gross amount of interest as savings income in the tax year when it is received.

11 Income taxed as trade profits: II - basis periods

Introduction

1.   This chapter deals with the basis of assessment of income of a trade carried on by an individual. The rules applicable to a partnership are discussed in Chapter 15.   The basis period rules are contained in ITTOIA 2005.   A profits basis period is the period used for measuring the trade profit that is matched to a tax year.

Trade profit assessment for a tax year

2.   This topic is covered under the following headings:

General rule

Commencement provisions

Cessation provisions

General rule

3.   The general rule is that the basis period for measuring the trade profits of a tax year is the period of 12 months ending with the business's accounting date in that tax year. This is called the 'current year basis'.

The accounting date means a date, normally annually, on which a balance sheet is drawn up, on generally accepted accounting principles, and the income statement of the business is then arrived at based on the change in net assets (adjusted for drawings and capital introduced) on that balance sheet compared with the last balance sheet.

Even if a sole trader omits to draw up a balance sheet, in principle one must be produced for tax purposes if the accruals basis is to be properly applied to measure accounting profit for a period of account. Businesses over a certain size are required to submit their balance sheets with the self-assessment return but very small businesses are not required to do so. (See Chapter 10 section 23 for a comment on new profit-accounting proposals for micro-businesses from 2013/14.)

Commencement provisions

4.   When an individual starts trading, the following rules apply for determining the profits of the first two or three tax years in which a continuing trade exists.

a) Profits of the first tax year are measured as the 'actual' profits of the period from the date of commencement of trading to the following 5th April. If the chosen accounting date is not 5 April (or 31 March), time- apportionment is used to measure assessable profit up to the end of the first tax year. This time-apportionment assumes that profits accrued evenly over the whole of the first period of account.

b) Profits of the second year are normally either:

    i)   profits for the 12 months ending with the accounting date in that year; this basis applies if there is an accounting date in the second tax year, and it is the end of a trading period of twelve months or more;

    or

    ii) profits of the 12 months from the date of commencement. This applies if there is an accounting date in the second tax year, but it is not the end of a trading period of at least twelve months.

Where there is no accounting date in the second tax year, because the first period of account ends in the third tax year, then the second tax year's assessable profit is measured with hindsight, using time-apportionment of available accounts, for the period covering 6 April to 5 April.

c) For subsequent years the profits assessable for each tax year are the profits for the 12 months ending with the accounting date in the tax year.

Example

T commenced trading on the 1st June 2009 with the following tax adjusted profits for the first 3 periods of account:

	£
1.6.2009 – 31.5.2010	6,000
1.6.2010 – 31.5.2011	10,000
1.6.2011 – 31.5.2012	12,000

Compute the taxable profits for relevant tax years.

Solution

Tax year	Basis period	Assessed amount
2009/10	1.6.09 – 5.4.10 (10/12 × 6,000)	5,000
2010/11	1.6.09 – 31.5.10 (12 months to 31.5.10)	6,000
2011/12	1.6.10 – 31.5.11 (12 months to 31.5.11)	10,000
2012/13	1.6.11 – 31.5.12 (12 months to 31.5.12)	12,000

Notes

i)   The second year is assessed on the profit of the 12 month accounting period ending in the second year i.e. 12 months to 30th May 2010.

ii)   The second tax year contains an 'overlap period' where profits are measured for a second time. This is the period 1 June 2009 to 5 April 2010 with overlap profit of 10/12 x 6,000 = 5,000.

iii)   The amount of overlap profits is recovered on the earlier of the following:

a) a change of accounting date that results in a period of account more than 12 months or

b) the cessation of trading.

iv) Calculations should strictly be made in days and not months, although for the examinations of professional accounting bodies, calculations in whole months are usual.

HMRC have stated that an accounting date of 31 March may be treated as 5 April, so long as this rule is consistently applied for all tax years.

v) The assessed profits less the overlap profits to be recovered are therefore equal to the actual profits $(33,000 - 5,000) = 28,000$.

Example

A commenced trading on the 1st July 2009 and has the following tax adjusted results for the first 3 periods of account:

	£
1.7.2009 – 31.12.2010	24,000
1.1.2011 – 31.12.2011	30,000
1.1.2012 – 31.12.2012	40,000

Compute the taxable profits for all relevant tax years.

Solution

Tax year	Basis period	Assessed amount
2009/10	1.5.09 – 5.4.10 ($9/18 \times 24,000$)	12,000
2010/11	1.1.10 – 31.12.10 ($12/18 \times 24,000$)	16,000
2011/12	1.1.11 – 31.12.11 (12 months to 31.12.11)	30,000
2012/13	1.1.12 – 31.12.12 (12 months to 31.12.12)	40,000

Notes

i) The second year is assessed on the profits of the 12 months ending 31st December 2010.

ii) The overlap period is from 1 January 2010 to 5 April 2010, with profits of $3/18 \times 24,000 = 4,000$.

iii) Assessed profits less the overlap profits to be recovered are thus equal to the actual profits.

$(12,000 + 16,000 + 30,000 + 40,000) - 4,000 = 94,000$

Example

T started business on the 1st January 2010 with first accounts for the 16 months to 30th April 2011 and thereafter:

£

1.1.2010 – 30.4.2011	32,000
1.5.2011 – 30.4.2012	28,000

Compute the taxable profits for relevant tax years.

Solution

Tax year	Basis period	Assessed amount
2009/10	1.1.10 – 5.4.10 (3/16 × 32,000)	6,000
2010/11	6.4.10 – 5.4.11 (12/16 × 32,000)	24,000
2011/12	1.5.10 – 30.4.11 (12/16 × 32,000)	24,000
2012/13	1.5.11 – 30.4.12 (12 months to 30.4.12)	28,000

Notes

i)   There is no period of account ending in the second year 2010/11, therefore the actual basis applies.

ii)   The overlap period is 1 May 2010 – 5 April 2011 i.e. 11 months

      11/16 × 32,000 = 22,000

iii) Assessed profits less the overlap profits are thus equal to the actual profits

      (6,000 + 24,000 + 24,000 + 28,000) – 22,000 = 60,000

Cessation provisions

5.   The profits of the tax year in which cessation takes place are measured as follows.

   i)   The final tax year has a basis period from the end of the previous basis period to the date of cessation.

   ii)   Any profits from the overlap period on commencement not previously recouped are deducted from the profits of the final basis period.

   iii) The effect of the above is that over the life of a business only its actual taxable profits will be assessed.

Example

Q commenced trading on the 1st June 2007 and sold the business on the 30th April 2012 with the following tax adjusted results.

	£
1.6.2007 – 31.5.2008	6,000
1.6.2008 – 31.5.2009	10,000
1.6.2009 – 31.5.2010	12,000
1.6.2010 – 31.5.2011	16,000
1.6.2011 – 30.4.2012	8,000

Compute the assessable trading income for all tax years of the trade.

Solution

Tax year	Basis period	Assessed amount
2007/08	1.6.07 – 5.4.08 (10/12 × 6,000)	5,000
2008/09	1.6.07 – 31.5.08	6,000
2009/10	1.6.08 – 31.5.09	10,000
2010/11	1.6.09 – 31.5.10	12,000
2011/12	1.6.10 – 31.5.11	16,000
2012/13	1.6.11–30.4.12 (8,000–5,000 overlap)	3,000

Notes:

i)   The overlap period is 1 June 2007 – 5 April 2008 i.e. 10 months.

Overlap profit = 10/12 × 6,000 = 5,000

ii) The final period of profits is from 1 June 2011 to 30 April 2012 assessed in 2012/2013 i.e. £8,000. Overlap profits of £5,000 are deducted leaving a net assessment of £3,000.

iii) Total profits over the life of the business are £52,000 which is equal to the taxable profits assessed.

Student self-testing questions

1.

(i) Hilary commenced business on 1 August 2008 and made up her first accounts for the twelve months to 31 July 2009. Her profits adjusted for tax purposes were:

12 months ended 31 July	Adjusted profit
	£
2009	24,000
2010	40,000
2011	32,000
2012	36,000

(ii) Julia commenced business on 1 January 2010, making up her first accounts to 31 October 2010, then annually to that date. Her profits as adjusted for tax purposes were:

	£
10 months ended 31 October 2010	42,000
Year ended 31 October 2011	52,000
Year ended 31 October 2012	65,000

(iii) James began business on 1 September 2010 and made up his first accounts to 31 January 2009. His profits adjusted for tax purposes were:

	£
5 months ended 31 January 2010	24,000
Year ended 31 January 2011	60,000
Year ended 31 January 2012	72,000

(iv) Jeremy began business on the 1 February 2009 and made up his first accounts to 31 July 2010, eighteen months later. His profits adjusted for tax purposes were:

	£
Eighteen months ended 31 July 2010	56,000
Year ended 31 July 2011	40,000
Year ended 31 July 2012	45,000

Requirement: In each case calculate the measured assessable trade profits in the first, second and third tax years and any overlap profits arising. You may make calculations in whole months.

Solution

1) Hilary

1st year	08/09	1 August '08 - 5 April '09 = 8 months	
		8/12 x 24,000	<u>16,000</u>
2nd year	09/10	Is there an accounting date ending in 09/10?	
		Yes 31/7/09	
		The accounting period is greater than or equal to 1 year and therefore the basis of assessment is 12 months to the accounting date in the 2nd tax year.	<u>24,000</u>
		Year ended 31/7/09	
3rd year	10/11	As there was an accounting date ending in the 2nd tax year the basis of assessment is the year ended 31/7/10	<u>40,000</u>
Overlap profit		1/8/08 - 5/4/09 = 8 months (8/12 x 24,000)	16,000

2)   Julia

1st year	09/10	1 Jan '10 - 5 April '10 = 3 months 3/10 x 42,000	<u>12,600</u>
2nd year	10/11	Is there an accounting date ending in 10/11? Yes 31/10/10	42,000
			<u>8,667</u>
		The accounting date is less than 1 year therefore the basis of assessment is the first 12 months of trading	<u>50,667</u>
		10 months ended 31/10/10 plus Nov & Dec '10	
		Assessment is therefore:	
		10 months ended 31/10/10 + 2/12 x 52,000	
3rd year	11/12	As there was an accounting date ending in the 2nd tax year the basis of assessment is the year ended 31/10/11	<u>52,000</u>
Overlap profits		1/1/10 - 5/4/10	12,600
		1/11/10 - 31/12/10 (2/12 x £52,000)	8,667
			21,267

3)   James

1st year	09/10	1 September 2009 - 5 April 2010	
		= 7 months (£24,000 + (2/12 x £60,000)	<u>34,000</u>
2nd year	10/11	Is there an accounting date ending in 10/11? Yes, year ended 31/1/11	
		The accounting date is greater than or equal to 1 year after commencement therefore the basis of assessment is the year to the new accounting date	<u>60,000</u>
3rd year	11/12	As there was an accounting date ending in the 2nd tax year the basis of assessment is the year ended 31/1/12	<u>72,000</u>
Overlap profits		1/2/10 - 5/4/10 (2/12 x 60,000)	10,000

4)   Jeremy

1st year	08/09	1 February 2009 - 5 April 2009 2/18 x 56,000	<u>6,222</u>
2nd year	09/10	Is there an accounting date ending in 09/10? No. Therefore the basis of assessment is profits from 6/4/09 - 5/4/10	<u>37,333</u>
		12/18 x £56,000	
3rd year	10/11	Basis of assessment for the 3rd tax year is 12 months to the accounting date in the 3rd tax year i.e. 31 July 2010 12/18 x £56,000	<u>37,333</u>

| Overlap profits | The profits from 1 August 2009 to 5 April 2010 have been measured in both 09/10 and 10/11. | 24,889 |
| | Overlap profits are therefore £24,889 (8/18 x 56,000). | |

2. Mr E

In the spring of 2013, Mr E was considering starting a new business and had prepared a business plan. This showed that the business would commence trading on 1 July 2013, and that the pattern of profits would be:

Period to 31 December 2013	£600 per month
Twelve months to 31 December 2014	£1,200 per month
Thereafter	£2,400 per month

Mr E is considering two alternative dates on which to make up accounts each year, 31 March or 30 April.

(Note that he is not considering any other date and will not be making up accounts to 31 December.)

Required:

a) Compute the amounts which will be assessable as income from trading for each of the first three tax years under each of the two above alternative accounting dates. **(10 marks)**

b) Indicate the main advantages and disadvantages of each alternative. **(5 marks)**

(CIMA updated)

Solution

Accounting profits arising under the 2 proposed dates:

		£
31 March accounting date		
1 July 2013 - 31 March 2014	(6 x £600) + (3 x £1,200)	7,200
Year ended 31 March 2015	(9 x £1,200) + (3 x £2,400)	18,000
Year ended 31 March 2016	(12 x £2,400)	28,800
30 April accounting date		
10 months to 30 April 2014	(6 x £600) + (4 x £1,200)	8,400
Year ended 30 April 2015	(8 x £1,200) + (4 x £2,400)	19,200
Year ended 30 April 2016	(12 x £2,400)	28,800

Based on the accounting profits, the tax year measures of trading income will be as follows:

31 March accounting date:

	Basis period	Assessable profits £
2013/2014	1 July 2013 - 5 April 2014	7,200
2014/2015	12 months to 31 March 2015	18,000
2015/2016	12 months to 31 March 2016	28,800
		54,000

30 April accounting date:

	Basis period	Calculation	Assessable profit £
2013/2014	1 July 2013 - 5 April 2014	9/10 x 8,400	7,560
2014/2015	1 July 2013 - 30 June 2014	8,400 + (2/12 x 19,200)	11,600
2015/2016	Year ended 30 April 2015		19,200
			38,360

(b)

30 April

The 30 April accounting date gives a lower amount of total assessable profits for the first three years of assessment. There is a greater interval between earning profits and paying taxes.

(The difference in tax liability occurs because the business's profits are rising. If there were the same profit every month exactly, it would make little difference which accounting reference date was chosen.)

With the 30 April reference date, profits in the periods 1 July 2013 to 5 April 2014 (£7,560) and 1 May 2014 to 30 June 2014 (£3,200) are counted twice in the first three tax years – creating 'overlap profits' of (7,560+3,200) = £10,760.

Relief for overlap profits is obtained either on cessation or on a change of accounting date.

31 March

The 31 March reference date gives no 'overlap' profits.

It has higher total assessable profits in early years giving rise to earlier tax liabilities on profits earned. The reason why it gives higher profits is because profits are rising over the first three years.

Hence there is a cash flow disadvantage compared to selecting a 30 April reference date.

Questions without answers

1. Chatru commenced trading on 1 November 2008. His first accounts were made up to 30 April 2010 and thereafter to 30 April annually. He ceased trading on 31 March 2013.

    His trading results, adjusted for income tax purposes were:

	£
1.11.08-30.4.10	40,500
Year ended 30.4.11	12,000
Year ended 30.4.12	24,000
Period to 31.3.13	46,000

    Requirements:

    Calculate the assessable income for all years in question

    Calculate whether there would have been an income tax benefit in Chatru continuing to trade one extra month and making up final accounts to his normal accounting date, on the assumption that his tax-adjusted profit for April 2013 was £4,200.

    11 marks

    (ACCA updated)

2. Nan Pearson died on 30 June 2012 aged 58. She had been employed as a design engineer by Map plc, a company which specialises in the construction of motor bikes.

    The following is supplied:

    (1) Nan's salary, paid on the last day of each month, was £40,000 pa from which 5% was paid to an approved staff pension fund. The company's contribution was 8%. PAYE of £1,500 was deducted from the salary during 2012/13.

    (2) Her other income comprised the following.

	Year ended 5 April 2012	6 April 2012 to 30 June 2012
	£	£
Net interest received from a building society on a deposit account	1,264	1,440
Dividends received from UK companies net received excluding the tax credit	3,888	4,248

Arthur Pearson, Nan's husband, had been employed until his retirement in March 2008 at age 55. Since that date he undertook some self-employed bookkeeping activities and recent tax adjusted profits of this business are as follows:

	£
Year to 30 April 2009	5,000
Year to 30 April 2010	4,100
Year to 30 April 2011	5,900
Year to 30 April 2012	6,700

No tax has yet been paid on Arthur's income from trading for 2012/13

(3)   Arthur received net bank interest of £124 on 30 June 2011 and £104 on 30 June 2012.

The following events took place after Nan's death.

(1)   A payment of £140,000, being the sum assured on Nan's life under the Map plc's pension scheme, was paid to Arthur.

(2)   A pension of £22,980 (gross) per annum, payable on the first day of each month, was paid to Arthur by Map plc. The first payment was made on 1 July 2012 and a BR code was used by the company for PAYE purposes (i.e. basic rate tax was deducted from the pension by Map plc).

Arthur used the £140,000 assurance policy receipt to acquire and furnish a small studio apartment on 1 February 2013. He let this apartment under a ten year lease from 1 March 2013, the incoming tenant paying a premium of £4,000. The rent of £5,500 a year is payable quarterly in advance and was received when due. Arthur incurred the following expenses in connection with the letting:

	£
Interior decorating prior to letting	790
Year's insurance of premises and contents - 1 March 2013	384
Managing agent's fee (for tenancy agreement and March 2013 management)	250

Requirement:

Prepare income tax computations for 2012/13 for

(a) Nan Pearson, showing income tax payable or refundable (10 marks)

(b) Arthur Pearson, showing the final income tax position and indicating any final amounts of tax to be paid or repaid.   (6 marks)

(Total: 16 marks)

12 Income taxed as trade profits: III - change of accounting date

Introduction

1.   This chapter is concerned with the effects of a change of accounting date on the income taxed as trade profits for a tax year, under the basis period rules already described.

Detailed rules

2.   An outline of the rules in respect of a change of accounting date follows:

   a)   HMRC will ignore any change of accounting date and require separate balance sheets as before for the original annual basis periods unless all of the three undermentioned circumstances apply.

      i)   The first period of account (i.e. period for which business accounts are made up) ending with the new date does not exceed 18 months.

      ii) Notice of the change is given to an officer of HMRC in a personal tax return on or before the day on which that return is required to be delivered.

      Either

      1)   no accounting change resulting in a change of basis period has been made in any of the previous five tax years;

      or

      2)   the change is made for bona fide commercial reasons. In this case notice in (ii) above must set out the reasons for the change and HMRC do not, within 60 days, give notice to the trader that they are not satisfied that the change is made for bona fide commercial reasons.

   b)   There is a right of appeal against HMRC's decision not to accept a second change in five years as being for commercial reasons.

   c)   Obtaining a tax advantage by an accounting date change is not accepted as a valid commercial reason for a change.

   d)   Where all the conditions are satisfied, or the accounting change is made in the second or third tax year of the business, the basis period for the tax year of the change is as follows.

      i)   If the year is the second tax year of the business, the basis period is the twelve months ending with the new accounting date falling in that tax year (unless the period from commencement of the business to the new date in the second year is less than twelve months, in which case the basis is the first twelve months of the business).

Overlap relief will arise to the extent that profits are brought into charge twice as a result of this rule.

ii) If the 'relevant period' is a period of less than twelve months, the basis period is the twelve months ending with the new date in the tax year. Further overlap profits will arise to the extent that profits are brought into charge twice as a result of this rule. These overlap profits will be added to any previous overlap profits

iii) If the 'relevant period' is a period of more than twelve months, the basis period consists of the relevant period, less any overlap relief available to deduct.

The 'relevant period' is the period beginning immediately after the end of the basis period for the preceding year and ending with the new date in the year.

In summary, when the accounting date change involves a move of the accounting date later in the tax year, previous overlap is released, and when it involves a move of the accounting date to earlier in the year, new overlap is created.

	Difference between end of preceding basis period and new accounting date	Basis period
1st year	< 12 months	12 months to new A/C date
1st year	> 12 months	Period to new A/C date
2nd year	—	12 months to new A/C date

Profits for the period of overlap will need to be computed when a change of accounting date takes place.

Example

A starts in business on 1st July 2008 and produces accounts to 5th April until 5 April 2011, when a new date of 30th June 2011 is the next accounting date.

		£
Accounts	1.7.08 – 5.4.09	10,000
	6.4.09 – 5.4.10	12,000
	6.4.10 – 5.4.11	15,000
	6.4.11 – 30.6.11	2,000
	1.7.11 – 30.6.12	6,000

Compute the assessments.

Solution

		£
2008/09	1.7.08 – 5.4.09	10,000
2009/10	12 months to 5.4.10	12,000
2010/11	12 months to 5.4.11	15,000
2011/12	12 months to 30.6.11	
	1.7.10 – 5.4.11 = 9 months	
	9/12 × 15,000 =	11,250
	6.4.11 – 30.6.11 =	2,000 13,250
2012/13	1.7.11 – 30.6.12 =	6,000

Notes

i) Overlap Memorandum

There was no overlap profit arising on the commencement of the business, as a 5 April accounting date was adopted.

Overlap relief on change of accounting date:

Overlap period 1.7.2010 – 5.4.2011

$$= 9/12 \times 15,000 = \quad \underline{11,250}$$

Amount carried forward as overlap profits   11,250

ii) Total profit assessed less overlap relief

= £45,000 : (10,000 + 12,000 + 15,000 + 13,250 + 6,000) – 11,250.

Example

V started business on the 1st January 2008 with the following results.

6 months to 30.6.2008	20,000
12 months to 30.6.2009	40,000
12 months to 30.6.2010	50,000
18 months to 31.12.2011	75,000
12 months to 31.12.2012	60,000

Compute the assessable trading profits for all tax years, the overlap profit carried forward and the overlap relief.

Solution

Years	Period		£
2007/2008	1.1.08 – 5.4.08		
	3/6 × 20,000 =		10,000
2008/2009	First 12 months trading		
	20,000 + ((6/12) × 40,000)		
	20,000 + 20,000		40,000
2009/10	CY 30.6.2009		40,000
2010/11	CY 30.6.2010		50,000
2011/12	1.7.2010 – 31.12.2011		
	total for period	75,000	
	less overlap released	(20,000)	55,000
2012/13	CY 31.12.2012		60,000

Notes

i) Overlap Memorandum

Original overlap profits (1.1.08–5.4.08)+(1.7.08–31.12.08) = 9 months

$$= 10,000 + 20,000 = \qquad 30,000$$

2011/12 overlap released 1.7.10 – 31.12.11 = 549 days

$$18 – 12 = 6 \text{ months}$$

$$6/9 × 30,000 = \qquad (20,000)$$

Reduced overlap carried forward at 2012/13   10,000

ii) Total profit assessed less overlap relief

= £245,000 : (10,000 + 40,000 + 40,000 + 50,000 + 55,000 + 60,000) – 10,000

Example

B has been in business for many years with the following results.

12 months to 31.12.2008	10,000
12 months to 31.12.2009	30,000
12 months to 31.12.2010	20,000
6 months to 30.6.2011	12,000
12 months to 30.6.2012	36,000

Compute the assessable trading profits for all tax years and the overlap relief arising on the change of accounting date and carried forward by the taxpayer.

Solution

Years	Period	£
2008/09	12 months to 31.12.2008	10,000
2009/10	12 months to 31.12.2009	30,000
2010/11	12 months to 31.12.2010	20,000
2011/12	12 months to 30.6.2011:	
	12,000 + ((6/12) × 20,000)	
	12,000 + 10,000	22,082
2012/13	30.6.2011	36,000

Overlap relief 1.7.10 – 31.12.10

$6/12 × 20,000 \quad = \quad \underline{10,000}$

Total assessed profits less overlap relief = (10,000 + 30,000 + 20,000 + 22,082 + 36,000) – 10,000 = £108,000.

Student self-testing question

A starts in business on 1st May 2007 making accounts up to 5th April each year until 2011 when a new date of 30th November 2011 is chosen as the accounting date.

Business periods of account	Adjusted profits (£)
1.5.07 – 5.4.08	10,000
6.4.08 – 5.4.09	12,000
6.4.09 – 5.4.10	14,000
6.4.10 – 5.4.11	16,000
6.4.11 – 30.11.11	8,000
1.12.11 – 30.11.12	20,000

Compute the measured assessable trading profits for all tax years.

Solution

			£
2007/08	1.5.07 – 5.4.08		10,000
2008/09	12 months to 5.4.09		12,000
2009/10	12 months to 5.4.10		14,000
2010/11	12 months to 5.4.11		16,000
2011/12	12 months to 30.11.11		
	6.4.11– 30.11.11	8,000	
	1.12.09 – 5.4.10 = 4 months		
	4/12 x 16,000 =	<u>5,333</u>	13,333
2012/13	1.12.11 – 30.11.12 =		20,000
Overlap relief 1.12.11 – 30.11.12			5,333
Carried forward			5,333

Total profits = 85,333 – 5,333 = £80,000

Question without answer

1. X starts trading on 1st December 2008 with the following results:

	£
Period to 5th April 2009	7,000
Year to 5th April 2010	10,000
Year to 5th April 2011	15,000
6 months to 30th September 2011	8,000
Year to 30th September 2012	20,000

Compute the measured assessable trading profits for all tax years.

13 Capital allowances

Introduction

1.   The chapter is about the allowances available to a taxpayer in respect of capital expenditure on fixed assets. These allowances, which are called capital allowances, consist of a mixture of annual and other allowances which are available in respect of qualifying expenditure incurred under the following headings.

Plant and machinery

Business premises renovation (only for expenditure before 11 April 2012)

Know-how (not available to companies)

Scientific research assets

Patent rights (not available to companies)

The main statute is the Capital Allowances Act 2001, as amended by subsequent Finance Acts.

The UK government has a tendency to alter capital allowances rules often, for reasons of economic policy. It is an area of law which is not subject to EU scrutiny as 'State Aid', which means changes can be given effect very quickly.

The chapter is divided into the following sections:

Part I	–	Plant and machinery
Part II	–	Other assets

Examples in this chapter which cover a number of periods of account may be projected into the future. This is to avoid confusion that could result from including obsolete allowances, or transitional rules of no future significance, in workings shown for earlier tax years.

Nearly all of the capital allowance rules for tangible assets, described in this chapter, apply in the same way for corporate taxpayers. Where there are differences, the difference is noted. (See Chapter 18 for more points on companies' capital allowances.)

PART I – Plant and machinery – general conditions

2.   a) Allowances are available under this heading if a person carries on a qualifying activity and incurs qualifying expenditure.

   b) 'Qualifying activity' has the following meaning

   i)   a trade, profession or vocation,

   ii)   an ordinary property business,

   iii)   a furnished holiday lettings business,

   iv)   an overseas property business,

v)   the management of an investment company,

vi)   special leasing of plant or machinery,

vii)   an employment or office.

c) Expenditure is qualifying expenditure if –

i)   it is capital expenditure on the provision of plant or machinery wholly or partly for the purposes of the qualifying activity carried on by the person incurring the expenditure, and

ii)   the person incurring the expenditure owns the plant or machinery as a result of incurring it.

Qualifying expenditure

3.   a) Plant and machinery is not conclusively defined in tax statute though Schedule AA1 to the CAA 2001 attempted to codify existing case law. The definition most frequently referred to is that contained in a non-tax case, Yarmouth v France 1887 QBD. The case was brought under the Employers' Liability Act 1880, and consideration given as to whether or not a horse was plant and machinery. In the course of his judgement, Lindley LJ made the following statement:

'... in its ordinary sense it includes whatever apparatus is used by a business man for carrying on his business, not his stock in trade which he buys or makes for sale, but all goods and chattels, fixed or moveable, live or dead, which he keeps for permanent employment in his business.'

b)   In another important case it was stated that 'plant' excludes buildings and parts of buildings to the extent they are the 'setting' of the trade, rather than the 'apparatus' of the trade.

c)   Capital expenditure on alterations to an existing building, incidental to the installation of plant, may be treated as plant and machinery, where a qualifying activity is carried on.

d)   Expenditure on the thermal insulation of an industrial building.

e)   Fire safety expenditure.

f)   Personal security expenditure.

g)   Buildings and structures – see below.

Features integral to a building – the special rate pool

4.   Since 2008 certain features integral to a building, thermal insulation and long-life assets (see section 14) are placed for capital allowances purposes in a separate 'special rate pool'.

The writing down allowance is at a lower rate for this pool, compared to other items of plant and machinery.

The special rate pool also includes cars with carbon dioxide emissions exceeding 160g/km, acquired for business use after 31 March 2009 (5 April 2009 for sole traders/partnerships).

Features integral to a building are defined as: electrical systems; cold water systems; heating, ventilation, air cooling or purification systems including related floors and ceilings; lifts, escalators and moving walkways; external solar shading; active facades.

Allowances are available for both initial expenditure and replacement expenditure on integral features. 'Replacement' is expenditure on replacing or renewing over 50% of the asset within a 12 month period. Where capital allowances apply under this rule, a normal repairs deduction is not available as a deductible expense against profits.

Plant and machinery – buildings (to 5 April 2008 for Income Tax and 31 March 2008 for Corporation Tax)

5. Prior to the rules on 'features integral to a building' which could be included in the special rate pool, the following rules applied to distinguish trade plant and machinery from buildings in which that plant and machinery was incorporated:

Plant and machinery did not include:

i) buildings – see List A (references to Sch AAI CAA 2001)

ii) fixed structures – see List B

iii) interests in land.

Note The items included in list C could be claimed as plant and machinery of a trade, subject to the case-law criteria.

List A: Buildings

1. Walls, floors, ceilings, doors, gates, shutters, windows and stairs
2. Main services, and systems, of water, electricity and gas
3. Waste disposal systems
4. Sewerage and drainage systems
5. Shafts or other structures in which lifts, hoists, escalators and moving walkways are installed
6. Fire safety systems

List B: Structures

1. Any tunnel, bridge, viaduct, aqueduct, embankment or cutting
2. Any way or hard standing, such as a pavement, road, railway or tramway, a park for vehicles or containers, or an airstrip or runway
3. Any inland navigation, including a canal or basin or a navigable river
4. Any dam, reservoir or barrage (including any sluices, gates, generators and other equipment associated with it)

5. Any dock

6. Any dike, sea wall, weir or drainage ditch

7. Any structure not within any other item in this column

List C: Assets which can be included in buildings, but expenditure on which is unaffected by the buildings rules

i.e. These items could still be claimed **as plant and machinery**, subject to established case law principles. Note that some of these items are 'features integral to a building' which since April 2008 must get writing down allowance at the lower 'special' rate. The rest of the items on this list C remain potentially identifiable as plant and machinery in the general pool. Also, existing assets in these categories could still be included in the general pool brought forward, and account for some plant proceeds on disposal of a building.

'List C'

1. Electrical, cold water, gas and sewerage systems –
   a) provided mainly to meet the particular requirements of the trade, or
   b) provided mainly to serve particular machinery or plant used for the purposes of trade

2. Space or water heating systems; powered systems of ventilation; air cooling or air purification; and any ceiling or floor comprised in such systems

3. Manufacturing or processing equipment; storage equipment, including cold rooms; display equipment; and counters, checkouts and similar equipment

4. Cookers, washing machines, dishwashers, refrigerators and similar; washbasins, sinks, baths, showers, sanitary ware and similar equipment; furniture and furnishings

5. Lifts, hoists, escalators and moving stairways

6. Sound insulation provided mainly to meet the particular requirements of the trade

7. Computer, telecommunications and surveillance systems (including wiring or other links)

8. Refrigeration or cooling equipment

9. Sprinkler and other equipment for extinguishing or containing fire; fire alarm systems

10. Burglar alarm systems

11. Any machinery (including devices for providing motive power) not within any other item in this column

12. Strong rooms in bank or building society premises; safes

13. Partition walls, where moveable and intended to be moved in the course of the trade

14. Decorative assets provided for the enjoyment of the public in the hotel, restaurant or similar trades

15. Advertising hoardings; signs, displays and similar assets

16. Alteration of land for the purpose only of installing machinery or plant

17. Provision of dry docks

18. Provision of any jetty or similar structure provided mainly to carry machinery or plant

19. Provision of pipelines

20. Provision of towers used to support floodlights

21. Provision of any reservoir incorporated into a water treatment works

22. Provision of silos used for temporary storage or on the provision of storage tanks

23. Provision of slurry pits or silage clamps

24. Provision of swimming pools, including diving boards, slides and any structure supporting them

25. Provision of fish tanks or fish ponds

26. Provision of rails, sleepers and ballast for a railway or tramway

27. Swimming pools

28. Cold stores

29. Any glass house with integral environment controls

30. Movable buildings intended to be moved in the course of the qualifying activity

Cases on plant and machinery

6. The following is a summary of some of the cases concerned with the definition of plant and machinery. Cases prior to 2001 were influential in the drawing up of lists A B and C above :

1. Jarrold v John Good & Sons Ltd 1962 CA 40 TC 681. In this case movable metal partitioning used to divide office accommodation was held to be plant.

2. CIR v Barclay Curle & Co. Ltd 1969 H.L. 45 TC 221. The company constructed a dry dock, the whole cost of which, including excavation, was held to be plant.

3. Cooke v Beach Station Caravans Ltd 1974 CD 49 TC 524. The company constructed a swimming pool with an elaborate system of filtration, as one of the amenities at a caravan park. The cost, which included excavation, was held to be plant of the leisure business.

4. St Johns School v Ward 1974 CA 49 TC 524. A special purpose prefabricated structure, for use as a laboratory and gymnasium in a school, was held not to be plant.

5. Schofield v R & H Hall Ltd 1974 NI 49 TC 538. A grain importer built a concrete silo with gantries, conveyors and chutes, which was held to be plant.

6. Benson v The Yard Arm Club Ltd 1978 CD STC 408. The purchase and conversion of an old ferry boat into a floating restaurant was held not to be plant, but the setting of the business.

7. Dixon v Fitch's Garage Ltd 1975 CD STC 480. A metal canopy covering the service area of a petrol filling station was held to be a shelter, and not plant.

8. Munby v Furlong 1977 CA STC 232. Books purchased by a barrister to create a library in his practice were held to be plant.

9. Leeds Permanent Building Society 1982 CD Decorative screens incorporating the society's name in a building were held to be plant.

10. Wimpy International Ltd v Warland 1988 CA Expenditure on items of decoration installed in the company's restaurants was held partly to be plant and machinery. However, item 14 in List C now expands the principles found in that case.

11. J D Wetherspoon plc v HMRC 2012 UKUT 42 (TCC)– a recent important tax appeal case on what is 'plant' expenditure, and what is 'buildings', when refurbishing pubs. The Upper Tribunal (Tax and Chancery Chamber) issued judgment on 31 January 2012.

    The case at first instance was heard in 2007 and so the judgement relates to the 'plant' rules before the 2008 reforms, when the 'special rate pool' came in. The judgment includes much useful guidance on the 'plant or buildings?' distinction for capital allowances on fitting out pubs and restaurants. For example it was held that expenditure on new wall tiling is generally on buildings (so no capital allowances). However tiling is plant where installed for a clear trading purpose - in this case, to protect the kitchen wall against splashes from cooking pans . In contrast, tiling in the customer toilets was held simply to be a general type of wall covering and not plant. In the pub itself, timber panelling on internal walls, which the taxpayer argued was plant installed for a trading reason - to create pub 'atmosphere' - , was held not to be plant, because it was not sufficiently special or distinctive to be distinguished from ordinary wall covering. The Wimpy case from 1988 (10 above) was referred to in detail.

12. Hunt v Henry Quick Ltd: King v Bridisco Ltd CHD. 1992 STC 633. The construction of mezzanine platforms in a warehouse was held to be plant and machinery, as they had a trade function.

13. Gray v Seymour's Garden Centre C.H.D. 1993. The construction of a special horticultural greenhouse was held not to be plant and machinery.

14. Attwood v Anduff C.A. 1997. The expenditure on a purpose built car wash site was held not to be plant and machinery. However, while structural expenditure on the site was not accepted as plant, car wash machinery clearly would be plant.

15. Shove v Lingfield Park C.D. 2003. An artificial all-weather track at a racecourse was held to be part of the premises and not plant.

When capital expenditure is incurred

7.   The expenditure is normally treated as incurred on the date on which the obligation to pay becomes unconditional. However, if payment in whole or in part is not required until more than four months after the date on which the obligation to pay becomes unconditional, then so much of the amount as can be deferred is taken to be incurred on that later date when the obligation to pay becomes unconditional. This is to prevent artificial acceleration of 'purchase dates' beyond a normal credit period, to obtain allowances in an earlier period.

Example

K orders an item of plant from X plc on the following terms:

31.12.2012 plant delivered and invoiced on same date to K.

21.1.2013   due date for payment by K, being the end of the month following date of delivery.

3.2.2013   K makes payment.

The expenditure is deemed to have been incurred by K on 31.12.2012.

Example

L orders an item of plant from T plc costing £50,000 as follows:

31.12.2012   plant delivered and invoiced on same date.

31.1.2013   90% of invoice amount due for payment.

30.6.2013   balance of 10% due for payment.

L is deemed to have incurred the expenditure as follows:

31.12.2012   90% × £50,000 i.e. £45,000

30.6.2013   10% × £50,000 i.e. £5,000

Allowances available

8.   The types of allowances which can be claimed in respect of expenditure on plant or machinery are:

annual investment allowance (AIA)

enhanced capital allowances (ECA) – also called 100% First Year Allowance (FYA) in the case of low emission cars

writing down allowance (WDA)

balancing allowance (BA)

sometimes the above are offset by a 'negative allowance' – a balancing charge (BC).

Annual investment allowance £25,000 (2011/12 £100,000)

9.   Annual investment allowance of 100% of expenditure up to £25,000 a year will be available on any category of plant and machinery other than cars, for all

categories of business. The limit was £100,000 per year up to 5 April 2012 for unincorporated taxpayers and 31 March 2012 for companies.

Annual Investment Allowance can be allocated to eligible assets in any order of the taxpayer's choice. The most efficient order of allocation is to the special rate pool first, then to the general pool, then short life assets and finally private use assets.

Enhanced capital allowances – 100% First Year Allowance for Energy/water saving plant

10. Enhanced capital allowances (ECAs) are designed to encourage the use of energy efficient equipment by giving a 100% allowance on purchase. Only products included on the UK Energy Technology Lists approved by the Department of Environment Transport and the Regions (DETR) will qualify. These lists are available at www.eca.gov.uk .

The allowance, which is available to all businesses, is also extended to qualifying energy saving assets purchased for leasing or hire to others.

Enhanced capital allowances – 100% FYA for Low-emission cars

11. a) A 100% FYA is available on the purchase of a new car if:

  i) it is a low-emission car i.e. emits not more than 110g/km of carbon dioxide, or

  ii) it is electrically propelled.

b) The 100% FYA is also available for plant and machinery to refuel vehicles with natural gas or hydrogen fuel, e.g. storage tanks, pumps, etc.

c) The allowance is extended to assets acquired to be leased, let or hired.

12. Enhanced capital allowances (ECA or 100% FYA) are also available for plant and machinery, excluding cars (other than Low Emissions cars), for use primarily within an Enterprise Zone.

General pool plant and machinery WDA –18% from April 2012 (2011/12 - 20%)

13. a) A writing down allowance (WDA) is available in respect of expenditure incurred in the capital allowances basis period (the accounting period for companies), other than assets attracting ECA or FYA in that year.

b) The allowance is available whether the plant or machinery is brought into use for the trade by the end of the basis period, so long as it was acquired for the trade.

c) WDA is given on a reducing balance basis on the unrelieved general pool of plant expenditure, after adjusting for in-year additions and disposals, other than additions qualifying for FYA / ECA, as shown in the specimen computation below (section 19).

d) Before computing WDA the pool is reduced by reference to the Total Disposal Receipts (TDR) (limited to the original cost) from any of the following events at any time during the chargeable period.

  i) The plant or machinery ceases to belong to the taxpayer.

  ii) The taxpayer loses possession of the plant or machinery in circumstances where it is reasonable to assume that the loss is permanent.

  iii) The plant or machinery ceases to exist as a result of destruction, etc.

  iv) The plant or machinery begins to be used wholly or partly for purposes other than those of the trade.

  v) The trade is permanently discontinued.

e) The balance remaining on the pool after deducting any proceeds of disposals is written down in the normal way. If the pool balance after deducting sale proceeds, and bringing in qualifying additions, is negative there is a balancing charge calculated to bring the balance on the pool to nil.

f) The taxpayer can claim any proportion of the allowances available, but must accept the full balancing charge arising on a disposal.

g) If a plant asset has any private use, the asset must be kept outside the pool. The 18% allowance is calculated in the normal way and deducted from the cost or written down value of the asset; the amount given as the full writing down allowance is then reduced accordingly for the private use element. A separate (single-asset) pool is required for each asset with a private use element so that private use can be accurately excluded from tax relief.

h) Companies do not have 'private use assets' as a company has no private identity. Assets used privately by directors or staff are in business use by the company and the private use is dealt with by the Benefits Code (see Chapter 7).

i) A writing down allowance is not available in the year of cessation of trading, though a balancing allowance may be.

j) If the balance remaining on the general pool before WDA in any year is less than £1,000, the taxpayer may take the whole amount remaining as WDA of that period, writing the pool down to nil.

k) A writing down allowance is not available in the same period as first year allowance on assets which received a partial first year allowance; but WDA is available in the same year as additional investment allowance, to the extent the asset expenditure is not already fully relieved by the allocated AIA.

l) Cars with CO_2 emissions of 160 g/km or less qualify for the 18% writing down allowance and are added to the general pool, but do not qualify for any AIA.

Special rate pool - 8% WDA from April 2012 (2011/12 - 10% WDA)

14. Assets in the special rate pool attract a writing down allowance of 8%. These assets are:

a) Features integral to a building;

b) Thermal insulation in a building;

c) Cars with CO_2 emissions of more than 160 g/km;

d) 'Long-life assets' – ie Machinery or plant which has an expected working life when new of 25 years or more.

Expenditure on long-life assets which does not exceed a minimum limit is excluded from the rules requiring the assets to be put in the SR pool.

   i) For companies, the minimum limit is £25,000 a year, divided by one plus the number of associated companies.

   ii) The minimum of £25,000 a year also applies to individuals, and to partnerships made up of individuals.

   iii) The exclusion for expenditure below the minimum limit does not apply to shared contributions to expenditure on machinery or plant, nor to expenditure on a share in machinery or plant, on machinery or plant for leasing, or on machinery and plant on which allowances have been given to a previous owner at the long-life asset rate.

The long-life assets category is not very significant for a small trader, because of the minimum value rules. It is more relevant for companies, which buy large assets such as ships, aeroplanes and helicopters, heavy cranes etc.

Separate pooling rules

15. A separate expenditure pool must be kept for each of the following classes of assets:

   i) the general pool of plant and machinery (as detailed above);

   ii) the special rate pool (as detailed above);

   iii) assets with any private use (one pool per asset);

   iv) short life assets where a de-pooling election has been made (one pool per asset, or per class of identical assets).

   v) cars (except low-emission cars) costing more than £12,000 acquired before 1/6 April 2009 are subject to transitional rules from FA 2008, and must remain in their own single-asset pools until April 2014 or earlier disposal.

Specimen capital allowances computation – working layout

16.

	£	General pool £	Special rate pool £
Unrelieved qualifying expenditure (WDV) brought forward from the last period of account		X	X
Qualifying expenditure (not eligible for AIA =cars)		X	X
Qualifying expenditure (eligible for AIA, but not eligible for 100% FYA)	X		
Less: Annual Investment Allowance (maximum £25k per year, pro-rated for long or short period of account)	(X)*		
Excess of expenditure over AIA - taken to pool or special rate pool or both, depending on asset type		X	
Available qualifying expenditure for WDA (before disposals)		X	X
Less: Total disposal receipts (limited to original cost of each asset, if this can still be traced)		(X)	(X)
		X	X
Less: Writing down allowances 18% or 8% (pro-rated for long or short period of account)		(X)*	(X)*
Qualifying expenditure for 100% ECA /FYA	X		
Less: First year allowance at 100% (not pro-rated for a short or long period of account)	(X)*	0	
Unrelieved qualifying expenditure (WDV) c/fwd		X	X

Notes

i)   The total of trading capital allowances available for a period of account to a taxpayer is the sum of the items marked * in the computation layout above.

ii) The above computation omits a single-asset pool, but this would be set up in the same way as the multi-asset pools by entering the cost of the asset in its own column. The annual WDA is then deducted from the single asset pool WDV.

iii) For the operation of balancing charges and balancing allowances, which do not occur in the specimen layout above, see section 21.

Capital allowances and accounts

17. For all businesses the following provisions apply.

    1) Capital allowances are given for a 'chargeable period' which is based on the period of account for individuals, and on the corporation tax accounting period for companies.

    2) Capital allowances are treated as a trading expense of the business in the chargeable period and any balancing charge is treated as a trading receipt. This means that the trade profit for tax purposes is after the deduction of capital allowances. However, the taxpayer is not obliged to claim the maximum allowances available. If lower capital allowances are claimed than are available, the unrelieved expenditure (written down values) carried forward to the next period will be correspondingly higher.

    3) Where the period of account for income tax purposes is not a 12 month period, the writing down allowance and the annual investment allowance are contracted or expanded on a pro-rata basis. e.g.

       Period of account, 8 months – writing down allowance   8/12 × 18%

       Maximum AIA (from April 2012 to November 2012)   8/12 x £25,000

       Period of account, 15 months – writing down allowance   15/12 × 18%

       Maximum AIA (from April 2012 to June 2013)   15/12 x £25,000

    4) The pro-rating rules above also apply to companies where the accounting period is shorter than 12 months. If a company has a period of account longer than 12 months then this is split into one corporation tax accounting period of 12 months and one short period covering the rest of the period of account. Therefore companies can never have WDAs and AIAs pro-rated upwards for long periods, but only downwards for short periods.

    5) ECAs, FYAs, balancing allowances or charges are not adjusted for long or short periods.

    6) On the commencement of a new unincorporated business, or on a change of accounting date, in order to deal with the taxable profits of the first and second years of assessment it will be necessary first to compute and deduct the capital allowances for the period(s) of account.

Example

P started trading on the 1st May 2012 with the following results:

Adjusted profits 1.5.12 – 30.4.2013	86,800
Adjusted profits 1.5.13 – 30.4.2014	155,900
General plant and machinery purchased 10.04.2013	35,000

Compute the capital allowances available assuming current rules continue to apply in future years, and show the assessable trading profits for the years 2012/13 to 2014/15.

Solution

Capital allowances period 1.5.12 – 30.4.13   General plant and machinery pool

Opening WDV		0
10.04.2013 additions	35,000	
Less: Annual investment allowance – maximum	(25,000)	
		10,000
		10,000
30.4.13 writing down allowance 18%		(1,800)
WDV 30.04.2013		8,200

Capital allowances period 1.5.13 – 30.4.14

30.4.2014 writing down allowance 18%		(1,476)
WDV 30.04.2014		6,724

Period of Account	Adjusted Profits	Capital Allowances	Taxable Profit
	£	£	£
1.5.12 – 30.4.13	86,800	26,800	60,000
1.5.13 – 30.4.14	155,900	1,476	154,424

Assessments

		£
2012/13 (1.5.12 – 5.4.13)	11/12 × 60,000	55,000
2013/14 (1.5.12 – 30.4.13)		60,000
2014/15 (1.5.13 – 30.4.14)		154,424

Notes

The overlap period is from 1.5.12 – 5.4.13, i.e. 11 months, or profits of £55,000. When the business ceases trading, an adjustment for this amount will be made in the final self-assessment of trading profits.

Example

Q started trading on 1 October 2012 with first accounts for the 15 months to 31 December 2013. Capital expenditure of £46,250 on general plant and machinery was incurred on 1 October 2012. Capital expenditure of £24,000 was incurred on features integral to a building on 1 November 2012. Adjusted profits, before capital allowances, for the 15 months amounted to £114,775.

		General pool	Special rate pool
Period of account			
Capital expenditure	1.10.2012	46,250	
	1.11.2012	24,000	
Annual investment allowance	25,000 x 15/12	(31,250)	
Transfer unrelieved cost to pool		39,000	0
Writing down allowance	18% x 15/12	(8,775)	
Written down value carried forward		30,225	0

Assessments

Adjusted profits 1.10.12 – 31.12.13		114,775
Capital allowances		
(31,250 + 8,775)		40,025
		74,750
2012/13 1.10.12 – 5.4.13		
74,750 x 6/15		29,900
2013/14 1.1.13 – 31.12.13		
74,750 x 12/15		59,800

Notes

i)   The capital allowances are computed for the period of account of 15 months.

ii)   Capital allowances are deducted from the profits of the period of account before computing the profits assessed in different tax years, using the basis period rules.

iii)   Overlap profits are January to March 2013: 74,750 x 3/15 = £14,950.

iv)   If the first period of account had been less than 12 months in duration, the WDA and AIA would have been pro-rated down.

v)   FYAs and ECAs are not scaled up or down for the length of a period of account.

Restriction on leasing costs for cars with high emissions

18. This is not strictly a capital allowances rule, but was introduced as a result of the capital allowances rules for cars. The legislators considered that, given the slower rate of writing down allowances for cars with high CO_2 emissions, businesses would lease these cars instead of buying them outright (obtaining a full expense deduction for the lease costs).

To discourage this, if a private car is leased or hired for trading purposes which emits more than 160 g/km of CO_2, then the hiring or leasing charge allowed as a business expense is restricted by 15%. This rule applies equally to incorporated and unincorporated businesses.

Example

C hires a car for £3,200 p.a. which emits 190 g/km CO_2. C uses the car 30% for private use.

Total of hire charge	3,200
Restriction for high emissions 15%	(480)
	2,720
Restriction for private use 30%	(816)
Allowable expense	£1,904

Plant acquired by hire purchase

19. With this method of purchase the interest element is allowed as an expense of trading. With regard to the capital element, capital allowances can be claimed:

a) Before the plant is brought in to use, for any instalment due.

b) When the plant is brought in to use, for all instalments outstanding, as if the whole of the balance of capital expenditure had been paid on at that date.

c) Where an HP agreement is not eventually completed after the plant has been brought into use, then an adjustment is made which claims back part of the allowance granted.

Leased plant and machinery

20. In general a lessor of plant and machinery is entitled to the full amount of capital allowances on eligible expenditure, and the rental payments of the lessee are an allowable business expense on an accruals basis (except for some cars, as noted in section 18 above).

Separate pooling arrangements apply to assets leased outside the UK, other than ships, aircraft and containers leased in the course of a UK trade.

Balancing charges and allowances: general rules

21. A balancing charge arises when the total disposal receipts (TDR) (limited to the original cost) of any pooled or non-pooled asset is greater than the amount of pool written down value existing for offset in the period of the sale.

Disposal value is the amount of the proceeds of sale, or where the asset is lost or destroyed, any insurance or compensation moneys received. In other circumstances, e.g. if plant is given away, the market price is used.

Where plant or machinery is demolished giving rise to a disposal treatment, the net cost of demolition can be added to the amount of unallowed expenditure at the time of the demolition.

A balancing allowance arises when the amount of pool written down value is greater than the total disposal receipts (TDR), but only in the following circumstances:

a) in the terminal period when trading permanently ceases

b) when there is, or is deemed to be, a cessation of trade, see below

c) when the asset has been de-pooled by election, or by reason of private use. (However, a balancing allowance is not given on a private use asset if it is sold to a connected person for less than its tax written down value.)

d) if a car which cost over £12,000 is in a single-asset pool dating from before April 2009, under the transitional rules for cars acquired before April 2009.

No balancing allowance is given on the sale of all remaining assets in the general or special rate pool unless the trade also ceases.

Deemed cessation of trading for capital allowances

22. For capital allowance technical purposes the triggering of balancing adjustments is done by deeming the assets in 'special pools' as forming a separate notional trade to that of any actual trade undertaken, so that on a disposal the notional trade is deemed to have ceased. This applies to the following categories:

a) private use assets

b) short life assets

c) ships

d) each letting of machinery otherwise than in the course of a trade of letting

Where capital allowances are computed on the basis of a deemed trade, this is assumed to be discontinued when a disposal is brought into account in respect of a single item or the last item in a pool of assets.

Example

B, who has been trading for many years, has the following data relating to his accounting year ended 31st March 2013.

		£
a)	Additions to general plant – 31.12.12	12,000
	Proceeds of sale of plant (original cost £1,500)	2,500
	Purchase of Renault car for sales manager purchased 31.1.2013	14,000
	CO_2 emissions of Renault car 180 g/km	
	Sale of Peugeot car used by sales staff (original cost £9,000)	4,500
	CO_2 emissions of Peugeot car 140 g/km	

b)   At the 1st April 2012 the tax written down value of assets was:

	£
Plant and machinery	15,000
Citroen car for B, purchased since May 2009 (private use 30%)	7,400

CO_2 emissions of Citroen car 150 g/km

Compute the capital allowances claimable for the AP to 31st March 2013.

Solution:

	general pool £	motor car (p.u.30%) £	special rate pool £
Written down value b/f 31.3.12	15,000	7,400	
Addition not qualifying AIA (staff car)	–	–	14,000
	15,000	7,400	14,000
Proceeds of asset sales (1,500 + 4,500)	(6,000)	–	–
	9,000	7,400	14,000
Addition AIA	12,000		
AIA 100% (under £25k)	(12,000)		
	0		
	9,000		
WDA 31.3.13	(1,620)	(1,332)	(1,120)
WDV c/f 31.3.13	7,380	6,068	12,880

Notes

i) The proceeds of sale of the plant are limited to the original cost of £1,500.

ii) The total allowances available to B for 2012/13 are:

	£
Plant pool AIA 12,000 + WDA 1,620	13,620
Car with private use 30%	932
Special rate pool	1,120
	15,672

iii) Plant purchased is eligible for AIA up to £25,000 of expenditure.

iv) Notice that the car with private use forms a separate pool and the WDA is first computed at the 18% rate and deducted in full within that pool, then restricted as regards the actual allowance given. This method allows for varying proportions of private use over the life of the asset.

v) A car with CO_2 emissions of more than 160 g/km is entitled to WDA of only 8%.

vi) Private use of cars by employees is irrelevant to the capital allowances position.

Plant and machinery – short-life assets

23. Short-life assets, other than cars, may be removed from the general pool ('de-pooled') at the option of the taxpayer. As a general rule, an election to de-pool will only be advantageous if the proceeds of sale are expected to be less than the written down value at the date of future disposal, so that the de-pooled treatment will give the chance of an immediate balancing allowance in the future chargeable period. De-pooling can last for a maximum of nine accounting (or basis) periods, but sometimes for only eight, depending on how dates interact.

The provisions on short life assets are as follows.

a) The rules apply in respect of plant and machinery from the general pool, but do not apply to motor cars, ships or assets leased to non-traders, or assets already required to be pooled separately.

b) Where the taxpayer expects to dispose of an item of plant or machinery at less than its tax written down value, within eight years of the end of the period of acquisition, then they can elect to have the item extracted from the general plant pool, and a separate pool created. The plant is treated as being in use for a separate notional trade.

c) The election to de-pool a short life asset or class of assets must be made within two years of the end of the period of acquisition.

d) Any balancing adjustment arising on the disposal is calculated separately.

e) If the item of plant or machinery has not been sold or scrapped by the end of eight years from the end of the year of acquisition then its tax written down value is transferred back to the general plant pool on the day after the 8th anniversary.

Example

T, who has traded for many years, has an accounting year end of 31 March. On the 1 May 2008 he purchases equipment for £8,788, electing for de-pooling.

Show the computations in the following circumstances:

a)   The plant is sold in the year to 31 March 2013 for £2,000.

b)   The plant is sold in the year to 31 March 2013 for £5,000.

c)   The equipment is not sold by the 31 March 2013.

Solution:	Capital allowances computation	£
2008/09	Basis period to 31.3.2009: cost	8,788
	Writing down allowance 20%	(1,757)
WDV 1.4.09		7,031
2009/10	BP to 31.3.10: Writing down allowance 20%	(1,406)
WDV 1.4.10		5,625
2010/11	BP to 31.3.11: Writing down allowance 20%	(1,125)

153

WDV 1.4.11		4,500
2011/12	BP to 31.3.12: Writing down allowance 20%	(900)
WDV 1.4.12		3,600

a) 2012/13 year to 31.3.2013.

Disposal proceeds	(2,000)
Written down value b/f 1.4.12	3,600
Balancing allowance	1,600

b) 2012/13 year to 31.3.2013.

Disposal proceeds	(5,000)
Written down value b/f 1.4.12	3,600
Balancing charge	(1,400)

c) As the item of plant has not been sold by 31.3.13, WDA of (18% x 3600) = £648 applies for the year to 31.3.13. If the plant is not sold within eight years of the end of the year of acquisition, the written down value must then be transferred at the end of that period to the general plant pool.

Notes

i) Where short life assets of a similar nature are acquired in fairly large numbers e.g. small tools or returnable containers, then the cost of the assets may be aggregated and treated as one sum.

ii) Where assets used in a trade are stocked in large numbers and individual identification is possible but not readily practicable, then the computation can be based on the number of each class of asset retained. Assets falling under this heading could be calculators, amusement machines and scientific instruments.

The renewals basis

24. This is really a non-statutory method of obtaining relief on expenditure on plant and machinery, quite distinct from the capital allowance system outlined above. In fact where the renewals basis is adopted then the capital allowance system does not apply. The main points arising are:

a) The initial cost of any item of plant or machinery does not give rise to any allowances whatsoever, and no writing down allowance is available with this basis.

b) When an item is replaced then the cost of the new item, less anything received for the old one, is allowed as a deduction in computing trade profit. Any element of improvement or addition is excluded, and can only be claimed when it is replaced. Subsequent replacements are dealt with on a similar basis.

c) A change from the renewals basis to the normal capital allowance system can be made at any time, but the decision must apply to all items of plant in that class. In the year of the change, capital allowances can be claimed, irrespective of whether the expenditure is on a replacement or not.

The renewals basis effectively gives 100% relief in the year of expenditure on the replacement of an asset, but no relief at all for the first investment in an asset.

PART II – Other assets

Renovation of business premises – disadvantaged areas

25. Initial Business Premises Renovation Allowance (BPRA) is given for 100% of qualifying expenditure incurred on or after 11 April 2007 and before 11 April 2012. The scheme allows people or companies, who own or lease property that has been vacant for a year or more in one of the designated disadvantaged areas of the UK, to claim immediate, full tax relief on their capital spending on conversion or renovation of that property to bring it back into business use.

Scientific research capital allowances

26. Allowances for capital expenditure on scientific research and development related to a trade carried on by a taxpayer are given against trading profits at 100% in the year the expenditure is incurred. The rules are as follows:

a) 'Research and development' means activities that fall to be treated as research and development in accordance with normal accounting practice.

b) Expenditure on research and development includes all expenditure incurred for:

i) carrying out research and development, or

ii) providing facilities for carrying out research and development.

But it does not include expenditure incurred in the acquisition of rights in research and development, or rights arising out of research and development.

c) 'Normal accounting practice' means normal accounting practice in relation to the accounts of companies incorporated in a part of the United Kingdom.

d) Capital expenditure under this heading would include buildings and plant and machinery, but not land.

e) The amount of the allowance is 100% of capital expenditure.

Balancing adjustments can arise when assets representing research and development expenditure cease to be used for such purposes and either they are sold or destroyed.

Note Companies, but not income tax payers, can also get special allowances on research and development expenses that are revenue in character, equal to more than the total cost of that research and development expenditure. See Chapter 19.

Student self-testing questions

Note: These questions all relate to unincorporated taxpayers' capital allowances. Questions involving capital allowances for companies will be found in and after part III.

1. Ryan incurred the following expenditure on plant and machinery in the year ended 31 December 2013:

		£
6 January 2013	New plant	51,000
11 February 2013	Second hand lorry	25,000
14 February 2013	Features integral to a building	1,500
17 July 2013	Ryan's car (30% private use)	13,000
14 August 2013	Car fleet for sales team (6 cars)	60,000

CO_2 emissions of all cars were 180 g/km.

Requirement: Calculate the capital allowances available to Ryan for the year ended 31 December 2013.

Solution

Year to 31 December 2013		General Pool £	Special rate pool £	Car,30% private, 180g emissions £
Qualifying expenditure incurred (not eligible for AIA) - cars	£		60,000	13,000
Qualifying expenditure (eligible for AIA but not 100% FYA)	77,500			
Less: Annual Investment Allowance (maximum)	(25,000)			
Excess of expenditure over £25,000		52,500		
Less: Writing down allowance 18% or 8%		(9,450)	(4,800)	(1,040) 70% business
(WDV) carried forward		43,050	55,200	11,960

	£
Allowances: Annual investment allowance	25,000
Writing down allowance 18%	9,450
Writing down allowance 8%	4,800
WDA 13,000 @ 8% = 1,040 x 70% business	<u>728</u>
	<u>39,978</u>

2. Tom commenced trading on 1 July 2012 and produced his first set of accounts to the period ended 30 September 2013. He purchased the following assets during this 15 month period:

		£
10 July 2012	Plant	53,750
18 July 2012	Car (private use 25%)	16,000
20 July 2012	Van	18,000
30 July 2012	Office furniture	2,000
1 August 2013	Computer equipment	5,400

CO_2 emissions of the cars were 180 g/km.

Requirement: Calculate the capital allowances available to Tom for the period of account.

Solution

15 month period of account 1 July 2012 to 30 September 2013	£	General Pool £	Car (25% private) £
Qualifying expenditure incurred (car) (not eligible for AIA)		-	16,000
Qualifying expenditure - AIA (not eligible for 100% FYA)	79,150		
Less: Annual Investment Allowance – maximum (£25,000 x 15/12)	(31,250)		
Excess of expenditure over £100,000		47,900	
Less: Writing down allowances 15/12 x 18% or 8% [= 22.5% and 10%]		(10,777)	(1,600) 75% business
Written down value (WDV) carried forward		37,123	14,400

Allowances	Annual investment allowance	31,250
	Writing down allowance 18% x 47,900 x 15/12	10,777
	WDA 8% x 16,000 x 15/12 x 75%	<u>1,200</u>

Questions without answers

1.   Wilton starts a trade on 1 March 2013 and has the following results before capital allowances

Period of account	Profits
1/3/13 - 31/7/14	80,651
1/8/14 - 31/7/15	123,600
1/8/15 - 31/7/16	164,000

General plant is bought as follows:-

Date	Cost
1/5/13	10,000
30/6/13	14,000
1/12/13	68,732
1/10/14	87,000
1/2/15	4,000

On 1 May 2015 plant which cost £14,000 was sold for £8,000

Requirement: Calculate assessments on profits from trading for the first five tax years. Assume no changes in future years to the plant and machinery capital allowance rules applying in 2012/13.

2.   Homer started a business on 1 February 2013 and prepared accounts for the 18-month period to 31 July 2014 and then to 31 July each year. Between 1/2/13 and 31/7/15 he had the following capital expenditure and disposals.

Additions			Disposals		
1/5/13	2nd hand plant	65,497			
1/5/13	Ford car	11,000			
13/6/13	lorry	9,000			
1/10/13	photocopier	7,000			
10/11/14	Office equipment	5,000	30/11/14	Photocopier (bought 1/10/13)	9,300
15/6/15	machinery	2,000			
20/6/15	VW car	16,000			
30/6/15	new lorry	18,000	30/6/15	Lorry (bought 13/6/13)	7,500

The private use of Homer's Ford and VW cars is 40%.

CO_2 emissions of the Ford car purchased on 1/5/13 were 190 g/km.

CO_2 emissions of the VW car purchased on 20/6/15 are 150 g/km.

Requirement: Calculate the maximum capital allowances available to Homer for the periods ending 31/7/14 and 31/7/15.

Assume no future changes to plant and machinery capital allowance rules applying in 2012/13.

14 Relief for trading and capital losses

Introduction

1. This chapter is concerned with the tax reliefs available to an income tax-payer who incurs a trading loss and also certain 'capital losses' that may be claimed against income. Losses by companies are covered separately in Chapter 22.

List of loss reliefs

2.

Trading loss set against total income of the same or prior tax year.	Section 64 ITA 2007
Trading loss carried forward and set against future trading income from the same trade.	Section 83 ITA 2007
Losses incurred in each of the first four years of trading set against total income of the three preceding tax years.	Section 72 ITA 2007
Terminal loss relief for losses of the last 12 months of a trade.	Section 89 ITA 2007
Relief for trading losses where a business is transferred to a limited company.	Section 86 ITA 2007
Relief for capital losses against income .	Section 131 ITA 2007
Relief for pre-trading expenditure (not technically a loss relief, but an expense relief, since 2005) .	Section 57 ITTOIA 2005
Trading loss set against capital gains.	section 261B TCGA 1992
Property rental business losses.	Section 117 ITA 2007

Set against 'other income' Sec 64 ITA 2007

3. The following points should be noted:

i) Capital allowances are deducted in computing adjusted taxable profits.

ii) Profits and losses are calculated by reference to periods of account, except the terminal loss computation for Section 89.

iii) The basis period rules apply to allocate losses to tax years, but there can be no 'overlap' so losses are only measured once.

iv) Any loss which would otherwise count in two basis periods can only count in the earlier period.

v) Relief against total income can be claimed in the tax year of the loss or the preceding tax year.

vi) Where Section 64 total income claims are made in respect of both years the taxpayer can choose which claim should be taken in priority. Partial claims are not permitted.

vii) Any unused loss is carried forward under Section 83.

Example

A, who has been in business for many years, has an adjusted loss from trading for the year ended 31st December 2012 of £12,000. Under the basis period rules this is a trade loss of tax year 2012/13.

For tax year 2011/12, A's self-assessed taxable income, before any loss claims, was as follows:

	£
Trade profits year to 31.12.2011	10,000
Property business profit	30,000

Compute A's income tax liability for 2011/12 on the assumption that he claims relief for the trading loss of 2012/13 in the previous tax year, under s64 ITA 2007.

Solution:

Income tax computation 2011/12	**£**
Trade profits	10,000
Property income	30,000
Total income	40,000
Section 64 loss relief from 2012/13	(12,000)
Net income	28,000
Personal allowance	(8,105)
Taxable income (non-savings)	19,895
Income tax liability: 19,895 @ 20%	3,979

Notes

i) Personal allowances are claimed after relief for a loss, so that there may be wasted personal allowances if a large trade loss is carried back.

ii) The whole of the loss for 2012/13 has been used against total income of the tax year preceding the loss tax year, i.e. 2011/12.

Capital allowances

4. Capital allowances are deducted in computing trade profits, but the taxpayer does not have to claim the full allowances available in computing his or her taxable profits. Unusable losses can therefore sometimes be avoided by forgoing capital allowances in a period.

Example

T, who started in business in January 2007, has an adjusted trading profit for the 12 months to 31st December 2012 of £795, and capital allowances available of £4,000. T has property income for 2012/13 of £8,600 and no other income.

Compute T's optimal loss claim and income tax liability for 2012/13.

Solution: Income tax computation 2012/13

	£
Property income	8,600
Trading profit after capital allowances (see working)	nil
Total income	8,600
Less Section 64 relief – claimed current year (see working)	(495)
Net income	8,105
Personal allowance	(8,105)
Taxable income	NIL

Trading loss.

Claimed Section 64 (795 profit – 1,290 capital allowances) = 495

Assessable trading profit	NIL

Note

T has claimed only £1,290 of his maximum capital allowances so that he does not waste his personal allowance in 2012/13.

The balance of the capital allowance unclaimed of (£4,000 – £1,290), increases the pool WDV carried forward at 1 January 2013, on which WDA can be claimed for y/e 31 December 2013.

Tax planning considerations in making a Section 64 claim

5.   The following points should be taken into consideration in deciding whether to make a claim for loss relief against total income under Section 64 for the current or prior year, or both, and in what order.

a)   *Loss of personal allowance*: Cannot be carried forward, or back.

b)   *Transfer of married couple's allowance, spouses aged 65 at 5.4.2000:* Can all be transferred to the spouse, on a joint election, although only obtaining relief at the 10% rate.

c)   *Loss of personal pension plan relief (see Chapter 16)*: Net relevant UK earnings are after deduction of loss relief.

d)   *Saving tax at higher rates*: A claim can be made for the tax year of the loss or the preceding year, or both in either order. The top tax rate of the taxpayer in these years may not be the same.

e)   *Reduction in Class 4 NIC*: Profits for Class 4 National Insurance purposes (see Chapter 17) are after deduction of loss reliefs set against trade income (s83), but are not reduced by loss reliefs set against total income (s64).

Carried forward – Section 83 ITA 2007

6.   To the extent that a trading loss has not been relieved by claims under section 64 or 72, which take priority, it may be carried forward and set against the first available profits of the same trade.

Any loss brought forward must be set off as soon as possible against trade profits, even where this causes a loss of personal allowances.

Example

Mr R has tax adjusted profits for the year to 31st December 2012 of £26,000, and no capital allowances. Trade losses brought forward under Section 83 amount to £3,105. R started in business on 1st July 2002, and has no other income.

Compute the income tax liability for 2012/13 of Mr R.

Solution: Income tax computation 2012/13

		£	£
(basis period year to 31.12.12)			
Trade profits		26,000	
Section 83 losses b/f		(3,105)	22,895
Personal allowance			(8,105)
Taxable income			14,790
Tax Liability	n/a	@ 10%	0
	14,790	@ 20%	2,958

Relief for losses in first four years of trading – Section 72 ITA 2007

7.   The relief which is available under this section is in addition to that under Sec 64 or 83, but is only available in the first four tax years of a new trade. The relief is as follows.

a)   Trading losses incurred in the first four tax years may be carried back and set against the total income of the taxpayer, in the previous three tax years in each case.

b)   The set-off under section 72 is against income of an earlier year before a later year, i.e. on a FIFO basis.

c)   The trade loss is calculated on the normal basis period rules for losses.

d)   Each loss is set against income of the first available year in the following order: non savings income, savings income, and dividend income of the claimant.

e)   A claim must be made by the filing date for the tax year after the loss is incurred.

f) Each claim is a separate claim for a separate tax year loss. It is not necessary to make the section 72 claim for all tax years if losses are incurred in all the first four years.

g) Where a claim is made for relief under Sec 64 and under Sec 72, then the loss cannot be apportioned between them. Butt v Haxby 1983 STC 239.

Example

P left his employment on the 31st December 2009 and commenced trading on the 1st January 2010 with the following results for tax purposes:

	£ (Loss)
12 months to 31.12.2010	(3,000)
12 months to 31.12.2011	(2,000)
12 months to 31.12.2012	(5,000)

Compute the losses available for set-off under section 72 and show the tax years in which they can be utilised.

Solution

2009/10	1.1.10 – 5.4.10 3/12 × 3,000 =		(750)
2010/11	Year ended 31.12.10	(3,000)	
	Less allocated to 2009/10	750	(2,250)
2011/12	Year ended 31.12.11		(2,000)
2012/13	Year ended 31.12.12		(5,000)

Loss relief available is as follows:

	2009/10	2010/11	2011/12	2012/13
	750	2,250	2,000	5,000
Set against total income				
2006/07	750	–	—	
2007/08	–	2,250	—	
2008/09	–	–	2,000	
2009/10	–	–	–	5,000

Notes

i) If the losses cannot be fully used by a section 72 claim then the balance can be carried forward in the usual way under Section 83.

Terminal loss relief – Section 89 ITA 2007

8. Under this section relief is available where a cessation of trading takes place, and a loss arises attributable to all or part of the last 12 months of trading. The rules for computing the loss are designed to be fair to all traders, regardless of what point in the final tax year they cease trading.

A terminal loss may optionally be carried back and set against the trading profits (less capital allowances) of the three tax years prior to the tax year in which the trade ceases. The terminal loss is made up of 3 elements:

(a)   The loss from 6 April to the date of cessation in the final tax year; plus

(b)   The loss for the other part of the final twelve months of trading; plus

(c)   Overlap profits.

Where part (b) of the calculation shows a profit it is ignored in calculating the terminal loss.

Example

S has overlap profits brought forward of £1,000, and ceased trading on 30th June 2012 with the following results:

Adjusted profits	£
9 months to 30.6.12	(1,500)
12 months to 30.9.11	1,200
12 months to 30.9.10	1,600

Compute the terminal loss available for relief.

Solution: Calculation of terminal loss – 12 months to 30.6.2012

		£	£
2012/13	(6.4.2012 – 30.6.2012)		
3/9 × (1,500)		(500)	(500)
2011/12	(1.7.2011 – 5.4.2012)		
1.10.2011 – 5.4.2012 6/9 × (1,500)		(1,000)	
1.7.2011 – 1.10.2011 3/12 × 1,200		300	(700)
Overlap profits			(1,000)
Terminal loss			(2,200)

9.   Some further points on terminal losses.

a)   Capital allowances claimed are deducted before terminal loss relief is applied.

b)   Terminal loss is computed after deducting capital allowances.

Transfer of a business to a limited company – Section 86 ITA 2007

10.   If a sole trader or partnership transfers its business to a limited company, there is a cessation of trade. Accordingly, trading losses at the date of transfer are not available for set-off against any future corporation tax profits of the new company.

However, Section 86 provides some relief where the following conditions are met.

a) The consideration for the business consists wholly or mainly in allotted shares of the company. In this case 80% is often taken to satisfy 'mainly'.

b) The shares are beneficially held by the transferor throughout the period of any tax year for which a claim under Section 86 is made.

c) The company carries on the same business throughout any tax year for which a claim is made.

Relief is available in respect of trading losses from a former business which can be carried forward and they can be set against income received by the transferor from the company. The losses must be set against earned income first, e.g. directors' fees or remuneration, and then investment income, e.g. dividends.

Example

D transfers his business to a limited company on the 1st August 2012 wholly for shares.

At that date the business has trading losses of £10,000. In the year 2012/13 D receives director's remuneration of £8,000 and a net dividend of £900 from the company.

Income tax computation 2012/13

	£
Income from employment	8,000
Less Section 86 loss	8,000
Dividend income (£900 x 100/90)	1,000
Less Section 86 loss	1,000

Notes

i) With this example there would be trade losses to carry forward to 2013/2014 of £1,000 providing the conditions noted above are satisfied.

ii) In claiming the Section 86 relief for 2012/13 D has lost his personal allowances which cannot be carried forward.

Relief against total income for capital losses on unquoted trading companies – Section 131 ITA 2007

11. Under this section a loss made by an individual on the disposal of any unquoted shares can be set against his or her income for income tax purposes. The loss must arise from a number of shares originally subscribed for on the formation of the company, and not from an inheritance or subsequent acquisition.

The claim is similar to a claim under Section 64 ITA 2007, but takes precedence over relief under that section. The company must be a UK trading company at the date of the disposal. A qualifying loss can only be claimed in the following circumstances:

a) on a disposal for full market value, or

b)   on a winding up, or

c)   on a claim that the shares have become of negligible value.

The loss is deducted from the taxpayer's income in the year in which the disposal takes place or in the preceding year.

This relief is also available where the unquoted shares sold at a loss were originally acquired under the Enterprise Investment Scheme (see also Chapter 6).

Example

Z and his wife have the following data relating to 2012/13.   £

Z Income from employment	45,000
Mrs Z Income from employment	8,600
Z Building society interest (net)	8,000
Z allowable loss under Sec 131 ITA 2007 arising from shares in A Ltd	3,000

Compute the income tax liability for 2012/13 of Z and his wife.

Solution: Income tax computation 2012/13

	Z £	Mrs Z £
Non savings income		
Income from employment Z	45,000	–
Income from employment Mrs Z	–	8,600
	45,000	8,600
Savings income		
Building society interest (gross)	10,000	–
	55,000	8,600
Less capital loss relief Sec 131	3,000	–
	52,000	8,600
Personal allowance	8,105	8,105
Taxable income	43,895	495

Tax liability

		Z	Mrs Z
n/a / n/a	@ 10 %	0	0
34,370 / 495	@ 20%	6,874	99
9,525 / –	@ 40%	3,810	–
43, 895 495		10,684	99

Notes

i) The relief for the capital loss is deducted from the earned income of Z in the computation. If this is insufficient it is set against his unearned income.

ii) As Z is paying tax at the 40% rate it would be tax efficient to transfer some of his investments to Mrs Z, to generate additional income in her own right.

Pre-trading expenditure

12. Relief is available for expenditure incurred by a person in the seven years before he or she commences to carry on a trade.

a) The expenditure must be allowable trading expenditure which would have been deducted in computing trading profits if incurred after the commencement of trading.

b) Pre-trading expenditure is treated as an expense of the trade.

c) The relief does not apply to pre-trading purchases of stock.

d) A trading loss in the first tax year caused by pre-trading expenditure relief may be relieved under Section 64, 83 and 72 ITA 2007 in the normal way.

Restrictions on claiming loss reliefs

13. a) A claim under Section 64 is only available to trades which were carried on with a view to profit, and on a commercial basis, in the tax year of the loss.

b) Farmers and market gardeners cannot obtain relief under Section 64 if in the previous five years their business has incurred successive trade losses, unless it can be shown that the trade is being carried on with a view to profit, and there is a reasonable expectation of profits in the future.

c) Loss relief under Section 83 is available in the earliest possible years only against the profits from the same trade, and not against total income or profits from any other trade.

d) From 2008/09 Income Tax loss relief against total income under section 64 is restricted to a maximum of £25,000 offset in a tax year, if an individual does not spend more than 10 hours per week on average working in the trade which incurred the loss. (This change was made to prevent 'hobby' traders getting unlimited reliefs for trading losses against other taxable income.)

Trading losses set against capital gains

14. Where a trading loss is incurred in a tax year, then to the extent that it has not been fully relieved by a total income claim under Section 64 ITA 2007, a claim for relief against net chargeable gains of the same year can be made. The amount set against capital gains cannot exceed the chargeable gains for the year, before deducting the CGT exemption amount of £10,600, for 2012/13.

Example

N has the following data relating to the year 2012/13:

	£
Trade loss for year to 31.3.13	(17,000)
Chargeable gains before exemption.	12,000

In the year to 5th April 2013 N has other taxable income totalling £16,000.

Compute the income tax liability for 2012/13, assuming N makes all possible current year loss claims.

Solution: Income tax computation 2012/13

	£
Total income	16,000
Less Section 64 claim	(16,000)
	— =

CGT computation 2012/13

	£
Chargeable gains	12,000
Less trading losses extended to gains (s280)	(1,000)
	11,000
Less annual exemption	(10,600)
Taxable chargeable gains	400

Notes

i) N's personal allowance of £8,105 for 2012/13 would be wasted.

ii) The trading loss of £17,000 has been dealt with as follows:

	£
Section 64 2012/13	16,000
Capital gains 2012/13	1,000

iii) The CGT on the remaining £400 is taxable at the 18% rate.

For details of CGT see Chapter 30.

Property business losses

15. 1) Any rental business loss of an individual is automatically carried forward and set against rental business profits of the next year. It cannot be carried back, or set against other income of the year.

2) Property business losses can only be set off against profits from property business (apart from (4) below).

3) From April 2011 furnished holiday lettings losses may only be set against income from the same furnished holiday letting business. Previously they could be treated as trade losses and added to a s64 claim.

4) Where a rental business loss is attributable to capital allowances then all or part of that attributable loss can be set against total income as relief for non-trade capital allowances against total income.

Example

K has a property business loss of £3,500 for the year 2012/13 after claiming landlord's capital allowances of £1,500.

	£
Loss relief available against total income	1,500

Notes

i) The £1,500 loss can be set against total income of 2012/13. The balance of £2,000 must be carried forward against future property business profits.

ii) Loss relief is limited to the smaller of the total property business loss and the capital allowances included in computing it.

Student self-testing questions

1. James receives £3,000 per year income from property. He makes up business accounts for trading annually to 31 December. His recent tax adjusted results from trading have been:

Year to 31 December 2010	Profit	£42,000
Year to 31 December 2011	Profit	£48,000
Year to 31 December 2012	Loss	(£100,000)
Year to 31 December 2013	Profit	£5,000

Requirement: Show the net income before personal allowances in each of the years after making a tax effective claim for loss relief.

Solution

Tax year	2010/11	2011/12	2012/13	2013/14
Period of a/c	31.12.2010	31.12.2011	31.12.2012	31.12.2013
Income from trading	42,000	48,000	Loss	5,000
S83				(5,000)
				0
Income from property	3,000	3,000	3,000	3,000
	45,000	51,000	3,000	3,000
S64		(51,000)		
Net income	45,000	0	3,000	3,000

Loss Memorandum:-

		£
2012	Loss arising	100,000
2011	S64 carry back against total income	(51,000)
2013	S83 carry forward against trade profit	(5,000)
c/fwd		44,000

Note: A s64 claim against total income of the current year would not be tax effective, as the total income of 2012/13 is covered by the personal allowance.

2. Nathaniel started trading on 1 October 2010 and prepared accounts to 31 December of each year from 2011.

His results for the first two accounting periods were: -

15 months to 31 December 2011	Loss 23,700
Year to 31 December 2012	Loss 19,320

Prior to becoming self -employed he had the following other income:-

2007/2008	12,200
2008/2009	12,500
2009/2010	12,800
6/4/2010 to 30/9/2010	6,900

Requirement: Calculate Nathaniel's net income for 2007/2008 to 2010/2011 using all available s72 claims.

Solution

Losses eligible for s72 Relief

Year	Basis period	Workings	Loss	Years for s72 claim
2010/11	1.10.10-5.4.11	23,700 x 6/15	9,480	07/08 – 09/10
2011/12	1.1.11-31.12.11	23,700 x 12/15 - 23700 x 3/15	14,220	08/09 – 10/11
2012/13	y/e 31.12.12		19,320	09/10 - 11/12

Using all possible s72 claims, total income is:

		2007/08	2008/09	200/10	2010/11
Income from trade					0
Other income		12,200	12,500	12,800	6,900
s 72 relief	2010/11 loss	(9,480)			
	2011/12 loss		(12,500)	(1,720)	
	2012/13 loss			(11,080)	(6,900)
Total income		2,720	0	0	0

c/fwd loss of 1,340 for year 2012/13

Questions without answers

1. Jensen started to trade on 6/4/2011. Projected results are:

    Year to 5 April

2012	Profit	24,000
2013 (projected)	Profit	32,000
2014 (projected)	Profit	36,000
2015 (projected)	Profit	30,000
2016 (projected)	Loss	(56,000)

    Business is expected to be profitable thereafter

    Jensen also has rental income of £12,000 per annum. Using the 2012/13 loss relief rules:

    a) **Outline how Jensen could get relief for the loss in 2015/16;**

    b) **Calculate the quickest way of relieving the loss.**

    c) **How would the situation change if Jensen ceased trading on 5/4/2016?**

2. Mister Y was employed as an auditor until 1/1/2012 and on that date started in business as a commodity dealer making up accounts to 30 June each year:

Income as auditor		Results as dealer (loss)	
2008/2009	20,000	1/1/12 to 30/6/12	(6,000)
2009/2010	22,000	Year to 30/6/13	(3,000)
2010/2011	24,000	Year to 30/6/14	(2,400)
2011/2012	22,000	Year to 30/6/15	nil

Requirement: Show the revised net income for all tax years if Mr Y claims loss relief as soon as possible.

3. A business ceased on 30 September 2013. Results were

Year to 31/12/2010	4,000
Year to 31/12/2011	800
Year to 31/12/2012	600
9 months to 30/9/2013	(3,900)
Overlap profits on commencement (unrelieved)	900

Requirement: Calculate the terminal loss and show how it is relieved against earlier profits.

15 Partnership taxation

Introduction

1. A partnership exists where two or more persons join together for business purposes forming an association which is not a separate legal entity for taxation purposes.

A trading or professional partnership is taxed as a collection of sole traders.

The main special features of partnership taxation relate to:

   a)   the allocation of profits for tax purposes,
   b)   the effect of changes in partnerships' members or profit-sharing arrangements, and
   c)   some loss restrictions for limited liability partnerships.

General provisions

2. The following provisions apply to any new partnership that has a trade or profession.

(The partnership tax rules in this chapter do not apply to partners in investment activities, including letting of property. These are simply treated as joint owners of an investment asset, and taxed on their respective shares of the income, net of allowable expenses, for each tax year.)

   a)   For income tax purposes a partnership of two or more individuals is not treated as a separate legal entity distinct from the partners. The effect of this is that each partner is assessed for income tax individually like a sole trader.

   b)   A 'partnership tax return' must also be completed for HMRC by the representative partner. This return is completed for a partnership period of account, not a tax year. It shows the adjustment of the firm's accounting profits for tax purposes, and the allocation of the adjusted profits to each partner, including capital allowances. The profits and capital allowances figures shown on the partnership return are then repeated as basis period data on the individual partners' self-assessment tax returns for a tax year.

   c)   Taxable profits of the partnership are calculated in the same way as for a sole trader, so that all partnership expenses and capital allowances are deducted from the profits before the allocation of net profits to the partners. Therefore partners cannot individually decide whether to claim full or reduced capital allowances, or to de-pool a short life asset; such decisions must be the same for all partners, and notified on the partnership tax return.

   d)   Profits are assessed on a current year basis, with the normal basis period being the period of account for the twelve months ending in the tax year. The rules for determination of the assessable trade profits of each partner in the first two or three tax years, and last tax year, in which he or she is a member of the partnership are exactly the same as the opening and closing tax years' basis period rules for a sole trader (see Chapter 11).

e) Partnership profits are allocated by reference to the partnership profit-sharing agreement applicable for the period of account, not the related tax year.

f) Where there is a change in the members of a partnership, so long as there is at least one partner carrying on the business both before and after the change, the change does not constitute a cessation of the partnership's trade for tax purposes (except for any partner who has left the partnership).

Adjustment and allocation of profits

3. As already noted, partnership accounting profits are adjusted for income tax purposes using the same principles as for a sole trader - see Chapter 10. Partners' 'salaries' and 'interest' earned on capital are taxed as trade income, affecting final shares of trade profits. So partners' salaries (if any) and interest (if any) are allocated first, and the balance of tax-adjusted net profit is then divided between partners in the agreed profit-sharing ratio.

Example

A and B formed a partnership in June 2007, sharing profits equally, after interest of 5% p.a. on their fixed capital accounts of £160,000 and £100,000 respectively, and a salary for A of £50,000. Tax-adjusted profits shown on the partnership return for the year ended 31st December 2011 were £150,000.

Show the allocation of profits for 2012/13.

Solution: Partnership computation 2012/13

Adjusted profits after capital allowances year to 31st December 2012 – £150,000

Allocation of profit 2012/13

	Total £	A £	B £
Interest on capital: 10%	13,000	8,000	5,000
Salary – A	50,000	50,000	–
	63,000	58,000	5,000
Balance shared equally	87,000	43,500	43,500
Share of trade profits	150,000	101,500	48,500

Notes

i) Each partner includes his share of profit, i.e. A. £101,500, B. £48,500, in his personal self-assessment tax return, being trading profits measured for 2012/13 based on the year to 31.12.12.

ii) All amounts shown in the partnership accounts for the year to 31st December 2012, for partners' salaries, share of profits already drawn, or interest on capital, will have been added back as proprietors' drawings in arriving at the taxable profit of £150,000 in the partnership tax return.

Example of opening year rules

C and D entered into partnership on the 1st June 2008 with the following results:

	£	£
	Adjusted profits	Capital allowances
1.6.2008 – 31.5.2009	20,000	2,000
1.6.2009 – 31.5.2010	30,000	5,000
1.6.2010 – 31.5.2011	40,000	15,000
1.6.2011 – 31.5.2012	50,000	10,000

The partners have agreed to share profits equally.

Show the individual partners' assessable trading profits for the relevant tax years.

Solution

	Partnership C and D	Assessments	A	B
2008/09	Period of account 1.6.08 – 5.4.09 10/12 × (20,000 – 2,000)	15,000	7,500	7,500
2009/10	Period of account 1.6.08 - 31.5.09 (20,000 – 2,000)	18,000	9,000	9,000
2010/11	Period of account 1.6.09 - 31.5.10 (30,000 – 5,000)	25,000	12,500	12,500
2011/12	Period of account 1.6.10 - 31.5.11 (40,000 – 15,000)	25,000	12,500	12,500
2012/13	Period of account 1.6.11– 31.5.12 (50,000 – 10,000)	40,000	20,000	20,000

Notes

i) The overlap period is 1.6.08 to 5.4.09, with overlap profits of £7,500 being carried forward by each partner (this is counting in whole months, which is acceptable for accounting exams; the overlap figure is £7,595 each if one counts the exact days, which is the correct position in tax law). When the partnership ceases, or a partner leaves and is replaced by another, then the leaving partner's final profits assessment from the partnership will be reduced by his overlap relief.

ii) Paying income tax and class 4 NI liability is the responsibility of the individuals in the partnership and not the partnership itself. However, many partnerships do account for and pay all income tax and class 4 NI for the partners, treating them as drawings from current account.

iii) We can check the overlap against total profits assessed for each partner :

Total profits assessed for 5 tax years (58 months of trading) = £61,500

based on £54,000 net assessable profits for 4 x 12 months to 31 May 2012

Profits counted twice = first 10 months = £7,500

£7,500 = overlap carried forward by each partner (54,000 + 7,500 = 61,500)

Changes in a partnership

4. The basis period rules apply separately for each new partner who joins, and for each retiring (ceasing) partner. The trade is a source of income which is starting or ceasing for the individual, but the other partners are unaffected by a partner joining or leaving the partnership, so long as they themselves continue trading.

If there is a change in profit-sharing ratio during a period of account, for exam purposes it may be assumed that all income and expenses in that period of account accrued evenly. In practice, the final information about the allocated profit shares of partners, for a period of account when there is a change in either the partners or their profit shares, or both, will be effective as reported to HMRC on the partnership tax return.

Example

X and Y started in partnership on 1st July 2005, sharing profits equally. Their accounts are made up to 31st December each year. On 1st January 2008, Z was admitted as an equal partner, the profit ratio then becoming one-third each.

Tax-adjusted profits for the years to 31st December 2008 were as follows:

	£
1.7.2005 – 31.12.2005	20,000
12 months to 31.12.06	40,000
12 months to 31.12.07	50,000
12 months to 31.12.08	60,000

Show the assessable trading profit of each partner for tax years 2005/06 to 2008/09. Calculations may be made to the nearest month.

Solution

Tax Year	Basis period	£	Total £	X £	Y £	Z £
2005/06	(1.7.05 – 31.12.05)	20,000				
	1.1.06 – 5.4.06 (3/12 × 40,000)	10,000	30,000	15,000	15,000	–
2006/07	12 months to 31.12.06		40,000	20,000	20,000	–
2007/08	X: 12 months to 31.12.07		50,000	25,000		–
	Y: ditto				25,000	

Z: opening year rules:

1.1.08 – 5.4.08	$3/12 \times 60,000 \times \frac{1}{3}$	5,000	– –	5,000

	Total for 2007/08	55,000	25,000	25,000	5,000
2008/09 12 months to 31.12.08		60,000	20,000	20,000	20,000

Notes

i)   When Z is admitted on 1st January 2008, there is continuation of the trade for the others.

ii)   The partners are assessed individually on their shares of the profits.

iii) Z is treated as starting in self-employment on 1st January 2008 and his individual overlap profit must be computed based on that start date. His overlap will be the profits counted in both 2007/08 and 2008/09. This is as follows:

1.1.08 – 5.4.08 = 95 days (say 3 months)

$3/12 \times 60,000$ (i.e. profits to 31.12.2008) $\times \frac{1}{3}$ (Z's share)   = 5,000

iv)   When a partner leaves, his or her overlap profits are adjusted in his or her final assessment.

v)   Overlap carried forward by X and Y = £10,000 each : by Z = £5,000

Basis periods

	X + Y	Z
2005/06	1.7.05 – 5.4.06	–
2006/07	1.1.06 – 31.12.06	–
2007/08	1.1.07 – 31.12.07	1.1.08 – 5.4.08
2008/09	1.1.08– 31.12.08	1.1.08 – 31.12.08

Example

Using the data for X, Y and Z in the above example, and the following further tax-adjusted results:

	£
12 months to 31.12.09	80,000
12 months to 31.12.10	90,000
12 months to 31.12.11	100,000
12 months to 31.12.12	140,000

Z leaves the partnership on the 30th September 2011.

Show the assessable trade profits of the partners for all tax years.

Solution

	Total	X	Y	Z
2009/10 to 31.12.09	80,000	26,667	26,667	26,666
2010/11 to 31.12.10	90,000	30,000	30,000	30,000
2011/12: ratio changes when Z leaves				

1.1.10 – 30.9.11:

9/12 × 100,000 1:1:1	75,000	25,000	25,000	25,000
Less overlap relief Z				(5,000)
(note (i))				20,000
1.10.11 – 31.12.11(only 2 partners)				
3/12 × 100,000 1:1	25,000	12,500	12,500	–
X and Y's assessable profit		37,500	37,500	
	100,000			
2012/13 1.1 to 31.12.12 (2 partners)	140,000	70,000	70,000	–

Notes

i) Z's assessment for the year 2011/12 comprises: £

9 months profit share from 1st Jan 2010 – 30th Sept 2011 =   25,000

Less overlap relief (see previous example)   (5,000)

20,000

ii) X and Y do not cease trading on the retirement of Z.

iii) **Basis periods**

	X + Y + Z	X + Y	Z
2009/10	1.1.09 – 31.12.09		
2010/11	1.1.10 – 31.12.10		
2011/12		1.1.11 – 31.12.11	1.1.11 – 30.09.11
2012/13		1.1.12 – 31.12.12	

Partnership taxed and untaxed income – notional business

5. a) Any other taxed or untaxed income of the partnership, after duly being allocated to individual partners, is treated as coming from a 'second notional business'. This second notional business commences when an individual becomes a partner and is treated as permanently discontinued only when the individual ceases to be a partner. It is taxed by applying the same basis period rules – including the possibility of 'overlap' profits – as apply to the principal partnership trade profits.

b) Where a partnership receives rents from subletting business accommodation, these rents can be treated as income of the primary trade (instead of forming income of a second deemed trade) in the following circumstances:

i) the accommodation must be temporarily surplus to current business requirements;

ii) the premises must be used partly for the business and partly let, in other words, rents from a separate property which is wholly surplus must be dealt with as property income;

iii)   the rental income must be comparatively small;

iv)   the rents must be in respect of the letting of surplus business accommodation only and not of land.

Partnership losses

6.   a) Partnership losses as computed for tax purposes are apportioned between the partners in the same proportion as they share profits.

b)   Where the business as a whole makes a profit as computed for tax purposes, but after allocation of prior shares (e.g. salaries) an individual partner makes a loss then this cannot be used for normal loss claim relief.

c)   If the partnership as a whole has a profit, but an initial allocation using the commercial profit sharing arrangement for all the partners produces a mixture of profits and losses for different partners, the actual total partnership profit (or loss) must be re-allocated so that only the net profit-making partners get any profit and no partners get a loss. The loss re-allocation is made in proportion to the notional profit (or loss) initially allocated to the profit making partners.

d)   If the partnership as a a whole has a trading loss this may be shared between partners according to the profit- (loss-) sharing agreement. The trade loss of each partner may then be dealt with as for a sole trader, i.e.:

i)   Set off against total income. Section 64.

ii)   Carried forward against share of future partnership profits. Section 83.

iii)   Used in a terminal loss claim. Section 89.

iv)   Used in an opening years Section 72 claim by that partner

v)   Used in connection with the transfer of the partnership trade to a limited company. Section 86.

Example

X, Y and Z have been in partnership for many years with a regular accounting period to 31st December.

Profits are shared equally, after the provision of salaries to X and Y of £50,000.

Adjusted profits for the year ended 31st December 2012, before salaries, amounted to £70,000.

Show the allocation of profits for 2012/13.

Solution: X,Y,Z partnership profit allocation 2012/13

Stage 1:	Total	X	Y	Z
Salaries	100,000	50,000	50,000	–
Balance of profit (loss)				
(70,000 – 100,000)	(30,000)	(10,000)	(10,000)	(10,000)
Net allocation	70,000	40,000	40,000	(10,000)

As this gives Z a notional loss but the partnership as a whole did not make a loss, for tax purposes the loss is reallocated to the profit-making partners.

i.e. X and Y take 40,000 / 80,000 or $\times \dfrac{1}{2}$ of the loss each.

In effect, Z's notional loss is allocated to X and Y proportionately, i.e. £5,000 each

	Total	X	Y	Z
Original allocation as above	70,000	40,000	40,000	(10,000)
Re-allocation to remove Z loss	–	(5,000)	(5,000)	10,000
Net allocation for tax returns	70,000	35,000	35,000	–

A practical point for partnership accounting arises from this example, If the partnership accounts treat Z's partnership current account on the basis that he has taken a a loss share of £10,000 for the year and X and Y have taken a profit allocation of £40,000 each, then Z may ask the other partners to make him a cash payment each. This payment would reflect the fact that they have each saved tax and NI at their marginal rates on £5,000 of actual partnership income, due to the loss reallocation rules. In effect, X and Y have had relief for Z's loss for tax purposes. If X and Y agreed to make such a payment (eg calculated at their marginal tax and NI rates), then that is a personal post-tax payment and not shown in any of the partners' tax returns or income tax computations.

Student self-testing question

Mars and Venus commenced in partnership on 1 July 2010 and decided to produce their accounts to 30 June annually. On 1 January 2012, Pluto joined the partnership.

The partnership's accounts show the following adjusted profits:

	£
Year ended 30 June 2011	100,000
Year ended 30 June 2012	135,000
Year ended 30 June 2013	180,000

Requirement: Show the trading income assessable on the individual partners for all the tax years affected by the above information, assuming that profits are shared equally. **(11 marks)**

Solution

		Mars	Venus	Pluto	TOTAL
		£	£	£	£
A/c to 30 June 2011		50,000	50,000	-	100,000
A/c to 30 June 2012	6/12	33,750	33,750	-	67,500
	6/12	22,500	22,500	22,500	67,500
		56,250	56,250	22,500	135,000
A/c to 30 June 2013		60,000	60,000	60,000	180,000

Mars and Venus will both be assessed as follows:

2010/11	£50,000 x 9/12	£37,500
2011/12	A/c to 30 June 2011	£50,000
2012/13	A/c to 30 June 2012	£56,250
2013/14	A/c to 30 June 2013	£60,000

Overlap profits carried forward are £37,500 for each of Mars and Venus.

Pluto will be assessed as follows:

2011/12	£22,500 x 3/6		£11,250
2012/13		£22,500	
	£60,000 x 6/12	£30,000	£52,500
2013/14	A/c to 30 June 2013		£60,000
Overlap relief on:	£11,250		
	£30,000		
	£41,250		

Question without answer

Vera and Jack commenced in business on 1 October 2008 as hotel proprietors, sharing profits equally. On 1 October 2010 their son Terry joined the partnership and from that date each of the partners was entitled to one-third of the profits. The profits of the partnership adjusted for income tax, are:

Period ended	30 June 2009	£30,000
Year ended	30 June 2010	£45,000
Year ended	30 June 2011	£50,000
Year ended	30 June 2012	£60,000

Requirement

Calculate the assessable profits for each of the partners for all relevant tax years from 2008/2009 to 2012/13 (7 marks)

Calculate the overlap profits for each of the partners. (4 marks)

16 Personal investment – pensions

Introduction

1.   This chapter is concerned with the income tax aspects of a UK individual's saving towards a retirement pension.   Contributions to pension saving are encouraged by the tax system so tax relief is given on contributions up to generous limits.   Approved schemes where an underlying fund exists (see below) also have the tax advantage that no income tax or capital gains tax is paid on investments while held in the pension fund.

It is important to understand the difference in treatment of contributions to:
* occupational pension schemes, for individuals in certain employments; and
* personal (or 'stakeholder') pension schemes, for those in employment, self-employment or no employment.

To qualify for tax relief, a pension scheme must meet conditions which are considered socially desirable, for example with regard to the maximum pension it offers and the way in which entitlements accrue. With exceptions for ill-health retirement and for certain specialised professions, a pension scheme will not be approved if its rules allow any value to be received by an individual member below the age of at least 55.

This chapter is not concerned with the taxation of pensions already in payment to pensioners. Income received by members from their pension schemes is generally treated as employment income (see Chapters 7 and 8) and subject to PAYE.

Background - UK tax-approved pension schemes from 1 April 2004

2.   The tax system for pension savings in the UK was simplified in 2004. Apart from arrangements that are still running from before 2004 (not covered further here), there are now two basic kinds of approved pension scheme to which taxpayers can contribute pension savings and get income tax relief on what they put in. These two types are:

a)   **Registered occupational schemes** These are linked to particular employers or groups of employers, and only open to qualifying employees. Contributions to them are paid gross by employers and employees. The employer deducts the employee's contributions before the employee receives the relevant pay.

If only the employer pays into the scheme, it is called 'non-contributory' (because the employee does not have to contribute). The new 'annual allowance charge' may impose a tax on the employee for employer's contributions if the total value of accumulated pension rights to date exceeds certain limits. Other than that, there is no need to include any pension contributions made by the employer in an employee's total income computation.

The employee's contributions to an occupational scheme are deductible from employment income as an expense of employment (see Chapter 7).

In funded occupational schemes (where there is an underlying fund of investments held to pay future pensions), investments are normally pooled for the benefit of all members. Therefore no specific funds belong to a member until his or her pension rights vest (i.e. the pension becomes payable). In unfunded occupational schemes (eg some civil service and teachers' pension schemes) there is no underlying pool of investments. The pension payable from an unfunded public scheme is a promise by the Government, to be funded from future taxation.

Income tax relief is still given on an employee's contributions to unfunded public sector occupational schemes, such as schoolteachers' or police pensions. This relief is given even though such 'pension contributions', which earn future entitlement to a public sector pension, are not being invested at all.

b) **Registered stakeholder schemes or 'Personal Pension Plans'**.   In these schemes, a specific fund is kept invested for each contributing member. They are available to anyone and not attached to a particular employer, though an employer may contribute to a PPP on behalf of an employee. All PPP contributions are treated as paid to the scheme's trustees net of basic rate tax. The value ultimately received by the scheme then includes an additional sum of 20/80 of the contribution, reclaimed by the PPP manager from the Government, and representing the basic rate income tax relief due on all contributions.

Up to £2,880 a year (net) - £3,600 a year (gross) is the maximum gross amount which may be saved in a personal (stakeholder) pension scheme by someone who has no 'relevant earnings'. The member does not even need to be a taxpayer to benefit from the £720 'tax relief top-up' that is added by the Government to a net contribution of £2,880 that is made to a stakeholder or personal pension scheme.

It is possible to set up group personal pension plans (GPPPs) for groups of members sharing the same employer or a group of employers. This saves on administration costs. UK Employers are increasingly closing their occupational pension schemes and offering their staff GPPPs instead. In this case, the employer can deduct an employee's GPPP contributions from pay, but the amount passed over to the GPPP is treated as paid net of basic rate tax. It does not qualify for relief as a specific expense of employment, because that only applies for contributions to occupational (salary-related) schemes.

An employee can also make further net-of-tax payments into a GPPP directly (not by deduction from payroll), so long as the total contributed does not exceed the annual or lifetime limits.

A Self Invested Personal Pension (SIPP) is a normal personal pension plan (so the member's contributions are again paid in net of basic rate tax) but with a SIPP, the member can direct the fund manager where exactly to invest his or her fund (subject to rules about suitable investments for approved pension funds).

Contribution rules

3.   The maximum allowable contribution payable by an individual contributing member of a pension scheme of any kind for each tax year is the greater of:

    £3,600 gross; or

100 per cent of 'relevant UK earnings', but subject to the annual allowance maximum (see section 4).

'Relevant UK earnings' are defined as:

income from employment;

chargeable income derived from the carrying on or exercise of a trade, profession or vocation (whether individually or as a partner acting personally in a partnership);

earnings of overseas Crown employees that are subject to UK tax;

income from furnished holiday lettings;

patent or copyright income of the original artist, author or inventor.

There is no limit to the contributions that can be paid by an employer on behalf of a scheme member who is an employee, provided these meet the maximum annual allowance provisions (below). Employer contributions obtain tax relief for the employer as trade expenses only in the employer's accounting period in which they are actually paid.

Annual allowance – all individuals 2012/13

4. The maximum amount of pension contributions relievable for tax purposes in the tax year 2012/13 is fixed at £50,000 (even if the relevant UK earnings are higher than this). The annual allowance includes both employee and employer contributions. It was the same amount in 2011/12.

Unused annual allowance can be carried forward for up to 3 tax years.

Contributions in excess of the annual allowance can still enter a pension scheme – (assuming the provider will accept them –as a policy some schemes refuse them). All such excess annual contributions, if made and accepted, are taxed on the employee as income enjoyed, at the 40% rate.

Lifetime allowance – all individuals 2012/13

5. The lifetime allowance during the year 2012/13 is £1.5m, reduced from £1.8m in 2011/12.

This is the amount against which the value of an individual's prospective pension benefits is tested each year, until pension payments begin.

Consequences of a taxpayer exceeding the annual or lifetime allowance

6. An employer's, an employee's, or a self-employed person's contributions to a defined contribution (money purchase) scheme, which are in excess of the annual allowance, are taxed as income of the employee at 40%. All PPPs are money purchase schemes and so are some occupational schemes.

Employer's or employee's contributions to a defined benefit occupational scheme which increase the actuarial value of current benefits in a year to more than the lifetime allowance of £1.5 million are taxed as income of the employee at 40%, in the year of the contribution being made.

Unapproved pension schemes

7.   Unapproved invested pension schemes also exist. One kind is simply a pay-as-you-go arrangement, where the employer pays a pension out of current profits to former employees. In this case the employer gets tax relief when the pension is paid and then the employee is taxed on the payment as pension income paid directly by the employer. The other kind is a funded arrangement known as an Employer-Financed Retirement Benefit Scheme (EFRBS for short). They have very different tax treatment from approved schemes.

i)   An employer's contributions to an EFRBS receive no tax relief when made and there is no tax relief on the funds invested.

ii)   Investment income and capital gains of an EFRBS are all taxable at the rate applicable to trusts. Trusts taxation is not covered in detail in this book. The income tax rate applying to an EFRBS is 50% (on dividends it is 42.5% less the 10% tax credit). The tax on capital gains of an EFRBS is 28%.

iii)   When pension payments are made from an EFRBS, a tax credit for the 50% income tax paid by the trust can be claimed by the pension beneficiary, so long as the pension clearly comes from UK taxed income of the trust.

However, contributions to unapproved schemes do not count towards the annual allowance, nor will the fund's accrued value count towards the lifetime allowance. This exclusion may make an EFRBS attractive for very highly-paid employees who have already reached the lifetime limit for approved pension savings.

Stakeholder pensions

8.   These schemes were originally announced in 2000 as intended for 'workers on modest incomes' who did not have access to an occupational or private pension scheme. However, since the 2004 simplification, the term 'stakeholder pensions' (whether or not used in practice) effectively describes almost all money-purchase personal pension plans, except SIPPS (see above).

All but the smallest employers must offer staff access to a stakeholder pension from October 2001, unless they offer an occupational scheme. Unlike occupational pension schemes, the employer has no choice about whether to provide a minimum stakeholder scheme.

Stakeholder pension contributions attract a similar tax relief to occupational pension scheme contributions, though the administration is different. All contributions are paid in net of basic rate tax, which the scheme recovers directly from HMRC. This means that contributions are deducted from net pay rather than gross pay, as is the case for occupational pension scheme contributions.

An employer of at least five employees must offer a stakeholder pension scheme to employees. However, an employer does not have to offer the scheme to an employee who:

is under 18 years old

is within five years of retirement age

is not resident in the UK

earns less than the lower earnings limit for National Insurance (NI) purposes

has less than three months' service.

Employees must be offered the chance to join a stakeholder pension scheme within three months of starting work. They cannot be compelled to join nor can they be a member of a salary-related occupational pension scheme and a stakeholder pension scheme at the same time. However, an employee may be a member of a stakeholder pension scheme at the same time as having a personal pension or being a member of a money purchase occupational pension scheme.

An employee in a stakeholder scheme must be allowed to:

choose his or her own level of contributions

vary those contributions at will

make one-off payments of £10 or more

stop and start making contributions at will, without penalty.

The contribution must always be at least £10.

A stakeholder pension scheme member may contribute up to £3,600 gross into a scheme, regardless of his or her earnings. This allows those with low incomes or high unearned income to benefit from some element of pensions tax relief.

(It also allows family members, if they wish, to pay into a personal/stakeholder pension for a child and get a 20% subsidy from the state via the tax repayment. However, it should be borne in mind that approval rules about minimum retirement ages for members of stakeholder schemes mean that it is likely that a fund started for a child will not become accessible for a very long time after the first contributions are made.)

Unlike with Gift Aid, there is no requirement that a person who has contributed to a stakeholder pension plan 'net of basic rate tax' actually hands that tax over to the tax authorities. The fund provider can still claim back the basic rate tax notionally deducted, even if the contributing member paid no income tax or CGT for the year when the net contribution up to £2,880 was paid to the fund.

Personal Pension Plans

9. Since 2006, any other PPP effectively works the same way as specifically labelled 'stakeholder' pension plans.

As with stakeholder pensions (in fact all personal pension plans from 1 April 2004), the administrator of an HMRC-approved personal pension plan can **only** accept pension contributions **net** of basic rate tax relief. The contributing member therefore receives the basic rate tax relief at source.

Where higher or additional rate relief is due, the basic rate band is extended in a similar way as to give higher rates of relief on Gift Aid donations (see Chapter 5).

Contributions to Occupational Pension Schemes

10. Contributions to occupational schemes are deducted gross from pay.

On the personal tax computation they should be shown as a specific deduction against earnings of the employment. This effectively gives income tax relief at the highest marginal rate, as the contributions expense is deducted in computing total income.

Pension contributions (whether occupational or PPPs) are not a deductible expense from gross pay/ profits for the purposes of National Insurance.

Student self-testing questions

1. Christa is sole proprietor of a beauty salon. Her tax adjusted trading profits for the year to 5 April 2013 are £180,000, and she has no other income. Christa makes net contributions of £14,400 to a personal pension during the year.

Required: Calculate Christa's income tax liability for 2012/13.

Solution: Christa, Income tax computation 2012/13

	£
Income from trading (= total income/ net income)	180,000
Personal allowance (ANI > £117k, so reduced to nil)	0
Taxable income (all non-savings)	180,000

Income Tax:	£	£		
Basic rate on non-savings		34,370	@ 20%	6,874
Extend basic rate band				
for gross PPPs: £14,400				
x 100/80		18,000	@ 20%	3,600
Basic rate band limit		52,370		
Higher rate on non-savings		115,630	@ 40%	46,252
Extend higher rate band for	150,000			
PPPs as before : £14,400 x 100/80	18,000			
Higher rate band limit		168,000		
Additional rate on non-savings		12,000	@ 50%	6,000
		180,000		
Total income tax liability				£62,726

2. Olivia is an employee whose only income during 2012/13 is a salary of £180,000. She contributes 10% of her gross salary to an approved occupational pension scheme.

Required: Calculate Olivia's income tax liability for 2012/13.

Solution

	£	£
Salary	180,000	
Less: pension contributions	18,000	
Income from employment		162,000
Personal allowance (fully abated)		0
Taxable income		162,000

Income Tax	£		£
Basic rate	34,370	@ 20%	6,874
Higher rate	115,630	@ 40%	46,252
	150,000		
Additional rate	12,000	@ 50%	6,000
	162,000		
Income tax liability			£59,126

17 National Insurance contributions and social security

Introduction

1.   National Insurance is now regarded as a tax on earnings, although in original concept it was a contribution towards State benefits, principally the State old age pension. This chapter is concerned with National Insurance and related aspects of the UK Social Security system, under the following main headings:

Classes of contribution	Statutory sick pay	Taxable state income
Gross pay	Statutory maternity pay	Non-taxable state income
Directors	Tax Credits	Class 4 contributions
Class 1 A NIC – benefits, cars and fuel		

Note   The Contributions Agency, which collects some classes of National Insurance, is a branch of HMRC.

Classes of contribution

2.   The classes of contribution payable are as follows:

Class 1   Paid by employed earners and their employers, based on earnings

Class 1A   Employers' annual contribution paid on benefits-in-kind

Class 1B   Employers' contribution paid on PAYE settlements

Class 2   Payable by self-employed workers at a flat rate

Class 3   Non-employed persons (voluntary NI)

Class 4   Self-employed persons, additional contribution, based on 'profits'

All employed persons and their employers must pay Class 1 contributions.

The weekly earnings thresholds and rates to find Class 1 NI contributions from 6th April 2011 are given below. Equivalent monthly thresholds apply to those paid monthly, and annual thresholds (equivalent to those for Class 4 NI) apply to company directors, whose NI earnings period is the tax year (see section 5).

For simplicity, the accounting professional bodies allow thresholds for Class 1 to be applied on an annual basis in tax examinations (unless the employee changes job during the tax year).

An employed person is someone gainfully employed either under a contract of service, or as the holder of an office as defined for income tax purposes, e.g. a company director.

A self-employed person is liable for Class 2 and Class 4 contributions. The Class 2 contribution is a flat rate per week, now payable by direct debit every 6 months, and collected in January and July. Before July 2011 Class 2 was paid either monthly or quarterly.

Class 4 NI is a percentage of the annual 'profits', as determined for income tax purposes. It is self-assessed on the tax return, and paid along with income tax.

Class 3 contributions are voluntary contributions, payable at a weekly flat rate. They preserve entitlement to some social security benefits including UK State Pension. Class 3 may be paid up to 6 years after the relevant tax year.

Employees must be aged 16 or over before any liability to National Insurance arises.

For employees who are over State pension age (currently 65 for men and 60 for women but due to equalise and then rise in stages to 68 in future) the NI position is as follows:

   i)   Primary contributions (employees' NIC) are not due on earnings paid after the 65th birthday, or state pension age if earlier;

   ii)   Secondary contributions (employers' NICS) continue as before even after state retirement age is reached.

Employer's Class 1A contributions apply to all taxable benefits in kind except:

   i)   where Class 1 NI contributions are already due (e.g. on cash vouchers)

   ii)   those covered by a P11D dispensation

   iii)   those included in a PAYE settlement

   iv)   those provided for non-P11D employees

   v)   those otherwise not required to be reported through the P11D return.

Gross pay

3.   Gross pay for Class 1 National Insurance purposes includes:

           Wages/salaries

           Bonus payments

           Fees

           Overtime pay

           Sick pay and maternity /paternity pay

           Petrol allowances - unless credited and charged to a company account

           Cash allowances generally

           Cash vouchers

           Anything else readily convertible to money, e.g. quoted shares, or commodities that can be sold on a readily-traded market

As noted in the previous section, non-cash benefits are not part of Gross Pay for National Insurance, and are liable not to Class 1, but to class 1A National Insurance. Class 1A NI is paid on benefits in kind by the employer, at the end of the tax year. Non-cash benefits incur no NI liability for the employee.

National Insurance contributions – gross pay

4.   Class 1 Employed earners from 6th April 2012

£ per week earnings	Not contracted-out	Contracted-out Salary-related (COSR)
Employee		
Up to £146 a week – primary earnings threshold	Nil	Nil
Between £146 and £817 a week	12.0%	10.6%
Over £817 a week	2.0%	2.0%
Employer		
Up to £144 a week – secondary earnings threshold	Nil	Nil
Between £144 and £817 a week	13.8%	10.4%
Over £817 a week	13.8%	13.8%
Rebate on earnings between £107 (the LEL) and £144 a week	Nil	3.4%

Further Notes on terms relevant to Class 1 calculations

i) The employee's contributions are known as Primary Class 1, and the employer's contributions as Secondary Class 1 contributions.

ii) The COSR rate applies to employees who are in a salary-related (defined-benefit) occupational pension scheme that is 'contracted out' of the State Second Pension (S2P – formerly called SERPS).

iii) COSR – refers to 'contracted-out salary-related' status of a pension scheme.

iv) LEL – employee's Lower Earnings Limit, £5,565. p.a. This is enacted as an annual limit for company directors and a weekly/monthly limit for others. Earnings above LEL must be recorded on the employer's NI record, even though no NI is due by the employee or employer until pay exceeds the ET.

v)   UEL – employee's Upper Earnings Limit £42,475. p.a. (2011/12 £42,475 - unchanged). This is the pay level at which a lower rate of NI becomes payable by the employee. The UEL is applied as a weekly or monthly figure to all employees except company directors.

vi)   ET – Employees' Earnings Threshold, annual level £7,605 p.a. (2011/12 £7,225). This is the level at which main rate NI becomes payable by employees. For employers the ET is £2 less per week in 2012/13 (£104 less per year).

In accounting exams, the Class 4 annual UEL and ET are given but the Class 1 annual figures for company directors may not be. The Class 4 UEL and ET are similar and in accounting exams these may be used as an approximation for the actual Class 1 annual equivalent UEL and ET for non-directors.

Class 1A   13.8% on non-cash benefits (paid by employers)

Class 2   Weekly rate £2.65 (2011/12 £2.50). Collected 6-monthly on 31 July and 31 January in the tax year. No liability if earnings are below £5,595 for the tax year, and a certificate of exception is obtained.

Class 3   Weekly rate £13.25. (2011/12 £12.60)

Class 4   See below.

Directors

5.   The NI earnings period for employees is the interval at which regular payments are made, normally a multiple of weeks or months. For directors the earnings period is annual, whether they are paid weekly, monthly or at other intervals. The following rules should be noted.

i)   For directors the earnings period runs from 6th April to the following 5th April.

ii)   Directors in post at 6th April have an annual earnings period, even if they cease to be directors in the course of the year.

iii) Where a director is appointed after 6th April then the earnings period is pro-rated using a 52-week period for the whole tax year.

Example

Algy is a Director of K Ltd. He receives a salary of £50,000 in 2012/13, paid six-monthly. The company operates a salary-related pension scheme, which is contracted out of S2P. Compute the primary and secondary NI contributions payable.

Solution: Algy National Insurance contributions 2012/13 (COSR rates)

(Director, so annual earnings period)

	Primary contributions – employee		£
ET	7,605	@ 0%	–
	34,870	@ 10.6%	3,696
	42,475		
	7,525	@ 2.0%	150
	50,000		3,846

Secondary contributions – employer

		£
7,485	@ 0%	–
34,990	@ 10.4%	3,639
42,475		3,639
7,525	@ 13.8%	1,038
50,000		4,677

Note

Once the earnings paid in the tax year exceed the upper earnings limit, any additional cash remuneration paid to a director will incur all employee's Class 1 NI at the lower rate of 2%.

Class 4 contributions

6. The following are the main features of this class of contribution.

    a) Contributions are calculated by the taxpayer on the self-assessment tax return and collected by HMRC together with all other self-assessed income tax.

    b) Where a partnership exists, then each partner's liability is calculated separately and paid separately, as for income tax (see Chapter 15).

    c) The contributions are based on the trade profits as determined in accordance with Chapter 11, with the following deductions:

        i)   Capital allowances (balancing charges are added)

        ii) Loss relief under Sections 83 and 89, ITA 2007.

    d) Personal allowances and pension payments of any kind are not deductible.

    e) The rate of contribution is 9.0% of profits in between £7,605 and £42,475 for 2012/13, plus 2% on profits above £42,475.

    f) Where the profits of farmers are averaged, the revised amounts are used for Class 4 purposes. However, when trading income or total profits are reduced by a trade loss carried back (see Chapter 14), the Class 4 NIC paid in the earlier year is unaffected.

    g) Interest on late payment of Class 4 NICs is charged at the usual rate of interest for income tax paid late.

Where an individual is both employed and self-employed, Class 1 contributions will be paid on the employment earnings and Class 2 and Class 4 (in principle) are payable on the self-employed earnings. However, it is possible to apply for a 'deferment' of the remaining Class 2 and 4, which in practice means a permanent reduction. For example, if the employment earnings already incur employee's NI at 12% on the whole maximum earnings band of (42,475 − 7,605), then the Class 4 due from the same person is only payable at 2%. The principle of deferment prevents an individual paying more NI because income is split between employment and self-employment, than they would pay if all income came from employment.

Example

Xavier has been trading for many years with an accounting year-end to the 30th June. He has the following data relating to the income tax year 2012/13:

		£
Trade profits to 30.6.2012		40,000
Capital allowances		2,965
Building society interest (net)		800

Calculate the income tax and Class 2 and 4 NI payable by self-assessment for 2012/13.

Solution: Xavier income tax, class 2 and 4 NI computation 2012/13

		£	£
Income taxed as trade profits		40,000	
Less capital allowances		(2,965)	37,035
Building society interest (gross)			1,000
Net income			38,035
Personal allowance			(8,105)
Taxable income			29,930
Tax liability n/a @ 10%			0
On non-savings	28,930 @ 20%		5,786
On savings	1,000 @ 20%		200
	29,930		5,986
Less income tax deducted from Building society interest			(200)
Tax payable by self-assessment			£5,786
Class 4 NIC contributions payable:			£
Trade profits			40,000
Less capital allowances			(2,965)
			37,035
Class 4 (£37,035 – 7,605) = 29,430 @ 9.0%			2,649
Class 2 NIC 52 @ £2.65			138
Total self-employed NI payable			£2,787

Directors liable for company's contributions

7.   Where a company has failed to pay NICs on time and the failure appears to be attributable to fraud or neglect by one or more individuals who were officers of the company (culpable officers), the outstanding NICs may be sought from the culpable officers.

Statutory sick pay, statutory maternity pay, etc

8.   Employers are responsible for paying statutory sick pay (SSP), statutory maternity, paternity, and adoption pay to their employees. The detailed rules for computing these entitlements change regularly. To qualify for SSP, a worker must be earning at least the lower earnings limit of £107 per week for 2012/13.

Employers can claim SSP reimbursement against their NI contributions payable if and to the extent that their SSP payments for an income tax month exceed 13% of their gross Class 1 contribution liability for that month. This can help a small business when a large proportion of the workforce is ill at the same time.

Both employers' and employees' Class 1 contributions count here.

Other payments similar to SSP work the same way in outline. Entitlement arises if earning above the LEL. Payments received are all subject to National Insurance and income tax, in the same way as wages and salaries. In addition, small employers can recover most of their SMP etc by setting if off against PAYE income tax and NI due.

Statutory paternity pay

A father may take 2 weeks paid paternity leave at the lower of 90% of average weekly earnings and £135.45 per week (2012/13 figure).

Child benefit

9.   Child benefit is a social security benefit paid to the person primarily responsible for caring for a child. The 2012/13 rate is £20.30 a week for the eldest child and £13.40 a week for each subsequent child. Children under 16 qualify automatically but this can be extended up to 19 if still in school education.

Following the practice long established, until 6 January 2013, child benefit is not affected by the income of the carer, and is not taxable.

From 7 January 2013 onwards, a taxpayer who has adjusted net income of over £50,000 a year will be subject to a new 'tax charge', where they or their partner receive child benefit. If both partners have adjusted net income of over £50,000, only the partner with the higher income is liable for the charge.

The charge will be 1% of the child benefit award for each £100 of income between £50,000 and £60,000. The charge on taxpayers with income above £60,000 will equal the amount of child benefit paid.

In 2012/13 the full amount of income for the year, and the amount of child benefit paid from 7 January 2013 to the end of the tax year, will be used to calculate the charge.

Child tax credit

10.   Child tax credit is a separate social security benefit, based on income. It is non-taxable and has no effect on other income tax liabilities.

Working tax credit

11.   Working tax credit is a social security benefit for people with low incomes from employment or self- employment. Again this income does not have any effect on tax liabilities.

Student self-testing questions on employment income income tax, PAYE and National Insurance

(These questions expect students to refer to Chapters 7-8 as well as 17.)

1. William Wong is the finance director of Glossy Ltd. The company runs a publishing business. The following information is available for the tax year 2012–13:

(1) William is paid director's remuneration of £2,400 per month by Glossy Ltd.

(2) In addition to his director's remuneration, William received two bonus payments from Glossy Ltd during the tax year 2012–13. The first bonus of £22,000 was paid on 30 June 2011, in respect of the year ended 31 December 2011. William became entitled to this bonus on 15 March 2012.

The second bonus of £37,000 was paid on 31 March 2013 and was in respect of the year ended 31 December 2012. William became entitled to this second bonus on 15 March 2013.

(3) From 6 April 2012 until 31 December 2012, William used his private motor car for business purposes. During this period, William drove 12,000 miles in the performance of his duties for Glossy Ltd, for which the company paid an allowance of 30 pence per mile. The relevant HMRC authorised mileage rates are 45 pence per mile for the first 10,000 miles, and 25 pence per mile thereafter.

(4) From 1 January 2013 to 5 April 2013, Glossy Ltd provided William with a diesel powered company motor car with a list price of £46,000. The motor car cost Glossy Ltd £44,500, and it has an official CO_2 emission rate of 234 g/km. Glossy Ltd also provided William with fuel for his private journeys.

(5) William was unable to drive his motor car for two weeks during February 2013 because of an accident, so Glossy Ltd provided him with a chauffeur, at a total cost of £1,800.

(6) Throughout the tax year 2012–13 Glossy Ltd provided William with a television for his personal use that had originally cost £3,825.

(7) Glossy Ltd has provided William with living accommodation since 1 January 2011. The property was purchased in 1998 for £90,000, and was valued at £210,000 on 1 January 2011. It has an annual value of £10,400.

(8) Glossy Ltd pays an annual insurance premium of £680 to cover William against any liabilities that might arise in relation to his directorship.

(9) During May 2012 William spent ten nights overseas on company business. Glossy Ltd paid him a daily allowance of £10 to cover the cost of personal expenses such as telephone calls to William's family.

(10) William pays an annual professional subscription of £450 to the Institute of Finance Directors, an Inland Revenue approved professional body, and a membership fee of £800 to a golf club. He uses the golf club to entertain clients of Glossy Ltd.

(11) William has not 'contracted out' of the State Second Pension scheme.

Required:

(a) State the rules that determine when a bonus paid to a director is treated as being received for tax purposes. **(3 marks)**

(b) Calculate William's taxable income for the tax year 2012–13. **(15 marks)**

(c) Calculate the total amount of both Class 1 and Class 1A national insurance contributions that will finally have been paid by both William and Glossy Ltd in respect of William's earnings and benefits for the tax year 2012–13. **(5 marks)**

(d) Advise William of the forms that Glossy Ltd must provide to him following the end of the tax year 2012–13 in respect of his earnings and benefits for that year, and state the dates by which these forms have to be provided to him. **(2 marks), (25 marks)**

(ACCA updated)

Solution

(a)   The earliest of:

   (1) The date that the bonus is paid.

   (2) The date that entitlement to the bonus arises.

   (3) The date when the bonus is credited in the company's accounts

   (4) The end of the period of account if the bonus relates to that period, and has been determined before the end of the period.

   (5) The date that the bonus is determined if the period of account it relates to has already ended.

(b)   William – Taxable income computation 2012–13

		£	£
Director's remuneration	(2,400 x 12)		28,800
Bonus			37,000
			65,800
Benefits (see notes below):			
Car benefit		4,025	
Chauffeur		1,800	
Fuel benefit		1,767	
Television	(3,825 at 20%)	765	
Living accommodation			
– Annual value		10,400	
– Additional benefit		5,400	24,157
			89,957
Expenses			

Mileage allowance	1,400	
Professional subscription	450	1,850
		88,107
		8,105
		£80,002

(1) The first bonus of £22,000 will have been treated as received during 2011/12.

(2) The relevant percentage for the car benefit is restricted to the maximum of 35%.

(3) The motor car was only available for three months of 2012–13 so the benefit is £4,025 (46,000 x 35% x 3/12). The list price must be used even though a lesser amount was actually paid.

(4) The car benefit does not cover the cost of a chauffeur, so this is an additional benefit.

(5) The fuel benefit is £1,767 (20,200 x 35% x 3/12).

(6) The living accommodation cost in excess of £75,000, so there will be an additional 'expensive accommodation' benefit. Since the property was purchased more than six years before first being provided to William, the benefit is based on the market value of £210,000.

(7) The additional benefit is therefore £5,400 (210,000 – 75,000) = 135,000 at 4%.

(8) The provision of liability insurance does not give rise to a taxable benefit, nor does the payment of the overseas overnight allowance, since it is not above the de minimis limit of £10 per night.

(9) The mileage allowance received will be tax-free, and William can make the following expense claim:

10,000 miles at 45p	4,500	
2,000 miles at 25p	500	
	5,000	
Mileage allowance		
12,000 at 30p	3,600	
	£1,400	

(10) The golf club membership is not an allowable deduction despite being used to entertain customers.

(c) NIC

Employee Class 1	(42,475 – 7,605) =	34,870 @ 12%	£4,184
	(65,800 – 42,475)=	23,325 @ 2%	£466
Employer Class 1	(65,800 – 7,485) =	58,315 @ 13.8%	£8,047
Employer Class 1A	(on benefits)	24,157 @ 13.8%	£3,333

(d) (1) Form P60 employee's certificate of pay, income tax and NIC must be given to William by 31 May 2013.

(2) A copy of form P11D detailing expense payments and benefits in kind must be given to William by 6 July 2013.

Questions without answers

1. You should assume that today's date is 15 March 2012.

Ali Patel has been employed by Box plc since 1 January 2009, and is currently paid an annual salary of £36,000. On 6 April 2012, Ali is to be temporarily relocated for a period of twelve months from Box plc's head office to one of its branch offices. He has been offered two alternative remuneration packages:

First remuneration package

(1) Ali will continue to live near Box plc's head office, and will commute on a daily basis to the branch office using his private motor car.

(2) He will be paid additional salary of £500 per month.

(3) Box plc will pay Ali an allowance of 38 pence per mile for the 1,600 miles that Ali will drive each month commuting to the branch office.

HMRC authorised mileage rates are 45 pence per mile for the first 10,000 business miles driven each year, and 25 pence per mile thereafter. Ali's additional cost of commuting for 2012–13 will be £1,800.

Second remuneration package

(1) Box plc will provide Ali with rent-free living accommodation near the branch office.

(2) The property will be rented by Box plc at a cost of £800 per month. The annual value of the property is £4,600.

(3) Ali will rent out his main residence near Box plc's head office, and this will result in income from property of £6,000 for 2012–13.

Required:

(a) Calculate Ali's income tax liability and Class 1 national insurance contributions for 2012–13, if he:

   (i) Accepts the first remuneration package offered by Box plc;
   (6 marks)

   (ii) Accepts the second remuneration package offered by Box plc.
   (5 marks)

(b) Advise Ali as to which remuneration package is the most beneficial from a financial perspective. Your answer should be supported by a calculation of the amount of income, net of income tax and employee's Class 1 national insurance contributions, which he would receive for 2012/13 under each alternative. (4 marks)

(15 marks)

(ACCA updated)

End of section questions without answers

1. Evaluate the advantages, disadvantages and feasibility of replacing the taxation of income by: a direct expenditure tax; an annual wealth tax.

2. For the purposes of this question you should assume that today's date is 15 March 2012:

Carol Courier is employed by Quick-Speed plc as a delivery driver, and is paid a salary of £26,000. She contributes 5% of gross salary into Quick-Speed plc's HMRC approved occupational pension scheme, which is not contracted out of the state additional pension.

As an alternative to being employed, Quick-Speed plc have offered Carol the opportunity to work for the company on a self-employed basis. The details of the proposed arrangement for the year ended 5 April 2013 are as follows:

(1) Carol will commence being self-employed on 6 April 2012.

(2) Her income from Quick-Speed plc is expected to be £38,000.

(3) When not working for Quick-Speed plc, Carol will be allowed to work for other clients. Her income from this work is expected to be £4,500.

(4) Carol will lease a delivery van from Quick-Speed plc, and 100% of the mileage will be for business purposes. The cost of leasing and running the delivery van will be £4,400.

(5) When she is unavailable Carol will have to provide a replacement driver to deliver for Quick-Speed plc. This will cost her £2,800.

(6) Carol will contribute the equivalent of £2,000 gross into a personal pension scheme during 2012-13. This will provide her with similar benefits to the occupational pension scheme provided by Quick-Speed plc.

Required:

(a) Assuming that Carol does not accept the offer from Quick-Speed plc and continues to be employed by the company, calculate her income tax and Class 1 NIC liability for 2012-13. **(5 marks)**

(b) Assuming that Carol accepts the offer to work for Quick-Speed on a self-employed basis from 6 April 2012 onwards, calculate her income tax, Class 2 NIC and Class 4 NIC liability for 2012-13. **(6 marks)**

(c) Advise Carol as to whether it will be beneficial to accept the offer to work for Quick-Speed plc on a self-employed basis. Your answer should be supported by a calculation of the amount by which Carol's income for 2012-13 (net of outgoings, income tax and NIC) will increase or decrease if she accepts the offer. **(4 marks)**

(d) Critically comment on whether Carol would be considered an employee or self-employed under current HMRC policy. **(5 marks)**

(20 marks)

(ACCA updated)

3. On 31 December 2012 Foo Dee resigned as an employee of Gastronomic-Food plc. The company had employed her as a chef since 2000. On 1 January 2013 Foo commenced self-employment running her own restaurant, preparing accounts to 30 September. The following information is available for 2012–13:

Employment

(1) During the period 6 April 2012 to 31 December 2012 Foo's total gross salary from her employment with Gastronomic-Food plc was £38,000. Income tax of £7,707 was deducted from this figure under PAYE.

(2) Foo used her private motor car for both business and private purposes during the period from 6 April 2012 to 31 December 2012. She received no reimbursement from Gastronomic-Food plc for any of the expenditure incurred. Foo's total mileage during this period was 15,000 miles, made up as follows:

Normal daily travel between home and permanent workplace	4,650
Travel between home and permanent workplace in order to turn off a fire alarm	120
Travel between permanent workplace and Gastronomic-Food plc's suppliers	750
Travel between home and a temporary workplace for a period of two months	3,800
Private travel	5,680
	15,000

The relevant HM Revenue & Customs authorised mileage rates to be used as the basis of any expense claim are 45 pence per mile for the first 10,000 miles, and 25 pence per mile thereafter.

(3) On 1 October 2012 Gastronomic-Food plc paid £12,900 towards Foo's removal expenses when she was permanently relocated to a different restaurant owned by the company. The £12,900 covered the cost of disposing of Foo's old property and of acquiring her new property.

(4) Foo contributed 6% of her gross salary of £38,000 into Gastronomic-Food plc's HMRC-approved occupational pension scheme, which is not contracted out.

Self-employment

(1) Foo's profit and loss account for her restaurant business for the nine-month period ended 30 September 2013 is as follows:

Gross profit		128,200
Depreciation	3,500	
Motor expenses (note 2)	4,200	
Property expenses (note 3)	12,800	
Other expenses (all allowable)	50,700	71,200
Net profit		£57,000

(2) During the period 1 January 2013 to 30 September 2013 Foo drove a total of 6,000 miles, of which 2,000 were for private journeys.

(3) Foo purchased her restaurant on 1 January 2013. She lives in a flat that is situated above the restaurant, and one-quarter of the total property expenses of £12,800 relate to this flat.

(4) On 1 January 2013 Foo purchased a motor car with CO_2 emissions of 140 g/km for £16,667 (see note 2 above) and equipment for £3,600.

Other income

(1) During the tax year 2012–13 Foo received building society interest of £640 and dividends of £360. These were the actual cash amounts received.

Other information

(1) Foo contributed £1,600 (net) into a personal pension scheme during the period 1 January 2013 to 5 April 2013.

(2) She did not make any payments on account of income tax in respect of the tax year 2012–13.

Required:

(a) **Calculate Foo's tax adjusted trading profit for the nine-month period ended 30 September 2013.** **(6 marks)**

(b)(i) Calculate the income tax payable by Foo for the tax year 2012–13. **(13 marks)**

(ii)Calculate Foo's balancing payment for the tax year 2012–13 and her payments on account for the tax year 2013–14, stating the relevant due dates. (Ignore national insurance contributions.) **(3 marks)**

(c) **Advise Foo of the consequences of not making the balancing payment for the tax year 2012–13 until 31 May 2014.** (Assume the HMRC interest rate on late paid income tax is 3.0%) **(3 marks)**
(25 marks)
(ACCA updated)

4. Sue Macker was made redundant from her employment on 15 March 2012. She is a vintage motor car enthusiast, and so decided to take this opportunity to indulge her hobby.

On 6 April 2012 Sue took out a bank loan of £75,000 at an annual interest rate of 10%, rented a workshop for twelve months at a rent of £400 per month, and purchased equipment at a cost of £13,500.

On 10 April 2012 Sue purchased four dilapidated vintage motor cars for £8,000 each. The restoration of the four motor cars was completed on 10 March 2013 at a cost of £12,000 per motor car. Sue immediately sold all of the motor cars for a total of £200,000.

Sue was then offered employment elsewhere in the country commencing on 6 April 2013. She therefore sold the equipment for £5,800 on 20 March 2012, and repaid the bank loan on 5 April 2013.

Because she has just been indulging her hobby, Sue believes that the disposal of the vintage motor cars during the tax year 2012–13 should be exempt from tax. She has done some research on the Internet and has discovered that whether or not she is treated as carrying on a trade will be determined according to the six following 'badges of trade':

(1) The subject matter of the transaction.

(2) The length of ownership.

(3) Frequency of similar transactions.

(4) Work done on the property.

(5) Circumstances responsible for the realisation.

(6) Motive.

Sue had no other income during the tax year 2012–13 except as indicated above.

Required:

(a) **Briefly explain the meaning of each of the six 'badges of trade' listed above.** (You are not expected to quote from decided cases.)   **(3 marks)**

(b) **Briefly explain why Sue is likely to be treated as carrying on a trade in respect of her vintage motor car activities.**   **(3 marks)**

(c) **Calculate Sue's income tax liability and her Class 2 and Class 4 national insurance contributions for the tax year 2012–13, if she is treated as carrying on a trade in respect of her vintage motor car activities.** (Ignore VAT.)   **(7 marks)**

(d) **Explain why it would be beneficial if Sue were instead treated as not carrying on a trade in respect of her vintage motor car activities.**   **(2 marks)**

(15 marks)

(ACCA updated)

5. Tony Note

Tony Note is self-employed running a music shop. His profit and loss account for the year ended 5 April 2013 is as follows:

	£	£
Gross profit		198,000
Expenses		
Depreciation	2,640	
Motor expenses (note 1)	9,800	

Professional fees (note 2)	4,680	
Repairs and renewals (note 3)	670	
Travelling and entertaining (note 4)	4,630	
Wages and salaries (note 5)	77,200	
Other expenses (note 6)	78,780	
		(178,400)
Net profit		19,600

Note 1 – Motor expenses
During the year ended 5 April 2013 Tony drove a total of 20,000 miles, of which 2,500 were driven when he went on holiday to Europe. The balance of the mileage is 20% for private journeys and 80% for business journeys.

Note 2 – Professional fees
The figure for professional fees consists of £920 for accountancy, £620 for personal financial planning advice, £540 for debt collection, and £2,600 for fees in connection with an unsuccessful application for planning permission to enlarge Tony's freehold music shop.

Note 3 – Repairs and renewals
The figure for repairs and renewals consists of £270 for a replacement hard drive for the shop's computer, and £400 for a new printer for this computer.

Note 4 – Travelling and entertaining
The figure for travelling and entertaining consists of £3,680 for Tony's business travelling expenses, £480 for entertaining suppliers, and £470 for entertaining employees.

Note 5 – Wages and salaries
The figure for wages and salaries includes a salary of £22,000 paid to Tony's wife. She works in the music shop as a sales assistant. The other sales assistants doing the same job are paid a salary of £18,000 p.a.

Note 6 – Other expenses
The figure for other expenses includes £75 in respect of a wedding present to an employee, £710 for Tony's health club subscription, £60 for a donation to a political party, and £180 for a trade subscription to the Guild of Musical Instrument Retailers.

Note 7 – Use of office
Tony uses one of the six rooms in his private house as an office for when he works at home. The total running costs of the house for the year ended 5 April 2013 were £4,320.

Note 8 – Private telephone
Tony uses his private telephone to make business telephone calls. The total cost of the private telephone for the year ended 5 April 2013 was £680, and 25% of this

related to business telephone calls. The cost of the private telephone is not included in the profit and loss account expenses of £178,400.

Note 9 – Goods for own use
During the year ended 5 April 2013 Tony took goods out of the music shop for his personal use without paying for them, and no entry has been made in the accounts to record this. The goods cost £600, and had a selling price of £950.

Note 10 – Plant and machinery
The tax written down values for capital allowances purposes at 6 April 2012 were as follows:

	£	
General pool	9,250	
Renault motor car	15,000	CO_2 emissions 150 g/km

The Renault car is used by Tony.

Required:

(a) Calculate Tony's tax adjusted trading profit for the year ended 5 April 2013. **(16 marks)**

(b) Calculate Tony's income tax liability for the tax year 2012/13.

(2 marks)

(18 marks)

(ACCA updated)

Part III

Corporation Tax

18   General principles

Introduction

1. Corporation Tax is a direct tax on the income and capital gains of companies and other corporate bodies. In this chapter the main elements of the corporation tax system are outlined. It begins with some basic expressions, then forms of organisation liable and exempt from corporation tax are examined, followed by corporation tax self-assessment. The remainder of the chapter deals with the corporation tax accounting periods, and the rates of tax. A summary of corporation tax rates and a specimen computation are provided at the end.

2. Corporation tax as a separate form of business taxation was introduced by the FA 1965. However, an entirely new set of rules for the determination of business income was not provided, and the substance of the income tax system was preserved, especially in the original rules for measuring companies' taxable income, and recognition of interest paid and received.

From the 1990s, company tax was reformed, so that the rules for certain types of transaction (such as borrowing for trade purposes) no longer mirror the income tax rules for the same type of transaction carried out by an individual. These corporate tax changes were influenced by several developments: partly by improvements in accounting standards, meaning that company directors had less choice about when to account for a company's revenue and costs; partly by the UK's move to corporation tax self-assessment; and partly by the Government's wish to counter tax planning structures which exploited timing and measurement differences which existed under the previous systems for recognising financial profits and costs (including cross-border tax differences, where transactions involved a non-UK counterparty).

Company tax rules on corporate finance, leasing and debt arrangements, including gains and losses on financial derivatives and foreign currency holdings, now follow, as far as possible, the required financial accounting treatment of such profits and losses (but with some restrictions for 'estimated' losses). There is a 'loan relationships tax regime' and a 'leasing tax regime' designed specifically for corporation tax. These rules cover financing transactions, other than those involving equity shares. The reformed system also covers profits and losses on foreign currency exchange transactions. Further reforms are still made periodically to the foreign currency, loan relationship and leasing tax regimes, if specific tax avoidance tactics are identified by HMRC.

For more on the loan relationships regime see Chapter 19 sections 6-7.

Also, from 1 April 2002, companies are subject to a different tax regime from unincorporated businesses for intangible non-current assets that are 'intellectual property', such as goodwill, patents, and know-how (See Chapter 19 section 8).

UK companies also qualify for extra tax reliefs for revenue expenditure on Research and Development (R&D) compared to unincorporated businesses (see Chapter 19 section 5).

The Corporation Tax Acts 2009 and 2010 changed some of the main terminology of corporation tax without actually changing the rules, and represent the first time in UK tax law that the corporation tax rules were placed in separate statutes on their own. (However, the term 'the Corporation Tax Acts' is defined, by CTA 2010, as also covering Income Tax statutes, so far as these contain rules that also apply to companies.)

However, rules for computing (though not for taxing) corporate capital gains are still contained in the Taxation of Chargeable Gains Act 1992, a statute which does still cover both individuals and companies, though for individuals it has been very significantly amended by subsequent Finance Acts. (See Chapters 26 to 33.)

The UK Government in November 2010 issued an important consultative policy document called 'Corporate Tax Reform: Delivering a More Competitive System' which sets out further major reforms planned for the UK's corporate tax system during the expected life of the current Government (i.e. by FY 2015). The full document is available online from http://www.hm-treasury.gov.uk. Specific proposals for the 'patent box' tax regime, a lower CT rate for intellectual property royalty income of UK companies, are not covered further in this book, as they have not yet been included in legislation. Recent and pending reforms to other 'foreign profits' tax rules are seen by the UK Government as important for the UK's future attractiveness as a headquarters location for multinational groups. The new foreign profits regime is discussed (at a general awareness level) in Chapter 25.

Basic expressions in corporation tax law

3. Financial year

A financial year runs from the 1st April to the following 31st March, and each year is known by reference to the calendar year in which the 1st April occurs. Thus the financial year 2012 covers the period from the 1st April 2012 to the 31st March 2013. Corporation tax rates are fixed by reference to financial years.

Accounting period

Companies do not self-assess CT for financial years, but for corporation tax accounting periods, which are linked to their financial reporting periods. A CT accounting period can never exceed 12 months in length, but can be shorter.

Close company

This is a company which is owned or controlled by a small number of persons (called participators) and their close family members. Private family companies usually fall into this category. The corporation tax consequences of a company being close are now quite limited. A loan by a close company to a participator that lasts past the year-end incurs a liability on the company to pay a temporary additional tax payment to HMRC which is refundable once the loan is repaid or replaced by a dividend. This provision is not discussed further here. Other special income tax and CGT rules on benefits received affect the participators in a close company, and they can obtain income tax relief for interest on a loan to purchase shares in a close company.

Close investment holding company (CIHC for short)

This means a close company, other than one whose business consists substantially of trading activities (for this purpose 'trading' includes acquiring and letting land or property to unconnected persons), except a company which is the managing or parent company of a group whose other companies all have a trade. CIHCs are excluded from the small profits rate, and their participators are logically also excluded from any share tax reliefs that require the company to be a trading company.

Further key definitions

4. Total Profits

Paraphrasing slightly, the Corporation Tax Act 2010 defines 'total profits' as:

i) all of a company's income from any source that is within the charge to CT, after giving effect to specific expense reliefs available against particular sources of income, plus

ii) all of a company's chargeable gains that fall within the charge to CT, after giving effect to any specific deductions and tax reliefs available against chargeable gains.

Taxable Total Profit 'TTP' (formerly 'Profits Chargeable to Corporation Tax', 'PCTCT')

This is a new term introduced by the CTA2010, and used in CT accounting periods ending after 31 March 2010. It is defined as:

i) Total profits, less

ii) Amounts which can be relieved against total profits.

The term at (ii) covers certain loss reliefs, other special deductions, and qualifying charitable donations (see specimen computation at the end of this chapter). Where more than one such deduction is claimed, the order of set-off is usually fixed.

Group relief

This is the term used to describe the voluntary set-off of a trade loss, excess management expenses, excess charitable donations, a net non-trade loan relationship deficit, or certain other net costs, of one member of a group of companies ('group' as specifically defined for group relief) against the profits of another member of the same group. See Chapter 24 for details.

Franked investment income (FII)

When a UK resident company receives a qualifying distribution (broadly, an income dividend) from another company, the amount of the payment is notionally increased by the UK dividend tax credit (currently 1/9). The result of this calculation is known as 'franked investment income' (FII).

FII is not liable to corporation tax in the hands of a UK resident company, but may affect the corporation tax rate paid on all other taxable profits. See Chapter 19.

Under Finance Act 2009, foreign dividends are FII from 1 July 2009 (23 November 2008 for dividends from non-UK companies resident in the European Union). Foreign dividends are therefore now grossed by 1/9 to convert them to FII for CT purposes, just like UK dividends.

Group FII

This is FII from a company (UK or foreign resident) in which the recipient company has a direct or indirect **controlling** holding (> 50%). It is disregarded in computing Augmented Profits. The reason given for this rule is that such a company already counts as an associate in deciding the upper profits limits applying to determine the CT rate of both companies on their UK taxable profits.

Augmented Profits

This is the term used to determine whether a company pays corporation tax at the main rate, or a lower rate. It is equal to:

Taxable Total Profits, plus FII, but excluding Group FII.

Associated companies

For corporation tax purposes, these are defined as companies under the same ultimate control as the company in question. More detail is in Chapter 23.

Main rate of corporation tax

This is set in the Finance Act each year. For Financial Year 2012 (FY2012) it is 24%, reduced from 26% in FY2011. It is applied to taxable total profits to find the CT liability for an accounting period. (See section 16 below for accounting periods falling in two financial years with different CT rates.)

Small profits rate of corporation tax (formerly 'Small companies rate')

This is a lower rate of CT payable by companies with 'augmented profits' falling under certain levels. It is set in the Finance Act each year. For Financial Year 2012 it is 20%. This is unchanged from FY2011. For policy reasons the small profits rate has usually been kept close to the basic rate of income tax, and at present it is exactly the same.

Further details on applying CT rates are in sections 15 to 17 below. Worked examples of the small profits rate, and the marginal rate relief for companies with profits in the marginal band, are in Chapter 23.

Organisations liable to corporation tax (CTA 2009)

5. a) Companies resident in the UK are chargeable to CT on their taxable total profits (as defined for CT purposes), wherever in the world the profits arise. A company is resident in the UK if it is incorporated here. It is also UK resident if it is incorporated elsewhere, but has its place of 'central management and control' in the UK.

The Finance Act 2011 contains an irrevocable opt-out election by which a UK resident company can choose to exclude the profits of an overseas branch or permanent establishment from inclusion in the UK company's worldwide profits charged to UK CT. The downside of this election is that net expenses /losses of the overseas branch cease to be allowed against UK profits, and UK capital allowances (see Chapter 20) are no longer available on plant and machinery of the overseas branch. This legislation will substantially change the options for UK tax on foreign branches of UK companies. See Chapter 25 for more on taxation of foreign branches.

b) Companies not resident in the UK are chargeable to corporation tax on the profits of any UK permanent establishment of that company which carries on a trade in the UK.   See section 6 below.

c) 'Unincorporated associations' are liable to corporation tax. This term excludes partnerships and local authority associations but includes any form of club or society, including voluntary associations, if there is a trading or profit intention. If the club or society is non-profit making or charitable, tax exemption may apply. See section 7 below.

d) Building societies, provident societies, and insurance companies. Special rules apply to these organisations.

e) Corporate members of partnerships: If a company enters into a trading partnership, it is charged to corporation tax in respect of its share of the partnership profits, but partners who are individuals pay income tax or capital gains tax on their profit shares. See Chapter 15 for taxation of partnerships in general.

Non-resident companies

6. a) A company not resident in the United Kingdom is within the charge to corporation tax if, and only if, it carries on a trade in the United Kingdom through a permanent establishment in the United Kingdom.

b) If it does so, it is chargeable to corporation tax, subject to any exceptions provided for by the Corporation Tax Acts, on all profits, wherever arising, which are attributable to the UK permanent establishment. These profits are the company's 'total profits' for the purposes of corporation tax.

c) CTA2009 provides that the UK permanent establishment's profits reported on its CT self-assessment must be computed on the 'separate enterprise principle'. This means that all transactions between a UK branch operation and its foreign headquarters or parent group must be priced 'on arm's length terms', that is at the same transfer prices as would have been agreed between unconnected parties.

d) If a foreign resident company has investment or property income derived from UK assets, but no UK trade through a permanent establishment, then it is liable only to basic rate income tax, not corporation tax, on its UK income only (subject to any Double Tax Treaty which may exempt this income from UK tax). A company with no trade in the UK is not liable to UK tax on its chargeable gains.

e) For the purposes of the Corporation Tax Acts a company has a permanent establishment in a territory if, and only if –

    i) it has a fixed place of business there through which the business of the company is wholly or partly carried on, or

    ii) an agent acting on behalf of the company has and habitually exercises there authority to do business on behalf of the company.

f) A fixed place of business includes:

a place of management;

a branch;

an office;

a factory;

a workshop;

an installation or structure for the exploration of natural resources;

a mine, an oil or gas well, a quarry or any other place of extraction of natural resources;

a building site or construction or installation project.

Organisations exempt from corporation tax

7. a) Partnerships (except for the profit share of a corporate partner – see above).

    b) Local authorities.

    c) Approved pension schemes.

    d) Charities. A charity, which is defined as 'any body of persons or trust established for charitable purposes' is exempt from corporation tax in so far as its income is applied to charitable purposes only. If a charity carries on a trade then any profits arising will be exempt providing that:

        i) they are applied solely for the purposes of the charity, and

        ii) either the trade is exercised out of a primary purpose of the charity, or the work is mainly carried out by the beneficiaries of the charity.

    e) Agricultural and scientific societies.

    f) The Crown.

Notice of chargeability to corporation tax

8. A company must give notice to HMRC of the beginning of its first CT accounting period which brings it into the charge to corporation tax. The notice which must be in writing must be given within three months of the beginning of the accounting period (henceforth AP, or CTAP where there is any possibility of confusion with other types of accounting period). For a new company, the information is given on form CT41G which is sent by HMRC to all newly-incorporated UK companies.

Self-assessment – CT return (Form CT600)

9. The main features of the corporation tax self-assessment (CTSA) system are as follows:

a) The payment of CT and the filing of the company's tax return are separate activities. For required tax payment dates, see paragraph 10 onwards.

b) Between 3 and 7 weeks after the end of a company's AP(or what HMRC think is the end of an accounting period), HMRC issues a notice (form CT603) requiring the company to deliver a tax return for the specified period.

  For accounting periods ending after 31 March 2010, the filing of the CTSA return (Form CT600) and accompanying financial statements and computations must be done entirely online, using HMRC-approved software. Except for charities, the company's financial statements must be filed in iXBRL format. Charities may file their financial statements as a pdf file (Acrobat). Tax computations linking the financial statements to the figures in the Form CT600 must also be filed in iXBRL. This is a tagged electronic format readable by both humans and computers, and allows automated software to check key figures in the financial statements to the company tax computations and self-assessment return. HMRC provides free software to set up accounts and computations in iXBRL and approved commercial packages are also available which can be integrated with computerised accounting systems.

  Online CT filing does not apply for periods ending before 31 March 2010. However most companies were already accustomed to filing their financial statements with HMRC in pdf format in those periods.

  There is an intention ultimately to combine the submission of company tax returns with the online submission of accounts to Companies House in the UK so that it is all achievable with a single online filing, but at present this is not yet the case. The date when accounts are required at Companies House is currently earlier than the date when CT returns are required.

c) Whether filed in paper form or online, the CTSA return includes:

  i) a self-assessment of CT payable for the accounting period

  ii) formal claims for allowances and reliefs

  iii) supplementary pages, if applicable, in respect of:

    loans to participators by close companies CT600A

    controlled foreign companies CT600B

    group and consortium relief CT600C

    insurance companies CT600D

    additional details where the company is a charity CT600E

For limited companies, the financial statements must also be sent in iXBRL form together with any computations required to show how the financial statements link to the figures entered in the CT return.

Bodies that are liable to CT, but are not limited companies, should send whatever form of accounts they are required to prepare. Any additional computations necessary to link these accounts to the CTSA return figures should also be provided.

d) The latest filing date for a CTSA return is 12 months from the end of the accounting period, or in the case of a period of account that covers more than one accounting period, twelve months from the end of the period of account. The directors are at liberty to file the CTSA return earlier than the latest filing date.

e) The company can amend its submitted CTSA return by giving a notice of amendment, within 12 months after the filing date. An amendment may include additional claims for relief, or the withdrawal of previously submitted claims.

f) HMRC can amend the submitted tax return to correct obvious errors or omissions, without launching a formal enquiry. This cannot be done more than nine months after the actual filing date, and the company may, if it wishes, appeal.

g) HMRC has up to twelve months from the actual filing date to raise an aspect enquiry (limited in scope), or a full enquiry, into a submitted CT return and to propose its own amendments as a result of an enquiry. HMRC also has up to twelve months from the date of a submitted amendment to a return, to enquire into the amendment.

h) Penalties are automatically due if the corporation tax return is filed late. There are flat-rate and tax-related penalties depending on the extent of the delay in filing the corporation tax return:

Period of delay (months)	Penalties
1 – 3	£100
3 – 6	£200
6 – 9	£200 + 10% of tax unpaid
9 –	£200 + 20% of tax unpaid

For 3 or more late returns in a row, the flat rate penalties are increased from £100 and £200 to £500 and £1,000.

Penalties are also charged for an incorrect return, under the regime introduced in the Finance Act 2007, explained in Chapter 3, Section 12.

Payments on account of corporation tax

10. a) 'Large' companies, defined as those which paid CT at the full rate in the previous accounting period, are required to make quarterly instalment payments of their corporation tax liability for an accounting period. It is the responsibility of the company's management to estimate these payments on account.

b) A company is 'large' for a corporation tax accounting period (CTAP) if its corporation tax augmented profits are equal to or exceed the 'upper profits limit' – currently defined as £1.5m. However, this limit is reduced for associated companies and pro-rated for short accounting periods.

c) If there are associated companies, then the £1.5m limit for augmented profits is divided by the total number of associated companies, including the taxpayer company. Thus a parent company with 4 active subsidiaries has an upper relevant limit of $\frac{1,500,000}{5}$ i.e. £300,000. See Chapter 23 for more on reducing the upper profits limit where there are associated companies, or a short accounting period.

d) A company that becomes 'large' during a CTAP does not have to make CT instalment payments for that period, provided:

i) it was not a large company in the previous CTAP, and

ii) its taxable total profits for that CTAP do not exceed £10million (this limit is divided where appropriate by the number of associated companies in the group, and apportioned for a short CTAP).

e) No company is required to make instalment payments if its CT liability for the current CTAP is already known to be less than £10,000.

f) Subject to the exceptions above, CT must be paid by 'large' companies in four quarterly instalments, based on anticipated current year's taxable total profits, as follows:

Instalment	Due date
1st	6 months + 14 days after start of CTAP
2nd	9 months + 14 days after start of CTAP
3rd	14 days after end of CTAP
4th	3 months + 14 days after end of CTAP

Thus a company with a 31st March year end pays CT instalments on 14th October, 14th January, 14th April and 14th July following the year end.

g) If management CT estimates are accurate then 100% of the CT liability is paid by four instalments of 25% each.

h)   If management estimates are inaccurate, over and underpayments are liable to interest at different rates (currently 4% per year for underpayments, and 0.5% per year for overpayments).

i)   Interest arising on over- or under-payments of CT is taxable/tax-deductible for the company as a non-trading loan relationship surplus/deficit for CT purposes. Interest on CT is regarded as normal commercial charge or receipt for the time value of the money, and does not count as a penalty or imply non-compliance by the company with its tax obligations.

j)   Groups of companies are able to arrange to pay single CT instalments on behalf of the whole group, without having to specify exactly which companies' final liability each instalment relates to. The allocation of the group's instalment payments to individual companies can be settled when the companies' individual CT returns are finalised.

k)   Companies which are not 'large' must pay all corporation tax by nine months and one day after the end of the CT accounting period, and do not incur any interest on late payment until this date.

l)   Note that for all companies, the CT due payment date falls before the last submission date for the CT return. A company whose directors cannot determine the expected CT liability until the final CT return date should therefore either make an estimated overpayment of CT which can be refunded later, or accept the cost of interest currently at 4% on any CT not paid by the original due date.

Interest on overpaid tax and on correct tax paid early

11.   Interest paid by HMRC on overpaid CT subsequently repaid is known as repayment interest.   Interest paid by HMRC on overestimated quarterly instalments paid early (but not repaid because it is matched to a liability falling due later) is known as credit interest. The rate of both is 0.5% per year from 29th September 2009 but can be varied by HMRC in line with market conditions. Credit interest cannot be earned before, at the earliest, the first instalment payment date for an accounting period. Other than this rule, repayment and credit interest are computed from the date of actual payment to either the due date or the date of refund. All interest paid by HMRC to companies is taxable as income of a non-trade loan relationship.

Financial years and accounting periods

12.   As already noted, CT is charged on the profits of companies for the UK Government financial year which runs from 1 April. A UK Government financial year is known by the calendar year in which it begins, e.g:

Financial year	Period
2011	1st April 2011 – 31st March 2012
2012	1st April 2012 – 31st March 2013

The corporation tax rates and the marginal relief fraction for a financial year (see more details in section 15) are enacted in the Finance Act for that financial year.

The Provisional Collection of Taxes Act 1968, as amended in 2011, allows HMRC, and requires corporate taxpayers, to apply new tax rates and other rules in a Finance Bill that is still before Parliament, with those actions being legally ratified by legislation enacted by 6 October in that financial year. Until the passing of Finance Act 2011 in July 2011, the extent of the PCTA was only 6 August in the financial year.

Corporation tax accounting periods

13. a) A corporation tax accounting period (CTAP) is the period for which CT liability is computed, and can never exceed 12 months in length.

b) A CTAP begins in the following circumstances:

i) When a company comes within the scope of UK CT – for example, by starting a UK trade, acquiring its first source of taxable income (if incorporated in the UK), or becoming resident in the UK (if not previously so resident);

ii) immediately after the end of the last accounting period, provided the company remains within the scope of UK CT.

c) A CTAP ends when the earliest of the following events occurs.

i) The company reaches its reporting year end (i.e. its accounting reference date).

ii) The anniversary of the end of the last CTAP before the current one.

iii) The company starts or stops trading (a CTAP ends, and a new one begins, when all trade starts or stops, even if other business activities continue).

iv) The company ceases to be within the scope of CT (for example, by selling its trade and all its income-producing assets, or in the case of non-resident companies, by ceasing to trade in the UK or to carry on exploration or exploitation activities in the UK sector of the North Sea).

v) The company goes into liquidation (once a company is in liquidation, its CTAPs run for consecutive periods of 12 months until the completion of the winding-up).

vi) The company starts or stops being resident in the UK.

Periods of account longer than 12 months

14.   If a company's period of account covers two or more CTAPs, the various types of taxable profits, gains, losses and reliefs must be allocated correctly to the CTAPs.

Where a period of account exceeds twelve months, say 15 months, it is by law split into two accounting periods, the first of 12 months and one of three months.

Example

K Ltd has regularly prepared accounts to the 31st December. On 1st January 2012 the directors decide that the year-end shall be 31st March, and the next set of accounts will be for the period of fifteen months to the 31st March 2013.

Corporation tax accounting periods	Periods of account
12 months to 31st December 2011	12 months to 31st December 2011
12 months to 31st December 2012 3 months to 31st March 2013	} 15 months to 31st March 2013
12 months to 31st March 2014	12 months to 31st March 2014

Note

There will be two CT returns for the 15-month period of account:
12 months to 31.12.2012;   and 3 months to 31.3.2013.

15.   The following rules apply to allocate income, capital gains, FII and reliefs to CT accounting periods (CTAPs) in a long period of account

i)   Assessable (taxable) trading income/profit is computed by adjusting accounting profits for the whole period of account, **before** deducting capital allowances or adding CAs balancing charges (see Chapter 20). The assessable trading income, before CAs, is then allocated to the CTAPs by time-apportionment, regardless of known fluctuations in sales or profitability.

ii) Capital allowances and CAs balancing charges are calculated separately for each CTAP, and deducted in that period to the extent claimed.

iii) Income from land and buildings (property business income) is computed for each CTAP on a business accounting (accruals) basis, applied for that period. Lease premiums received are treated on a receipts not accruals basis.

iv) Chargeable gains are assessable, and capital losses arise, in the CTAP in which the disposal contract was made. Capital losses of the later CTAP cannot be carried back and set against capital gains of the earlier one.

v)   Qualifying charitable donations are deducted from the total profits of the CTAP in which they were paid.

vi) Surpluses and deficits on *non-trade* loan relationships, and other non-trading profits or expenses governed by special tax regimes reflecting financial accounting rules (see Chapter 19) are allocated to CTAPs on the same basis that they would be recognised in the company's financial accounts if financial accounts were drawn up for that same period. For example if an interest-bearing bank deposit account was closed after the first six months of a long period of account, the non-trading interest surplus arising would all be allocated to the first CTAP included and none of it to the second CTAP.

vii) However interest payable on *trading* loan relationships follows the trade profits rules (covered at (i) above) and therefore is allocated pro rata to CTAPs as an expense of trading, regardless of when it was incurred.

Corporation Tax rates

16. There are two rates of corporation tax, the small profits rate ('Small Companies Rate' until 31 March 2010) and the full or main rate. The level of augmented profits determines which rate applies, and there is marginal relief to smooth the average rate of CT between small profits rate and main rate where profits fall in the intermediate zone.

This method is a form of progressive taxation varying the average rate of CT according to how profitable the company is (including FII). The average rate of CT rises smoothly as taxable profits plus FII increase. Once the upper relevant profits amount is reached, the rate cannot go up any more.

Recent CT rates and profits limits/ marginal relief fractions:

Financial years	FY08	FY09	FY10	FY11	FY12
Year to 31st March	2009	2010	2011	2012	2013
Full rate	28%	28%	28%	26%	24%
Small profits rate	21%	21%	21%	20%	20%
Marginal relief fraction	7/400	7/400	7/400	3/200	1/100
Lower relevant amount	300,000	300,000	300,000	300,000	300,000
Upper relevant amount	1,500,000	1,500,000	1,500,000	1,500,000	1,500,000

Marginal relief formula: tax the company's profits at main rate first, then deduct:

$$(U - A) \times \frac{N}{A} \times \text{ the marginal relief fraction}$$

where N = Taxable total profit, U = upper relevant amount, A = Augmented profits

Several worked examples of CT calculations with marginal relief are in Chapter 23.

Effective marginal CT rates for FY 2011:

0 – 300,000	20%
300,001 – 1,500,000	27.5%
1,500,001 –	26%

Effective marginal CT rates for FY 2012:

0 – 300,000	20%
300,001 – 1,500,000	25%
1,500,001 –	24%

For illustrative examples and self-test questions on marginal relief and small profits rates, see Chapter 23.

Change in the rate of CT part way through a CTAP

17. If a company's CTAP does not coincide with the financial year, and there is a change in the rate or rates of CT, the taxable total profits for the CTAP must be apportioned between the two financial years on a time basis, before adding on FII, then tax is computed at different rates for each fraction of a financial year.

The CT rates changed on 1 April 2012, so CTAPs that straddle the date 1 April 2012 are taxed by apportioning the taxable total profit between the two financial years, applying the correct rates of tax, and treating the total as the single CT liability for the CTAP.

Example

D Ltd, a trading company, whose 12 month ended on the 30th June 2012, has taxable total profits for that period of £2,000,000 and no associated companies. As the CT full profits rate is 26% for FY2011 and 24% for FY2012, D's CT liability computation is as follows:

	£	£
Taxable total profits		
1.7.2011 to 31.3.2012 $^{274}/_{365} \times 2{,}000{,}000$	1,501,370	
1.4.2012 to 30.6.2012 $^{91}/_{365} \times 2{,}000{,}000$	498,630	2,000,000
Corporation tax payable		
Financial year 2011 to 31.3.2012 1,501,370 @ 26%		390,356
Financial year 2012 to 31.3.2013 498,630 @ 24%		119,671
Total CT liability		510,027

The full profits rate applies in this case, and it changed on 1st April 2012.

<u>Note</u> Although it is correct to apportion taxable profits of a CTAP to FYs using exact days, and this is done by commercial corporation tax software, it is acceptable to do the calculation in whole months for the tax exams of UK professional accounting bodies.

18. Specimen corporation tax computation (based on CT600 form)

INCOME AND GAINS	£	£
Tax-adjusted trading profits	–	
Less capital allowances	–	
Less Trade losses brought forward against trading profits	–	
Subtotal: Net trading profits		–
ADD: Net non-trade loan relationship surplus *		
(typically interest receivable and similar income)		–
ADD: Overseas income		–

ADD: Miscellaneous Income   –

ADD: Income from which income tax has been deducted   –

	£	£

ADD: Non-trading gains on intangible fixed assets   –

ADD: Income from UK land and buildings   –

ADD: Chargeable gains, net of allowable capital losses   –

SUBTOTAL – NON-TRADE PROFITS   –

DEDUCTIONS SPECIFICALLY FROM NON-TRADE PROFITS:

    Non-trade loan relationship deficit *   –

    Non-trade capital allowances   –

        –

TOTAL PROFITS   –

LESS: DEDUCTIONS AND RELIEFS FROM TOTAL PROFITS:

    Losses on unquoted shares   –

    Trading losses set against total profits   –

    Excess management expenses   –

Profit before qualifying charitable donations and group relief   –

LESS: Qualifying charitable donations paid   –

LESS: Group relief claimed   –

= TAXABLE TOTAL PROFITS   –

CORPORATION TAX :

Financial year   2011 @ 26% (20% if SPR applies)   –

         2012 @ 24% (20% if SPR applies)   –

Total corporation tax before reliefs and set-offs in terms of tax   –

    LESS: Marginal small profits relief   –

    LESS: Double taxation relief   –

NET CORPORATION TAX LIABILITY   –

Add Tax due on profits of CFCs (see Chapter 25)   –

Less: relief for Income Tax suffered by deduction from income   –

= CORPORATION TAX DUE   –

Note: * non-trade loan deficits suffered are firstly netted against non-trade loan relationships income, and any negative balance is then taken to the non-trade loan deficit line.

Student self-testing questions

1. Tina Limited has TTP of £3,200,000 for the year ended 30 September 2012.

Requirement

Calculate the corporation tax liability for year ended 30 September 2012.

Answer

		£
FY 2011	3,200,000 x 6/12 x 26% =	416,000
FY 2012	3,200,000 x 6/12 x 24% =	384,000
		£800,000

19   The charge to corporation tax

Introduction

1. This chapter is concerned with the determination of CT total profits before deductions and reliefs, which is an important stage in the determination of taxable total profit.

The chapter examines the most important components in the CT total profits computation as demonstrated in the specimen CT computation at the end of Chapter 18. The chapter concludes with a comprehensive example of the adjustment of accounting profits to trading profits for corporation tax purposes.

Generally accepted accounting practice

2. United Kingdom tax law requires that tax computations are prepared in accordance with generally accepted accounting practice. Generally accepted accounting practice is defined as being the accounting practice that is used in preparing accounts which are intended to give a 'true and fair' view (section 836A, Taxes Act 1988). The various financial reporting standards issued by the United Kingdom/International accounting bodies generally require that the relevant financial reporting standard needs to be applied to all transactions of a reporting entity whose financial statements are intended to give a true and fair view.

Sources of income

3. Income is brought into Total Profits under the following headings;

    Trading profits

    Profits and gains from non-trading loan relationships

    Overseas non-trading income (under CTA2009 overseas trading income is included with UK trading profits)

    Other/ Miscellaneous Income

    Income from which income tax has been deducted

    Non-trading gains on intangible fixed assets

    Income from land and buildings

    Chargeable gains, net of allowable capital losses

Trading profits

4. The following points should be noted under this heading.

    a) The general principles of what is tax-deductible trading expenditure for sole traders (see Chapter 10) also apply to companies; except where a specifically different rule exists for corporation tax. Profits and losses arising from trade loan relationships form part of trading profits. Companies do not have a private or personal existence and therefore there is not usually scope for expenses to be apportioned between private and business use. Expenses of providing private benefits or assets for loan to staff or directors are allowable for the company as trade or management expenses, being part of allowable staff remuneration costs. (The private benefit element may be assessable on the director or employee under income tax rules – see Chapter 8.)

b) Petroleum revenue tax (a separate tax only paid by companies involved in UK oil extraction) is a deductible expense for corporation tax purposes.

c) Incidental costs of obtaining loan finance, including costs in connection with the issue of convertible loan stock, are allowed as a deduction in computing trading income. This applies even to long-term non-trading loan finance and would include such costs as professional fees, accountants' reports, commissions, advertising and communication costs related to bond or debenture issues, or any other borrowings, secured or not.

d) Pre-incorporation expenses incurred up to seven years prior to the actual commencement of trading can be treated as being incurred on the first day of trading. Eligible expenditure includes all expenses which, had the company already been trading, would have been allowed as a trading expense, such as rent, rates, staff wages and salaries, but not initial company formation expenses, stamp duties, or capital expenditure (though capital allowances may be available).

e) Unpaid remuneration:

   i) A deduction for employees' or directors' remuneration is not allowed in the computation of trading profits if the remuneration was paid more than nine months after the end of the period of account. Instead a deduction is allowed in the period of account when paid.

   ii) 'Payment' in this case is based on the same rules used to determine when remuneration is received by the director or employee for the purpose of taxes on earnings (and PAYE). See Chapter 7 on this.

   iii) Where the corporation tax return is submitted before the end of the nine month period, any remuneration unpaid at that time should be added back in calculating the taxable profits. If the remuneration is subsequently paid before the end of the nine month period, an adjustment can be made to the submitted return within two years of the end of the period of account.

f) Just as for sole traders and partnerships that pay staff pension contribution for their employees (see Chapter 10), pension contributions paid by a company to a separate pension plan or fund on behalf of employees or directors may not be deducted on the accruals basis, but only when the payment has been made. This can also mean that a deduction is due in the tax computation of a company for employer's pension contributions that have been accrued in earlier years' accounts but were paid in the current AP.

g) A company's taxable profits are computed without any adjustment in respect of dividends paid or other distributions made out of its profits.

h)   For tax relief on amortisation of intangible fixed assets, see section 9 below.

Research and development reliefs and credits – 225% for SMEs/130% for large companies

5. Relief is available for qualifying research and development expenditure (of a revenue nature) by UK companies, in an amount that is greater than the cost actually incurred. The rate is 225% for small or medium sized companies and 130% for large companies. These terms are defined as for company law financial reporting purposes, and have nothing to do with the 'large profits' or 'small profits' company as defined for CT rates.

The following is an outline of the rules on R&D tax credits:

a)   Rates of R&D tax credits:

    i)   225% of qualifying R&D expenditure (200% before 1 April 2012) for small or medium sized companies

    ii)   130% of qualifying R&D expenditure for large companies

b)   Minimum threshold level of expenditure to qualify in any year – £10,000.

c)   A company's qualifying R&D expenditure is deductible in an AP if it relates to an actual trade or a future or potential trade. That is, either:

    i)   it is allowable as a deduction in computing for tax purposes the profits for that period of a trade carried on by the company, or

    ii)   it would have been allowable as such a deduction, had the company, at the time the expenditure was incurred, been carrying on a trade consisting of the activities in respect of which it was incurred.

d)   'Qualifying R&D expenditure' of company means expenditure that meets the following conditions:

    i)   it is not of a capital nature.

    ii)   it is attributable to relevant research and development directly undertaken by the company, or on its behalf.

    iii) it is incurred on staffing costs, or on consumable stores (including power, fuel, water, and software or is qualifying expenditure on sub-contracted research and development.

    iv)   any intellectual property created as a result of the research and development to which the expenditure is attributable is, or will be, vested in the company (whether alone or with other persons). This condition was removed for SME companies' R&D relief with effect from FY 2010.

    v)   the expenditure is not incurred by the company in carrying on activities the carrying on of which is contracted out to the company by any person.

    vi)   the expenditure is not subsidised.

e) Where:

i) A company is entitled to R&D tax relief for an accounting period,

ii) it is carrying on a trade in that period, and

iii) it has qualifying R&D expenditure that is allowable as a deduction in computing for tax purposes the profits of the trade for that period, it may (on making a claim) treat that qualifying R&D expenditure as if it were an amount equal to 225%/130% of the actual amount.

The effect of making an R&D claim, if the company is profitable, is that tax is saved equal to between 20% and 24% of the qualifying R&D expenditure for an SME, and at 3/10 of these rates if the company is a large company.

If the company making the claim is an SME and is not profitable, so R&D tax credits simply increase trade losses, then the Board may elect to receive immediate payment from the government for the tax value of the excess R&D credits, instead of allowing them to be carried forward or back as part of a trade .

Surplus on non-trading loan relationships

6. The income taxable under this heading is as follows.

a) Interest Income. Bank and building society interest should normally be paid gross to a corporate account-holder, and is taxable under this heading on an accruals basis. If a company does receive UK deposit interest net, i.e. with 20% deducted at source, the gross amount is still chargeable to corporation tax, and the income tax is credited elsewhere (see below).

b) Other finance income from non-trade loan relationships. Measurement is based on the amount treated under GAAP (either International or UK GAAP is acceptable) as the receivable amount for the CTAP (e.g. the gradual credits recognised each year under IAS39/FRS25 as the redemption profit on a 5-year corporate bond that is redeemable at a premium). So there is no need to adjust finance income totals shown in the income statement for such items for tax purposes.

Upward revaluations of debt instruments recognised through profit and loss account are also taxable as surplus on loan relationships.

Loan relationships of companies are never chargeable assets for the calculation of chargeable gains for Corporation Tax. Thus for example the write-off or waiver of a non- trade loan to another company is a deficit on a non trade loan relationship, not a capital loss.

Where income is received after deduction of income tax at source, since the gross amount is chargeable to corporation tax, the income tax deducted at source is recoverable as follows:

a) It can be set against any income tax payable in respect of payments made by the company under deduction of basic rate tax at source – e.g. payment of patent royalties to a non-incorporated royalty recipient.

b) If relief is not fully available under (a) then any excess may be deducted from the main corporation tax liability, or if this is exceeded, a cash repayment may be obtained.

Income tax that has to be deducted from payments of royalties etc. by companies, together with any related income tax claimed by offset under a) above, is accounted for under the 'quarterly return system' outlined in Chapter 21.

Loan relationships

7. a) In general a loan relationship exists whenever there is a creditor or debtor for a debt which is regarded as a loan under general law. A company-issued bond, other loan security or debentures would fall within this definition.

b) The definition in (a) above also covers company holdings of Government gilt-edged securities, building society PIBS (permanent interest-bearing shares), and corporate bonds and corporate debts. Bank interest receivable by a trading company (other than a company whose trade is banking) is also taxed as a non-trading credit.

c) To give effect to the loan relationship tax rules there are two methods of accounting which companies are authorised to use, mirroring current accounting standards on financial instruments.

   i) an accruals basis;

   ii) a market-to-market basis - by which a loan relationship is accounted for in each AP at a fair value in the balance sheet and any movement is taken to profit and loss account.

   As a general rule, companies follow the chosen accounts treatment for taxation purposes.

d) Where companies enter into a loan relationship for the purposes of a trade, then all profits, losses and costs relating to the loan relationship are treated as receipts or expenses of that trade and therefore included in the calculation of trade profits or losses.

e) Where a company enters into a loan relationship which is of a non-trade nature, i.e. it is not a loan relationship in the course of activities forming an integral part of the trade, then any net income is taxed as interest income and any net loss is dealt with as below:

   i) by offset against the company's other income and gains chargeable to corporation tax for that accounting period; or

   ii) by surrender as group relief to other United Kingdom group companies (see Chapter 24); or

   iii) by carry back on a last in first out basis against the company's previous three years' net profits arising from its loan relationship, to the extent that such profits arise on a company's non-trading foreign exchange and financial instrument transactions; or

   iv) by carry-forward against its future non-trading profits (including capital gains). This treatment is also extended to losses arising from non-trading foreign exchange and financial instrument transactions.

f)   The loan relationships rules apply to all UK companies in the charge to corporation tax, including UK branches of overseas companies.

g)   A company issuing corporate debt is able to obtain tax relief for interest on an accruals basis, provided the interest is paid within 12 months of the accounting year end.

Intangible fixed assets

8.   Companies (but not unincorporated businesses) are able to obtain tax relief for the cost of intangible assets/ intellectual property, in most cases based on the amortisation or impairment charged in the accounts.

Intangible assets include:

i)   patents, trade marks, registered designs, copyright or design rights;

ii)   database rights, computers and software licences, know how;

iii)   goodwill, excluding that arising on consolidation after purchase of shares.

Intangible assets for this purpose do not include leases of property or land

a)   Expenditure on intellectual property is any expenditure incurred on the acquisition, creation, maintenance, preservation or enhancement of that property. It includes abortive expenditure and expenditure on establishing and defending title to that property. It also includes royalties paid for the use of the intellectual property. Whether or not the expenditure is treated as capital expenditure in the financial statements is irrelevant, except that capital expenditure on tangible assets is specifically excluded.

b)   The system provides that a 'tax debit' (normally an item of tax deductible expenditure) in respect of intellectual property can arise in five ways:

   i.   as expenditure written off as it is incurred;

   ii.   as amortisation of capitalised intellectual property;

   iii.   as a write-down following an impairment review;

   iv.   as a reversal of a tax credit from a previous accounting period;

   v.   as losses on realisation of intellectual property.

c)   A tax credit can arise on the following occasions:

   i.   receipts recognised in the profit and loss account as they accrue;

   ii.   revaluations of intellectual property;

   iii.   credits in respect of negative goodwill;

   iv.   reversal of a tax debit in previous accounting periods;

   v.   gains on realisation of intellectual property.

d)   The rules only apply to assets created or acquired after the 31st March 2002. These assets are called chargeable intangible assets. All other IFAs held by a company on the 1st April 2002 called existing assets, continue to be dealt with under the existing rules (i.e. mainly on a CGT basis) so long as the assets remain in the hands of the same 'economic family'.

e)   Where the IFAs are not held for trade purposes, the taxable and relievable amounts are pooled to produce a net non-trading gain or loss.

Corporate Venturing Scheme

9. This scheme was an incentive to 'business angels' which worked for companies rather like the Enterprise Investment Scheme (EIS) works for income tax. It has been closed to new claims from 1 April 2011.   Under this scheme, companies obtained 20% corporation tax relief on amounts subscribed for new ordinary shares in small higher-risk trading companies which are then held for at least three years. A loss on disposal of qualifying CVS shares (net of the 20% relief) can still be set against income.

Only investments in unquoted companies qualify for relief, but relief will not be withdrawn if the company later becomes quoted, provided there were no arrangements in place or planned, at the time the investment was made, for seeking a listing.

Relief will not be withdrawn merely because the investee company goes into receivership.

Property income

10.   Companies' property business income is measured on the same basis as the property of individuals, except that companies do not deduct mortgage interest on loans to purchase letting property specifically against their rental income, but treat it as a general non-trade loan relationship deficit.

Also, a company accounts for its property business income according to its own CTAPs and not (as individuals and trusts do) to a prescribed year-end of 5 April. The rules for offset of property income losses are also different – see section 11 below and Chapter 22.

Other rules are similar to those for property business income of individuals (see Chapter 9), but are summarised here for convenience.

a)   Rental income and expenses are computed on an accruals basis, with a deduction for all expenditure wholly and exclusively incurred for the letting business.

b)   Furnished lettings, holiday and non-holiday, are taxed as income from property and the 10% wear and tear allowance is available as an alternative to claiming for renewals of furnishings and kitchen utensils etc.

c)   Overseas property income is taxed as 'other' income, and available for double tax relief, but is measured using the same rules as for UK property business income.

d)   Profits and losses on all lettings are pooled as the business is taxed as a single letting business.

e)   The company intangible asset regime does not apply to intangible assets that bundle rights over land or buildings (i.e. typically leases, but also options over land): these assets have their own tax rules (see below).

f)   Capital allowances where available are deducted as a business expense. These are not available on the property or let contents, except on furniture and kitchen appliances etc for qualifying furnished holiday lets. In other cases they are only available for the cost of capital plant and machinery used by the landlord to maintain the property.

11. Rental losses of a company are relieved in the same way as management expenses, i.e. against current period total profits. They may also be surrendered as group relief or carried forward against future property income. This provides companies with a broader scope of property business loss relief than is available for individuals.

Lease premiums

12.   For convenience the following paragraphs repeat points already made in Chapter 9, covering let property lease premiums which are liable partly as rental income if the related lease duration is less than 51 years. Companies are much more likely to receive (or pay) lease premiums in the current commercial environment than indivduals are.

One way of looking at lease premiums is to regard them as a capitalised part of future rental income which would otherwise have been received by way of annual rent. They include any sum whether payable to the immediate or a superior landlord, arising in connection with the granting of a lease, but not arising from an assignment of an existing lease.

(Under an assignment the lessee takes the position of the original lessee, with the same terms and conditions.)

Where a new lease is granted (but not when an existing lease is assigned) at a premium for a period not exceeding 50 years, then the landlord is deemed for income tax or corporation tax purposes to receive rental income equal to the premium, less an allowance of 2% of the premium for each complete year of the lease remaining, excluding the first 12 month period.

Example

B Ltd granted a lease for 24 years of its warehouse to a trader on the following terms:

A lease premium of £12,000 to be paid on 1.1.2012 and an annual rent of £1,000;

Allowable letting expenditure for AP ended 31st December 2012 was £5,800.

Corporation Tax AP 31.12.2012

	£	£
Lease premium received	12,000	
Less 2% × 12,000 × (24 – 1)		
i.e. 1/50 × 12,000 × 23	(5,520)	6,480
Annual rent		1,000
		7,480
Less allowable expenses		(5,800)
Property income liable to corporation tax		1,680

In effect the lease premium is discounted by reference to its duration, and the longer the unexpired portion, the greater the discount. Thus if a lease had 49 years to run the discount would be:

$$(49 – 1) \times 2\% \text{ i.e. } 96\%.$$

The amount of the taxable premium may also be determined by use of the formula:

$$P - \frac{(P \times Y)}{50}$$

P = amount of premium paid; Y = number of completed 12 months other than the first.

Lease premiums and the lessee

13.   Where the lessee makes a payment of a lease premium at the start of a lease, then a proportion of that premium may be set against the following:

a)   any trading income, providing the premises are used for business purposes.

b)   any rental income or lease premium received from any sub-lease granted by the lessee.

In effect the amount of the premium assessed as income of the lessor can be charged as an expense of trading by the lessee, the deductible expense being spread over the remaining life of the lease.

Example

S Ltd is granted a lease of premises to be used for trading purposes, for a period of 20 years, at an annual rent of £6000 p.a. plus an initial lease premium of £32,000.

	£
Lease premium	32,000
Less 2% × 32,000 × (20 – 1) i.e. 38% × 32,000	(12,160)
Lease premium taxed on lessor as income	19,840

Relief available to S Ltd for notional rent for trade purposes $= \dfrac{19840}{20}$ i.e.£992 p.a.

Overseas income

14. Income from overseas activities of UK companies is generally computed on UK tax principles. Other awareness points on international issues for UK companies are covered in Chapter 25. The new irrevocable election to exclude the results of all a UK company's foreign branches from inclusion in the UK profits of the main company was mentioned in Chapter 18 section 5.

Capital gains tax

15. UK resident companies are not liable to capital gains tax as such, but they are liable to corporation tax on chargeable gains which must be computed in accordance with the appropriate CGT rules, covered in Part IV.

All chargeable gains are taxed at the relevant corporation tax rate on TTP.

Example

K Ltd has taxable total profits of £1,500,000 for its accounting year ended 31st March 2013, and a chargeable gain of £500,000.

Compute the corporation tax payable.

Solution: K Ltd corporation tax computation. CTAP to 31.3.2013   £

Corporation tax trading profits	1,500,000
Chargeable gain	500,000
Taxable total profits	2,000,000
Corporation tax @ 24% (main rate applies)	480,000

Comprehensive example – adjustment of trading profit for a company

16. Note: In following the example below, the reader should refer to both the foregoing sections and the contents of Chapter 10 on the adjustment of trading profits for income tax purposes.

For example, companies are still subject to the income tax rules on allowable expenses of trading and on the disallowance of capital items and capital improvements included in repairs. They must also disallow certain business gifts, customer and supplier entertaining, illegal payments, some car leasing payments, and movements on general provisions.

Example

S plc has the following results in respect of the year ended 31st March 2013.

	£	£
Sales		283,165
Factory cost of sales		(127,333)
Factory profit		155,832

Expenses:	General administration	37,021	
	Marketing	28,197	
	Distribution	16,031	
	Financial	22,000	(103,249)
			52,583
Non-sales revenue			14,723
Profit before tax			67,306
Corporation tax			(30,000)
Profit after tax			37,306

Additional information: £

Factory cost of sales includes:

Depreciation	17,832
Permanent partitioning of works office	3,179
Repairs to new premises to make usable	1,621

General expenses include:	Legal costs of tax appeal	627
	Legal costs of share issue	175
	Stamp duty – property	1,200
	Fines on employees for parking tickets	250

		£
Marketing expenses include:	Trade debts written off	1,211
	Loan to ex-employee written off	250
	Increase in general bad debt provision	5,000
	Increase in specific bad debt provision	1,000
	Promotional gifts (£45 each, not food or drink, and with company name on)	1,800
	Advertising on TV	6,000

Financial expenses include:	Bank interest on overdraft	1,100
	Bank charges	238
	Donation to political party	250
	Subscriptions to trade associations	1,250
	Redundancy payment to staff	11,000

Non-sales revenue comprises:	Profit on sale of assets	323
	Bad debts recovered	1,700
	Agency commission income	12,700

Compute the adjusted profits for corporation tax purposes, ignoring capital allowances.

Solution: S plc adjustment of profits. AP to 31st March 2013

	£	£
Profit before tax		67,306
Add back items disallowed:		
(see notes 1 to 10):		
Depreciation	17,832	
Partitioning	3,179	
Repairs	1,621	
General administration:		
Legal expenses	627	
Legal expenses	175	
Stamp duty – property	1,200	
Marketing expenses:		
Loan to ex-employee written off	250	
Increase in general bad debt provision	5,000	
Financial expenses:		
Political donation	250	
		30,134
Less profit on sale of fixed assets		(323)
Adjusted trading profit		97,117

Notes

1. Depreciation £17,832 – added back, capital allowances claimed in lieu.
2. Partitioning £3,879 –plant and machinery, see Jarrold v Johnson & Sons 1962 40 TC 681.
3. Repairs £1,621 – see Law Shipping Co. Ltd, and Odeon Theatres Ltd cases.
4. Legal expenses £627 – expenses of a tax appeal are not allowed.
5. Legal expenses £175 – capital expenditure (because it relates to a share issue) - This would be allowable as loan finance expenses if on a bond/loan stock issue.
6. Stamp duty £1,200 – capital expenditure not revenue.
7. Loan to ex-employee written off £250 – making loans to individuals is not the company's trade so this is not a trading expense. (customer bad debt write-offs are part of the trade, and loans to current employees that are waived would fall under the category of staff pay)
8. Increase in general provision for bad debts £5,000.
9. Donation to political party £250 – not an expense of trading.
10. Profit on sale of fixed assets £323 – this is not a taxable revenue receipt; in effect it is negative depreciation. No taxable capital gain will arise if the assets qualified for capital allowances and were sold for less than cost, or if they were chattels sold for below £6,000, or cars.

See also Chapter 10, section 7 for some case law on disallowable expenses.

Student self-testing question

1. T Ltd has the following results for the year ended 30th June 2012

	£	£
Sales		160,000
Cost of sales		(40,000)
Gross profit		120,000
Wages and salaries	42,000	
Rent and rates	4,287	
Insurance and telephone	1,721	
Repairs and renewals	35,000	
Heating and lighting	2,897	
Professional charges	3,250	
Bank interest payable on business overdraft	1,155	
Subscriptions and donations	1,200	
Directors' remuneration	22,000	
Patent renewal fees	1,000	
Bad debts	1,250	
Sales commission	5,680	
Loss on sale of assets	1,000	
Miscellaneous expenses	7,251	(129,691)
Net Trading loss		(9,691)
Other income:		
Discounts received	1,123	
Foreign exchange surplus	12,107	
Dividends received	1,620	
Rents receivable less outgoings	651	15,501
Trading profit before taxation		5,810

Additional information:

	£
Repairs and renewals:	
Repairs to newly acquired premises	
of which £10,000 was necessary to make them usable	27,000
Furnace relining – provision for future expenditure	8,000
Professional charges:	
Audit and accounting	1,250
Architect's fees for new factory design	1,750
Legal costs for renewal of short lease	250
Subscriptions and donations:	
Donation to golf club used by staff	500
Subscriptions to trade associations	150
Gift aid payment to charity	550

Wages and salaries of staff:

Salaries and national insurance	32,000
Staff Bonuses (paid in May 2013)	10,000

Directors' remuneration:

Salary paid in year	14,000
Pension scheme accrued payment due at year-end (paid 31.8.12)	4,000

Bad debts:

Trade debts written off	250
Increase in general provision	1,000

Entertaining:

Office party	410
Theatre tickets for foreign customers	991
Removal expenses of new managing director	850
Compensation to customers for damage from company's product	5,000

Exchange surplus:

Profit from currency dealings arising from trade	12,107

Rents receivable less outgoings:

Net rents from letting part of factory	1,000
Deficit on property let to retired employee at a nominal rent	(349)

Compute the trading profits for taxation purposes for the CTAP to 30th June 2012.

Solution: T Ltd AP to 30th June 2012

	£	£
Trading profit per accounts		5,810
Add items disallowed:		
Repairs and renewals	18,000	
Professional charges	1,750	
Donation to golf club	500	
Gift aid to charity	550	
Pension provision unpaid at year end	4,000	
Bad debt provision (general)	1,000	
Loss on sale of asset	1,000	
Theatre tickets - entertaining	991	
Staff bonuses (unpaid after 9 months)	10,000	37,791
		43,601
Less dividends received (not taxable in hands of a company)	1,620	
Rents receivable (not trade income)	651	(2,271)
Trading profit for taxation purposes		41,330

Notes to answer

1. Repairs to make the premises initially usable are not allowable. Round sum provision for future costs is also disallowed.

2. Architect's fees for new factory are capital expenditure on the factory building.

3. Donation to golf club, although used by staff, is not welfare or sports expenditure.

4. The gift aid to the charity is not allowed as a trading expense, but is deducted as a qualifying charitable donation from total profits in the taxable total profits computation.

5. Pension contributions are not allowed unless actually paid in the AP.

6. The increase in the bad debt provision is general and therefore not allowed: It will be allowed in future if applied to write off specific bad debts.

7. Losses on the sales of fixed assets are not trading expenses.

8. The theatre tickets are disallowed entertaining expenses.

9. Dividends received by a company are not liable to corporation tax.

10 Rents receivable are taxable as income from property, not trading income.

11. As the exchange surplus has arisen through trading, it is taxable as a trading receipt and on an accounts basis.

12. As the staff bonus was paid more than nine months after the year end, it is not allowed against taxable profits until the next accounting period.

Questions without answers

1. Z plc has the following results for the year ended 31st March 2013.

	£	£
Trading profits		1,900,000
Bank deposit interest (gross)	1,500	
Building society interest (gross)	1,700	3,200
		1,903,200
Less allowable expenses	50,000	
Director's remuneration	25,000	
Depreciation	✗ 8,000	(83,000)
Profit before tax		1,820,200

Compute the taxable total profit, showing each separate category of income, and the corporation tax payable.

2. Carrot Limited, a company resident in the United Kingdom, makes up accounts annually to 30 September. The information listed below relates to Carrot Ltd's twelve month AP ended 30 September 2012.

INCOME	£
Trading profit (already adjusted for tax purposes)	1,120,000
Rents receivable	40,000
Dividends received from non-group companies	138,600
Building Society interest receivable	48,000
Capital gains	148,000

Requirement: Compute the TTP for Carrot Ltd and the corporation tax payable.

3. P Ltd's accounts for the 12 months to 31st December 2012 showed the following:

	£	£
Revenue		442,100
Less: Cost of sales		(214,000)
Gross profit		228,100
Net rents receivable on let property ✗ trading		750
Profit on sale of plant items ✗ trading		5,500
		234,350
Less: expenses		
Wages and salaries	90,500	
Rent, rates and insurance	6,000	
Motor expenses	2,000	
Legal expenses ✗ ✓	2,000	
Directors' remuneration ✗	35,000	
Audit charges	2,500	
Miscellaneous	1,300	
Depreciation ✗	6,000	
Amortisation of purchased goodwill ✓	14,000	
		(159,300)
Net profit		£75,050

Notes

i) Legal expenses comprise:

		£
	Debt collection ✔	600
	Advice on staff service agreements	250
	Issue of debentures ✓	1,150
		2,000

ii) Miscellaneous expenses comprise:

			£
	Subscriptions :	trade associations ✔	150
		political party ✗	440
	Staff outing		710
			1,300

iii) On 1st January 2012 the company acquired the Goodwill of an unincorporated business for £140,000, which it has decided to write off over 10 years. 140,000/10 = 14,000 ✓

iv) Capital allowances for the AP to 31.12.2012 have been agreed at £33,230 and are deductible in computing trading income. ✗ ✓

v) Gross profit has been computed after deducting £50,000 paid in December ✓ 2012 under a threat of blackmail of the chief executive.

Calculate the liability to corporation tax for the CTAP to 31st December 2012.

4. Valerie Ltd's accounts for the 12 months to 31 December 2012 showed the following:

	£
Sales turnover	729,150
Less: cost of goods sold	(401,000)
Gross profit	328,150
Net rents	1,000
Profit on sale of plant (2)	2,500
	331,650

Less expenses:	
Wages & salaries	140,000
Rent, rates and insurance	6,000
Motor expenses	4,000
Miscellaneous expenses (1)	2,000
Director's remuneration	40,000
Bad debts (4)	3,650
Audit fee	2,000

Depreciation	5,000
Premium on lease, written off (3)	14,000
	(216,650)
Net profit	£115,000

Notes

(1) Miscellaneous expenses comprise:

	£
Staff outing	600
Penalty for late VAT return	400
Wine given to customers	1,000

(2) The profit on sale of plant relates to a disposal which gave rise to a chargeable gain of £1,600.

(3) On the 1st July 2012 Valerie Ltd was granted the lease of additional factory premises for a period of 7 years on payment of a premium of £14,000.

(4) Bad debts expense account comprises the following:

	£
Specific provision	2,000
Loan to an ex-employee, written off	650
Increase in general bad debt provision	1,000

Requirement: Calculate TTP for the CTAP to 31 December 2012.

20   Capital allowances

Introduction

1. The capital allowance system, described in Chapter 13 in connection with income tax, is essentially the same for corporation tax. There is a difference in computing maximum writing down and annual investment allowances for a long period of account, as a CTAP cannot last longer than twelve months.

Another difference is that companies do not have private use assets.

The changes in Annual Investment Allowance and Writing Down Allowance rates that take effect from 6 April 2012 for income tax payers take effect for FY2012 for companies, i.e. from 1 April not 6 April. Where an AP straddles a change in WDA rates, the rate for the period is computed using a time apportioned average WDA rate. In order to focus on the main principles, the examples in this chapter are shown for APs that commence no earlier than 1 April 2012, so as to avoid confusion arising from the numerical effect of different WDA rates in a CTAP. An interactive tool is available on HMRC's website to assist taxpayers to find the averaged WDA rate for any CT accounting period ending after 1 April 2012.

Main features

2. a)   Capital allowances are available in respect of qualifying expenditure incurred in an accounting period.

b)   Capital allowances are deducted as an expense in arriving at the trading income. A balancing charge is treated as trading income.

c)   The pool system for plant and machinery and other assets is the same for companies as for individuals, but there is no depooling, or WDA disallowance, for private use made by staff or directors of a company asset.

d)   A company need not claim all the capital allowances available.

e)   If capital allowances claimed create or increase a trading loss then they are carried forward as an integral part of that trading loss (see Chapter 22).

f)   Where the   CTAP is more than 12 months' duration then the capital allowances are computed for each separate period; WDA rates and limits are not 'scaled up' as they are for income tax purposes (see Chapter 13).   However for short CTAPs, the WDA rates and the AIA limits are scaled down for companies.

g)   A 100% first year allowance, also known as Enhanced Capital Allowance (ECA) is available to certain environmentally-friendly assets of companies, just as for individual sole traders. This applies to the following expenditure:.

   i)   Approved Energy-saving and Water-saving plant and equipment (listed in Regulations);

   ii)   Low-emission cars – the limit is now set at 110g CO_2/km emissions.

h) From 1 April 2012 the Writing Down Allowance (WDA) is 18% per year (reducing balance) on the general pool of plant and machinery, which includes cars with CO_2 emissions of 160 g/km or less.

i) From 1 April 2012 the WDA is 8% per year (reducing balance) in the special rate pool. This pool includes plant which qualifies as 'features integral to a building', 'long life assets', and cars with CO_2 emissions above 160 g/km.

Features integral to a building can broadly be defined as:

i) electrical systems (including lighting systems);

ii) cold water systems;

ii) space or water heating systems, powered systems of ventilation, air cooling or air purification, and any floor or ceiling comprised in such systems;

iv) lifts, escalators, and moving walkways;

v) external solar shading; and

vi) active facades (which manage energy use)

j) Annual Investment Allowance (AIA) may be claimed by companies, as by sole traders, for expenditure on general pool or special rate pool assets, other than cars. This AIA is given in addition to (and before) the normal WDA on the same expenditure. Assets which have received 100% AIA in the year of purchase should still be tracked within their particular pool (either the general or special rate pool) as the proceeds of a future disposal must be allocated to the correct pool.

The AIA for a full twelve month period was reduced to £25,000 a year from 1 April 2012 (£100,000 to 31 March 2012). Examples in this book adopt the approach of ignoring future changes until they are enacted, in order to keep the examples simple, and then focusing on the new rules rather than exploring the residual effects of the old ones.

If there is a group of companies under common control, sharing a similar trade or having the same trading premises, then only one AIA limit applies between them all. This is to prevent splitting of the same business across multiple companies to get better access to AIA. The AIA may be allocated to any company or companies but HMRC must be told how total AIA claims within the group have been allocated. In general in the examples in this book it may be assumed that AIA is available in full to the company being looked at.

k) Like sole traders, companies can elect to 'de-pool' short life assets, namely plant from the general pool which will be used for less than 8 years (increased from 4 years in April 2011) in the trade, and where the directors expect the residual value to be lower than the tax written down value when the assets are sold or scrapped.

De-pooled short life assets receive the same WDA during their ownership as they would have done if left in the general pool. The difference comes when they are sold or scrapped as the single-asset pool is deemed to come to an end and a balancing allowance or charge is given on the difference between the disposal proceeds and the written down value before disposal. A balancing allowance could not have been received if the main trade did not end and the asset had been in the general pool.

Example

K plc has the following data relating to its AP ended 31st March 2013.

	£
Trading profits for tax purposes	1,865,550
Profit from land and property	173,200
Plant and machinery pool at 1.4.2012	88,000
Additions 1.8.2012 (general plant and machinery)	24,000

Compute the capital allowances and the corporation tax liability for the CTAP to 31st March 2013.

Solution

Capital allowances: plant and machinery	**Pool**
	£
Written down value b/f	88,000
Additions qualifying for AIA	24,000
AIA within £25,000 annual limit	(24,000)
	88,000
Writing down allowance @ 18%	(15,840)
Balance	72,160
Written down value c/f on general pool	72,160

Total allowances (24,000 + 15,840) = £39,840

Corporation tax computation CTAP 31.3.2013

	£
Trading profits	1,865,550
Less capital allowances	(39,840)
Net Trading profits	1,825,710
Income from land and buildings	173,200
Taxable Trading Profit	1,998,910
Corporation tax payable £1,998,910 @ 24% FY 2012	479,738

Example

Minty plc starts in business on 1 May 2012, making up accounts to 31 December 2012.

Additions to plant and machinery:		£
1 May 2012	BMW car CO_2 140 g/km	25,000
5 May 2012	Air cooling system	70,000
6 May 2012	Water saving plant	12,000
8 May 2012	Toyota car CO_2 105 g/km	15,000
9 May 2012	Photocopier	7,000
10 October 2012	VW car CO_2 190 g/km	16,000

Required: Calculate capital allowances for the AP 1 May to 31 December 2012.

Solution

		Workings £	General pool £	Special rate pool £	Allowances £
Additions for 100% ECA					
Water saving plant		12,000			
Toyota car	Low emissions	15,000			
		27,000			
ECA 100%		(27,000)	0		27,000
Additions for AIA					
Air cooling system		70,000			
Max £25k x 8/12		(16,667)		53,333	16,667
Photocopier			7,000		
Additions not for ECA or AIA					
BMW car	<160g/km		25,000		
VW car	>160g/km			16,000	
			32,000	69,333	
WDA @ 18%	5,760 x 8/12		(3,840)		3,840
WDA @ 8%	5,546 x 8/12			(3,698)	3,698
					£51,205
WDV	31/12/2012		28,160	65,635	

Example

Minty plc has the following disposals of plant and machinery for the year to 31 December 2013:

1 August 2013	VW car (cost £16,000)	£12,000
10 October 2013	Photocopier (cost £7,000)	£ 9,000

Required: Calculate capital allowances for the year to 31 December 2013.

Solution

			General pool £	Special rate pool £	Allowances £
WDV	01/01/2013		28,160	65,635	
Disposals					
VW car	proceeds			(12,000)	
Photocopier	proceeds	9,000			
	max cost		(7,000)		
			21,160	53,635	
WDA	@18%		(3,809)		3,809
WDA	@8%			(4,290)	4,290
					£8,099
WDV	31/12/2013		17,351	49,345	

Student self-testing question

1 Cinders Ltd has a general pool balance brought forward of expenditure of £200,000 at 1 May 2012, and makes up its accounts to 30 April each year.

On 5 June 2012 the company buys a laser cutter costing £95,000 and elects for it to be treated as a short life asset.

On 30 September 2014 the laser cutter is sold for £24,000.

Required: Calculate capital allowances for the years to 30 April 2013, 2014, and 2015

Solution

y/e 30/04/13

			General pool £	Short life asset £	Allowances £
WDV b/f			200,000		
Addition	Cutter	95,000			
AIA		(25,000)		70,000	25,000
WDA 18%			(36,000)		
WDA 18%				(12,600)	48,600
					73,600
WDV	30/04/13		164,000	57,400	

y/e 30/04/14

WDA 18%		(29,520)	(10,332)	39,582
WDV	30/04/14	134,480	47,068	

y/e 30/04/15

Disposal			(24,000)	
Balancing Allowance			(23,068)	23,068
WDA 18%		(24,206)		24,206
				47,274
WDV	30/04/15	110,274	0	

Question without answer

1. Wineglass Ltd purchased the following assets in respect of the six-month period ended 31 March 2013:

	£
1 October 2012 Office equipment	3,400
5 October 2012 Machinery	62,200
11 October 2012 Installation of cold water system	27,200
18 February 2013 Motor car with CO_2 emissions 140g/km	10,600

The motor car purchased on 18 February 2013 is used by the sales manager, and 15% of the mileage is for private journeys.

The cold water system is a 'feature integral to a building'. 8;

There was no pooled expenditure brought forward at 1 April 2012. ✗

Required: Calculate capital allowances available to Wineglass Ltd for the period to 31 March 2013.

21 Company Gift Aid /quarterly returns

Introduction

1. This chapter is concerned with the quarterly return system under which companies may have to collect and account for income tax on behalf of other taxpayers.

It also covers relief for qualifying charitable donations of companies, formerly known as relief for non-trade charges on income, and still alternatively called Company Gift Aid.

2. Qualifying charitable donations are allowed as a deduction in computing the taxable total profit for an AP. In equation form:

Taxable total profit   =   Profits – Trading losses etc.

                                     – Qualifying charitable donations

                                     – Group relief

Qualifying charitable donations are therefore deducted from total profits after trading losses etc. and before group relief.

Gift aid payments

3. Payments made by a company to a charity are covered by the Gift Aid Scheme. Under these rules:

i)   The company does not deduct income tax at the basic rate when making the payment.

ii)   The payment does not enter the quarterly CT61 scheme.

iii)   The payment is treated as a qualifying charitable donation.

iv)   The charity recipient cannot recover any income tax in respect of the amount it receives as this is the full amount of the donation.

v)   There is no limit on the amount of charitable donations that could be made in this way by a company but if it pays more than its net total profits (After deductions and reliefs), the CT relief may be lost. Relief for charitable donations cannot be carried forward or back to another accounting period. However it can be surrendered as part of group relief (see Chapter 24). It is also likely under company law that a company would require the consent of its shareholders to any significant charitable donations.

Qualifying donations – additional relief

4. Companies (other than close companies) can also treat as qualifying charitable donations gifts to a charity up to a maximum of $2\frac{1}{2}\%$ of dividends paid on ordinary share capital, during the company's accounting period.

The above relief is in addition to any gifts made by way of Gift Aid payments.

Eligible deductions

5. To be eligible for deduction from profits the qualifying charitable donations must comply with the following conditions.

a)   They must be actually paid in the accounting period, and not accrued - except for a covenanted donation by a charity trading company to a charity which is its parent.

b)   The payments must be ultimately borne by the company making the payment.

c)   They must be paid out of the company's profits brought into charge to corporation tax.

Adjustment to accounts

6. As the normal company accounts do not distinguish between qualifying charitable donations and other charitable expenses it is necessary to 'add back' qualifying charitable donations, because only qualifying charitable donations actually paid in the AP are allowed, whereas for accounts purposes an element of accrual might have been made. If the payments relate to an earlier accounting period, they are nevertheless allowed as a qualifying charitable donation in the AP when the payments are made.

Collection of income tax on payments which are not distributions

7. The principles of the system for the collection of income tax that must be withheld by a company when it makes certain payments, and must later be accounted for to HMRC, are as follows.

Return periods

a) A company must make returns to HMRC in respect of each of its accounting periods of any payments made to others (not accruals) subject to the deduction of income tax at source, and of any income received (not accrued) which has been taxed at source.

b) The returns must be made for a quarter and the dates prescribed are 31st March, 30th June, 30th September, and 31st December. These are known as standard return periods, and if a company's AP does not coincide with any of the quarterly dates, then an additional return is required at its year-end.

Income tax is deductible from the following payments made by companies:

Yearly interest (paid to an individual)

Property Rents paid directly to non-UK resident landlords (including a non UK resident company): however, this requirement is lifted if the rent is paid via a UK agent

Interest paid on deposit or savings accounts held by individuals with banks/ buildings societies

Payment to an individual of the income element of an annuity

Patent royalties paid to individuals

Note: Payments of interest, royalties, annual payments and annuities to companies by other companies are made gross without any tax deduction so long as the recipient company is within charge to corporation tax.

Example

S Ltd has an accounting year ending on the 30th November 2012. The return periods relating to that AP are as follows:

2011	1st December to 31st December
2012	1st January to 31st March
	1st April to 30th June
	1st July to 30th September
	1st October to 30th November

The company here has five return periods and each return must be submitted within fourteen days of the end of the return period. If there are no transactions in the period a nil return is not required.

c) The return forms must show particulars of payments made in the period, and income tax deducted is due on the return date without the making of any formal assessment. Particulars of any income must also be included on the returns, and any income tax suffered at source is offset, on the company quarterly returns, against any income tax the company has retained, under legal obligation, from payments of the types listed at 7(b).

The position at the end of a return period

8. a) If the income tax suffered in a return period exceeds the income tax retained from payments made then no income tax need be paid over for the quarter. The net excess of income tax suffered at source on income may be carried back and set against any income tax accounted for and paid on earlier quarterly returns in the same accounting period. This generates a repayment which cannot exceed the amount of income tax already accounted for and paid over relating to net-of-tax payments made in the accounting period.

b) If (as is generally the case) cumulative income tax suffered by the company on taxed income does not exceed its income tax retained on payments made, then the net amount of income tax withheld on payments, less any suffered on income, is payable to HMRC on the due date.

c) Once all quarterly returns required have been submitted, and if income tax retained by company on payments to others has all been offset within the same CTAP against income tax suffered at source by the company itself, then any net income tax which the company has suffered on income received may be treated as CT already paid. Therefore, net income tax suffered is set off on the submitted CT return against the company's final CT liability for the AP (see last part of specimen computation at end of Chapter 18).

Example

F Ltd has a CTAP ended 31st March 2013 and during the year the following transactions took place.

2012	April 11th	Debenture interest paid to individuals	8,000
	June 30th	Interest received (net)	4,000
	August 7th	Bank interest paid	12,000
	October 11th	Debenture interest paid to individuals	8,000
2013	January 1st	Interest received (net)	4,000

All transactions are shown net as entered in the company's bank account.

Show the quarterly returns for the year to 31st March 2013.

Solution

Quarter	Gross paid £	Income tax retained (20%) £	Gross received £	Income tax suffered (20%) £	Net income tax paid or repaid £
30.6.12	(10,000)	2,000	5,000	(1,000)	1,000
30.9.12	–	–	–	–	–
31.12.12	(10,000)	2,000	–	–	2,000
31.3.13	–	–	5,000	(1,000)	(1,000)
Total	(20,000)	4,000	10,000	(2,000)	2,000

Notes

i) In the fourth quarter, the excess of income tax suffered can be set against the payment made in quarter 1 or 3. This generates a repayment of £1,000 of income tax (previously accounted for and paid over) to the company for the 4th quarterly period.

ii) Interest paid by companies on bank borrowings is not subject to deduction of income tax and is, therefore, excluded from the quarterly return system.

iii) The 'total' line shows the company's cumulative position for the whole AP.

The position at the end of an accounting period

9. This may be summarised as follows.

a) Income tax suffered on income received net > income tax paid on outgoing net payments.

  i) Excess can be set against corporation tax payable on the profits of the accounting period.

  ii) If the excess is greater than the corporation tax payable then a cash repayment can be obtained.

b) Income tax deducted from income received net < income tax paid on outgoing net payments.

  i) In this case since the excess has already been paid over within the quarterly return system, no further adjustment is necessary.

  ii) Note that as stated in Chapter 18, a UK trading company is not liable to Income tax (IT) on its own income, as it pays Corporation Tax.

  Any BRIT paid over by companies on the quarterly returns is income tax paid out of the gross payment, on behalf of either individuals or non-resident companies.

That a company may deduct, from the basic rate income tax due on net payments it has made, any basic rate tax suffered at source on its own income in the same AP, is a cash flow convenience.

An individual, or a non-resident investment company, that receives interest, royalties or rents net from a UK company should also receive a tax certificate from the company showing the amount of tax withheld by law at 20%. This tax suffered is then creditable against the recipient's own income tax liability, whether the certifying company actually paid the tax to HMRC or simply offset it against the tax suffered at source on its own income.

Example

B Ltd has an AP ended 31st March 2013 and during that year, the following transactions took place.

2012	June 10	Interest on unsecured loan stock paid – individuals (net)	1,600
	July 19	Interest received (net)	2,000
	Aug 31	Building society interest received (gross)	2,500
	Dec 10	Interest on unsecured loan stock paid – individuals (net)	1,600
2013	Jan 19	Interest received (net)	2,000

The adjusted trading profits for the year ended 31st March 2013 amounted to £1,795,300 before any adjustment for loan interest paid. The unsecured loan interest is used for trade purposes. Property income in respect of the same period was £1,200.

Show the quarterly returns for the year to 31st March 2013 and the corporation tax computation for the same period.

Solution

Quarter	Gross paid £	Income tax retained (20%) £	Gross received £	Income tax suffered (20%) £	Net tax paid or repaid £	Net tax suffered at source, c/fwd £
30.6.12	(2,000)	400	–	–	400	–
30.9.12	–	–	2,500	(500)	(400)	(100)
31.12.12	(2,000)	400	–	–	300	–
31.3.13	–	–	2,500	(500)	(300)	(200)
Total	(4,000)	800	5,000	(1,000)	–	–

Corporation tax computation AP to 31.3.2013

Trading profits (1,795,300 – 4,000)	1,791,300
Property income	1,200
Income taxed at source	5,000
Building society interest	2,500
Taxable trading profit	1,800,000
Corporation tax @ 24%	432,000
Less excess income tax as above	(200)
	431,800

Notes

i.   The repayment of £400 for quarter 2 is limited to the amount of IT already paid for quarter 1. The £100 balance (500-400) of unrelieved tax suffered on net income in q2 is carried forward to q3. In quarter 3, this £100 is offset against the £400 of IT retained on net payments made, meaning that only £300 of tax has to be paid over with the 3rd quarterly return.

ii)   The £300 paid over for quarter 3 is then all refunded in quarter 4, following receipt of net-of-tax interest on which £500 of IT has been withheld. After the £300 repayment claimed for the fourth quarter, a net £200 of income tax suffered on income over the 4 quarters remains unrelieved. This net £200 is relieved by offset against the CT liability.

iii.   As there was an excess of taxed income suffered, the income tax unrecovered is set against the corporation tax payable. From a cash flow point of view, the benefit will not be felt until the corporation tax becomes payable.

Student self-testing question

K Ltd has the following data relating to its AP ended 31st March 2013.

	£
Operating profits	1,550,000
Building society interest receivable and received (gross)	2,000
Private loan interest receivable (received but net of 20% tax)	10,000
Gift aid payment made	40,000
Debenture interest payable and paid (gross), to investors who are not individuals, on a trade loan	20,000

Compute the corporation tax payable for the CTAP to 31st March 2013.

Solution

Corporation tax computation AP to 31.3.2013

	£
Trading profits (1,550,000 – 20,000 trade interest payable)	1,530,000
Surplus on non trade loan relationships:	
Interest receivable (10,000 + 2,000)	12,000
Total profits	1,542,000
Qualifying charitable donation	
Gift aid payment	(40,000)
Taxable total profit	1,502,000
Corporation tax liability	
1,502,000 @ 24%	360,480
Less relief for income tax suffered on loan interest received	(2,000)
Corporation tax payable	358,480

Notes

i) A Gift Aid payment by a company is made gross to the charity, not under tax deduction.

ii) There were no payments made in the year from which K Ltd did have to deduct income tax and therefore the tax suffered on the loan interest received has not been reclaimed through the quarterly return system by the end of the accounting period.

iii) It is likely that K Ltd's private loan debtor withheld basic rate tax from interest if it was unsure about K Ltd's UK corporation tax status. The normal pattern for companies such as K Ltd is to receive bank interest gross, and other interest may be paid to companies gross as long as the payer has proof that the recipient company is within the charge to UK CT.

22 Relief for losses

Introduction

1. This chapter examines the various forms of loss relief available to a company which is not a member of a group of companies. The main emphasis is given to loss reliefs available in respect of trading losses. Non-trading loan relationship deficits are covered. Relief available in connection with property business losses and chargeable gains is also covered.

A company can claim to set a trading loss against other income in several ways. In summary form they may be depicted as follow:

Set against profits (income and gains) of the same period. Sec 37

Carried back and set against profits (income and gains) of the previous year. Sec 37

Carried forward and set against future trading income from the same source. Sec 45

Surrendered as group relief. Sec 130 (current year)

List of loss reliefs

2. i) Trade losses — set against taxable total profit of the same accounting period. Sec 37.

ii) Trade losses — set against taxable total profit of the previous year. Sec 37. (Also see Note above)

iii) Trade losses — carried forward and set against future trade income. Sec 45.

iv) Trade losses — terminal loss relief. Sec 39.

v) Trade losses — surrendered to a 75% subsidiary (and consortium company) by way of group relief. See Chapter 24.

vi) Trade losses — transfer to successor company along with trade.

vii) Non-trading loan relationship deficit — set against total profits.

viii) Pre-trading expenditure — treated as expenditure on 1st day of trading.

Trade losses

3. It is perhaps worth recalling that a trading loss is arrived at after deducting capital allowances which sometimes differ from accounting depreciation expensed. Either large capital allowances, or interest costs arising from a

trading loan relationship may turn an 'operating profit' in the financial accounts (stated before borrowing costs) into a trading 'loss' for tax purposes.

Trade losses Section 37

a)   Under this section a company which has incurred a loss in its trade (excluding any loss brought forward) in any accounting period, may claim to set off that loss against total profits (i.e. including chargeable gains) of the same accounting period.

b)   Any balance of loss remaining after this set off in the current period can be set off against total profits of APs falling within the previous twelve months.

c)   A total profits claim for the current year must be made before claiming total profits relief for any preceding year.

d)   A claim under this section must be made within two years of the end of the AP in which the loss is incurred, or within such longer period as HMRC may allow.

e)   Relief for the loss under Section 37 appears in the computation before Gift Aid donations and group relief are deducted.

f)   Even if the AP of the loss is less than 12 months' duration, the loss can nevertheless be carried back 12 months, so long as a current period claim is made first.

Example

Q Ltd has the following corporation tax profit/loss for its accounting years ended 31st March 2012 and 2013 and makes both the available claims for loss relief under Section 37.

Show the computations.

Q Ltd

	31.3.12 £	31.3.13 £
Trading profit/(loss)	80,000	(30,000)
Income from property	10,000	11,000
Chargeable gains	9,000	2,100
Non-trading loan relationship deficit	–	(2,000)

Solution

Claim for relief under Section 37

	£	£
Trading profit	80,000	
Income from property	10,000	11,000
Chargeable gains	9,000	2,100
Non-trading loan relationship deficit	-	(2,000)
Total profits	99,000	11,100
Less Section 37 loss claim	(18,900)	(11,100)
Assessment	80,100	-

Loss memorandum	£
The trading loss of £30,000 has been utilised as follows:	
Set against total profits for the year to 31.3.2013	11,100
Set against total profits for the year to 31.3.2012	18,900
	30,000

Notes

i)   After making a claim under Section 37 for the year to 31st March 2013 it is not obligatory also to make the second claim to carry the losses back to the previous CTAP to March 2012.

ii) However, the carry-back relief, if claimed, is only available after a current period loss claim has been made.

iii) It is not possible to claim a partial relief for the year to 31st March 2013 and also claim relief for the period to 31st March 2012.

iv) The non-trading loan relationship deficit is deducted before the loss relief – see 8 below.

Trade losses carried forward against future trade profits, Section 45 CA 2010

4. Where a company incurs a trading loss in any accounting period, then if no other claim for relief is made by the taxpayer (e.g. under Section 37), the loss will be dealt with as follows:

a)   It will be carried forward to succeeding accounting periods so long as the company continues to trade.

b)   A loss carried forward is only deductible from future trading income, not from total profits.

c)   The trading income/profit of a succeeding period is automatically treated as being reduced by trading losses brought forward.

d)   A claim under this section must technically be made within four years (or before FY 2010, six years) of the end of the AP in which the loss was incurred. In practice section 45 relief is given automatically by the self assessment system to the extent optional loss relief claims are not made which would take priority (including a group relief loss surrender – see Chapter 24).

e) Anti-avoidance legislation provides that there may be a disallowance of trading losses carried forward if there is a change of ultimate ownership of the company and also a major change in the nature or conduct of the trade within three years either side of the change of ownership .

Example

D Ltd has the following results for the two years ended 30th June 2013.

	30.6.12 £	30.6.13 £
Trade profits/(loss)	(120,000)	70,000
Interest income	30,000	40,000
Chargeable gain	60,000	10,000

The company makes a claim under Sections 37 and 45 CTA 2010.

Compute the taxable total profit after loss reliefs.

Solution

	30.6.12 £	30.6.13 £
Trade profits	–	70,000
Less Section 45 (second claim, in order of priority)	–	(30,000)
	–	40,000
Interest income	30,000	40,000
Chargeable gain	60,000	10,000
Total profits	90,000	90,000
Less Section 37 (first claim, in order of priority)	(90,000)	
Taxable total profit	–	90,000

Notes

i) The trading loss of £120,000 incurred in the AP to 30th June 2012 has been utilised as indicated below.

		£
Accounting period to 30.6.12	Section 37	90,000
Accounting period to 30.6.13	Section 45	30,000
		120,000

ii) The trading loss carried forward to 30.6.13 is deducted from trading profits and not total profits.

Terminal loss relief Section 39 CTA 2010

5. Trading losses arising in the twelve months prior to the cessation of trading can be carried back against total profits of the previous thirty six months on a LIFO basis.

A claim for relief must be made within two years of the end of the CTAP in which the loss is made or within such later period as HMRC may allow.

Note that:

(a) there is no limit on the amount of losses that can be carried back under section 39 as long as they relate to the last twelve months of trading. ;

(b) the company must have ceased trading before this claim can be made;

(c) the loss available for carry-back is computed for exactly twelve months , which may involve more than one CTAP and apportioning the loss of the earlier one.

Example

Z Ltd has the following data for the four years ended 31st March 2013 when it ceased trading.

	31.3.10	31.3.11	31.3.12	31.3.13
	£	£	£	£
Trading profits	55,000	30,000	65,000	(180,000)
Income from property	7,000	8,000	9,000	9,000
Capital gains				1,000

The company makes a claim for loss relief under sections 37 (current period) and 39.

Show the final taxable profits.

Solution: Z Ltd APs ended 31st March

	2010	2011	2012	2013
	£	£	£	£
Trading profits	55,000	30,000	65,000	loss
Income from property	7,000	8,000	9,000	9,000
Capital gains	–	–	–	1,000
Total profits	62,000	38,000	74,000	10,000
Less section 37 claim				(10,000)
Section 39 claim (LIFO)	(58,000)	(38,000)	(74,000)	-
Taxable profits	4,000	–	–	-

Note

Loss Memorandum:	£	£
Trade loss to 31.3.2013		180,000
Section 37 31.3.13	10,000	
Section 39 31.3.12	74,000	
Section 39 31.3.11	38,000	
Section 39 31.3.10	58,000	180,000

Transfer of losses

6. When a company ceases trading and another company takes over the same trade, unrelieved trade losses can be carried forward to the successor company providing that certain conditions are met, which are:

a) On or at any time within two years after the succession and within one year prior thereto, at least 75% of the interest in the trade is held by the same persons. This means that three quarters of the ordinary share capital in both companies must be held by the same persons throughout the three-year period. Throughout the same period the same trade must be carried on by a company in charge to corporation tax.

b) It follows from this provision that the transfer of a trade from an individual to a company precludes the transfer of trading losses between the entities. However, in that case under Section 86 ITTOIA 2005 some relief for an individual is available whereby part of a business loss may be set against income which he or she receives from the company. See Chapter 14.

Where there is a transfer of trade then the following applies.

a) The trade is not treated as if it had been discontinued and a new one started.

b) Loss relief under Section 39 is not available to the company ceasing to trade. If the second company ceases to trade within four years of the succession, then loss relief can be carried back, where appropriate, to the first company.

c) Relief under Section 45 for the carry forward of losses is available, subject to any claim by the company ceasing to trade, under Section 37 i.e. set off against total profits .

   Where a trade or part thereof is transferred between two companies, then relief to the successor for losses brought forward is restricted where the amount of the 'relevant liability' immediately before the transfer exceeds the open market value of the 'relevant assets' at that time.

d) No capital allowances balancing adjustments are raised on the transfer.

e) Unused capital allowances can also be carried forward.

f) Losses cannot be carried forward where at any time before the change in ownership the scale of activity becomes small or negligible and the change takes place before any considerable revival has occurred.

g) Other losses or capital losses cannot be transferred.

Non-trading loan relationship / foreign exchange deficit

7. Interest incurred and receivable plus any other debits and credits relating to non-trade borrowing and lending must be pooled to produce either a non-trading credit or deficit for the period. This also includes any non-trading foreign exchange debt differences.

A net non-trading credit is included as interest income.

A net non-trading deficit is relieved by one or more of the following methods:

i)   By offset against the company's taxable profits (in whole or part) for the same period. A current year non-trading deficit is deducted against taxable profits before: any current year trading loss offset under Section 37; charges on income; and a non-trading deficit carried back from a subsequent period.

ii) Against the taxable profits of fellow group members under the group relief provisions.

iii) By carry-back (in whole or part) against the company's interest income loan relationships profits falling within the previous 12 months.

iv) By carry-forward for offset against the company's non-trading profits for the next accounting period. (For this purpose, non-trading profits represent the company's total profits except those constituting trading income.)

The above reliefs must be claimed within two years of the end of the relevant CTAP or such further period as HMRC may allow. Any surplus non-trading deficit remaining after the above claims is automatically carried forward as a non-trading debit for the next accounting period.

Example

Q Ltd has the following data relating to the year ended 31st December 2012.

	£
Adjusted trading profit	93,000
Income from property	5,000
Non-trade interest cost incurred	65,000
Non-trade interest received	15,000

Compute the taxable total profits for the CTAP to 31st December 2012.

Solution: Q Ltd corporation tax computation AP 31.12.12

	£
Trading profits	93,000
Income from property	5,000
	98,000
Non-trading deficit	(50,000)
TTP	48,000

Notes

i)   The non-trade LR deficit comprises:

non-trade interest paid	65,000
less non-trade interest received	15,000
	50,000

ii) The excess non-trade LR deficit is deducted from total profits and taken off before group relief. (Refer to the specimen CT computation at the end of Chapter 18)

Pre-trading expenditure

8. Relief is available for expenditure by a company in the seven years before it commences to carry on a trade.

a)   The expenditure must be allowable trading expenditure which would have been deducted in computing trading income if incurred after commencement of trading.

b)   Such expenditure is treated as a trading expenditure on the first day on which the trade commences.

c)   The relief does not apply to pre-trading purchases of inventory (trading stock).

Chargeable gains

9. The amount of any chargeable gain arising in a CTAP is reduced by any allowable capital losses of the same AP and then by those brought forward from a previous period. A company can never carry any capital losses back to an earlier accounting period.

Example

R Ltd has the following data relating to its CTAP to 31st March 2013.

	£
Capital losses brought forward 1.4.12	3,000
AP to 31.3.2013	
Trading profits	41,000
Chargeable gains	22,000

Compute the corporation tax payable.

Solution: R Ltd CTAP to 31st March 2013

	£	£
Trading profits		41,000
Chargeable gains	22,000	
Less capital losses b/f	(3,000)	19,000
Total profits/ Taxable total profit		60,000
Corporation tax payable: 60,000 @ 20%		12,000

Other Non-trading losses – relief

10.   Non-trading loan relationship deficit

See section 7 above.

Loss on property business

Relief can be taken for losses against current year total profits. See Chapter 19.

Capital losses

May be set against chargeable gains of same CTAP, or carried forward. They cannot be set against total profits.

Management expenses

Relief for expenses of management may be claimed where a company has a recognised business activity of managing investments. Excess management expenses may be set against total profits.

Student self-testing questions

1. Trailer Limited has the following results for the two years to 31 August 2012

	y/e 31.8.11	y/e 31.8.12
	£	£
Trading profit/(loss)	(21,000)	17,000
Interest income - non trade relationship	6,000	9,000
Capital loss	(2,000)	
Chargeable gains		7,000

Requirement: Calculate TTP for the 2 periods, assuming that the loss is relieved under S45 (carry-forward relief), and showing any losses carried forward at 1 September 2012.

Suggested solution

	31/8/11	31/8/12
	£	£
Trading profit	-	17,000
Less : S45 relief		(17,000)
		NIL
Interest income	6,000	9,000
Chargeable gains (£7,000 - £2,000)		5,000
	6,000	14,000
TTP	6,000	14,000

Loss memorandum

	£
Loss for year ended 31/8/11	21,000
Relieved year ended 31/8/12 (S45)	(17,000)
Available for further carry-forward under S45	4,000

2. Caravan Limited has the following results for the accounting years ended 31 March 2012 and 31 March 2013.

	Year to 31/3/12 £	Year to 31/3/13 £
Trading profit/(loss)	39,000	(49,700)
Income from property	2,000	1,500
Qualifying charitable donations (gross)	500	500

Requirement: Calculate TTP for both periods, assuming that relief under S37 (against total profits) is claimed for the loss in the period ended 31 March 2013. Show any losses available to carry forward at 1 April 2013.

Suggested solution

Caravan Limited: TTP computation for 2 years ending 31 March 2013

	Year ended 31/3/12 £	Year ended 31/3/13 £
Trading profit	39,000	-
Income from property	2,000	1,500
Total profits	41,000	1,500
S37 relief (the setoff for the current year must be claimed before the carry-back claim)	(41,000)	(1,500)
TTP	-	-
Unrelieved Gift Aid payments (Caravan loses tax relief, but the charity still gets the same donation)	500	500

Loss memorandum	£
Loss for the year ended 31/3/13	49,700
Less S37 year ended 31/3/13	(1,500)
S37 year ended 31/3/12	(41,000)
Loss to carry forward	7,200

3. Buttercup Limited made up accounts to 30 September and ceased to trade on 31 March 2013. Results have been as follows:

	30/9/10	30/9/11	30/9/12	Period ended 31/3/13
Trading profit/(loss)	5,200	4,700	3,200	(30,500)
Income from property	2,000	1,800	1,900	500

Interest income - non trading	750	900	840	400
Chargeable gains	3,000	-	2,000	-
Qualifying charitable donations:				
-Gift Aid payment	300	300	300	300

Requirement: Show the TTP for all years, assuming the loss is relieved under S39 terminal loss relief.

Suggested solution

	30/9/10 £	30/9/11 £	30/9/12 £	31/3/13 £
Trading profit	5,200	4,700	3,200	-
Income from property	2,000	1,800	1,900	500
Interest income	750	900	840	400
Chargeable gains	3,000	-	2,000	-
Loss relief in aggregation (see 1)			(1,600)	
Less S39 loss offset (see 2)	(10,950)	(7,400)	(6,340)	(900)
TP	0	0	0	0
Gift Aid	-	-	-	-
TTP	Nil	Nil	Nil	Nil
Unrelieved Gift Aid Payment	300	300	300	300

(1) Computer terminal loss under section 89:

	£
Trade Loss of final 6 months 31/3/13	(30,500)
Less trade profits of prior 6 months (3,200 x 6/12)	1,600
= terminal trade loss of final 12 months	(28,900)

(2) Make S39 terminal loss claim:
Set against other profits, LIFO:

6 months to 31/3/13	900
6 months to 31/3/12 (balance of 7,940)	6,340
y/e 30/9/11	7,400
y/e 30/9/10	10,950
Loss remaining unrelieved	(3,310)

Questions without answers

1. Uncut Undergrowth Limited (UUL) is a United Kingdom resident company which has been manufacturing garden machinery since 1999. It has no associated companies. The company results are summarised as follows:

	Year Ended 30/6/12	6 months to 31/12/12	Year Ended 31/12/13	Year Ended 31/12/14
	£	£	£	£
Trading Profit/(Loss)	25,000	(51,000)	(362,500)	87,000
Non-trade loan interest received (gross amount)	-	15,000	22,000	-
Bank interest received -non trade relationship	-	-	-	10,000
Income from property	25,000	-	-	-
Chargeable gains	-	-	30,000	-
Gift Aid payment to charity	1,000	1,000	1,000	1,000

On 1 July 2011 there were no trading losses brought forward, but £40,000 of prior capital losses were still unrelieved.

Requirements

(a) Calculate the corporation tax liabilities for all years in the question, after giving maximum relief at the earliest time for the trading losses sustained and any other reliefs. (11 marks)

(b) Show any balances carried forward. (5 marks)

NB: All apportionments may be made to the nearest month.

Note Use FY 2012 tax rates for all years in this question.

(ACCA updated)

2. Loser Ltd's results for the year ended 30 June 2012, the nine month period ended 31 March 2013, the year ended 31 March 2014 and the year ended 31 March 2015 are as follows:

	Year ended 30 June 2012	Period ended 31 Mar 2013	Year ended 31 Mar 2014	Year ended 31 Mar 2015
	£	£	£	£
Trading profit/(loss)	90,200	(33,000)	34,600	(85,500)
Income from property	(3,600)	4,500	8,100	5,600
Gift Aid payments	(1,400)	(800)	(1,200)	(1,100)

Required:

(a) State the factors that will influence a company's choice of loss relief claims. You are not expected to consider group relief.

(3 marks)

(b) Assuming that Loser Ltd claims relief for its losses as early as possible, calculate the company's Taxable Total Profits for:

the year ended 30 June 2012,

the nine month period ended 31 March 2013,

the year ended 31 March 2014 and

the year ended 31 March 2015.

Your answer should show any amount of unrelieved losses as at 31 March 2015. (10 marks)

(c) Explain how your answer to (b) would have differed if Loser Ltd had ceased trading on 31 March 2015. (2 marks)

(15 marks)

(ACCA updated)

Student note: Some of these questions contain brief elements of tax on the capital gains of companies, and this topic is covered in Chapters 26-33.

23 Corporation tax rates and the small (profits) company

Introduction

1. This chapter is concerned with the taxation of 'small profits companies', known until 1 April 2010 simply as 'small companies' for corporation tax rate purposes. The new name was introduced by the Corporation Tax Act 2010 to reflect the fact that a company with 'small' profits, as defined, in a particular year may in all other respects be quite a 'large' company.

Regarding what are the 'profits' for 'small profits rate' purposes, this means the augmented profits as defined by CTA2010, that is to say the taxable total profit plus FII but not group FII.

This chapter begins with a brief recent history of small profits rates.

The UK government has made many changes in the rates of corporation tax for 'small (profits) companies' over recent years. Before FY2006 there were special rules for companies with profits under £50,000. There was a 0% starting rate, marginal relief for very small profits from £10,000 to £50,000, and a 'non-corporate distribution rate' to tax profits more highly where dividends were paid to individuals rather than left in the company.

All of these special rules for companies with profits under £50,000 were abolished in April 2006. The Labour Government then announced an intention to raise the small companies rate in stages to 22% but the final stage of this was never implemented due to the 2008 recession.

The Coalition Government that was elected in 2010 restored the small profits rate of CT to 20%, from FY 2011. This is the same as the basic rate of income tax. However the planned reduction in the main rate of Corporation tax will leave the difference between SPR and main rates at the lowest it has ever been (currently it is only a 4% difference) and it may be that the future of corporation tax could include the end of the small profits rate and the complications it causes to the effective marginal rate of tax which companies face on marginal profits after they rise out of the small profits band.

Though the small profits CT rate did not change from 31 March to 1 April 2012, the marginal relief fraction did change and so companies in the marginal profits band will still need to work out CT liabilities separately for the two financial years included in a CTAP commencing from May 2011.

Basic rates

2. Rates

	Financial years	
	2012	**2011**
	to 31.3.2013	**to 31.3.2012**
Small company augmented profits level	0-300,000	0-300,000
Small profits rate	20%	20%
Marginal relief band	300,001–1,500,000	300,001–1,500,000

Augmented Profits between £0 and £300,000 are taxed at the small profits rate of 20%. Profits in between £300,000 and £1,500,000 are taxed at the main rate of corporation tax, subject to marginal relief (see section 4). These profits limits are subject to adjustments for associated companies, already mentioned in examined in the next chapter.

Definition of profits

3. The definition of profits for the small profits rate is the sum of:

   a) taxable total profit, i.e. total profits less allowable deductions and group relief, **plus**

   b) franked investment income, excluding FII from group companies.

Example

Beta Ltd has the following data relating to the year ended 31st March 2013.

Trading profits	£3,500
Chargeable gains	£4,700

Calculate the corporation tax payable for the AP to 31st March 2013.

Solution: Corporation tax computation AP to 31.3.2013

	£
Trading profits	3,500
Chargeable gain	4,700
Total profits/Taxable total profit/Augmented Profits	8,200
Corporation tax payable £8,200 @ 20%:	1,640

Example

AP Ltd has the following income and charges relating to the year ended 31st March 2013.

	£
Trading profits	127,000
Chargeable gain	3,500
Gift Aid donations	1,500
Dividends received	14,400

Calculate the corporation tax payable for the AP to 31st March 2013.

Solution: Corporation tax computation AP to 31.3.13

		£
Trading profits		127,000
Chargeable gain		3,500
Total profits		130,500
Less qualifying charitable donations		1,500
Taxable total profit		129,000
Add franked investment income 14,400 + (10/90 × 14,400)		16,000
Augmented profits		145,000
Corporation tax payable:		
£129,000 @ 20%		25,800

Marginal relief – small profits rate

4. Where the augmented profits exceed the lower relevant amount of £300,000, but fall below the upper relevant amount of £1,500,000, then the position is as follows:

a)   First tax is computed on TTP at the full rate of 24%.

b)   Then Marginal relief is deducted (a relief in terms of tax) using the formula:

$$(U - A) \times \text{N}/\text{A} \times \text{the fraction}$$

U   =   Upper relevant amount i.e. £1,500,000 (for both FY11 and FY12).

A   =   Augmented profits = taxable total profits + non-group FII

N   =   Taxable total profits i.e. all profits chargeable to corporation tax.

c)   The fraction is determined with respect to financial years, and the recent years are as follows:

Financial years	Marginal relief fraction
FY2010 to 31.3.2011	7/400
FY2011 to 31.3.2012	3/200
FY2012 to 31.3.2013	1/100

The fraction is set so as to achieve a smoothly increasing average rate of CT on profits between the defined lower and upper relevant amounts.

d)   Thus in respect of accounting periods for the financial year to the 31st March 2013 the formula is:

$$(1{,}500{,}000 - A) \times \frac{\text{N}}{\text{A}} \times \frac{1}{100}$$

Example – marginal relief

Z Ltd has the undermentioned data relating to its accounting year ended 31.3.2013.

	£
Trading profits	453,100
Chargeable gains	2,250
Gift Aid donations	5,350
Dividend received	1,800
Dividend paid	24,000

Compute the corporation tax liability.

Solution: Calculation of augmented profits:

	£	
Trading profits	453,100	
Chargeable gain	2,250	
	455,350	
Less qualifying charitable donations	(5,350)	
Taxable total profit	450,000	(N)
Add franked investment income	2,000	
Augmented profits	452,000	(A)

Computation of marginal relief:

$$(1,500,000 - 452,000) \times \frac{450,000}{452,000} \times 1/100 \qquad \underline{10,434}$$

Z Ltd Corporation tax computation AP 31.3.2013

	£
Trading profits	453,100
Chargeable gains	2,250
Total profits	455,350
Less qualifying charitable donations	(5,350)
Taxable total profit	450,000
Corporation tax @ 24% ×450,000	108,000
Less marginal relief (above)	(10,434)
Corporation tax payable	97,566

Notes

i)   From this example it can be seen that the marginal relief is a calculated amount which is deducted from the tax on taxable profits computed at the full rate of 24%.

ii)   As A > £300,000 and < £1,500,000, marginal relief should be claimed.

Marginal rates of corporation tax

5. The marginal rate of corporation tax refers to the rate of corporation tax borne on profits in between £300,000 and £1,500,000, and for the financial year to 31st March 2013 this is 25% (year to 31 March 2012 27.5%).

If the difference between the full and small profits rates reduces then the marginal rate between the defined profit limits goes down too (assuming the profits limits do not alter).

This can be demonstrated as follows:

	£ FY2012	£ FY2011
Tax on £1,500,000	at 24% 360,000	at 26% 390,000
Less tax on (£300,000)	at 20% (60,000)	at 20% (60,000)
Subtracting		
Difference		
= tax on £1,200,000 marginal band	300,000	330,000
	25%	27.5%

Example for FY 2012

B Ltd has taxable total profits of £400,000 for the year ended 31st March 2013. Calculate the corporation tax payable and show the marginal rate of tax.

Solution

	£
Taxable total profits	400,000
Corporation tax @ 24%	96,000
Less marginal relief	
(1,500,000 – 400,000) × 1 / 100	(11,000)
	85,000

Corporation tax liability

Although the statutory formula must be used in submitted CT computations involving marginal relief, when carrying out projected income calculations, or for tax planning purposes, a CT liability at marginal rates on £400,000 of taxable profit can be viewed as equivalent to:

£	£
300,000 @ 20%	60,000
100,000 @ 25% (marginal rate)	25,000
400,000	85,000

The marginal rate of 25% on company profits in the marginal rate band compares with a marginal rate of income tax for 2012/13 of 40% (the higher rate) or 50% (the additional rate) for the proprietor of a successful unincorporated business (plus, usually, 2% Class 4 NIC).

Associated companies

6. A company is treated as an associate of another at a given time, if at that time, or at any time within one year previously, either one of the two has control over the other, or both are under the same control. Control is generally established with a shareholding of more than 50%. Control is also established if the parent company is entitled to acquire:

a) the greater part of the share capital or issued share capital, or voting power of the associate company.

b) such part of the issued share capital as would entitle the parent company to receive the greater part of the income of the associate company if it were distributed amongst the participators, ignoring the rights of loan creditors.

c) such rights as would on a winding up of the company, or in any other circumstance, entitle the parent company to the greater part of the assets of the company, available for distribution among the participators.

If a company has one or more associated companies in the accounting period, then the upper and lower relevant maximum and minimum amounts are divided equally between the company and the number of associates. Thus a company with two associates would have to allocate the relevant amounts threefold:

FY 2012, to 31.3.2013	Lower level	Upper level
	£	£
The company	100,000	500,000
First associate	100,000	500,000
Second associate	100,000	500,000
	300,000	1,500,000

In determining the number of associated companies the following points should be noted.

a) An associated company which has not been active at any time in the accounting period (i.e. a dormant company) is disregarded.

b) A company which is only an associate for part of an accounting period is counted.

c) All active companies are counted separately in the total, even if they were associated companies for different parts of the accounting period.

2. Overseas companies are included in determining the number of associates.

Example

D Ltd, a company resident in the United Kingdom, owns 80% of the equity share capital of S Ltd., 52% of the ordinary share capital of J Ltd. and 25% of the ordinary share capital of N Ltd. The company prepares accounts to the year ended 31 December and provides the following information in respect of its AP of twelve months ended 31 December 2012:

INCOME	£
Trading profits	260,000
Bank interest	140,000
Capital gains	50,000
Rental income	200,000

Requirement: Compute the corporation tax liability for the above accounting period.

Solution

D, S & J are associates for the purposes of tax; N is not.

Divide upper and lower limits by 3:

£300,000 / 3	Lower £100,000
£1,500,000 / 3	Upper £500,000

Calculation of TTP

Trading profits	260,000
Interest income	140,000
Income from property	200,000
Chargeable Gains	50,000
TTP	650,000

The company is taxed at full rate because 'profits' are £650,000 ('profits' = TTP as there are no dividends). The CT liability would need to be apportioned:

FY11: 1.1.2012 to 31.3.2012 3/12 x £650,000 x 26%	42,250
FY12: 1.4.2012 to 31.12.2012 9/12 x £650,000 x 24%	117,000
Total corporation tax liability	159,250

Accounting periods of less than 12 months

7. As already indicated, for corporation tax purposes a company's accounting period cannot exceed 12 months in duration. If the AP is less than 12 months in length then the relevant profits amounts are reduced accordingly.

Thus with an AP of three months' duration ending in the financial year to 31.3.2013 the lower profit level would be £300,000/4 i.e. £75,000, and the upper profit level would be 1,500,000/4 i.e. £375,000.

If the situation arises where a company has an AP of less than 12 months' length, and has an associated company, then the respective profit levels are first divided by the number of companies and then reduced in proportion to the length of the short accounting period.

Student self-testing questions

1. Harold Limited has the following results for the year ended 31 March 2013.

	£
TTP	150,000
Dividend received on 1 September 2012	15,000

Requirement: Calculate CT liability for the year ended 31 March 2013.

Solution

	£
TTP	150,000
FII (£15,000 x 100/90)	16,667
Profits	166,667

Less than £300,000 therefore tax at small profits rate

FY12	£
150,000 x 20%	30,000

2. Hannah Limited has the following results for the year ended 31 March 2013.

TTP	250,000
Dividend received on 1 September 2012	50,000

Requirement: Calculate CT liability for the year ended 31 March 2013.

Solution

	£
TTP	250,000
FII (£50,000 x 100/90)	55,556
Profits	305,556

Therefore marginal relief band

FY11	£
250,000 x 24%	60,000
(1,500,000 - 305,556) x 250,000/305,556 x 1/100	(9,773)
	50,227

3. Freddie Limited makes up accounts to the year ended 30 June. It has no associated companies. For the year ended 30 June 2012 the corporation tax return shows the following:

TTP	1,245,000
Dividend income (received on 1 June 2012)	50,000

Requirement: Calculate the corporation tax liability for the AP ended 30 June 2012

Solution

	£
TTP	1,245,000
FII (£50,000 x 100/90)	55,556
Augmented Profits	1,300,556

The CT needs to be worked out separately for Financial Years, because the main rate of CT (and the marginal fraction) changed on 1 April 2012.

Augmented profits FY2011 = 9/12 x £1,300,556 = £975,417

Augmented profits FY2012 = 3/12 x £1,300,556 = £325,139
Pro-rated lower limit in each financial year:
    FY11 1.7.11-31.3.12 (9 months) - £300,000 x 9/12 = £225,000
    FY12 1.4.12-30.6.12 (3 months) - £300,000 x 3/12 = £75,000
Pro-rated upper limit in each financial year:
    FY11 1.7.11-31.3.12(similarly) £1,500,000 x 9/12 = £1,125,000
    FY12 1.4.12-30.6.12 (similarly) - £1,500,000 x 3/12 = £375,000
Augmented profit is in the marginal band in both years. Therefore marginal relief applies. The value of Freddie's marginal relief would be bigger, and its average CT rate lower, if augmented profits were closer to £300k than £1.5m.

Freddie Ltd Corporation tax liability:	£
FY11:	
Tax at full rate on TTP of (1,245,000 x 9/12) = £933,750 x 26%	242,775
Less marginal relief (1,125,000-975,417) x 933,750/975,417 x 3/200	(2,148)
FY12:	
Tax at full rate on TTP of (1,245,000 x 3/12) = £311,250 x 24%	74,700
Less marginal relief (375,000-311,250) x 311,250/375,000 x 1/100	(529)
Corporation tax liability for the CTAP to 30 June 2012	314,798

Average rate of CT net of marginal relief (314,798/1,245,000)	25.3%
(CT averaged full rate for the same period without any MR	
= (9/12 x 26%) + (3/12 x 24%)	25.5%

4. K plc has the undermentioned data relating to its AP ended 31st March 2013.

	£
Trading profits	327,000
Income from property	13,000
Chargeable gains	45,000
Gift Aid donations paid	10,000
Dividend received 31.12.12	18,000
Dividend paid 31.12.12	24,000

Calculate the corporation tax liability for the AP to 31st March 2013.

Solution: Corporation tax computation AP to 31.3.2013

	£	
Trading profits	327,000	
Income from property	13,000	
Chargeable gains	45,000	
	385,000	
Less qualifying charitable donations	(10,000)	
Taxable total profit	375,000	= N
Corporation tax at full rate	£	
£375,000 @ 24%	90,000	
Less marginal relief	(10,490)	
Corporation tax payable	79,510	

Note: Marginal relief computation.

$$N = 375,000$$

$$A = N + FII = 375,000 + 20,000 = 395,000$$

$$(1,500,000 - 395,000) \times \frac{375,000}{395,000} \times 1/100$$

$$= 1,105,000 \times \frac{375}{395} \times 1/100 = 10,490.$$

Questions without answers

1. James Limited has 2 associated companies and a TTP for the year ended 31 March 2013 of £200,000.

Requirement Calculate the corporation tax liability in respect of the year ended 31 March 2013.

2. D Ltd, which has no associated companies for tax purposes, has the following data relating to its accounting year ended 31st March 2013.

	£
Operating profits	440,000
Interest income (non-trading)	10,000
Income from property	20,000
Chargeable gain	20,000
Debenture interest paid (gross) trading in nature	10,000
Dividend received 31.12.12	4,500
Dividend paid 31.12.12	24,000

Compute the corporation tax liability for the AP to 31st March 2013.

3. The following information has been extracted from the records of Nerston Ltd, a UK resident company with no associated companies, for its trading year to 31st March 2013.

	£
Operating profits	18,000
Income from property	20,000
Debenture interest paid gross: trading purposes	3,200
Chargeable gain	2,400
Dividends paid in the year	30,000

Compute corporation tax payable for the AP to 31st March 2013.

4. N Ltd has owned 60% of the share capital of D Ltd for several years. Both companies are trading companies resident in the UK.

The following information relates to the ten month AP to 31 January 2013 of N Ltd:

	£
Adjusted trading profit (before capital allowances)	177,000
Bank interest receivable – non-trading	5,000
Capital gains	10,000
Rental income	5,000

The balances brought forward at 1 April 2012 for capital allowances purposes were as follows:

General pool	Car pool all 145g/km	Post-31.3.09 Renault car, CO_2 165g/km
£42,887	£16,000	£18,000

During the above period machinery was sold for £10,000 (original cost £11,000) and new desks were bought for £6,000 on 1st May 2012. The Renault car with CO_2 emissions of 165g/km was traded in for £10,000 against the cost of a new Skoda car with CO_2 emissions of 170g/km costing £12,000 on 1st June 2012.

Requirement

(a) **Compute the maximum capital allowances which N Ltd may claim for the ten month AP to 31 January 2013.**

(b) **Compute N Ltd's corporation tax liability for the ten month accounting period.**

5. DLT Ltd is a resident in the UK. It has one associated company. The board decided to alter the company's accounting date and prepared accounts for the 14 months from 1 April 2012 to 31 May 2013. The following relates to this period.

INCOME	£	£
Trading profit (before capital allowances)		420,000
Rents receivable		
- Year to 31 March 2013	52,000	
- 1 April to 31 May 2013	25,000	
		77,000
Bank interest receivable, all received July 2012*		48,000
Capital gains		
- October 2012	120,000	
- May 2013	150,000	
		270,000

The written down balances for capital allowances purposes brought forward at 1 April 2012 were:

	£
General pool	177,780
Citroen car CO_2 180g/km	22,500

Capital transactions during the above period were as follows:

Purchases:		
10/10/12	Lorry	24,000
05/01/13	Energy saving machinery	12,033
Disposals		
02/01/13	Citroen car sold for	11,000

*The bank interest wholly relates to the year ended 31/12/12.

Requirement: Compute the corporation tax liability payable in respect of the above accounting profits.

6. Upbeat Ukuleles Limited is a United Kingdom resident company, which has been manufacturing musical instruments for many years. It has no associated companies. The company has previously made up accounts to 30 June but has now changed its accounting date to 30 September.

The company's results for the 15 month period to 30 September 2013 are:

	£
Trading profits (as adjusted for taxation before capital allowances)	1,320,000
Debenture interest receivable (notes 3)	20,000
Bank interest receivable (note 4)	6,000
Chargeable gain (notes 5 and 6)	10,000
Gift aid payment (note 7)	5,000
Dividends received from UK companies (note 8)	30,000

Notes

1. Capital allowances

   On 1 July 2012 the tax written-down value of the plant and machinery in the capital allowances pool was £100,000. There were no additions or sales in the period of account to 30 September 2013.

2. On 1 July 2012 the company had trading losses brought forward of £800,000.

3. The debenture was acquired in July 2013.

4. Bank interest receivable (non-trading relationship)

	£
Accrued interest brought forward as a debtor, 1 July 2012	(1,000)
Received 30.11.12	3,000
Received 30.5.13	2,000
Accrued to 30.9.13 (carried forward as a debtor)	2,000
Interest per income statement	6,000

5. Chargeable gain. The chargeable gain of £10,000 is in respect of shares disposed of on 31 December 2012.

6. On 1 July 2012 the company had capital losses brought forward of £12,500.

7. Gift Aid Payment. £5,000 was paid to a charity on 31 December 2012.

8. Dividends received

	£
25.4.13	18,000
29.9.13	12,000
	30,000

Requirement: Calculate the corporation tax liabilities for the 15 month period ended 30 September 2013. **(22 marks)**

Note. All apportionments may be made to the nearest month. (ACCA updated)

24 Groups and consortia

Introduction

1. This chapter considers extra corporation tax rules that apply where a company is a member of a group or consortium.

Topics to be considered

2. a) Group relief
(75% subsidiaries and consortia)

The set-off of trading losses against profits within a group, known as group relief.

b) Inter-company transfer of assets
(75% subsidiaries)

The transfer of assets between group companies without any chargeable gain or loss arising.

c) Company reconstructions

Without change of ownership.

d) Change in ownership

Disallowance of trading losses.

Group relief (groups and consortia) Section 130 CTA 2010

3. Group relief is a very flexible loss relief option within groups of companies. One company in a qualifying group of companies may surrender any specified amount(s) of its trading losses, excess charitable donations, non-trade loan deficits, or surplus management expenses, and other companies in the same group may claim the amounts to reduce their own taxable profits for UK CT. The provisions on group relief are now found in the CTA 2010, Sections 130 onwards.

Meaning of group – world wide

4. Two companies are members of the same group relief group if the following four conditions all prevail.

a) One is the 75% subsidiary of the other, or both are 75% subsidiaries of a third company. A 75% subsidiary is defined under Section 838 TA 1988 in terms of the direct or indirect ownership of not less than 75% of the ordinary share capital, ordinary shares meaning all shares other than fixed rate preference shares. From the FY 2009 under the Finance Act 2009 an amendment to the 75% rule was introduced to remove the reference to fixed rate preference shares. This is to ensure that corporations issuing new preference shares to external investors do not lose the right to group relief. The term 'fixed rate preference shares' is replaced with 'relevant preference shares'.

b) The parent company is beneficially entitled to not less than 75% of the profits available for distribution to equity holders of the subsidiary company. An equity holder is any person who holds ordinary shares or is a loan creditor in respect of a loan which is not a commercial loan. Loan creditor has the same meaning as that used in connection with close companies except that the proviso in favour of bank normal borrowings is not excluded and therefore is within the definition for the purposes of these conditions. A normal commercial loan is one which carries a reasonable rate of interest, with no rights to conversion.

c) The parent company would be entitled beneficially to not less than 75% of any assets of the subsidiary company available to its equity shareholders on a winding up.

d) The meaning of 'group' for group relief includes non UK subsidiaries, and UK branches of overseas companies. This means that control for group relief can be traced through non-UK intermediate companies.

However in general there is no point in seeking to include non UK companies in a group relief claiming relationship if they are not within the charge to UK corporation tax.

As regards overseas companies surrendering losses to the UK, following the European Court of Justice Judgement in the Marks and Spencer case a small extension to the group relief rules was made from FY 2006. Relief may be claimed for losses from subsidiaries within the European Economic Area (EEA) or having a permanent establishment within the EEA (including indirectly held subsidiaries) if the tax loss cannot ever be relieved in the country of the loss. The loss surrender must be computed in line with UK tax rules. In practice few companies with loss-making overseas subsidiaries will satisfy these tight conditions (in the M&S case the loss-making Italian and French subsidiaries had actually closed and this made it impossible for them to relieve their losses by local carry-forward against profits).

Example of applying the 75% control rule to see if a GR relationship exists

B Ltd owns 75% of the ordinary share capital of W Ltd, which in turn owns 75% of the ordinary share capital of Z Ltd.

Since B Ltd would only be entitled to 56.25% of the profits available for distribution by Z Ltd the three companies do not constitute a group for the purposes of group relief. B Ltd and W Ltd however would constitute a group, as would W Ltd and Z Ltd. So B cannot surrender GR losses to Z and Z cannot surrender GR losses to B. But W can surrender or claim losses from either of the other two.

Example

T Ltd is the UK parent of two 100% subsidiaries, A Inc and B Inc, both being USA resident companies. B Inc owns 75% each of two UK companies, D Ltd and E Ltd.

T Ltd and its USA subsidiaries, and the sub-subsidiaries D and E, all constitute a group relief group for tax purposes. Therefore GR losses could be surrendered from T Ltd, D Ltd and E Ltd to either of the other two UK resident companies. As A Inc and B Inc are outside the European Economic Area they cannot partake in GR surrenders, even under the limited scope introduced after the M & S case. However they are members of the group for control purposes.

Meaning of consortia – world wide

5. A company is owned by a consortium if 75% or more of its ordinary share capital is beneficially owned by companies, none of which:

a)   beneficially owns less than 5% of the ordinary share capital,

b)   would be entitled to less than 5% of any profits available for distribution to equity holders,

c)   would be entitled to less than 5% of any assets available to equity holders on the wind up.

6. Group relief is also available to a consortium of companies in the following circumstances:

a)   Where the company surrendering the loss is a trading or holding company owned by a consortium (not being a 75% subsidiary of any company) and the claimant company is a member of the consortium. A loss may also be surrendered from a member of the consortium to the trading or holding company.

b)   Where a trading company is the 90% subsidiary of a holding company, which itself is owned by a consortium.

Example

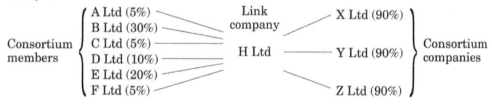

A loss in X, Y or Z could be transferred to the consortium members in proportion to their interests. In addition a loss by any of the consortium members could be claimed by X, Y or Z, and in this case the amount would be restricted to the profits of each claimant proportionately. However, see Section 12 below.

What may be surrendered as group relief

7. The following may be given by a surrendering company as group relief:

a)   trading losses computed as for set off in accordance with Section 37 i.e. excluding any losses brought forward, but after claims for capital allowances.

b)   any excess of capital allowances normally given against income of a special class, such as agricultural buildings allowances.

c)   any charitable donations not relieved against total profits

d)   any excess of management expenses of an investment company, other than a close investment holding company.

e)   a net loss arising from a loan relationship.

No amounts arising from earlier or succeeding accounting periods can be surrendered.

The surrendering company does not have to make any claim for loss relief, e.g. under Section 37, before surrendering losses to GR claimants, although this is frequently done in practice.

The claimant

8. In the CTAP of the claimant company, the surrendered loss may be set against the claimant's total profits including chargeable gains determined as follows:

a)   After taking into consideration any relief for losses from trading brought forward from previous years under Section 45. These would be deducted in arriving at the normal trading profits.

b)   After taking into consideration any loss relief under Section 37 for the current accounting period, whether claimed or not.

c)   Before any loss relief under Section 37 in respect of a loss brought back from a subsequent accounting period.

d)   After deducting qualifying charitable donations .

e)   Group relief is only available to companies resident in the UK or trading here through a branch.

Relief is to be set against the current profits of the claimant, and it cannot be either carried forward or backward to other accounting periods.

General points

9. a) Group relief is limited to the smaller of the surrendering company's losses relief, or the claimant company's profits available for group relief. Where the surrendering company's losses are greater than the claimant's available profits then the excess cannot be carried forward or backward as group relief. This does not prevent any other form of loss relief being obtained by the surrendering company, e.g. carry forward under Section 45.

b)   More than one company in the group may make a claim relating to the same surrendering company.

c)   If any payment takes place between the claimant and the surrendering company, and such a payment is not necessary to support a claim, then this transaction is:

i)   ignored for all corporation tax purposes as regards both payer and recipient

ii)   not treated as a distribution.

Example

H Ltd has a wholly owned subsidiary company M Ltd and the results of both companies for their current CTAP of the same 12 months are given below:

	H Ltd £	M Ltd £
Trading profits	(75,000)	70,000
Less loss b/f under Section 45	–	30,000
	(75,000)	40,000
Interest income	15,000	–
Chargeable gain	10,000	5,000
Gift Aid donations	–	25,000

H Ltd decides to make a claim for loss relief under Section 37 and to surrender as much as possible of the balance of its loss to M Ltd.

Show the effects of the claims on H Ltd and M Ltd.

Solution   **H Ltd**

	£
Interest income	15,000
Chargeable gain	10,000
	25,000
Less Section 37 claim	(25,000)
Taxable total profit	=
Utilization of losses	
Available trade loss	75,000
Less Section 37	(25,000)
Available for group relief	50,000
Less surrendered to M Ltd under Section 130	(20,000)
Carried forward under Section 45	30,000

M Ltd

	£
Trading profits	40,000
Chargeable gain	5,000
	45,000
Less qualifying charitable donations	25,000
Profits before group relief	20,000
Group relief claimed under Section 130	(20,000)
Taxable profits after group relief	0

Smaller amount taken for group relief

Notes

i)   In this example the group relief is limited to the claimant's profits of £20,000, as these are the lower amount.

ii)   Group relief is deducted after qualifying charitable donations by the claimant.

Overlapping periods

10. Where the accounting periods of the surrendering company and the claimant company do not coincide, but they have been members of the same group throughout their respective accounting periods, then the group relief is in effect restricted to the proportion of the loss/profit of the overlapping period. This may, in fact, cover two accounting periods of either company.

Example

X Ltd has a 75% subsidiary, Y Ltd, and the results of both companies for the last two accounting periods are as follows:

X Ltd

AP to 31.3.2012 Trading profit		10,000
AP to 31.3.2013 Trading profit/(loss)		(16,000)

Y Ltd

AP to 31.12.2012 taxable profits		6,000
AP to 31.12.2013 taxable profits		24,000

Compute the group relief available.

Solution

In this example the period of the loss by X Ltd covers two accounting periods of Y Ltd and it will be necessary to determine the lower of the profit or loss in each corresponding period.

Group relief available

	£	£
Overlapping period 1.4.2012 to 31.12.2012		
X Ltd (3/4 × 16,000)	(12,000)	
Y Ltd (3/4 × 6,000)	4,500	
Restricted to the lower amount		4,500
Overlapping period 1.1.2013 to 31.3.2013	£	£
X Ltd (¼ × 16,000)	(4,000)	
Y Ltd (¼ × 24,000)	6,000	
Restricted to the lower amount		4,000
Total		8,500

a) An overlapping period is the period throughout which both the claimant and the surrendering companies meet the qualifying conditions for group relief (as to membership of the group or consortium) and which is a common period within the corporation tax accounting periods of both companies.

b) The maximum loss to be surrendered is the smaller of the unused part of the total available or the unrelieved part of the total profit of the claimant company in the overlapping period.

c) The unused part of the loss is the part remaining after prior surrenders of loss. This assumes that the total loss available for the overlapping period is computed and successive surrenders of loss are deducted from that total until the whole of the loss for the overlapping period is exhausted.

d) The unrelieved part of the total profit assumes an apportionment of the total profit for the entire CTAP between the amount for the overlapping period and the balance. The profit for the overlapping period is then taken and successive group relief claims are deducted from it until, cumulatively, the profit is exhausted.

Companies joining or leaving a group

11. Group relief is generally only available if the claimant and surrendering companies are members of the same group (or fulfil the conditions relating to a consortium) throughout the accounting periods of both companies. However, when a company either joins or leaves a group or consortium, then some relief is available and a new accounting period, for group relief purposes only, is deemed to end or commence on the occurrence of that event.

Normally the profits/losses are apportioned on a time basis. However, if it appears that such an apportionment would produce an unreasonable result, then a more reasonable basis must be used.

Example

D Ltd, a trading company, acquires a 100% interest in W Ltd on the 30th June 2012. Both companies have the same year end and the results for the year to 31st December 2012 are as follows:

	D Ltd £	W Ltd £
Trading profit	12,000	(40,000)
Interest income	3,000	–
Chargeable gain	15,000	–
Chargeable loss	–	(10,000)

Compute the amount of group relief available.

Solution

On the acquisition of W Ltd who then with D Ltd forms a group, there is deemed to be a commencement of an accounting period for group relief purposes.

	£
Loss to be surrendered by W Ltd	
Loss for 12 months to 31.12.2012	40,000
Proportion for deemed accounting period from	
1.7.2012 to 31.12.2012 $6/12 \times 40,000$	20,000

Loss to be claimed by D Ltd

Trading profit	12,000
Interest income	3,000
Chargeable gain	15,000
	30,000

Proportion from 1.7.2012 $^6/12 \times 30,000 =$ 15,000

Since this is smaller than the amount of the loss of the surrendering company, this is the maximum available for group relief.

The computations for the year to 31st December 2012 are:

£

D Ltd

Taxable profits as above	30,000
Less group relief	(15,000)
Taxable total profit after group relief	15,000

W Ltd

Trading loss	40,000
Less surrendered	(15,000)
Unused loss	25,000

Notes

i)   The balance of the loss of W Ltd is not available for future group relief, but it can be used by W Ltd under Section 37 or 45.

ii) The capital loss of W Ltd may not be set against the chargeable gain of any other company.

Similar provisions apply when a company leaves a group, and the profits and losses up to the date of the departure must be apportioned to determine the amount of any group relief available.

Consortium relief

12. Where there is a consortium of companies as defined in section 6 above, the following relief may be available:

   a)   surrender to consortium members

   b)   surrender by the consortium members

   c)   a mixture of group/consortium relief

   d)   relief through a link company.

Relief is only available to a UK member of a consortium which can include overseas members.

Surrender to a consortium member

13. K Ltd is owned by four companies A Ltd (20%), B Ltd (30%), C Ltd (10%) and D Ltd (40%).

If K Ltd incurs a trading loss it may be surrendered to the consortium members A, B, C, D in proportion to their shareholding in K Ltd. Thus if K Ltd makes a loss of £20,000, the amount that can be surrendered to the consortium members is:

		£
A Ltd	20% × 20,000	4,000
B Ltd	30% × 20,000	6,000
C Ltd	10% × 20,000	2,000
D Ltd	40% × 20,000	8,000
		20,000

The amount of the loss that can be surrendered by K Ltd is reduced to the extent that it has profits of the same accounting period available to relieve the loss under Section 37. It should be noted that K Ltd does not have to make the claim under Section 37 but the consortium relief is restricted as though this had taken place whereas with group relief this restriction does not apply.

Surrender by the consortium members

14. Where a consortium member makes a loss then this can be surrendered to the consortium company. However, in this case the amount that can be surrendered is limited to the percentage of the profits of the consortium company.

Example

If C Ltd makes a loss then the amount that can be surrendered to T Ltd is restricted to 35% of the profit of T Ltd.

For example, if C Ltd makes a loss of £25,000 and T Ltd has profits of £50,000 then the amount of the loss that can be surrendered is limited to 35% x £50,000 i.e. £17,500.

In this case it is not necessary for C Ltd to consider any other profits available for set-off under Section 37.

A mixture of group/consortium relief

15. The position is as follows.

a) Where a consortium owned company is also a member of a group of companies then that company is known as a 'group/consortium company'.

b) If a group/consortium company incurs a loss then the amount that can be surrendered pro rata to the consortium members must first be reduced by:

   i) any potential claim under Section 37 (set-off against other profits of the same period)

   ii) any potential group relief claims that could be made under Section 130.

   The potential loss claims do not have to be made, but their availability restricts the loss to be surrendered by the group/consortium company.

c) Where the group/consortium company has taxable profits and wishes to claim loss relief from any of its consortium members, then the available profits must first be reduced by any potential group loss claims within the group/consortium company's own group.

d) If the accounting periods of the members of the group/consortium are not co-terminous then an overlapping period arises and the relief claimed cannot be more than the consortium members' proportionate share in the equity of the consortium subsidiary.

Example

X Ltd (25%) Y Ltd (45%) Z Ltd (30%)

A Ltd ⟶ (Group/consortium company)

B Ltd (75%) C Ltd (75%)

A, B and C constitute a group for group relief purposes
A is called the group/consortium company
A is a consortium company owned by X Ltd, Y Ltd and Z Ltd.

The following results relate to the year ended 31.12.2012.

			£
A Ltd	Trading loss		80,000
	Chargeable gain		12,000
B Ltd	Trading profits		25,000
C Ltd	Trading loss		10,000
	Chargeable gains		3,000

Compute the amounts that could be surrendered to X Ltd.

Solution

			£	£
a)	A Ltd trading loss			80,000
	Less potential reliefs:			
	Section 37 A Ltd		12,000	
	Section 130 B Ltd		25,000	
	Section 130 C Ltd		3,000	(40,000)
				40,000
	25% × 40,000 =			10,000
b)	A Ltd trading loss			80,000
	Less potential reliefs:			
	Section 37 A Ltd		12,000	
	Section 130 B Ltd		18,000	(30,000)
				50,000
	25% × 50,000 =			12,500

Notes

i)   In (a) the intra-group relief claimable by B & C and the possible claim under Section 37 by C has not been exercised.

ii)   In (b) the amount of potential group relief is after taking:

| C Ltd Section 37 | £10,000 – £3,000 | = | £7,000 loss |
| B Ltd group relief with C Ltd | £25,000 – £7,000 | = | £18,000 profit. |

Relief through a link company

16.   A link company is defined as a company which is a member both of a consortium and of a group.

Example

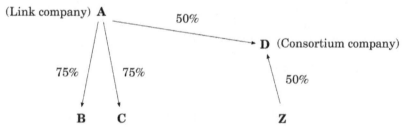

A, B and C constitute a group for group relief purposes.

A and Z jointly own the consortium company D.

A is a member of a group and a consortium.

Example

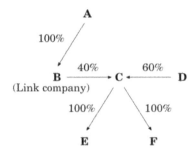

A and B constitute a group. C, E and F constitute a group. C is owned by a consortium of two members B and D. C is also a group consortium company.

In respect of the year ending 31st December 2012 the companies have the following results:

	£	
A Ltd	100,000	
B Ltd	(30,000)	loss
C Ltd	(20,000)	loss
D Ltd	Nil	
E Ltd	12,000	
F Ltd	(4,000)	loss

Calculate the possible claims for group relief and consortium relief.

Solution: CTAP to 31st December 2012

E Ltd Profits before relief			12,000
Less Group relief surrendered by F		4,000	
do.	C	8,000	(12,000)
Assessment			–

A Ltd	Profits before relief		100,000
	Less Group relief surrendered by B	30,000	
	Consortium relief C:		
	40% × (20,000 – 8,000)	4,800	(34,800)
	Profits chargeable to corporation tax		65,200

Notes

The consortium relief available to A Ltd from C Ltd is the lower of:

A Ltd profits after group relief i.e.	100,000 – 30,000	=	70,000
B Ltd share of C Ltd loss i.e.	40% (20,000 – 8,000)	=	4,800

Group payments of interest etc. – intercompany transactions

17.   Payments of interest, royalty payments and annual payments and annuities, are made without the deduction of income tax where the companies concerned are within charge to UK corporation tax, or in the case of interest and royalty payments, where the recipient is an EU company. Unlike the treatment of intra-group payments for consolidated accounting purposes, all companies in a group are charged o separate CT on an entity basis.

Group Chargeable Gains rules including transfer of assets between group companies

18.

a)   Until recently there was no kind of 'group relief' for chargeable gains and capital losses between different members of a group of companies. This situation has changed recently. See Part IV for how to compute companies' chargeable gains.

b)   Where one member of a CGT group makes a chargeable asset disposal, the company actually disposing of the asset and another company in the group can elect that the asset disposal outside the group be treated as being made by the other company. The election must be made within two years after the end of the accounting period in which the actual disposal is made. This can achieve the offset of chargeable gains against brought forward capital losses in a different company. However there are anti avoidance rules relating to 'pre entry' losses, i.e. losses realised or accruing before a company joined the CGT group, which cannot be used in this way. The further rules in this field are too complex for a book at introductory level.

c)   The most important point to note on CGT and groups is that as a general rule, when a company disposes of a chargeable asset outside the CGT group, it makes a chargeable gain or loss on normal principles. However, if a chargeable asset disposal is made by one member of a CGT group to another group company, that transaction automatically takes place for tax purposes at **no gain and no loss**. This applies regardless of actual payment made for the asset by the acquirer.

d)   A no gain no loss (NGNL) disposal is achieved by deeming the consideration for the disposal of the asset to be an amount at which neither a gain nor a loss accrues to the company disposing of the asset. Normally this means that the amount paid between the companies is deemed for CGT to be the original cost, plus enhancement expenditure, plus all indexation allowance to date.

When the asset is ultimately disposed of outside the group, the liability to corporation tax on any gain would arise in the company that actually sold the asset (or another group company, if the election at (b) above is made). The allowable cost would be the deemed cost at which the asset was acquired intra-group.

Companies defined as being in the same 'CGT group '

19. a) A Capital Gains Tax group comprises a principal company and all of its 75% subsidiaries. Unlike with section 130 group losses relief, a company cannot be a member of more than one 'CGT group' at the same time.

b) A 75% subsidiary means a company whose ordinary share capital is owned by another company either directly or indirectly to the extent of at least 75%. Again ordinary share capital comprises all shares other than relevant preference shares.

c) A company which is itself a 75% subsidiary of another company cannot be the principal company of a CGT group. It is the 75% parent company which is the principal company. This may have an impact on which other companies further down a group are counted in the same CGT group : a sub-subsidiary which is not in a ≥50% indirect relationship with the principal company (one particular company, as defined), as well as a ≥ 75% relationship with its own holding company, is excluded from the CGT group.

d) Members of a consortium are not eligible for treatment as a CGT group, nor are close investment holding companies, unless the transfer is between two close investment holding companies.

Assets available for group treatment

20. The disposal of any chargeable asset between group companies should attract no gain or loss treatment, but there are some exceptions given in the Act which are as follows.

a) Where the disposal is of redeemable preference shares in a company (these are normally not chargeable assets in the hands of a company anyway, if accounted for as debt instruments).

b) Where the disposal is of a debt due from a member of a group (now superseded by the loan relationships rules under which debts are not chargeable assets for companies).

c) Where the disposal arises from a capital distribution on the liquidation of a company.

d) Where the company is a dual resident member of a group of companies and any gain made by that company on the disposal would be exempt from tax under a double tax treaty.

If the transfer is of an asset which the recipient company appropriates to its inventory (trading stock), then that company is deemed to have received a capital asset and immediately transferred that asset to its inventory (trading stock). There would thus be no capital gain or loss arising on the inter-company transfer, as it would fall within the provisions noted above.

Where the asset transferred to a group company was inventory (trading stock) of the transferor company, then the latter is treated as having appropriated the asset as a capital asset immediately prior to the disposal. The value placed on the asset for trading purposes under Section 161 TCGA 1992 would be the transfer value giving rise to a 'no gain or loss' situation.

Other points

21. a) When an asset is disposed of by a group company to a company outside the group, then any capital allowances granted to any member of the group relating to the asset are taken into consideration in computing any gain or loss.

b) If a company to which an asset has been transferred at no gain and no loss ceases to be a member of a group within six years of the date of the transfer the position is as follows:

    i) At the date of the acquisition of the asset by the company leaving the group, or if later the beginning of the accounting period when the company left the group, it is deemed to have sold and reacquired the asset at its market value at the date when it acquired the asset from the other group member.

    ii) There will therefore, be a chargeable gain or loss on the difference between the market value at the time of the intra-group asset transfer, and the original cost to the group of the asset.

This provision does not apply if a company ceases membership of a group by being wound up.

c) The provisions of Section 152 TCGA 1992 (rollover relief) are extended to CGT groups which enables all trades carried on by the group to be treated as one for the purposes of the sale of assets 'used in the trade' and purchase of replacement assets 'used in the trade'.

For further details see Chapter 33.

Student self-testing questions

1. The results of A Ltd and its wholly owned subsidiary B Ltd for the three years ended 31st March 2013 are as follows:

		31.3.2011	31.3.2012	31.3.2013
		£	£	£
A Ltd	Trading profit/(loss)	1,200	(7,500)	4,800
	Income from property	500	500	500
B Ltd	Trading profit	2,500	3,500	5,000

A Ltd makes a claim for loss relief under Section 37 and then claims group relief under Section 130.

Show the computations of taxable total profit.

Solution:

	31.3.2011	31.3.2012	31.3.2013
A Ltd	£	£	£
Trading profit	1,200	–	4,800
Less Section 45	–	–	1,800
	1,200	–	3,000
Income from property	500	500	500
	1,700	500	3,500
Less Section 37	(1,700)	(500)	–
Taxable total profit	–	–	3,500
B Ltd			
Trading profit	2,500	3,500	5,000
Less group relief Section 130	–	(3,500)	–
Taxable total profit	2,500	–	5,000

Loss memorandum		£	£
Loss year to 31st March 2012			7,500
Section 37	31.3.2012	500	
Section 37	31.3.2011	1,700	
Section 37	31.3.2013	1,800	
Section 130	31.3.2012	3,500	
(group relief surrendered to B Ltd)			(7,500)

Note. The maximum amount has been surrendered to B Ltd.

2. Arch Ltd owns 100% of the share capital of Bow Ltd and Can Ltd. The results of each company for the year ended 31 March 2013 are as follows:

	Arch Ltd	Bow Ltd	Can Ltd
	£	£	£
Tax adjusted trading profit/(loss)	(125,000)	650,000	130,000

Required

a) **Explain the group relationship that must exist in order that group relief can be claimed.** (3 marks)

b) **Explain how group relief should be allocated between the respective claimant companies in order to maximise the potential benefit obtained from the relief.** (4 marks)

c) Assuming that reliefs are claimed in the most favourable manner, calculate the corporation tax liabilities of Arch Ltd, Bow Ltd and Can Ltd for the year ended 31 March 2013. **(8 marks)**

(ACCA updated)

Solution

(a) (1) One company must be a 75% subsidiary of the other, or both companies must be 75% subsidiaries of a third company

(2) The holding company must have an effective interest of at least 75% of the subsidiary's share capital, excluding relevant preference shares.

(3) The holding company must have the right to receive at least 75% of the subsidiary's distributable profits and net assets on a winding up.

(b) (1) Group relief should be allocated to the company(s) with the highest marginal rate of tax first. The upper and lower limits for marginal relief for this group are £1,500,000 / 3 = £500,000 and £300,000 / 3 = £100,000. Profits of between £500,000 and £100,000 are taxed at the marginal rate of 25%. Next those companies that are taxed at the 24% rate should be given relief.

(c)	£	£	£
	Arch Ltd	Bow Ltd	Can Ltd
Trading profit	-	650,000	130,000
Less group relief	-	(95,000)	(30,000)
TTP	-	555,000	100,000
Tax @ 20%			20,000
Tax @ 24%		133,200	

Questions without answers

1. Animal Ltd is the holding company for a group of companies. The results of each group company for the year ended 31 March 2013 are as follows:

	Tax adjusted trading profit/(loss)	Income from property	Franked Investment Income
	£	£	£
Animal Ltd	450,000	5,000	20,000
Bat Ltd	65,000	15,000	–
Cat Ltd	85,000	–	–
Dog Ltd	100,000	–	–
Elk Ltd	–	–	–
Fox Ltd	60,000	–	5,000
Gnu Ltd	(200,000)	–	–

Animal Ltd owned 100% of each subsidiary company's ordinary share capital throughout the year ended 31 March 2013 with the following exceptions:

(1)   Animal Ltd only owned 90% of Bat Ltd's ordinary share capital.

(2)   Animal Ltd's shareholding in Cat Ltd was disposed of on 31 December 2012.

       The trading profit of £85,000 is for the year ended 31 March 2013.

(3)   Animal Ltd's shareholding in Dog Ltd was acquired on 1 January 2013. The trading profit of £100,000 is for the year ended 31 March 2013.

(4)   Elk Ltd was a dormant company throughout the year ended 31 March 2013.

Required:

(a)   Explain the group relationship that must exist in order that group relief can be claimed.   (3 marks)

(b)   Explain why there are six associated companies in the Animal Ltd group of companies. Your answer should identify the six associated companies.   (3 marks)

(c)   Assuming that relief is claimed for Gnu Ltd's trading loss of £200,000 in the most favourable manner, calculate the taxable total profits of Animal Ltd, Bat Ltd, Cat Ltd, Dog Ltd and Fox Ltd for the year ended 31 March 2013.   (9 marks)

(15 marks)

(ACCA updated)

Student note: Some of these questions contain brief elements of capital gains tax and this topic is covered in Chapters 26-33.

25 International aspects

Introduction

1. This chapter deals, at an awareness level only, with aspects of corporation tax arising from overseas or international operations. These are described under the following main headings:

> Income from foreign sources
>
> Relief for withholding taxes (WHT) suffered on income or gains
>
> Double tax relief – general OECD principles
>
> Foreign dividends received after 1 July 2009 / 23 November 2008
>
> Foreign tax credit relief and other loss reliefs
>
> Controlled foreign companies (rules amended by Finance Act 2012).
>
> Transfer pricing – awareness issues.
>
> Differences between having a Foreign Branch and a Foreign Subsidiary
>
> 'Worldwide debt cap' - restriction on UK allowable interest costs from January 2010

Income from foreign sources

2. In principle, income from foreign sources is liable to CT in the same way as all other income of a UK resident company. Foreign interest receivable is within the loan relationship arrangements, and any profit on overseas loans is taxed as loan relationship surplus. Trading income from foreign branches (permanent establishments) is under the CTA2009 included in normal trade profits and not reported as a separate source of income (this was a minor legislative change). However where double taxation credit relief is being claimed it is still necessary to identify accurately the amount of foreign-taxed branch income. Income from overseas rentals is treated in the same way as UK property income. Chargeable gains realised on overseas assets are computed in the same way as other gains and are liable to UK corporation tax if the owner is a UK resident company. All of these types of foreign profits may be referred to in a claim for double tax relief against the UK corporation tax liability (see section).

Income from overseas sources that passes in cash payment may be subject to deduction of local withholding taxes (WHT) charged on certain payments leaving a tax jurisdiction (e.g. rents, royalties, licence fees or dividends). For all such receipts except dividends, the gross income is liable to UK corporation tax and so it must be grossed up for the foreign withholding tax suffered. Full relief is available for this withholding tax against UK CT, provided it has not been charged at a higher effective rate than the UK CT liability due on the same income. However, foreign dividends are not grossed up for actual foreign withholding taxes deducted, because they are not taxable income in the hands of a UK company. Instead the net dividend is grossed up by the UK notional tax credit for all dividends, of one-ninth (or multiplied by 100/90). See section 4 below.

Example

K Ltd has the following data relating to the 12 months CTAP to the 31st March 2013.

	£
Trading profits	1,280,000
Interest income receivable and received	
(net foreign interest after 15% withholding tax)	85,000
Chargeable gains	250,000

Calculate the UK CT payable for the AP to 31st March 2013, assuming double tax relief is claimed.

Solution

K Ltd corporation tax computation AP 31.3.2013

	£
Trading profits	1,280,000
Interest income (gross) $\frac{85,000}{85} \times \frac{100}{1}$	100,000
Chargeable gains	250,000
Total profits/taxable total profit	1,630,000

Corporation tax	£
1,630,000 @ 24%	391,200
Less double tax relief – withholding tax suffered	(15,000)
Corporation tax liability	376,200

Note

The double tax relief is the lower of the following:

UK CT @ 24% on foreign income £100,000	24,000
Foreign tax	15,000

Double tax relief – general OECD principles

3. Double Taxation Agreements ('Tax Treaties') provide negotiated means of determining the taxing rights of any two competing Governments (Taxing States), where the domestic tax rules of both States charge tax on the same income or gains.

The UK has an extensive network of Double Tax Treaties at Government level. These have been drafted so as to follow the OECD (Organisation for Economic Cooperation and Development) guidelines on Double Tax Treaties.

If there is no Double Tax Treaty with the relevant State, unilateral double taxation credit relief, which works on a similar basis to the commonest type of

Tax Treaty credit relief, is given by the UK Taxes Acts for foreign tax shown to have been suffered on income or gains which are also liable to tax in the UK.

The OECD principles state that the profits of a permanent establishment in another Taxing State should be primarily taxable in that other Taxing State. A permanent establishment covers a branch operation if there is the capacity for employees to conclude contracts there which bind the UK company. It also covers an appointed general agent (i.e. not an employee of the UK company) who has authority to conclude binding contracts in the foreign territory on behalf of the UK company.

Another OECD principle of double tax relief is that, in giving relief in the second Taxing State for tax suffered in the first, the second State may limit that relief to the amount of tax that would be paid on the same income in the second country. This principle is illustrated by the DTR calculations in the example at section 2 above. If the foreign withholding tax had been 30% (£30,000), then only £24,000 of it would have been available for offset against the UK tax liability. The rest of the foreign tax would still be paid, but would be shown in the company's accounts as additional tax on the foreign activity.

Foreign dividends received after 1 July 2009/ 23 November 2008

4. The Finance Act 2009 introduced a very important change to the tax treatment of dividends received by a UK company from companies resident outside the UK.

Formerly non-UK dividends were treated as taxable overseas investment income. From 1 July 2009 (23 November 2008 for companies in the European Economic Area) such dividends are treated the same way as UK dividends. Thus they are not taxable income in the hands of the UK recipient company. However, they now count as FII (unless paid by subsidiaries, and thus 'Group FII'), for the purposes of determining the augmented profits of the UK company. For this purpose the FII value is found by adding a notional 1/9 tax credit to the net dividend received.

Before those dates, FII treatment only applied to dividends from UK resident companies, and foreign dividends counted as taxable investment income that was included in the TTP figure in the UK.

To avoid disadvantaging existing international corporate structures, the treatment of specified foreign dividends as tax-exempt FII from July 2009 may be waived by a UK company, if the old treatment (as taxable foreign investment income, with double tax relief) is more beneficial to it under a Tax Treaty with relevant territory. The implications of an elective waiver of the foreign dividend exemption are not considered further here.

Foreign tax credit relief and other loss reliefs

5. Where a UK company has foreign income, then in order to preserve the maximum amount of DT relief, loss relief claims should be considered carefully.

Example

W Ltd and its wholly owned UK subsidiary X Ltd have the following results for the year ended 31st March 2013.

	W Ltd £	X Ltd £
Trading profits	(30,000)	80,000
Overseas Royalties	16,000	
(gross before withholding tax of 15%)		
Chargeable gains	2,000	1,000

Calculate the corporation tax payable in the following situations:

a) W Ltd claims loss relief under Section 37 and surrenders the maximum loss to X Ltd.

b) W Ltd makes no claim under Section 37 and surrenders as much loss as possible to X Ltd.

Solution

(a) **Corporation tax computations AP 31.3.2013**

	W Ltd £	X Ltd £
Trading profits	–	80,000
Overseas royalties	16,000	–
Chargeable gains	2,000	1,000
✱ shared loss relief	18,000	81,000
Less Section 37 (current year offset)	(18,000)	
Section 130 (group loss surrender)		(12,000)
TTP liable to CT	–	69,000
CT Payable @ 20%	–	13,800
Unrelieved foreign tax =	£2,400	

	W Ltd £	X Ltd £
(b) **Trading profits**	–	80,000
Overseas income	16,000	–
Chargeable gain	2,000	1,000
✱ loss relief transferred to subsid with most taxable inc.	18,000	81,000
Less Section 130 group loss surrender	–	(30,000)
TTP liable to CT	18,000	51,000
CT payable @ 20%	3,600	10,200
Less DTR	(2,400)	–
CT	1,200	10,200

Notes

i)   By X not claiming loss relief under Section 37 the full DT relief of £2,400 has been obtained by X.

Controlled foreign companies

6. UK resident companies with interests (even non-controlling interests) in a profitable 'controlled foreign company' (CFC) that is resident in a low-tax area may have to self-assess UK corporation tax on an apportionment of the profits of the CFC, on an arising basis.

The original rules about CFCs dated from 1984 but eventually ran into problems with European Union Treaty principles on Freedom of Establishment. They were also rendered less effective by the new foreign dividend exemption for parent companies from 2008/09. After a lengthy consultation substantial reforms have been enacted to the CFC system but at the time of writing they are not yet fully in force.

The new rules still require a UK company to declare on its CT self-assessment form any apportioned non-UK profits of a CFC which it has an interest, and to pay tax on these profits in the UK. However the exact definition of a CFC is changed by Finance act 2012.

Although the new legislation is in the 2012 Act, it will not come into force until at least January 2013 (on latest expectation). HMRC is still seeking input from affected corporate taxpayers until October 21012 on the exact operation of the new CFC regime The current guidance from HMRC on the CFC reforms and its intentions for implementing them is available (at the time of writing) on HMRC's website at the following web address:

   http://www.hmrc.gov.uk/drafts/cfc.htm.

The old definition of a CFC (which still applies in theory, until the new rules are brought into force) was:

a)   an overseas resident company which is under the control of persons resident in the UK, and,

b)   the overseas resident company is subject to a lower level of taxation in its country of residence than it would be in the UK. 'Lower' in this case means that the tax paid in the country of residence < 75% of the tax bill, had the company been resident in the UK.

c)   'Control' is deemed to exist where $\geq 40\%$ of the CFC is owned by a UK company.

d)   In 2008 the CFC regime was extended to corporations classified as Special Purpose Vehicles (SPV's) set up with the sole intention of avoiding UK corporation tax.

Tests of exclusion – until FA 2012 revised tests come into force

7. No direction will be made to apportion the profits of the CFC if that company satisfies any one of the following tests of exclusion.

a) Until 1 July 2009 only, 'the CFC pursues an acceptable distribution policy'. This ground for exclusion was removed when foreign dividends became exempt from UK corporation tax. Before that date the test meant that a trading CFC must have paid to UK residents by way of dividends at least 90% of its 'available profits', within a certain time after earning them. For non-trading CFCs, 90% of taxable profits less capital gains and foreign tax must be distributed.

b) 'The CFC is engaged in exempt activities'
A CFC is engaged in exempt activities if it has, throughout the accounting period, a business establishment in its territory of residence and its business affairs are effectively managed there. The latter is evidenced, amongst other things, if it has a sufficient number of employees in the territory to deal with its volume of business locally. Certain non-trading activities have to meet other criteria to benefit under this heading.

c) 'The CFC fulfils the public quotation condition'
This is met where the CFC has at least 35% of its shares which have voting power, quoted on a recognised stock exchange in the country of residence. As for close companies in the UK, this requirement is not met where 85% of the company's voting power is in the hands of its principal members.

d) 'The CFC satisfies the motive test'
There are two conditions to be met if the CFC is to satisfy the motive test.
   i) The existence of the CFC was not made mainly for the purposes of achieving a diversion of profits from the UK, and
   ii) Any reduction of UK tax resulting from transactions is either minimal or is not the main reason for undertaking those transactions.

e) 'The CFC has chargeable profits <£50,000'
Where the chargeable profits (calculated on the same basis as UK taxable total profits) of the CFC are less than £50,000 for a 12 month accounting period then it is excluded from apportionment.

Assessable profits

8. a) The CFC profit brought into UK taxable profits is the apportioned amount of the CFC's chargeable profits, computed on UK tax principles. Any overseas tax paid that is attributable to the apportioned profits is eligible for Double Tax Relief.

b) Deductions can be made against apportioned CFC profits where the UK company has reliefs which have not been fully utilised against its UK taxable profits. The reliefs are:
   i) relief for trading losses
   ii) group relief
   iii) relief for management expenses

c) No self-assessment need be made unless the amount apportioned to a UK company and its associates of the CFC's chargeable profits amount to at least 10% of the CFC's chargeable profits.

HMRC press releases have provided a list of what are known as 'excluded countries'. Where a company carries on a trade in one of these countries it is deemed to fall outside the charging provisions noted above.

CFCs – self-assessment

9.   The CTSA rules – i.e. corporation tax self-assessment rules – apply to CFCs. This means that UK companies have to include in their tax returns (Form CT600B) their share of a CFC's profits in accordance with the CFC rules. It is not necessary for HMRC to make a direction regarding a CFC, but HMRC do maintain information about possible CFCs and the UK companies believed to have controlling interests in them, so HMRC could initiate an enquiry into a CT return for the reason that CFC profits were omitted from a CT return.

International transfer pricing – tax issues

10. A UK company is required, when preparing its CT self-assessment, to consider all transactions with connected companies or businesses (e.g. a branch) and if necessary to revise the transfer prices used in those transactions and substitute an 'arm's length' basis, wherever this would increase the amount of UK taxable income.

The transfer pricing rules basically state that if any transaction is made with a related company (whether a trading supply of goods services or raw materials, a charge for rent, interest or a charge for management services) at a price that is not the level which would be reached between two unrelated parties negotiating at arm's length, and as a result the UK company (i.e. the company within the charge to UK tax) pays a higher amount of cost, or receives a lower amount of income, than would have applied under an arm's length pricing basis, then for tax purposes the arm's length transfer price (as agreed with HMRC) must be substituted. *— regulates companies trying to reduce tax by increasing costs & reducing income.*

The following additional rules apply

i)   The transfer pricing tax rules do not apply to Small and Medium-sized Enterprises, except in relation to transactions with a related business in a territory which does not have a double tax treaty with the UK containing 'a suitable non-discrimination' article.

ii)   For large groups (not SMEs), since 2004 similar transfer pricing tax rules apply between related group companies resident in the UK, as well as to international transactions.

iii)   In exceptional circumstances a medium-sized company may be required by HMRC to apply transfer pricing adjustments.

In practice HMRC will enter into 'advance pricing agreements' with multinational companies, typically lasting six years at a time These will agree the basis on which work in progress, raw materials or components, or other goods or services are to be priced when supplied to or purchased from a related non UK company under the same ultimate control.

Advance pricing agreements are very important for multinational groups to be sure that their methods of arriving at group internal transfer prices and entity profits on intra-group trading are acceptable to the taxing authorities in all the countries involved (not just the UK).

All Governments worldwide with developed tax systems have introduced similar transfer pricing review rules, in order to prevent the global profits of multinationals being disproportionately recognised for accounting purposes in countries with the lowest tax rates.

The largest settlements of transfer pricing tax enquiries to date have been made by pharmaceutical companies. In June 2010, a transfer pricing out-of-court settlement with UK HMRC of £505 million in back taxes by Astra Zeneca plc was announced, covering Astra Zeneca's business in the years 1995-2010. Glaxo plc reached some very high-value transfer pricing tax settlements in both Canada and the US the previous year, though the US liabilities have since been reduced on appeal.

Foreign branches of UK companies

11. Where a UK company carries on part of its trade through a foreign branch then the following rules apply:

a) The trade of the overseas branch is subject to UK corporation tax: the branch profits are taxed as part of the company's trading profits.

b) If the overseas branch is subject to foreign taxation (i.e. direct tax on its profits) then this is taken into consideration for double tax relief against UK tax on total profits.

c) The OECD principles allow the other Taxing State to tax the branch profits first, if the branch is a permanent establishment, as defined.

d) The transactions of the foreign branch with the UK parent should be priced on a 'separate enterprise' principle when computing the profits of the branch, and of the UK parent, for the purpose of DTR , i.e. when comparing overseas tax on the branch profits with UK tax on the same profits.

d) Capital allowances are available in the UK tax computations for plant and machinery purchased by the overseas branch

e) Net trading losses of the overseas branch are in effect relieved against the UK profits without the need for a formal claim, since both results are combined.

f) The existence of a foreign branch does not increase the number of associated companies for the purposes of the small profits rate of CT.

g) It is generally straightforward for income flows to pass between the branch and the parent HQ, unless exchange control restrictions exist in the foreign country. There is no need for formal declaration of a dividend or any specific transaction for the branch to send profits to the UK.

h) Branch net profit is taxable in the UK, whether or not it is remitted to the UK.

As noted in Chapter 18 Finance Act 2011 contains an election allowing a UK company to opt out of having its overseas branches' income and expenses included in its taxable worldwide profits. If the opt-out is made it is irrevocable. It also means the losses of overseas branches can no longer reduce UK profits by aggregation and that overseas tax paid by the branch will not be available for DTR. Capital allowances will no longer be available on branch assets.

The availability of this election alters the commercial and financial choices available in 2012 onwards to companies that have to choose between expanding overseas using a branch, and expanding by means of a newly-incorporated or purchased subsidiary company.

Foreign subsidiaries of UK companies

12. The tax features of trading through a foreign branch, in the absence of an irrevocable exemption election, may be contrasted with the position where a separate foreign company is incorporated or acquired by a UK company to handle its trade in a foreign country. In that case:

a) The profits of the overseas company will not be subject to UK corporation tax, unless it establishes a taxable presence in the UK (or it is a CFC – see (h) below).

b) Any foreign taxation paid by the overseas company on its profits (i.e. direct taxes) is not relievable in the UK against UK tax.

c) Any dividends paid by the subsidiary out of taxed profits will be tax-free dividend income of the parent in the UK, but not augmented profits (because it is group FII).

d) The transactions of the foreign subsidiary with the UK parent may be subject to tax transfer pricing rules to prevent suppression of profits that 'economically belong' in the UK. Foreign branches are of course subject to transfer pricing rules too. But in either case these rules do not apply if the UK company is an SME under financial reporting rules.

e) In contrast to a branch, no capital allowances are not available in the UK for plant and machinery owned and used by the subsidiary company.

f) Net tax losses of the overseas subsidiary cannot be surrendered as group relief (except under the limited circumstances of the Marks and Spencer case if it is located in the EEA.) (See Chapter 24, section 4.)

g) The subsidiary company will count as an extra associated company for the purposes of the small profits rate of CT.

h) Payments from the subsidiary company to the UK parent in the form of purchases of goods and services, management charges, rent or interest payments will be taxable income in the UK. However they will probably be allowable costs in the foreign country against profits taxed there.

i) If the subsidiary is located in a low tax area as defined, then it may be a CFC unless one of the exempting tests is satisfied.

Restrictions for UK companies on allowable interest – 'worldwide debt cap' rules

13.   The UK tax authorities have become concerned that global groups can take advantage of the leading role of London as a centre for debt finance, and the higher rates of CT in the UK than in some other countries, to borrow money in London which the group does not actually need to borrow, viewed at the world level.

In theory, surplus funds could be borrowed in the UK, with full UK tax relief on the interest at 24%, and then advanced to group companies outside the UK at a lower rate of interest than is being paid in the UK. The borrowed funds, or the profits and trading returns that they generate, may never come back to the UK but may remain as group cash deposited in a low-tax country (a 'tax haven').

To deal with this concern, UK companies belonging to groups over a certain size are subject to a new 'worldwide debt cap' test on their UK interest costs, effective from the first accounting period beginning on or after 1 January 2010. The final UK debt cap rules were enacted in 2009, after extensive consultation. It is likely that they will be further amended as the system beds down.

The basic rule is that a UK company over a certain size, and with over a certain level of borrowings, will not be able to deduct debt borrowing costs in UK corporation tax computations to the extent that these costs exceed the **total net borrowing cost** of the group worldwide for the same period, as shown in the consolidated accounts of the group.

There are exceptions for banks and insurance companies and other detailed additional rules.

Like the CFC rules discussed at 8 above it is likely that the new 'debt cap' rule for UK-deductible interest will act more as a deterrent to companies adopting targeted 'tax- abusive' group structures, than as a tax revenue raiser.

Student self-testing questions

1. Dingbat Ltd forecasts a tax-adjusted trading profit of £1,200,000 for the year ended 31 October 2013. Its directors are not expecting that it will earn any non-trading income or gains in the year. It has no associated companies.

Dingbat Ltd is planning to set up an overseas trading operation. The directors are unsure whether to set up a branch of Dingbat Ltd or a separate wholly-owned overseas company. In either case, the profit in the first accounting period would be the same, £140,000, and the overseas tax due on this profit would be £31,500. The overseas company would remit a dividend of half of its profit after tax.

Required:

Calculate the projected UK corporation tax liability of Dingbat Ltd and show the total tax paid out of the overseas profits (foreign and UK) for the year to 31 October 2013, after any available double tax relief:

(a) if the new operation is set up as an overseas branch, but no election is made by Dingbat Ltd to exclude the branch from UK taxation;

(b) if the operation is set up as an overseas subsidiary.

(Assume that corporation tax rates and limits will be the same in Financial Year 2013 as in Financial Year 2012.)

Solution:

(a) Overseas branch: Corporation tax liability of Dingbat Ltd:

		£
Trading profits	UK operation	1,200,000
	Branch operation	140,000
Taxable total profit		1,340,000
Upper limit (12 mths)	1,500,000	
Lower limit (12 mths)	300,000	
Corporation Tax	At 24% x £1,340k	321,600
Less Marginal relief	(1.5m-1.34m) x 1 / 100 x 1	(1,600)
UK CT	(effective rate 320/1340 = 23.9%)	320,000
Less double tax relief :	Check : 31.5k/140k = 22.5% which is less than 23.9% so no restriction on DTR	(31,500)
UK CT liability		288,500
Additional overseas tax liability		31,500
		320,000
Total tax on overseas profits	(23.9% x 140,000))	33,460

(b) Overseas subsidiary: CT liability of Dingbat Ltd

		£
Trading profits	UK company	1,200,000
	[Foreign dividend income is exempted]	
Taxable total profit		1,200,000
Upper limit (2 cos)	750,000	
Lower limit	150,000	
UK Corporation Tax	24% x £1200k	288,000
Additional overseas tax liability		31,500
		319,500
Total tax on overseas profits		31,500

Questions without answers

1. T Ltd, a UK company, owns 20% of A Inc, a foreign resident company. T Ltd has the following results for the year ended 31st March 2013:

	£
Trading profits	2,000,000
Chargeable gains	66,000
Overseas income :	
Dividend received from A Inc, net of 15% withholding taxes	85,000
Interest received from A Inc, net of 20% withholding taxes	160,000
Debenture interest paid (trading, gross)	140,000
Dividend paid	500,000

Compute the CT payable by T Ltd for the AP to 31st March 2013.

2. Wash plc is a UK resident company that manufactures kitchen equipment. The company's trading profit for the year ended 31 March 2013 is £1,600,000. Wash plc has a 100% owned subsidiary, Dry Inc. that is resident overseas. Dry Inc. sells kitchen equipment manufactured by Wash plc. The results for Dry Inc. for the year ended 31 March 2013 are as follows:

	£	£
Trading profit		580,000
Corporation tax		160,000
		420,000
Dividend paid – net	270,000	
– withholding tax	30,000	300,000
Retained profits		120,000

Dry Inc.'s dividend was paid during the year ended 31 March 2013. The company's overseas corporation tax liability for the year ended 31 March 2013 was £8,000 more than that provided for in the accounts.

All of the above figures are in pounds sterling.

i) **Calculate Wash plc's corporation tax liability for the year ended 31 March 2013.**

ii) **Explain the tax implications if Wash plc were to invoice Dry Inc. for the exported kitchen equipment at a price that was less than the market price.**

(ACCA updated)

End of section questions and answers

1. Tock Tick

Tock-Tick Ltd is a clock manufacturer. The company's summarised profit and loss account for the year ended 31 March 2013 is as follows:

	£
Gross profit	822,280
Operating expenses	
Bad debts (note 1)	9,390
Depreciation	99,890
Gifts and donations (note 2)	3,090
Professional fees (note 3)	12,400
Repairs and renewals (note 4)	128,200
Other expenses (note 5)	426,920
Total expenses	679,890
Operating profit	142,390
Profit from sale of fixed assets	
Disposal of office building (note 6)	78,100
Income from investments	
Loan interest receivable (note 7)	12,330
	232,820
Interest payable (note 8)	48,600
Profit before taxation	184,220

Note 1 – Bad debts

Bad debts are as follows:	£
Trade debts recovered from previous years	(1,680)
Trade debts written off	7,970
Decrease in specific bad debt provision	(3,100)
Increase in general provision for doubtful debts	6,200
	9,390

Note 2 – Gifts and donations

Gifts and donations are as follows:	£
Gifts to customers (pens costing £45 each displaying Tock-Tick Ltd's name)	1,080
Gifts to customers (food hampers costing £30 each)	720
Long service award to an employee	360
Donation to a national charity (made under the gift aid scheme)	600

Donation to a national charity	
(not made under the gift aid scheme)	250
Donation to a local charity	
(Tock-Tick Ltd received free advertising in the charity's magazine)	80
	3,090

Note 3 – Professional fees

Professional fees are as follows:	£
Accountancy and audit fee	5,400
Legal fees in connection with the issue of share capital	2,900
The cost of registering the company's trademark	800
Legal fees in connection with the renewal of a 35-year property lease	1,300
Debt collection	1,100
Legal fees in connection with a court action for not	
complying with health and safety legislation	900
	12,400

Note 4 – Repairs and renewals

The figure of £128,200 for repairs and renewals includes £41,800 for replacing the roof of an office building, which was in a bad state of repair, and £53,300 for extending the office building.

Note 5 – Other expenses

Other expenses include £2,160 for entertaining suppliers; £880 for counselling services provided to two employees who were made redundant; and the cost of seconding an employee to a charity of £6,400. The remaining expenses are all fully allowable.

Note 6 – Disposal of office building

The profit of £78,100 is in respect of a freehold office building that was sold on 20 February 2013 for £276,000.

The office building was purchased on 18 November 2002 for £197,900. Assume the indexation allowance from November 2002 to February 2013 is £75,700.

The building has always been used by Tock-Tick Ltd for trading purposes.

Note 7 – Loan interest receivable

The loan interest is in respect of a loan that was made on 1 July 2012. Interest of £8,280 was received on 31 December 2012, and interest of £4,050 was accrued but not yet received at 31 March 2013. The loan was made for non-trading purposes.

Note 8 – Interest payable

The interest payable is in respect of a five-year debenture loan that is used for trading purposes. Fixed interest is paid six-monthly to debenture holders. £24,300 was paid on 30 September 2011 and again on 31 March 2012.

Note 9 - Plant and machinery

On 1 April 2012 the tax written down values of plant and machinery were as follows:

	£
General pool	12,200
Renault car CO_2 170g/km (purchased May 2011)	20,800
Short-life asset	3,100

The following transactions took place during the year ended 31 March 2013:

	Cost/(Proceeds)
	£
28 May 2012 Sold the Renault car CO_2 170g/km	(24,800)
7 June 2012 Purchased a Honda car	14,400
1 August 2012 Sold the short-life asset	(460)
15 August 2012 Purchased equipment	6,700

The Renault car sold on 28 May 2012 for £24,800 originally cost £23,112. The Honda car purchased on 7 June 2012 is a low emission motor car (CO_2 emission rate of less than 110 grams per kilometre).

Required:

(a) Calculate Tock-Tick Ltd's tax adjusted Trading profit for the AP (year) ended 31 March 2013. Your computation should commence with the profit before taxation figure of £184,220. **(19 marks)**

(b) Calculate Tock-Tick Ltd's taxable total profits for the AP (year) ended 31 March 2013. **(5 marks)**

(c) State the effect on Tock-Tick Ltd's taxable total profits for the year ended 31 March 2013 if Tock-Tick Ltd claims the maximum possible group relief that it can receive from a 100%-owned subsidiary company Buzz Ltd, which made a trading loss of £62,400 for its twelve month AP which ended on 31 December 2012.

(4 marks)

(28 marks)

(ACCA updated)

Solution

1. Tock Tick Ltd

(a) Tock-Tick Ltd – Income from trading for the year ended 31 March 2013

	£	£
Profit before taxation		184,220
Depreciation		99,890
Bad debts – general provision		6,200
Gifts to customers – food hampers		720
Gift aid donation		600
Donation to national charity		250
Legal fees in connection with the issue of share capital		2,900

Legal fees in connection with the court action		900
Office extension		53,300
Entertaining		2,160
		351,140
Disposal of office building	78,100	
Loan interest received	12,330	
Capital allowances (working)	23,624	114,054
Trading profit		237,086

(1) Gifts to customers are an allowable deduction if they cost less than £50 per recipient per year, are not of food, drink, tobacco, or vouchers for exchangeable goods, and carry a conspicuous advertisement for the company making the gift.

(2) The long service award is deductible in calculating the trading profit.

(3) The gift aid donation is deducted in the corporation tax computation against total profits as a qualifying charitable donation, but is not an allowable trading expense in arriving at income from trading. The other national charity donation is not allowable because it was neither made under company gift aid declaration nor linked to local trade promotion.

(4) The legal costs of registering a trademark and of renewing a short-lease (less than 50 years) are allowable.

(5) The replacement of the roof is allowable since it amounts to repair and the whole structure is not being replaced. The office extension is not allowable, being capital in nature.

(6) The costs of counselling services for redundant employees and of seconding an employee to charity are allowable.

(7) Interest payable on a loan used for trading purposes is deductible in calculating the trading profit.

	Pool	Special rate pool (car)	Short-life asset	Allowances
	£	£	£	£
WDV brought forward	12,200	20,800	3,100	
Proceeds of disposals (max. cost)		(23,112)	(460)	
		(2,312)	2,640	
Balancing charge (pool exhausted)		2,312		(2,312)

Balancing allowance (SLA disposal)			(2,640)	2,640
Additions qualifying for AIA				
Equipment	6,700			
AIA	(6,700)	0		6,700
Low	14,400			
emission motor car				
100% FYA	(14,400)	0		14,400
		12,200		
WDA 18%		(2,196)		2,196
WDV carried forward		10,004		
Total allowances CTAP to 31.3.13				£23,624

(1) The sale proceeds for the motor car sold are restricted to original cost.
(2) It is necessary to take a balancing charge on the special rate pool as this cannot go forward with a negative WDV.

(b) Tock-Tick Ltd – Corporation tax computation for the year ended 31 March 2013

	£
Trading profit	237,086
Interest income – non-trade loan relationship	12,330
Net Chargeable gains (276,000 – 197,900 – 75,700)	2,400
	251,816
Qualifying charitable donation – Gift Aid	(600)
Taxable total profit	251,216

(c)
Group relief effect
(1) The accounting periods are not coterminous, so the claim for group relief would be restricted to the lower of £188,412 (£251,216 x 9/12) and £46,800 (£62,400 x 9/12).
(2) Tock-Tick Ltd's taxable total profit would therefore be reduced by £46,800.

Questions without answers

1.   Zoom plc

Zoom plc is a manufacturer of photographic equipment. The summarised draft profit and loss account of Zoom plc for the year ended 31 March 2013 is as follows:

	£	£
Operating profit (note 1)		813,980
Income from investments		
Bank interest (note 4)	26,820	
Loan interest (note 5)	22,500	
Rental income from property (note 6)	43,200	
Dividends (note 7)	49,500	
Total other income		142,020
		956,000
Interest payable (note 8)		(46,000)
Profit before taxation		910,000

Note 1 – Operating profit

Depreciation of £48,100 has been deducted in arriving at the operating profit of £813,980.

Note 2 – Plant and machinery

On 1 April 2012 the tax written down values of plant and machinery were as follows:

	£
General pool	19,600
Motor car CO_2 180g/km (purchased 1 April 2011)	20,200
Short-life asset (2 years old)	36,000

The following transactions took place during the year ended 31 March 2013:

		Cost/(Proceeds) £
15 April 2012	Purchased equipment	7,100
19 June 2012	Purchased a computer	2,280
29 July 2012	Sold the motor car	(24,200)
31 July 2012	Purchased motor car CO_2 150g/km (1)	16,600
3 August 2012	Sold a lorry	(9,800)
22 December 2012	Purchased motor car CO_2 140g/km (2)	10,800
1 February 2013	Purchased motor car (3)	14,200
28 February 2013	Sold the short-life asset	(8000)

The motor car sold on 29 July 2012 for £24,200 originally cost £22,445. The lorry sold on 3 August 2012 for £9,800 originally cost £17,200. Motor car (3) purchased on 1 February 2013 is a low emission motor car (CO_2 emission rate of less than 110 grams per kilometre).

Note 3 – Corporation Tax information

Zoom plc made quarterly instalment payments in respect of its corporation tax liability for the year ended 31 March 2013.

Zoom plc has three associated companies.

For the year ended 31 March 2012, Zoom plc had taxable total profits of £780,000.

Note 4 – Bank interest received

The bank interest was received on 31 March 2013 and there was no accrual brought forward or carried forward. The bank deposits are held for non-trading purposes.

Note 5 – Loan interest receivable

The loan was made for non-trading purposes on 1 July 2012. Loan interest of £15,000 was received on 31 December 2012, and interest of £7,500 was accrued at 31 March 2013.

Note 6 – Income from property

Zoom plc lets out two unfurnished office buildings that are surplus to requirements.

The first office building was let from 1 April 2012 until 31 January 2013 at a rent of £3,200 per month. On 31 January 2013 the tenant left owing two months rent which Zoom plc was unable to recover. This office building was not re-let until May 2013.

The second office building was not let from 1 April 2012 to 31 July 2012. During this period Zoom plc spent £4,800 on advertising for new tenants, and £5,200 on decorating the office building. On 1 August 2012 the office building was let at an annual rent of £26,400, payable in advance.

Zoom plc insured its two office buildings at a total cost of £3,360 for the year ended 31 December 2011, and £3,720 for the year ended 31 December 2012. The insurance is payable annually in advance.

Note 7 – Dividends received

The dividends were all received from unconnected UK companies. The figure of £49,500 is the actual cash amount received.

Note 8 – Interest payable

The interest is in respect of a debenture loan that has been used for trading purposes. Interest of £23,000 was paid on 30 September 2012 and again on 31 March 2013.

Required:

(a) (i) Calculate the amount of capital allowances that Zoom plc can claim for the year ended 31 March 2013.   (12 marks)

(ii) Prepare a computation for the year ended 31 March 2013 reconciling Zoom plc's profit before taxation with its taxable total profits. Your reconciliation should commence with the profit before taxation figure of £910,000, clearly identify the tax adjusted trading profit and the amount of profit from land and property, and end with the figure of taxable total profits (TTP).   (8 marks)

(b) Explain why Zoom plc was required to make quarterly instalment payments in respect of its corporation tax liability for the year ended 31 March 2013.   (3 marks)

(c) Calculate Zoom plc's corporation tax liability for the year ended 31 March 2013, and explain how and when this will have been paid. You should assume that the company's taxable profits accrued evenly throughout the year.   (3 marks)

(d) Explain how your answer to part (c) above would differ if Zoom plc had no associated companies. Your answer should include a calculation of the revised corporation tax liability for the year ended 31 March 2013.(4 marks)

(30 marks)

(ACCA December 2004 updated)

2. Scuba Ltd

Scuba Ltd is a manufacturer of diving equipment. The following information is relevant for the year ended 31 March 2013:

Operating profit

The operating profit is £162,400. The expenses that have been deducted in calculating this figure include the following:

	£
Depreciation and amortisation	45,200
Entertaining customers	7,410
Entertaining employees	2,470
Gifts to customers	
(diaries costing £25 each displaying Scuba Ltd's name)	1,350
Gifts to customers (food hampers costing £80 each)	1,600

Leasehold property

On 1 July 2012 Scuba Ltd acquired a leasehold office building that is used for business purposes. The company paid a premium of £80,000 for the grant of a twenty-year lease.

Plant and machinery

On 1 April 2012 the tax written down values of plant and machinery were as follows:

	£
General pool	47,200
Ford car CO_2 190g/km	22,400
Features integral to a building	276,900

The following transactions took place during the year ended 31 March 2013:

		(Cost/Proceeds) £
3 July 2012	Purchased machinery	7,300
10 July 2012	Purchased a computer	1,400
4 August 2012	Purchased a Skoda car CO_2 180g/km	10,400
18 November 2012	Purchased machinery	4,800
1 December 2012	Purchased a ventilation system (a feature integral to a building)	10,150
29 December 2012	Purchased computer software	1,100
15 February 2013	Sold a lorry	(12,400)

The Skoda car purchased on 4 August 2012 for £10,400 is used by the factory manager, and 40% of the mileage is for private journeys. The lorry sold on 15 February 2013 for £12,400 originally cost £19,800.

Income from property

Scuba Ltd lets a retail shop that is surplus to requirements. The shop was let until 31 March 2012 but was then empty from 1 April 2012 to 31 July 2012. During this period Scuba Ltd spent £6,200 on decorating the shop, and £1,700 on advertising for new tenants. The shop was let from 1 August 2012 to 31 March 2013 at a quarterly rent of £7,200, payable in advance.

Interest received

Interest of £435 was received from HMRC on 31 January 2013 in respect of the overpayment of corporation tax for the year ended 31 March 2011.

Profit on disposal of shares

On 8 February 2013 Scuba Ltd sold 5,000 £1 ordinary shares in Deep Blue Sea plc for £42,400. The shareholding had been purchased on 19 March 2007 for £26,900. The retail prices index (RPI) for March 2007 was 204.4, and for March 2013 it was 248.8 (estimated).

Other information

Scuba Ltd has no associated companies and has always had an accounting date of 31 December.

Required:

(a) Calculate Scuba Ltd's tax-adjusted trading profit for the year ended 31 March 2013. (21 marks)

(b) Calculate Scuba Ltd's taxable total profits and corporation tax liability for the year ended 31 March 2013. (6 marks)

(c) State the date by which Scuba Ltd must pay its corporation tax liability for the year ended 31 March 2013, and explain the implications for the company if this liability is paid three months late.

(3 marks)

(30 marks)

(ACCA updated)

Part IV

Taxation of chargeable gains

26 General principles

Introduction and brief history

1. UK Capital Gains Tax was brought in from the 6th April 1965. However, due to subsequent reforms, on a disposal of an asset held since before April 1982, there is now a discount from the gain liable to tax, to the extent that this gain is identified by CGT rules as having accrued before 1 April 1982. This date is the same for both individuals and companies. This reform was called the '1982 rebasing' of CGT, and occurred in 1988.

The basic principle of capital gains tax has always been that when an asset is sold, exchanged or gifted, any gain represented by the excess of the realised value over the historic cost is considered to be a taxable capital gain.

Legislation on the detailed computation of chargeable gains is in the Taxation of Chargeable Gains Act 1992, as amended.

However it is important to recognise that for individuals the regime is now different from the regime for companies, even though the rules are found in the same Act. One main difference is that individuals do not get adjustment of their CGT-allowable costs by monetary inflation even if they have owned an asset for a long time. Companies do get this relief in the form of the indexation allowance (assuming there is some inflation). This difference could be significant depending on the length of time an asset is owned and the rate of inflation over that time.

Indexation allowance

CGT indexation allowance (IA) was first introduced in 1982, and made more generous in 1985. Its purpose was to reflect rising prices, which were seen as causing inflationary gains to be unfairly taxed as real gains. For individuals, IA only operated fully until 1998, but for corporate taxpayers the 1985-type IA is still available and can add over 100% to the allowable cost of an asset when computing the gain. However, IA cannot create or increase an allowable capital loss.

Evolution of differences between individual and corporate taxpayers

From 1965 to 1988, capital gains were taxed at a flat rate of 30% for both individuals and companies. Variable tax rates on capital gains, aligned with the tax rates on other income / profits, were introduced in 1988. At this stage both indivduals and corporate taxpayers received indexation allowance in the same way.

In 1998, on-going indexation allowance was abolished for individuals (with indexation allowances already earned frozen at 1998 values until 2008/09 when the relief disappeared). The continuation of indexation allowance for corporate taxpayers meant a major divergence between the taxation system for capital gains of companies and that for capital gains of individuals.

From 1998 to 2008, individuals could claim CGT taper relief, reducing the chargeable gain, depending on the length of time an asset had been held. Taper relief was extremely generous if the asset was a 'business asset', as it went up to

75%, reducing the effective rate of CGT for a higher rate income tax payer from 40% to 10%.

CGT taper relief and 'frozen' indexation relief were removed in 2008. To compensate, the individual CGT rate was reduced to 18%, its lowest ever. Other complications dating from the 1988 rebasing legislation were also removed from the system in 2008. This move was a major simplification of CGT for individual taxpayers but meant that the capital gains tax system for corporate taxpayers was now very different from that for individuals.

To satisfy owners of private equity and other businesses, who had been expecting business asset taper relief to continue at an effective 10% rate, the Government amended the 2008 draft legislation to include a new CGT relief for 'entrepreneurs', restoring an effective CGT rate of 10% on up to £1 million of gains from disposal of qualifying businesses and shares.

The practical scope of this new 'Entrepreneurs' Relief' (ER) was very unclear at first, presenting a challenge for tax advisers. However its operation became clearer after the first self-assessment tax returns on which it could be claimed, those for 2008/09, were submitted and accepted in 2009 and 2010. The lifetime limit for ER gains has been raised in stages from the original £1m. For details of ER rules in 2012/13, see Chapter 27 section 10.

After a change of Government, the second 2010 Budget introduced a higher rate of 28% on gains realised after 22 June 2010, to the extent these exceeded the taxpayer's unused income tax basic rate band for the tax year. This higher 28% rate of CGT is unchanged in 2012/13, as are the lower CGT rate of 18% and the continuing ER rate of 10%.

There were no significant changes to CGT rules in the 2011 or 2012 Finance Acts other than that in April 2011 the lifetime limit for ER was increased to £10 million. For 2012/13 the personal CGT annual exemption (usually increased annually) is 'frozen' at the 2011/12 level, £10,600.

Companies meanwhile have had few changes to their chargeable gains regime since the 1990s, while the personal CGT regime has undergone frequent change. Companies simply pay corporation tax on their chargeable gains (after indexation allowance) as part of their taxable profits. (See Part 3 for corporation tax.)

Since CT rates have fallen since 2010 and are projected to continue to fall, the burden of CGT could be said to be shifting away from companies, while it has increased on affected individuals since 2010. However very few individuals actually pay any CGT at all, because for most people the annual exemption covers regular small investment gains, while longstanding exemptions for private residences, low-value personal chattels and private cars mean CGT is irrelevant to the only capital assets which most UK citizens ever own.

Having summarised the recent history of capital gains taxation, main features of the 2012/13 rules as they apply to individuals and companies are described in the rest of this chapter.

2.   For individuals, including sole traders and partnerships:

a)   Since April 2008, the capital gain realised by an individual on a chargeable asset is computed as the disposal proceeds (or deemed proceeds, for non-arm's length disposals), less the allowable capital disposal, acquisition and enhancement costs.

b)   In 2012/13 (and 2011/12), net personal capital gains, less allowable losses, are taxed:

   i)   at 10%, for gains on which entrepreneurs' relief is claimed and allowed;

   ii)   at 18%, to the extent that they can use that part of the individual's income tax basic rate band which is left after allocating the band first to taxable income, and also to gains qualifying for entrepreneurs' relief;

   iii)   at 28%, for any balance of net capital gains.

c)   Shares and securities acquired at different times, forming a single holding of identical assets, are 'pooled' together for CGT, and a weighted average cost is used to determine the allowable cost on disposal of a part of the holding. See Chapter 29.

For incorporated taxpayers in FY2012 the position is as follows:

a)   Chargeable gains are calculated by reference to the disposal proceeds, less any allowable costs, and then there may be deducted (but only to the extent that it does not increase or create a capital loss) an indexation allowance, based on the acquisition and enhancement costs. The company's net chargeable gains (gains less allowable losses) are included in total profits for corporation tax. See part 3 for detailed information on effective rates of corporation tax in FY 2011 and FY2012.

b)   As for individuals, shares and securities are 'pooled' together and a weighted average cost is used to determine the allowable cost on disposal of less than the complete holding. Indexation allowance on pooled shares is computed by a continuous indexation method, slightly different from IA calculations on other disposals. See Chapter 29 for the details.

Persons chargeable

3. The following classes of persons are liable to tax on capital gains, if resident, ordinarily resident or trading in the UK:

Individuals and personal representatives

Trusts and trustees

Companies, which compute capital gains under the same legislation (the Taxation of Chargeable Gains Act), but pay corporation tax not CGT

More detail about chargeable persons is given in Chapter 28.

Rates of tax on capital gains 2012/13

4.	Person	Exemption	Rate of tax
	Individuals	£10,600	10%, 18% or 28% (See detailed comments in sections 1 and 2 above)
	Companies	Nil	Chargeable gains taxed at company corporation tax rate within taxable total profits, i.e. small profits rate, marginal rate or full rate.

Chargeable assets

5. Under Sections 21 and 22 of the TCGA 1992 'all forms of property are assets for the purposes of capital gains tax, whether situated in the UK or not', including:

a)   options, debts, and incorporeal property in general

  (see section 6 below regarding application to companies)

b)   currency other than sterling

  (see section 6 below regarding application to companies)

c)   any form of property created by the person disposing of it, or coming to be owned without being acquired

d)   capital sums derived from assets.

Property

6. For individuals this term includes anything capable of being owned, such as freehold and leasehold land, shares and securities, and other tangible assets and intangible assets such as purchased and non-purchased goodwill. It also includes legal claims that have a value.

For companies the term 'property' in principle includes the same things as for individuals. However, having said that, the chargeable gains regime for companies specifically does not cover transactions involving such 'property' that are dealt with for corporation tax under the loan relationships rules or the intangible assets regime.

Companies' intangible fixed assets acquired after 31 March 2002 are outside the chargeable gains regime, and their debt relationships, including financial options and foreign currency deposits, are taxed as loan relationships, not as capital assets.

Options

7. Where a person (the grantor) grants an option over a chargeable asset to another person (the grantee) then this is a disposal by the first person of a chargeable asset, or alternatively the derivation of a capital sum from an asset. If the option is later exercised, any consideration received is added to any made

with the initial grant, to form a single disposal transaction. If it is not exercised then the capital sum is taxable proceeds.

Where some types of option are abandoned, then this is not a disposal by the grantee, so that he or she cannot establish a capital loss. However if the option was over equity shares or was an exchange-traded option (not held as part of a trading activity), TCGA allows a capital loss in certain circumstances. For companies, any transactions in options or other derivatives (eg swaps) relating to underlying debt arrangements are taxed as loan relationships. However equity share options come under the chargeable gains regime for companies.

Debts

8. The original CGT rules on debts now only apply to individuals. Since 1999 debts and loan relationships are not chargeable assets for companies.

UK Government securities (gilts, such as Treasury Stock) that are owned by individuals or trustees are specifically exempted from CGT. However, companies' holdings in gilts are taxable as commercial loan relationships.

Corporate bonds are also exempt from CGT if they are 'qualifying corporate bonds', which most are.

An ordinary debt is not a chargeable asset in the hands of the original creditor, his or her personal representative, or legatee. This means that a default on the debt is not a capital loss.

However an individual who acquires an existing debt for value from another person (by legal assignment), obtains a chargeable asset. If it is later collected at a higher value than the cost given, a chargeable gain arises. If it is redeemed at a lower value, a capital loss may be claimed (note that debt assignments usually involve a discount on face value). Capital treatment does not apply if the individual trades in debts, eg a commercial debt factor.

Provided HMRC accept the commercial nature of the original loan, a loan made by an individual to a UK resident trader, or a loan guarantee that is called in, if proved irrecoverable, can be claimed by an individual as an allowable capital loss.

Currency

9. Any currency other than sterling is in principle a chargeable asset for an individual (the capital gain or loss arises from the exchange difference, compared with the sterling cost, when it is reconverted to sterling). However there is a useful exemption for foreign currency 'acquired by an individual for personal use', so only holdings of an investment nature or unrelated to personal travel are chargeable assets in practice.

Created property – intangible fixed assets

10. For individuals this term includes such assets as goodwill, copyright, trademarks or know-how as chargeable assets. For the corporation tax treatment of intangible fixed assets see Chapter 18.

Patents are not chargeable assets, since any excess over cost realised on a sale is taxed as patent income under ITTOIA 2005.

For an individual, business 'know-how' is treated as a chargeable asset where disposed of along with any part of a trade, but not if disposed of alone, when it gives rise to a trading receipt.

Goodwill

11. 'Goodwill' for CGT means the excess value of a business transferred as a going concern, which is not attributable to separable assets of the business. Both purchased goodwill and self-created business goodwill are chargeable assets for individuals. Self-created goodwill has a nil cost in the hands of the creator, but is a chargeable asset that can give rise to a chargeable gain when disposed of for value along with the rest of the business.

For companies, goodwill acquired or created since 1 April 2002 is not a chargeable asset, as the corporate intangible assets regime takes priority. Also, there is no indexation allowance on the original cost when computing a company's gains under the intangible assets regime.

Capital sums

12. Capital receipts are defined to include:

a) Any capital sums received by way of compensation for damage or injury to assets, or for the loss, destruction or dissipation of assets, or for any depreciation of an asset;

b) Capital sums received under a policy of insurance of the risks of any kind of damage or injury to, or the loss or depreciation of assets;

c) Capital sums received in return for forfeiture or surrender of rights, or for refraining from exercising rights;

d) Capital sums received as consideration for use or exploitation of assets.

When a person derives any capital sum from an asset without disposing of the asset itself, this is treated as a part-disposal of the chargeable asset. If any part of the amount received is used to restore or replace the original asset then special reliefs apply. If the amount received is 'small', the taxpayer can elect to deduct the receipt from the cost of the asset instead of self-assessing a capital gain. (See further, Chapter 30).

Non-chargeable assets and exemptions

13. The following assets are either exempt assets, or chargeable assets on whose disposal there is no chargeable gain or allowable loss because of specific circumstances.

a) Private motor vehicles.

   This includes private cars and vintage cars purchased for investment.

b) Savings certificates.

All non-marketable securities are included under this heading such as National Savings Certificates, and Defence Bonds.

c)   Gambling winnings.

This covers winnings from pools, lotteries, premium bonds and bingo prizes.

d)   Decorations for valour.

These are exempt assets if disposed of by the individual to whom they were awarded, or their legatee. If purchased by anyone else they become chargeable assets.

e)   Currency.

As already noted, foreign currency acquired for personal use is exempt.

f)   Compensation.

Any compensation or damages obtained for any physical wrong or injury suffered by a person, or in connection with his or her profession or vocation.

g)   Life assurance and deferred annuities.

No chargeable gain arises on the disposal of any rights under a life assurance policy or deferred annuity, providing the disposal is made by the original owner. The acquisition of such rights from an original owner gives an individual acquirer a chargeable asset

h)   British government securities and 'qualifying corporate bonds' are exempt when held by individuals. (The same investments held by corporate investors fall under the loan relationship rules).

i)   Principal private residence of an individual. (See Chapter 30)

j)   Chattels bought and sold for less than £6,000. (See Chapter 30)

k)   Assets gifted to a recognised charity.

l)   Disposals conditionally exempt from IHT e.g. works of art given to public collections.

m)   Wasting chattels, i.e. Tangible movable property with useful life of less than 50 years, not used for trade purposes. (See Chapter 30.)

Exempt persons

14.   The under-mentioned persons are exempted from capital gains tax:

a)   Pension funds approved by HMRC.

b)   Registered charities providing the gains are used for charitable purposes.

c)   Registered friendly societies.

d)   Local authorities.

e)   Scientific research associations.

f)   Community amateur sports clubs.

Administration

15. A section of the self-assessment tax return is available for individual taxpayers to notify HMRC of chargeable gains and allowable losses. Appeals against HMRC decisions can be made through the Tribunal System (See Chapter 3: 11).

If no self-assessment return has been received for a tax year in which a gain has been realised that gives rise to a liability, it is the taxpayer's responsibility to notify the tax authorities of the gains by 31 October following the tax year, so that a return can be issued in time for the taxpayer to self-assess and pay the tax by 31 January following.

Companies report chargeable gains on the CT600 company tax return and payment is made as part of the normal corporation tax payment system.

Payment of tax

16. Capital gains tax is due when the final balancing payment is made under the income tax rules for self-assessment, as described in Chapter 2. The due date is as follows:

2011/12	-	31st January 2013
2012/13	-	31st January 2014

It is possible to pay capital gains tax by instalments where the consideration is payable over a period exceeding 18 months, and payment of capital gains tax in one sum would cause undue hardship. Payment of tax by ten equal instalments is also available in respect of tax due on gifts not eligible for holdover relief (See Chapter 33).

Rebasing

17. Under current rules, only gains or losses accruing from 31st March 1982 need be brought into charge to tax. Therefore most of the time, March 1982 market values are used instead of cost for any assets held at that date.

For more detail on rebasing, see Chapter 27 section 12.

Rebasing and Indexation – Incorporated entities

18. Where an asset was held on the 31st March 1982, indexation allowance is based on the higher of the original cost or the market value at 31st March 1982. In most cases the latter figure will be higher so original cost can be ignored.

Indexation cannot be used to create or increase a capital loss.

19. Layouts for capital gain / loss computations – companies and individuals

I. Chargeable assets held by incorporated entities

	FY 2012 £	y/e 31.03.13 £
Gross consideration or market value		–
Less: Incidental costs of disposal		–
Net proceeds of disposal		–
LESS: Allowable deductions:		
Initial cost of asset plus incidental purchase expenses	–	
Enhancement expenditure (i) (not repairs)	–	
Enhancement expenditure (ii)	–	
		–
Unindexed gain		–
Less: Indexation allowance – On initial cost plus expenses		–
On enhancement expenditure (i), (ii) etc		–
(note: indexation allowance cannot create or augment a capital loss)		
= Chargeable gain added to TTP		–

II. Chargeable assets held by individuals

	Tax year 2012/13 £	£
Gross consideration (or market value if connected party/gift)		–
Less: Incidental costs of disposal		–
Allowable deductions–		
Initial cost of asset plus incidental expenses	–	
Enhancement expenditure (not repairs)	–	
		–
Chargeable gain added to other gains/losses for the year		–

20. Retail Prices Index – used for indexation allowance under TCGA 1992

RPI	Jan	Feb	Mar	April	May	June	July	Aug	Sept	Oct	Nov	Dec
1982	–	–	79.44	81.04	81.62	81.85	81.88	81.90	81.85	82.26	82.66	82.51
1983	82.61	82.97	83.12	84.28	84.64	84.84	85.30	85.68	86.06	86.36	86.67	86.89
1984	86.84	87.20	87.48	88.64	88.97	89.20	89.10	89.94	90.11	90.67	90.95	90.87
1985	91.20	91.94	92.80	94.78	95.21	95.41	95.23	95.49	95.44	95.59	95.92	96.05
1986	96.25	96.60	96.73	97.67	97.85	97.79	97.52	97.82	98.30	98.45	99.29	99.62
1987	100.0	100.4	100.6	101.8	101.9	101.9	101.8	102.1	102.4	102.9	103.4	103.3
1988	103.3	103.7	104.1	105.8	106.2	106.6	106.7	107.9	108.4	109.5	110.0	110.3
1989	111.0	111.8	112.3	114.3	115.0	115.4	115.5	115.8	116.6	117.5	118.5	118.8
1990	119.5	120.2	121.4	125.1	126.2	126.7	126.8	128.1	129.3	130.3	130.0	129.9
1991	130.2	130.9	131.4	133.1	133.5	134.1	133.8	134.1	134.6	135.1	135.6	135.7
1992	135.6	136.3	136.7	138.8	139.3	139.3	138.8	138.9	139.4	139.9	139.7	139.2
1993	137.9	138.8	139.3	140.6	141.1	141.0	140.7	141.3	141.9	141.8	141.6	141.9
1994	141.3	142.1	142.5	144.2	144.7	144.7	144.0	144.7	145.0	145.2	145.3	146.0
1995	146.0	146.9	147.5	149.0	149.6	149.8	149.1	149.9	150.6	149.8	149.8	150.7
1996	150.2	150.9	151.5	152.6	152.9	153.0	152.4	153.1	153.8	153.8	153.9	154.4
1997	154.4	155.0	155.4	156.3	156.9	157.5	157.5	158.5	159.3	159.5	159.6	160.0
1998	159.5	160.3	160.8	162.6	163.5	163.4	163.0	163.7	164.4	164.5	164.4	164.4
1999	163.4	163.7	164.1	165.2	165.6	165.6	165.1	165.5	166.2	166.5	166.7	167.3
2000	166.6	167.5	168.4	170.1	170.7	171.1	170.5	170.5	171.7	171.6	172.1	172.2
2001	171.1	172.0	172.2	173.1	174.2	174.4	173.3	174.0	174.6	174.3	173.6	173.4
2002	173.3	173.8	174.5	175.7	176.2	176.2	175.9	176.4	171.6	177.9	178.2	178.5
2003	178.4	179.3	179.9	181.2	181.5	181.3	181.3	182.6	182.5	182.6	182.7	183.5
2004	183.1	183.8	184.6	185.7	186.5	186.8	186.8	187.4	188.1	188.6	189.0	189.9
2005	188.9	189.6	190.5	191.6	192.0	192.2	192.2	192.6	193.1	193.3	193.6	194.1
2006	193.4	194.2	195.0	196.5	197.7	198.5	198.5	199.2	200.1	200.4	201.1	202.7
2007	201.6	203.1	204.4	205.4	206.2	207.3	206.1	207.3	208.0	208.9	209.7	210.9
2008	209.8	211.4	212.1	214.0	215.1	216.8	216.5	217.2	218.4	217.7	216.0	212.9
2009	210.1	211.4	211.3	211.5	212.8	213.4	213.4	214.4	215.3	216.0	216.6	218.0
2010	217.9	219.2	220.7	222.8	223.6	224.1	223.6	224.5	225.3	225.8	226.8	228.4
2011	229.0	231.3	232.5	234.4	235.2	235.2	234.7	236.1	237.9	238.0	238.5	239.4
2012	238.0	239.9	240.8	242.5	242.4	241.8						

27   The basic rules of computation

Introduction

1. This chapter is concerned with the basic rules of computation used in the taxation of capital or chargeable gains. It begins with an examination of the meaning of consideration and market price, and the allowable cost deductions which apply to both individuals and incorporated entities. The chapter goes on to consider the computational rules on disposal of an asset by an individual in 2012/13. The chapter concludes with the somewhat different rules for taxing the disposal of an asset by an incorporated entity, including indexation allowance.

Consideration and market price

2. As a general principle a chargeable gain is computed by deducting from the total consideration obtained the initial cost of acquisition, any allowable expenditure, and (for corporate gains only) the 'indexation allowance'. Consideration is taken to be the gross sales price without any deduction for expenses of sale. However, in the following cases the disposal is deemed to be at market price:

a)   where the disposal is by way of a gift or a part-gift (sale at undervalue);

b)   where the transaction is not at arm's length, e.g. between connected persons (excluding connected persons who are husband and wife, civil partners, or CGT-grouped companies, where the disposal is deemed to be at a price giving 'no-gain-and-no-loss');

c)   where an asset cannot be readily valued, or is acquired in connection with a loss of employment;

d)   on a transfer into a settlement by a settlor.

3. Where the market value is used in place of actual payment for the deemed proceeds of a disposal, then the person who acquires the asset is also treated as acquiring at the market value, which becomes their CGT allowable cost.

Market value means the price which assets might reasonably be expected to fetch in a sale on the open market. There is a special department of HMRC called the Valuation Office Agency which gets involved in market value rulings if the market value evidence submitted by the taxpayer is not accepted without query. Special statutory rules apply in finding the market value of some assets for CGT, as noted below.

Deferred consideration

4. Even if the consideration is payable by instalments, the whole of the consideration is brought into account with no discount for the future receipt of monies. Where all or part of the consideration is deferred because it cannot be quantified at the date of the original disposal contract, the value of the right to receive that additional amount is separately worked out and is included as proceeds along with the ascertainable consideration at the date of the original disposal. The same value for this legal right (known as a 'chose in action', and treated as a separate intangible asset for CGT purposes) is deducted as an allowable cost from the deferred consideration when later determined and paid. So in effect the receipt of the final deferred consideration is treated as the disposal of the asset created by the legal right.

Allowable deductions

5. The following may be deducted from the consideration to arrive at the capital gain or allowable loss:

a)   The cost of acquisition, including incidental expenditure.

b)   Any enhancement expenditure, but not repairs or maintenance.

c)   Expenditure incurred in establishing or protecting the right to any asset.

d)   Incidental costs of disposal (see 6 below).

e)   The indexation allowance, only for corporate taxpayers (see 10 below).

6. Incidental costs include: fees, commission, or professional charges such as legal accountancy or valuation advice: costs of transfer and conveyance including stamp duty: advertising to find a buyer or seller. The following items of expenditure are specifically disallowed:

a)   Costs of repair and maintenance.

b)   Costs of insurance against any damage injury or loss of an asset.

c)   Any expenditure allowed as a deduction in computing trading income.

d)   Any expenditure recouped from the Crown or public or local authority.

Entrepreneurs' relief

7. For chargeable assets disposed of after 5th April 2008 by individuals or trustees, entrepreneurs' relief (ER) reduces the tax on qualifying business gains.

ER is not automatic and must be claimed. It is available in respect of gains made by individuals on the disposal of:

a)   all or part of a trading business which the individual carries on alone or in partnership;

b)   individual assets of the individual's or partnership's trading business, following the cessation of the business (the relief is available for one year after cessation);

c)   shares in (and securities of) the individual's 'personal' trading company (or holding company of a trading group). The relief is given on gains on disposals of shares in (and securities of) a trading company (or the holding company of a trading group) provided that throughout a one-year qualifying period before the disposal, the individual making the disposal:

   i)   is an officer or employee of the company, or of a company in the same group of companies; and

ii) owns at least 5 per cent of the ordinary share capital of the company, and that holding enables the individual to exercise at least 5 per cent of the voting rights in that company.

d) assets owned by the individual and used rent-free by his / her 'personal' trading company (or group), or trading partnership.

e) The rules for ER extend to assets held by trustees and personal representatives.

f) The aim of ER is to create a charge to capital gains tax at an effective rate of 10%. For disposals after 22 June 2010 there is a separate rate of ER tax at 10% (For disposals up to 22 June 2010 the same effective rate was achieved by 5/9ths of the gain being chargeable at 18%). There is a lifetime limit on ER gains of £10m from 6 April 2011.

The basic computation for individuals

8. This section illustrates a basic computation for an individual.

a) The basic computation for an individual who disposes of an asset that does not qualify for entrepreneurs' relief is illustrated as follows:

Example 1:

Peter purchased a house that was not his main residence, in January 1987 for £50,000. He incurred legal fees and survey fees of £500 on the acquisition of this property. In September 1991 Peter added an extension to the property at a cost of £15,000. He sold the house on 1st May 2012 for £350,000, incurring legal fees and selling costs amounting to £2,000. Peter has no other disposals for the tax year 2012-2013. Peter's taxable income for 2012-13 is £32,000, and he made net contributions of £1,600 to a personal pension scheme.

Compute the chargeable gain and capital gains tax payable on the disposal.

Suggested solution

	£	£
Proceeds from sale		350,000
Allowable deductions:		
Initial cost	50,000	
Costs of acquisition	500	
Enhancement expenditure, September 1991	15,000	
Incidental costs of disposal	2,000	(67,500)
Chargeable gain		282,500
Less annual exemption		(10,600)
Gain subject to capital gains tax		271,900
Capital gains tax @ 18% of £4,370 (see working)		786
Capital gains tax @ 28% of £267,530		74,908
Total CGT payable		£75,694

Working to support CGT rates above: £
Income tax basic rate band 2012/13 34,370
Extension to basic rate band for Peter
(See Part 2, income tax computations):
Grossed up personal pension contributions £1,600 x 100/80 2,000
Peter's basic rate income tax band 36,370
Taxable income (32,000)
Basic rate band available for taxation of gains at 18% £4,370

b) The basic computation for an individual who disposes of a business asset that qualifies for ER is shown in the following example:

Example 2:

Simon purchased a retail shop selling electrical goods in October 1985 for £85,000. He incurred acquisition costs of £1,500. In September 2000 the shop was extended and structurally improved at a cost of £30,000. Simon has been running this business as a trade since buying the shop. On 1st June 2012 Simon sold the shop and the trade for £750,000, incurring legal costs and other selling expenses of £3,500. Simon has no other capital gains during the tax year, and has made no previous claims for entrepreneurs' relief. Compute the chargeable gain and the capital gains tax payable.

Suggested solution £ £
Proceeds from sale 750,000
Allowable deductions:
Initial cost 85,000
Costs of acquisition 1,500
Enhancement expenditure, September 2000 30,000
Incidental costs of disposal 3,500 (120,000)
Chargeable gain 630,000
Less annual exemption (10,600)
Gain subject to capital gains tax 619,400
Capital gains tax @ 10% 61,940

Notes:

i) This is a sale of a trade, together with the main chargeable asset used for the trade, therefore both disposals qualify for entrepreneurs' relief.

From a CGT computational point of view it is not critical to separate the disposal into the shop and the trade goodwill, if both are sold together (though for stamp duty purposes it is likely that a clear price allocation would be set out in the legal documents). It is assumed none of the sale proceeds mentioned related to non-chargeable trade assets such as stock or trade debtors.

ii) Simon has used up £630,000 of his lifetime allowance for capital gains tax entrepreneurs' relief purposes. He therefore has a lifetime balance left for entrepreneurs' relief of £9,370,000 at 2 June 2012.

Part-disposals

9. On a part-disposal of an asset (other than a holding of shares or securities), the attributable cost of acquisition of the part disposed of is determined by the following general formula:

$$\text{Attributable cost} \ = \ \text{Cost of acquisition} \times \frac{A}{A + B}$$

A is the consideration for the disposal, excluding any expenses of sale.

B is the market value of the un-disposed portion.

Indexation allowance – Incorporated entities

10. For incorporated entities an indexation allowance applies in computing the gain.. The main general provisions relating to disposals are as follows.

a) The indexation allowance is calculated by reference to the change in the Retail Price Index between the date of the disposal and:

   i) the date of acquisition, or

   ii) the 31st March 1982 if that is later than the date of acquisition.

b) The indexation applies to the initial cost of acquisition and any enhancement expenditure but not to the incidental costs of disposal.

c) Where an asset was held on the 31st March 1982 indexation is automatically applied to the market value at that date or the actual allowable expenditure, whichever is the greater.

d) On a part-disposal, indexation allowance is calculated based on the fractional part of the total cost that was used in the calculation of the unindexed gain. The allowable cost carried forward for the part not disposed of is not indexed at that stage.

e) The indexation allowance cannot be used to create or increase a capital loss.

Calculation of indexation allowance

11. The 'indexation factor' is calculated according to the following formula, and rounded by statute to three decimal places. See the official RPI table provided at the end of Chapter 26.

$$\frac{\text{RPI in month of disposal} - \text{RPI in month of acquisition (or if later 31}^{\text{st}}\text{ March 1982)}}{\text{RPI in month of acquisition (or if later 31}^{\text{st}}\text{ March 1982)}}$$

Example

Q Ltd purchased an office for use in its trading business for £10,000 in January 1983. Legal charges and other allowable costs of acquisition amounted to £500. In January 1984 an extension to the property was built for £3,000, and major repairs undertaken amounting to £1,000. The whole property was sold for £100,000 on 28th January 2012 with incidental costs of disposal of £1,500. RPI January 1983 = 82.61, January 1984 = 86.84, January 2012 = 238.0.

Required: Compute the chargeable gain arising to Q Ltd on the disposal of the office.

Suggested solution

CGT computation		£	£
Proceeds of sale			100,000
Less: Expenses of disposal			(1,500)
			98,500
Less: Cost of acquisition (1983)		10,000	
Expenses of acquisition (1983)		500	
Enhancement expenditure (1984)		3,000	
			(13,500)
Un-indexed gain			85,000
Indexation allowance to January 2012 (See working)			(24,973)
Chargeable gain added to TTP			60,027

Working : Indexation allowance:

On Cost January 1983	£10,500		
$\dfrac{238.0 - 82.61}{82.61} =$	$1.881 \times 10,500 =$		19,750
On Enhancement cost January 1984	£3,000		
$\dfrac{238.0 - 86.84}{86.84} =$	$1.741 \times 3,000 =$		5,223
Total indexation allowance			24,973

Notes:

i)   The gain will be taxable at Q Ltd's corporation tax rate, as part of taxable total profits.

Assets held on 31st March 1982 – rebasing

12.   For assets held on 31st March 1982, the following rules apply when computing a chargeable gain

a)   The gain on cost is compared with the gain which would apply if the asset is assumed to have been sold on 31st March 1982 and immediately re-acquired at its market value at that date. This is called the re-basing comparison.

b)   For incorporated entities, indexation allowance is then deducted for the period from March 1982 up to disposal, but the factor is multiplied in both cases by the same figure, which is the **higher** of the 1982 market value and the actual cost.

c)   As indexation allowance cannot be used to increase a loss on disposal, therefore the remaining indexation allowance is unavailable once a gain has been reduced to zero.

d)   If both calculations result in a gain, the chargeable gain is the lower gain. If both of them give a loss, the allowable loss is the lower loss. If one gives a loss and the other a gain, or either of them gives a nil result, then the chargeable gain is nil.

e)   The above comparison is not done if the taxpayer made a CGs rebasing election under Finance Act 1988 in which case all computations for pre-April 1982 assets are based only on market values at 31 March 1982 without any regards to the original cost records. A rebasing election had to be made during the 2 tax years after the first relevant disposal after 1/6 April 1988 of a chargeable asset owned since before 1 April 1982.

Example

X purchased a painting in 1979 for £10,000 which he sells for £85,000 in August 2012, after incurring expenses of disposal amounting to £5,000. The market value at 31st March 1982 was £36,000.

Calculate the chargeable gain and the CGT on it, assuming that X has no other gains in 2012/13, and taxable income totalling £40,000.

Solution: Capital gains tax computation 2012/13

	Re-basing 31.3.82	Original cost
	£	£
Proceeds of sale	90,000	90,000
Cost of disposal	(5,000)	(5,000)
	85,000	85,000
Less cost of acquisition/	–	(10,000)
MV at 31.3.82	(36,000)	
Gain	49,000	75,000

Take the lower of the two gains:	£49,000
Realised in August 2012	
Less: Annual exemption	(10,600)
Chargeable gain subject to CGT	38,400
Remaining IT basic rate band	NIL
Subject to capital gains tax @ 28%	£10,752

Note

i)   The smaller gain of £38,400 obtained from re-basing will be taken as the chargeable gain. Where the March 1982 value is greater, a computation on original cost is not normally required.

Indexation – losses

13. The Indexation allowance claimed by corporations cannot be used to turn a gain into a loss or to increase a loss.

Example

B Ltd owns freehold property which has a market value of £20,000 on 31st March 1982. The property was sold on 30th January 2012 for:

      a) £300,000   b) £50,000

Compute the chargeable gain/loss.

Solution: B Ltd chargeable gain/loss computation

a)	Proceeds of sale	300,000
	March 1982 value	(20,000)
	Unindexed gain	280,000
	IA $\dfrac{238.0 - 79.44}{79.44} = 1.996 \times 20,000 =$	39,920
	Chargeable gain	240,080
b)	Proceeds of sale	50,000
	March 1982 value	(20,000)
	Unindexed gain	30,000
	IA of £39,920 restricted to	30,000
	No gain/loss	nil

Disposals treated by law as no gain / no loss

14. The following transactions are treated as no gain/no loss disposals. Other no gain/no loss transactions, such as on certain company reconstructions, are outside the scope of this book.

    i)   Acquisitions of quoted securities before 6th April 1965 where the substitution of the market value at 6th April 1965 converts a gain into a loss or vice versa.

    ii)   Disposals between spouses or civil partners who were not permanently separated throughout the tax year in question.

    iii)   Transfers of chargeable assets between companies in the same capital gains group. See Chapter 33, section 7.

Student self-testing question

1.   Z purchased a painting for £100,000 in August 1984 which he sold for £200,000 on the 3rd March 2013. Selling expenses amounted to £10,550.

Compute the capital gains tax payable on 31 January 2014, assuming no other chargeable disposals in the year, and that Z's 2012/13 taxable income is £49,000.

Suggested solution: Z CGT computation 2012/13

	£	£
Proceeds of sale		200,000
Less cost of acquisition	100,000	
Selling expenses	10,550	(110,550)
Gain		89,450
Annual exemption		(10,600)
Gain subject to CGT		78,850
Capital gains tax @ 28%		22,078

Question without answer

1. A shareholding qualifying for entrepreneurs' relief was acquired by an individual in February 1988 at a cost of £70,000. The individual has not made any disposals since April 2008. The shareholding was sold in January 2013 for sale proceeds of:

   i)   £15,500,000

   ii)   £850,000

Requirement

Compute the capital gains tax payable in each case, assuming the individual has £50,000 of taxable income for 2012/13.

28 Chargeable persons

Introduction

1. This chapter is concerned with the persons who are liable to capital gains tax (as opposed to corporation tax on chargeable gains). It considers individuals (including spouses/civil partners), trustees and personal representatives.

Individuals

An individual is liable to capital gains tax if he or she is resident, or ordinarily resident in the UK in an income tax year, wherever he or she may be domiciled.

For persons legally domiciled in the UK as well as resident or ordinarily resident in the UK, all chargeable gains worldwide are taxed on the arising basis and the date of disposal is the date of the legal contract becoming unconditional (or in the case of gifts, the effective date of transfer of ownership).

Remittance basis of assessment

2. An individual who is resident or ordinarily resident in the UK, but who is not domiciled in the UK, may elect to self-assess capital gains on foreign assets only to the extent that the proceeds from those gains are remitted to the UK. This is called the remittance basis. From 2008 a non-domiciled resident who claims UK taxation on the remittance basis does not benefit from a CGT annual exemption.

If remittance basis is selected for CGT, many detailed rules define remittances and match them to gains (e.g. for double taxation relief). In general the gain made on an asset is identified with the earliest possible remittance.

The CGT rate for gains taxed on non-domiciled residents on the remittance basis is 28% regardless of net income. Also, taxpayers who elect the remittance basis for CGT get no annual exemption.

In addition, as there is no concept of remitting loss, a non-domiciled individual who elects remittance basis obtains no relief for losses on foreign assets.

Therefore some non-domiciled residents who could choose remittance basis choose to be taxed on the arising basis in order to obtain relief for non-UK capital losses. For this purpose the terms residence, ordinary residence and domicile, have the same meaning as for income tax.

CGT Annual exemption

3. For all individuals, except non-domiciled residents taxed on the remittance basis, the first £10,600 of net gains in the income tax year is exempt.

For most trustees the first £5,300 of net gains in the year is exempt (this limit is subject to reduction for multiple trusts created on the same day)

The following points should be noted.

a)   In principle, for each tax year, chargeable gains and allowable losses for the whole year are first added together. Any annual exemption is deducted from the total net gains before considering losses brought forward which may also be deducted.

b)   If a taxpayer has no taxable income for the year, unused income allowances and reliefs cannot be deducted from net chargeable gains.

c)   The personal capital gains tax rate for 2012/13 is either 10% (disposals qualifying for entrepreneurs' relief), 18% or 28%, as noted in Chapter 26.

The CGT rate for all gains taxed on non-domiciled UK residents on the remittance basis is 28%. (See section 7.)

4.   A capital loss can only be offset against a capital gain of the same or a later year. Losses of the current year must be set against gains of the current year before being carried forward. The annual exemption amount of £10,600 is deducted from the net gains.

Losses brought forward can be set off against gains of the current year.

Losses brought forward are only utilised to the extent that they are used to reduce any gains to the £10,600 level.

The only time when capital losses can be carried back against gains of an earlier year is after death. (See section 6).

Example of loss offset – current year

Barry makes a chargeable gain from shares of £20,000 on 3 May 2012. He also incurred a capital loss in October 2012 of £2,500. The shares are not eligible for entrepreneurs' relief. Barry has taxable income of £48,000.

Compute Barry's CGT liability for 2012/13

Solution: Barry CGT computation 2012/13

	£
Chargeable gain	20,000
Less capital loss	(2,500)
Gain	17,500
Less annual exempt amount	(10,600)
Taxable gain	6,900
CGT payable 6,900 @ 28% =	1,932

Husband and wife

5.   All husband and wife tax rules apply equally to registered civil partners from the tax year 2005/06. The following points should be noted regarding CGT.

a)   Husband and wife are treated as separate individuals, each with a CGs annual exemption of £10,600 for 2012/13.

b)   Chargeable gains are recorded by husband and wife in their respective Self-Assessment Tax Returns (SATR).

c)   The transfer of chargeable assets between husband and wife in any tax year does not give rise to any CGT charge where they are living together in the tax year; however the next owner takes on the previous one's exact CGT base cost at the date of transfer.

d)   Losses of one spouse cannot be set against the gains of the other.

e)   Where assets are jointly owned then in the absence of a declaration of beneficial interest, the 50–50 rule applies and each is treated as owning 50% of the assets.

f)   Where a married couple live together they can have only one residence which can qualify as their principal private residence.

Example

Mr and Mrs Johnson have the following data relating to the year ended 5th April 2013:

	Mr J £	Mrs J £
Capital gains	15,200	14,000
Capital losses	–	1,000
Taxable income	50,000	18,000

Entrepreneurs' relief is not available.

Compute the CGT liabilities for 2012/13.

Solution: CGT computation 2012/13

	Mr J £	Mrs J £
Capital gains	15,200	14,000
Less losses	–	(1,000)
Net gains	15,200	13,000
Less annual exemption	(10,600)	(10,600)
Chargeable gains	4,600	2,400
CGT payable @ 28% / 18%	1,288	432

Trading losses set against chargeable gains

6. Where a trading loss is incurred in the year then to the extent that it has not been fully relieved against total income of the same or prior tax year, a claim for relief against any chargeable gain can be made. The amount to be claimed cannot exceed the chargeable gain for the year, before deducting the exemption amount of £10,600.

Example

Nick, who is single, has the following data relating to the year 2012/13:

	£
Trade profits 2012/13 (year to 31.3.2013)	15,000
Chargeable gains	12,500

In the year to 31st March 2014 Nick has a trading loss of £16,000, and no other income.

Compute the income tax liability and CGT liability for 2012/13.

Solution

Nick Income tax computation 2012/13

	£
Trade profits	15,000
Less loss relief (see Chapter 14)	(15,000)
Assessable income	–

CGT computation 2012/13

	£
Chargeable gains	12,500
Less trading loss claimed against current year gain	(1,000)
Chargeable gains	11,500
Less annual exemption	(10,600)
	900
CGT payable @ 18%	162

Notes

i)   Nick's personal allowance of £8,105 would be wasted.

ii) The trading loss of £16,000 has been dealt with as follows:

	£
Carry back 2012/13	15,000
Capital gains 2012/13	1,000

The trading loss for the year ended 31st March 2014 can be used in either 2012/13 or 2013/14. However, since there is no other income in the period to 31st March 2014 the carry back has been used. Nick could also have decided to carry the loss forward against future trading income (see Chapter 14).

Personal representatives and trustees

7. The executor or administrator of a deceased person's estate is deemed to have acquired all the chargeable assets at the market value at the date of death, but there is no disposal. Legatees are also deemed to have acquired assets passing to them, at their market value at the date of death, so that any transfer to a legatee is not a chargeable disposal.

Rates   The first £10,600 of net gains is exempt in the tax year in which the death occurs and the subsequent two tax years.

The 2012/13 CGT rate for personal representatives (trustees administering the estates of deceased people) should be 18% for the first £10,000 of gains, then 28%.

The 2012/13 rate for Trustees who are not personal representatives of a deceased person is 28%.

Losses   Losses of the personal representative cannot be set against previous gains of the deceased.

Losses of the deceased in the year of his or her death can be carried back against gains of the previous three tax years.

Within the time scale of the year of death and the next two years, losses need only be utilised to the extent that they reduce the net gains to the exempt amount.

Reform of overseas aspects of CGT for individuals

8. CGT is essentially a territorial tax based on residence. Overseas resident individuals and companies do not pay CGT on gains on UK chargeable assets unless they are assets of a trade based in the UK (a permanent establishment).

Since the 1990s there have been various reforms to CGT to counter tax planning to avoid CGT on gains of individuals who had both a UK and an overseas connection.

As a result of this and other reforms, UK personal CGT for taxpayers who are not primarily connected with the UK by all of tax residence, tax ordinary residence, and legal domicile is very complicated. It is also due to change in 2013/14. Therefore what follows is only a brief summary.

To date, the legal meaning of UK tax residence and ordinary residence have been largely established by case-law and HMRC practice. The Government has announced that new statutory rules defining UK tax residence will be included in Finance Bill 2013. (These rules were originally promised for 2012 but the timetable was put back in order to allow further consultation.) For example, the technique of becoming 'not ordinarily resident' in the UK for a relatively short period in order to avoid UK CGT on a specific disposal was made more difficult by the 'temporary non-residents' rule.

Current plans are that the legal concept of 'ordinary residence', which is something separate from 'residence', and on its own brings a taxpayer into UK CGT for a tax year, is to be removed from tax law in 2013/14. However, in 2012/13 the old non-statutory rules still apply.

Non-domiciled individuals and the remittance basis

The remittance basis election is made separately for each tax year. It is important to remember that unremitted gains dating from earlier tax years, when remittance basis was chosen, must be self-assessed in the tax year of later remittance to the UK. This applies even if the gain is remitted in a tax year when the arising basis applies for current gains. Gains taxable on the remittance basis are computed at the date of disposal in accordance with normal UK rules.

Non-domiciled UK residents who have ever made the remittance basis election even just for one tax year, must be very careful with their financial record keeping as evidence of the source of remitted funds is crucial if tax is not to be payable.

'Remittance' of a past gain does not just include remittance of cash. For example a remittance can be triggered by buying an asset overseas (such as a yacht) which is later brought to the UK, or paying bills in the UK with an overseas credit card.

Temporary non-residents

The following rules apply to individuals who become non-UK resident and non-UK ordinarily resident after 16th March 1998, but who stay away for less than five complete tax years. Such individuals are still liable to UK CGT on certain gains made during that period of temporary non-residence.

A gain or loss of the tax years between the years of departure and return ('the intervening years') in the UK will be taxed as a gain of the year of return, or allowed as a loss of the year of return provided that:

a)   the individual was resident or ordinarily resident for at least four out of seven tax years before the tax year of departure; and

b)   the intervening years do not exceed five tax years; and

c)   the gain or loss arose on an asset acquired by the individual before actual departure from UK.

Partners' capital gains

9. A partner is assessed individually in respect of his or her share of any chargeable gains accruing from the disposal of partnership assets. Therefore personal capital losses can be set against his or her share of any partnership capital gains, and vice versa.

Student self-testing question – married couples and CGT

Roger bought a painting for £15,000 in June 2008 which he sold for £65,000 on the 8th May 2012. Costs of disposal amounted to £2,200. Roger has taxable income of £52,000 for 2012/13.

Roger's wife Vanessa has capital losses of £3,500 for 2012/13.

Compute Roger's 2012/13 CGT liability.

Solution: CGT computation 2012/13

	£	£
Proceeds of sale 8.5.2012		65,000
Less Cost	15,000	
Cost of disposal	2,200	(17,200)
Gain		47,800
Less exempt amount		(10,600)
CGT assessment		37,200
CGT payable @ 37,200 @ 28%		10,416

Notes

i)   The losses of Vanessa can only be used against her own future gains.

Questions without answers

1. Frank has chargeable gains of £11,500 for the year 2012/13, and capital losses of £500. His wife sells a piece of land for £10,000 on 10th May 2012 being part of a larger plot purchased in 1995 for £3,000. The remaining part had a value of £30,000 on 10th May 2012. Frank's taxable income for 2012/13 is £21,300 and his wife Florence's is £1,000.

Compute the CGT liability for 2012/13 of Frank and Florence.

2. Arnold purchased a painting in 2000 for £20,000 which he sells for £50,000 in January 2013.

Arnold's wife Patricia owned a small business which she acquired for £16,000 on the 1st January 1989. On the 1st January 2013 she sells the business for £165,000, incurring disposal costs of £344.

Both Arnold and Patricia are both higher-rate income taxpayers in 2012/13.

Compute the CGT liability of Arnold and Patricia for 2012/2013.

29   Chargeable occasions

Introduction

1. A chargeable gain or loss arises on the occasion of a disposal of a chargeable asset. For this purpose a disposal takes place in the following circumstances, each of which is examined in this chapter:

> on a sale by contract
>
> on the compulsory acquisition of assets
>
> where capital sums are derived from assets destroyed or damaged, e.g. from insurance claims
>
> where assets have negligible value
>
> on the part-disposal of an asset
>
> by value shifting
>
> on a death
>
> where a gift is made

Disposal by contract

2. Where an asset is disposed of by way of a contract then the date of the disposal is the time the contract is made and not, if different, the time when the asset is conveyed or transferred. For shares and securities the date of the contract note is the disposal date, and for land and buildings and house property the date of the contract to sell is the relevant date, and not the date of completion.

Compulsory acquisition

3. Where there is a compulsory acquisition of an interest in land, then the date of the disposal is the date when the amount of compensation is formally agreed.

Capital sums derived from assets

4. Compensation or insurance monies received in respect of an asset, amounts to a disposal by the owner. Thus if A has property which is damaged or destroyed by fire, then any insurance money received constitutes a disposal for CGT purposes. However, this is varied to some extent where the capital sum is used for the following purposes:

a)   to restore a non-wasting asset or

b)   to replace a non-wasting asset lost or destroyed.

Doe the meaning of wasting and non-wasting assets, see Chapter 30.

Restoration of a non-wasting asset

5. If a capital sum is received in respect of a non-wasting asset, which is not lost or destroyed, the taxpayer can claim to have the sum deducted from the cost of acquisition, rather than treated as a part-disposal. Such a claim can only be made if:

a) the capital sum is used wholly for restoration, or the amount not restored is small relative to the capital sum or

b) the capital sum is small relative to the value of the asset.

Small is normally taken to be 5% or less.

Example

Terry purchased a picture for £35,000 in June 2009, which was damaged by fire in May 2012. Insurance proceeds of £1,000 were received in December 2012, the whole amount being spent on restoring the picture. T claims to have the sum of £1,000 not treated as a disposal. The value of the painting after the fire was estimated at £8,000.

Show the computation of the allowable expenditure carried forward.

Solution: Computation 2012/13

	£
Cost	35,000
Less insurance sum	(1,000)
	34,000
Add expenditure on restoration	1,000
Allowable expenditure c/f	35,000

Note

From a capital gains tax point of view, Terry is in exactly the same position as he was before the picture was damaged.

Example

Sam purchased a piece of antique furniture for £12,000 in May 2008. The item was damaged by water in January 2012 for which £1,500 was received by way of insurance in July 2012. The amount spent on restoration was (a) £1,500 (b) £1,430.

Compute the allowable costs in each case, on the assumption that Sam claims to apply the insurance payment to restoration, rather than have it treated as a capital receipt on part-disposal.

Solution

a) As the whole sum was spent on restoration there is no disposal if Sam claims, and no overall adjustment to the cost of the antique.

b) In this case the whole sum was not spent, but the unused amount of £70 is less than 5% of the capital sum, i.e. £75. The £70 not spent on restoration need not be treated as a disposal, but may be deducted from the allowed cost.

Computation 2012/13

	£	£
Cost of antique		12,000
Less insurance claim:		
Spent on restoration	1,430	
Not spent	70	(1,500)
		10,500
Add expenditure on restoration		1,430
Allowable expenditure		11,930

Note: This is equivalent to the cost less the amount not spent i.e. £12,000 − £70 = £11,930.

Example

Valerie has a collection of rare books purchased in February 2001 for £70,000 which were damaged by fire in May 2012 when they were estimated to be worth £100,000. The value of the collection as damaged by the fire was £70,000. In July 2012 Valerie received £30,000 insurance compensation and the collection was restored.

Compute the CGT effects of a) claiming for restoring and b) not claiming for restoring the book collection.

Solution

a) **Restoring:**   **CGT computation 2012/13**

	£
Original cost of collection	70,000
Less insurance claim	(30,000)
	40,000
Add expenditure on restoration	30,000
Allowed expenditure c/f	70,000

As the whole sum has been spent on restoration there is no disposal if Valerie so claims and no adjustment to the cost of acquisition.

b) **Not restoring: CGT computation 2012/13**

	£
Insurance proceeds	30,000
Apportioned cost $\dfrac{30,000}{30,000+70,000} \times 70,000$	(21,000)
Gain subject to CGT before annual exemption	9,000
Balance of original cost carried forward (70,000 − 21,000)	49,000
Add enhancement cost - restoration expense	30,000
Total allowable expenditure c/f, if no claim is made	79,000

Replacement of non-wasting assets

6. Where an asset is lost or destroyed and a capital sum is received by way of compensation, or under a policy of insurance, then if it is spent on a replacement asset within 12 months of the receipt of the sum (or such longer period as HMRC may allow), and the owner so claims, then:

a) the consideration for the disposal of the lost or damaged asset is taken to be such that neither a gain or loss arises.

b) the cost of the replacement asset is reduced by the excess of the capital sum over the total of the consideration used in (a) above, plus any residual or scrap value of the old asset.

Example

Quentin purchased a picture for £8,000 in 2001 which was destroyed by fire in July 2012. Insurance of £20,000 was received in December 2012 and Quentin decided to purchase another picture using the full amount of the insurance money. The scrap value of the picture was £100.

Show the computations, with and without a claim under Section 23.

Solution: CGT Computation 2012/13

a)   If no claim is made

	£	£
Capital sum received December 2012	20,000	
Add residual value	100	20,100
Cost		(8,000)
Chargeable gain subject to CGT		12,100

b)   If a claim is made

	£	£
Deemed proceeds of sale December 2012		8,000
Cost		(8,000)
No gain or loss		–
Replacement picture at cost		20,000
Capital sum received	20,000	
Less deemed proceeds	8,000	
	12,000	
Add scrap value	100	
Amount deducted from original cost		(12,100)
Allowable cost carried forward		7,900

Note

Where the whole sum is not spent on a replacement asset, then some relief is available providing that the amount not spent is less than the amount of the gain.

Assets whose value becomes negligible

7. The occasion of the entire loss, destruction, or extinction of an asset (wasting or non-wasting) amounts to a disposal of that asset, whether or not any capital sum is received. Where the value of an asset has become negligible, and HMRC accept that such is the case, then the owner may make a claim to the effect that the asset has been sold and immediately re-acquired for a consideration equal to the negligible value. Thus if P owns a building which is destroyed by fire, and it was not insured, then he may claim to have made a disposal and re-acquisition at the scrap value, including the land. An allowable loss for capital gains tax purposes would arise in the tax year for which the claim was made.

The replacement of business assets

8. Where a qualifying 'business asset' is disposed of, including the occasion of the receipt of a capital sum, then special provisions apply if the gross proceeds are either wholly or partially spent on other qualifying business assets. This 'rollover relief', which only relates to certain types of asset, is covered in Chapter 32.

Value shifting - shareholdings

9. Under these anti-avoidance rules a disposal of shares may be deemed to occur where for example the value of a controlling interest in a company is 'watered down' in such a way that the value is passed into other shares or rights, without the occurrence of a legal disposal. These rules are complex and are not further considered here.

Hire purchase

10. Where a person enters into a hire purchase or other capital transaction, giving the hire and use of an asset for a period of time, at the end of which they become the owner of the asset, the acquisition for CGT is deemed to take place at the beginning of the period of use even though it does not legally occur until a later date. However, if the contract ends before the property is legally transferred then no capital asset has been acquired and it is simply a hire contract.

For individuals, most assets acquired on hire purchase are cars or other exempt personal chattels (e.g. furniture). For companies, capital losses are more common than gains on HP assets. The rules on wasting chattels qualifying for capital allowances (see Chapter 30) mean that losses are given relief via capital allowances only, though gains over cost are taxable (e.g. gains on aircraft).

Part-disposals

11. In general any reference to a disposal of an asset in CGT legislation also includes a part-disposal, and where this occurs it is necessary to apportion the allowable cost of acquisition. The detailed rules for this are covered in Chapter 27 section 4, and Chapter 30 section 3.

Death

12. On the death of a person there is no disposal of any chargeable assets for capital gains tax purposes. The personal representative is deemed to have acquired any assets at their market value at the date of death, and any legatee also acquires the assets at the same market value, the date of acquisition being the date of death.

If a personal representative disposes of any assets other than to a legatee, e.g. in order to raise funds to pay any inheritance tax, then a chargeable occasion arises. However, in the year of death and in the two following years of assessment, the personal representative is entitled to the same annual exemptions as an individual.

Losses incurred by a personal representative cannot be set against any previous gains of the deceased. However, if the deceased had incurred any losses in the year of his or her death, then if they cannot be relieved in that year, then they can be carried back and set against gains in the previous three years.

See also Chapter 28 section 6.

Gifts

13. A gift of a chargeable asset amounts in CGT law to a disposal for value. For more on gifts and CGT, see Chapter 33.

Student self-testing question

Jane has a collection of rare prints which cost £3,000 in May 1983. They were damaged by water in November 2011 and Jane received £17,000 by way of insurance compensation in May 2012. She spent £15,000 on restoration. The value of the prints in a damaged state was £6,000.

Compute any CGT liability arising and the amount of allowable expenditure carried forward.

Solution: CGT computation 2012/13   £

	£
Capital sum received May 2012	17,000
Less spent on restoration of asset	(15,000)
Part-disposal proceeds	2,000
Proportion of cost allowable: $3,000 \times \dfrac{2,000}{2,000 + 6,000} =$	(750)
Gain subject to CGT	1,250

Allowable expenditure carried forward

Cost of acquisition	3,000
Less part-disposal cost	(750)
Balance of cost carried forward	£2,250

Question without answer

Zachariah had a painting which was badly damaged by fire in January 2012. The picture was originally purchased for £1,000 in July 1983. In May 2012 Zachariah received insurance compensation of £20,000 which he decides to spend on a new painting. The scrap value of the damaged painting was £50.

Show the CGT position for 2012/13 on the basis that:

a)   Zachariah makes a claim for replacement of the original asset under Section 23 TCGA 1992

b)   Zachariah makes no such claim.

30   Land and chattels

Introduction

1. This chapter deals with the CGT rules applicable to land and chattels under the following headings:

Freehold/leasehold land and buildings	Granting a lease from a freehold interest
Part-disposals of land	Private residence
Small part-disposals of land	Chattels
Disposals of short leases	

Freehold/long leasehold land and buildings

2. There are no special rules for the computation of capital gains arising on the disposal of assets under this heading.

A long lease is a lease with more than 50 years to run at the date of the transaction.

Land includes houses, hereditaments and buildings.

Where the property is also the main residence of an individual owner or joint owners, then the residence exemption is normally available. See below.

Part-disposals of land

3. Where there is a part-disposal of freehold or long leasehold land then unless the disposal is 'small', (see below) the normal part-disposal formula applies. This is in fact the CGT statutory formula used to apportion cost on a part-disposal of any chargeable asset, except holdings of shares and securities (see Chapter 29).

$$\textbf{Part disposal attributable cost} = \quad \textbf{Cost of whole asset} \quad \times \frac{\textbf{A}}{\textbf{A} + \textbf{B}}$$

Where A = gross disposal proceeds

B = Value of the part not disposed of at the date of the part-disposal

The 'cost of whole asset' figure used in the part-disposal cost formula

(a) includes incidental purchase expenses, and also enhancements to the extent reflected in the nature and condition of the part being disposed of;

(b) is compared with 1982 value if rebasing applies (see Chapter 27 section 12).

Example

G purchased a plot of land of 10 acres for £22,000 in May 1987, and an adjacent further 2 acres for £10,000 in June 2000. In December 2012 a sale of 5 acres was made for £60,000, from the original 10 acres, the remaining 5 acres being worth £75,000 at that time. The land was not used for business purposes.

Compute the capital gains tax payable, assuming no other disposals during the year and a taxable income for G of £55,000 in 2012/13.

Solution: CGT computation 2012/13   £

Proceeds of sale	60,000
Cost $22,000 \times \dfrac{60,000}{60,000 + 75,000}$	(9,778)
Gain	50,222
Annual exemption	(10,600)
Chargeable gain subject to capital gains tax	39,622
Capital gains tax @ 28%	11,094

In this case, since the disposal was wholly out of the first identifiable plot, there is no need to combine the acquisition costs of the two plots. The two remain separate assets for CGT.

If title to the plots had been merged, with the sale being 5 acres out of the total of 12 acres and the remaining 7 acres being valued at £85,000 at the date of disposal then the computation would be:

	£
Proceeds of sale	60,000
Cost $32,000 \times \dfrac{60,000}{60,000 + 85,000}$ =	(13,241)
Gain	46,759
Annual exemption	(10,600)
Chargeable gain subject to capital gains tax	36,159
Capital gains tax @ 28%	10,124

Small part-disposals of land

4. There are some special rules which relate to land where:

a) the value of the part-disposal does not exceed £20,000; and

b) the part-disposal is small relative to the market value of the entire property, before the disposal. 'Small' in this context means 20% of the value immediately prior to the disposal.

Given these conditions, the taxpayer can claim to have the proceeds of part-disposal deducted from the allowable cost of the whole property carried forward for CGT. In that case there is no chargeable gain recognised on the part-disposal.

The taxpayer's total consideration for disposals of land in a tax year must not exceed £20,000, for him or her to be eligible to claim relief under this section.

Example

Zara owns 10 acres of land which she acquired in April 1992 for £20,000. Incidental costs of the acquisition were £500. In August 2012 Zara sells 1.5 acres for £13,500, incurring disposal costs of £750. At the date of sale the remainder of the land had a market value of £135,500.

Compute the chargeable gain arising in 2012/13, showing the tax computations and the base cost carried forward

(a) On normal principles;

(b)   If Zara makes claims small part-disposal treatment under s.242 TCGA.

Solution:
(a) Zara CGT computation 2012/13

	£
August 2012 proceeds of sale	13,500
Deduct – Incidental cost of part-disposal	(750)
	12,750
Deduct – allowable cost: $\frac{13,500}{13,500 + 135,500} \times (20,000 + 500)$	(1,857)
Gain 2012/13	10,893

Base cost carried forward = (£20,500 - £1,857) = £18,643

(b) Alternative treatment: Claim under Section 242 TCGA 1992

	£
Cost of acquisition	20,500
Less net proceeds of sale August 2012 (13,500 – 750)	(12,750)
Revised allowed cost on a future disposal (CGT base cost)	7,750

Notes

i)   In this example, rather than claim relief under Section 242 it might well be better to accept the chargeable gain, since most of it falls within the annual exemption £10,600 for 2012/13, which might otherwise be unused.

ii)   The election under Section 242 TCGA 1992 can be made where the proceeds of sale are less than £20,000 and less than 20% of the value of the entire property before the disposal. Check:

$$\frac{\text{Disposal value}}{\text{Total value before sale}} = \frac{13,500}{13,500 + 135,500} = 9\%$$

Principal private residence exemption

5. A gain accruing to an individual on the disposal of his or her principal private residence (PPR) is exempt, in part or wholly, from capital gains tax.

Due to a relief withdrawn for new residences from 1988, exemption is also given for any gain on disposal of a residence that was provided for occupation by a dependent relative before 6 April 1988, if it is provided rent-free and without other consideration, and has been occupied by the dependent relative since before 6th April 1988.

'Residence' includes a dwelling house (or part) together with garden land up to half a hectare in area, or more if justified.

Full exemption is available where there has been a continuous period of ownership since 1 April 1982, or since purchase, whichever falls later, and the property has been occupied as a PPR for all of that ownership period.

If there have been identifiable periods when the owner's principal residence was elsewhere, all of the following are periods for which 'deemed occupation' may be claimed, and so can be included when determining how much of the time-apportioned gain qualifies for PPR exemption.

a) Actual periods of occupation as PPR.

b) Any period of absence during the last three years of ownership, provided that at some other time the residence was occupied as the principal private residence of the taxpayer. This deemed occupation period is the only one which applies even where the original PPR occupancy ended before 31st March 1982.

c) Absences for any reason, for periods which in total do not exceed three years, and are both preceded and followed by occupation as the PPR (see comment below).

d) Absence for any period of time during which the owner was in employment, carrying out duties abroad.

e) Absences amounting in total to not more than four years, during which the owner:

    i) lived elsewhere in the UK for reasons of employment because it was impossible to live at the property because of the distance to the place of employment, or

    ii) lived away from home at the employer's request, in order to perform his or her employment more effectively.

Absences under items (c) to (e) above only qualify as deemed occupation if the owner actually occupies the home both before and after the period of absence, and if there is no other property which is claimed as an alternative PPR during the absence period. However, if the owner is unable to resume residence at the end of a (d) or (e) qualifying absence period for reasons of employment, periods of absence under (d) and (e) can still qualify as periods of occupation.

Where the maximum period of absence under (c) and (e) is exceeded, then only the excess is treated as a period of non-occupation giving rise to a chargeable gain for part of the ownership period.

Where the property qualifies as occupied for only part of the ownership period (or the period since 31st March 1982, if less), the exempt portion of the gain is:

$$\frac{\text{Period of exemption as main residence}}{\text{Total period of ownership}} \times \text{Gain}$$

6. The following additional points should be noted.

a)   If part of any house (e.g. an office, or a consulting room) is used exclusively for business purposes, the part of any gain that relates proportionately to the business portion is not eligible for PPR exemption. Dual use of rooms for both business and private purposes however allows all rooms to be included in the property eligible for PPR exemption.

b)   If a house, or part of it, is let for residential purposes while the owner is not living there, then a further exemption called 'letting relief' can be claimed as deductible from the non-PPR portion of the gain. Letting relief is given up to the smallest of:

    i)   An amount equal to the gain already exempted by PPR rules;

    ii)   £40,000; and

    iii)   the remaining chargeable gain calculated as attributable to the let period or to the let proportion of the whole property.

Example

Alex purchased a house on 1st July 1988 for £25,806, in which he lived until the 31st March 1989. The property was then let for five years, followed by occupation by Alex until he sold the house for £600,000 on the 31st March 2013.

Compute the chargeable gain.

Solution: Alex CGT Computation 2012/13		**£**
Proceeds of sale		600,000
Cost of acquisition		(25,806)
Total gain before exemption		574,194
Less exemption:		
Proportion of total gain 273/297 (see working) x £574,194		(527,794)
Subtotal – non-exempt gain		46,400
Less letting relief – Lowest of:		**£**
maximum amount	40,000)	
gain otherwise exempt	527,794)	(40,000)
gain attributable to let period	46,400)	
= chargeable gain subject to CGT		
(before annual exemption)		6,400

Notes

		Years	Months	Total months
Period of ownership	1.7.88 – 31.3.13	24	9	297
Period of absence	1.4.89 – 31.3.94	5	–	60
Periods of occupancy	1.7.88 – 31.3.89	–	9	9
	1.4.94 – 31.3.13	19	–	228

	Months
Deemed occupancy, last three years	36
Maximum allowed absence preceded and followed by occupancy	36

Actual Occupancy (additional to last three years)

1.7.88 – 31.3.89		9
1.4.94 – 31.3.10		192	201
			273

c)   A husband and wife or civil partners can only have one residence between them for the purposes of the PPR and letting exemptions.

In a tax year throughout which spouses are permanently separated or divorced, each qualifies individually for the PPR exemption.

d)   In the absence of formal election, it is a question of fact which of several actual residences is the principal private residence of a couple, or of an individual. The taxpayer can make a formal election to specify which is to be regarded as the PPR but must do so within 2 calendar years of acquiring more than one possible PPR. If no election is made the decision as to which residence was the PPR can be made by HMRC when either property is later disposed of. It is not necessary that the taxpayer elects the property in which more time is spent as the PPR. However, residential properties are only eligible to be claimed as a PPR if there is the genuine character of a settled home, not an occasional and temporary residence, in the quality of the taxpayer's, or their family's, use of the property.

e)   Deemed occupation of a PPR can apply to an individual who lives in job-related accommodation (eg Army officers), but who intends in due course to occupy a house owned by that individual, as his or her main residence. This treatment also applies to self-employed people living in job-related accommodation.

Chattels

7. A chattel is a legal term for property that is tangible and movable. For capital gains tax purposes chattels on disposal fall into four categories.

a)   Chattels which are specifically exempt from capital gains tax on disposal, e.g. private cars, and decorations for valour (medals etc.).

b)   Chattels which are 'wasting assets' (section 8).

c)   Chattels, not being wasting assets, both bought and disposed of for £6,000 or less (the limit is applied to each chattel individually).

d)   all other chattels – which in general are subject to normal CGT rules but are subject to some special rules, linked to a) to c) above .

Chattels which are wasting assets

8. A wasting asset is one with an estimated useful life of less than 50 years at the time of the disposal. A chattel which is a wasting asset is exempt from capital gains tax unless:

a)   the asset has been used since first owned, for the purposes of a trade, profession or vocation, and capital allowances were available in respect of the expenditure, whether claimed or not, or

b)   it consists of commodities dealt with on a terminal market.

Where capital allowances have been claimed, then no chargeable gain will arise unless the disposal value is greater than the original cost. If the proceeds are less than £6,000 then the exemption noted below can be claimed.

The rationale for this exemption is that wasting chattels will typically be sold at a loss due to their wasting nature. If the gains were taxable then the losses would have to be allowed as capital losses which could be set against other gains. But this does not reflect economic reality as the value of a wasting asset would decline to nil over time in any case. Therefore non-trade wasting assets are exempt.

Where a wasting chattel has received capital allowances, any excess of cost over proceeds is recouped through capital allowances given (see Chapters 13 and 20). Therefore there is another kind of tax relief given for the capital loss. It is therefore symmetrical to treat any gain on original cost as a non-exempt gain, but subject to other chattels reliefs than the wasting asset one. The cost that qualified for capital allowances is used as the cost in the final CGT computation.

Chattels disposed of for £6,000 or less

9. Any gain arising on the disposal of a chattel, not being a wasting asset, is exempt if the gross disposal value is £6,000 or less.

Marginal relief where proceeds are up to £15,000 and the chattel cost under £6,000.

To avoid distortion of market pricing of chattels around the £6,000 CGT exemption limit, marginal relief applies to limit the maximum gain if disposal proceeds are somewhat greater than £6,000 and cost was less than £6,000. This marginal relief limits the maximum gain to:

$$\frac{5}{3} \times (\text{gross proceeds} - £6,000)$$

Thus the maximum assessable gain on a chattel is always the lower of:

i) $\frac{5}{3} \times$ (gross proceeds – £6,000) or

ii)   The actual gain i.e. gross proceeds less all allowable costs.

Some arithmetical checking shows that the maximum disposal proceeds where a marginal relief calculation and claim may save any CGT is just below £15,000

(5/2 x £6,000). This is proved as follows: with £15,000 proceeds and a cost of nil, the marginal relief gain (5/3 x £9,000 = £15,000) equals the actual gain (£15,000 minus nil). Therefore for chattel proceeds above £15,000, the relief is never effective, even if cost was below £6,000.

Example – CGT marginal relief on chattels

Harry buys a piece of pottery for £800 in 1992, which he sells in October 2012 for (a) £4,800, or (b) £6,800.

Compute the chargeable gains in both cases.

Solution: Harry CGT computation 2012/13

a)   As the proceeds of sale are less than £6,000 no chargeable gain arises.

b)   £

Proceeds of sale	6,800
Less: cost of acquisition	(800)
Chargeable gain on normal principles	6,000
Chattel, so limited to a maximum of $\frac{5}{3}(6,800 - 6,000)$	1,333
Net chargeable gain subject to CGT (before annual exemption)	1,333

Restriction of losses on chattels sold for less than £6,000

10.   If a chattel which cost more than £6,000 is sold for less than £6,000 then the allowable loss is calculated by reference to gross proceeds of £6,000 and not the actual disposal value.

If both the disposal price and the cost price are less than £6,000 then a loss is not allowed at all.

Rules exist to prevent avoidance by claiming separate chattels reliefs or exemptions on two or more chattels that form part of a set, eg a set of matching chairs. Any successive disposals of part of the set to the same or connected persons have to be treated as a single transaction for the purposes of the chattels rules, even if done in different tax years. This can means chattels relief and exemptions are not available if the cost and/or the disposal value of the whole set exceeds £6,000.

Student self-testing question

1.   In March 2013, Neil sells an oil painting, which he had acquired in June 1992 for £10,000. He sells the painting for:

a)   £7,200   b)   £5,700

Compute the allowable loss in each of the above cases.

Solution

a) The disposal is not exempt from CGT, as the proceeds exceed £6,000. The allowable loss is therefore calculated in the normal way as £2,800 (£10,000 − £7,200).

b) The asset was acquired for more than £6,000 and sold for less, therefore a restricted loss is allowed. The allowable loss is is calculated by substituting £6,000 for the gross disposal proceeds. The allowable loss is therefore £4,000 (£6,000 − £10,000), not the actual loss of £4,300.

Questions without answers

1. James purchased a house in Oxford, 'Millhouse', on 31st July 1987 and took up immediate residence. The house cost £50,000. On 1st January 1990 he went to work and live in the United States where he stayed until 30th June 1992. On 1st July 1992 James returned to the UK to work for his United States employers in Scotland where it was necessary for him to occupy rented accommodation. On 1st July 1993 his mother became seriously ill and James resigned from his job to go and live with her. His mother died on 30th September 1994 leaving her house to James. James decided to continue to live in his mother's house and finally sold 'Millhouse' on 30th June 2012 for £300,000.

Calculate the chargeable gain assessable on James for 2012/13. (ACCA)

2. Mr and Mrs Scott had the following transactions in assets in the year to 5 April 2013.

Mr Scott

Sold an antique for £7,250, incurring expenses of £250, on 1 December 2012, which he had bought in April 1992 for £2,950, including expenses of purchase.

Sold a holiday cottage on 1 November 2012, which had been bought for £31,000 on 3 April 1993. In May 1994 an integral garage costing £3,000 was added. The net proceeds of sale were £80,000.

Sold a vintage Rolls Royce car for £38,000 on 9 May 2012, which had cost £15,000 on 6 May 2002.

Mrs Scott

On 4 June 2012 sold an antique silver brooch for £4,800, incurring expenses of £54. It had cost £6,200, including expenses, on 5 April 2003.

Sold 5 acres of land on 14 October 2012 for £11,000, incurring expenses of £480. It was part of a 25 acre plot, which had been purchased on 14 March 1984 for £17,000, including expenses. The remaining 20 acres have been valued at £33,000.

Compute the capital gain accruing to Mr and Mrs Scott in each of the cases above.

3. Lord Scarlet carried out the following capital transactions in January 2013.

Sold a cricket bat, signed by the 1978 England test team, which he had bought at an auction in May 1992 for £1,400. The net proceeds, after paying auctioneer's fees of £520, were £11,520.

Sold £20,000 6.75% Treasury stock for £27,400. He had acquired the stock in September 2005 at par.

Sold an antique book for £3,000. He had bought it in May 1987 for £8,000.

Sold a one-third interest in a plot of land for £11,500. Lord Scarlet had acquired the land in June 1984 for £15,000. The value of the remaining two thirds interest in January 2013 was £28,000.

Compute the total capital gains tax payable by Lord Scarlet for 2012/13, if his taxable income for the year is £36,000.

31 Shares and securities

Introduction

1. This chapter is concerned with the CGT rules applicable to shares and securities. From 6th April 2008, following removal of CGT indexation allowance and taper relief for individuals, apportionment of cost of shares of the same class became much simpler. For corporate taxpayers, gains and losses on transactions in stocks and securities still require a calculation of indexation allowance using the weighted average cost of the shareholding.

This chapter commences with an overview of the current rules on calculating the CGT cost of holdings of shares or securities of the same type and class acquired at different times. It then examines bonus and rights issues and takeover bids.

Individuals

2. Since the simplification of CGT (6 April 2008), the following rules apply to compute the capital gains and the tax liability on disposals of shares and securities by individuals.

The pooling rules described below have not applied at all times since 1965. For instance, when taper relief was part of CGT, purchases were not pooled, due to the need to track the exact length of ownership applying on a share disposal.

a) Unless shares are bought and sold within a very short period (see (d) below), the whole shareholding of the same type of shares in a given company is treated as a single asset for CGT. Its statutory name is 'the section 104 holding' and its informal name is 'the share pool'. Matching rules apply to determine how many of the shares sold on a part-disposal come from the section 104 holding/ share pool – see section 3 below.

b) The cost of shares added to the section 104 holding (by purchase, subscription, inheritance, rights issue etc) increases the total allowable cost of the share pool. On a disposal of less than the whole holding, the allowable cost is apportioned on a weighted averaged basis to the proportion of the shares leaving the pool.

c) Shares owned since before 6 April 1965 are treated separately if the taxpayer does not wish to adopt general rebasing at 1982, but otherwise they form part of the section 104 holding. Details are not considered further here.

d) If a shareholding qualifies for entrepreneurs' relief (see Chapter 32 section 8) the gain on disposal is taxed at the reduced rate of 10%. Shares qualify for ER if throughout a one-year qualifying period, the individual making the disposal:

   i) is an officer or employee of the company, or of a company in the same group of companies; and

ii)   owns at least 5 per cent of the ordinary share capital of the company and that holding enables the individual to exercise at least 5 per cent of the voting rights in that company.

e)   Shares and securities held at or prior to 31st March 1982 are valued at their 31st March 1982 market value for the computation of the capital gain on disposal.

f)   When part of the shareholding is disposed of, the cost of acquisition relating to the disposal is the proportionate part of the cost of all the shares in the holding. A weighted average cost is computed.

g)   Shares that meet the income tax relief criteria as investments in the Enterprise Investment Scheme, Venture Capital Trusts and the Seed Enterprise Investment Scheme are exempt from capital gains tax.

Share matching rules for individuals

3.   When there is a part-disposal of some of the shareholding of a particular type of share in a given company, the following matching rules apply to decide which shares were sold, and therefore what they cost:

1)   Against any shares acquired on the same day as the disposal;
2)   Against any shares acquired within the following 30 days, taking the earlier acquisitions before the later;
3)   Against all past share acquisitions, with the cost calculated on a weighted average basis (this refers to the main pool of shares, known as the 's104 holding').

These matching rules prevent a taxpayer triggering an artificial gain by share disposals with very quick repurchase, to make use of the annual CGT exemption.

Before the thirty-day matching rule was enacted for individuals, 'bed and breakfasting' shares used to be a standard tactic in share portfolios, mainly in March before the end of the tax year. The taxpayer sold selected shares, whose market value was sitting above their averaged CGT cost, to trigger gains up to the CGT annual exemption, and then repurchased the same type of shares, typically the next day (as same-day share matching applied since 1965). The chargeable gains were covered by annual exemption, and the share pool's average cost was increased, thus saving CGT in future (or increasing allowable losses in future).

The Government decided this 'bed and breakfasting' was unacceptable tax planning, and so passed new matching rules to make it only work if the shares are not repurchased for 31 days thus exposing the taxpayer to genuine market volatility. (Though shares in another company in the same market sector could be purchased the same day, instead.)

Companies have no counterpart to the 'shares of the same type bought up to 30 days later' share-matching rule, as they do not get an annual exemption.

Examples of pooled shares weighted average cost - individuals

Example 1

Denis has the following transactions in the 25p ordinary shares of Z plc, a quoted trading company.

				£
6th May 1982	purchased	3,500	shares at cost	2,500
31st March 1984	purchased	1,000	shares at cost	1,500
3rd April 1998	purchased	2,000	shares at cost	7,500

Calculate the value of the section 104 holding at 6th April 2012.

Suggested solution

S.104 holding – (share pool) Denis ordinary shares in Z plc

		Number of shares	Qualifying expenditure
		£	£
6.5.82	Purchased	3,500	2,500
31.3.84	Purchased	1,000	1,500
3.4.98	Purchased	2,000	7,500
Pool at 6.4 2012		6,500	11,500

Notes:

i)   If all the shares were sold the qualifying expenditure would be the full £11,500.

ii) In accounting terms, the average cost per share at this point is 11,500÷6,500 = £1.77. However, using a per-share average cost for CG computations involving many shares introduces rounding errors. Also, TCGA 1992 technically deems the whole of the s.104 holding to be a <u>single asset</u> for CGT. This means that the proceeds and cost of a single share are not the relevant legal values for CGT, unless only one share was sold. Therefore, in tax exams, accounting students should use the statutory method, which deals with the whole pool together as one asset, and the shares sold as a part-disposal. Students should not work out a gain per share and then multiply by the total number of shares, even though it may give the same answer where rounding is minor.

iii) If part of the holding is disposed of, the allowable cost is always allocated pro-rata. For example, if 1,625 of the 6,500 shares are sold now, the apportioned cost of these for CGT is £2,875 (1625/6,500 x £11,500). The balance of cost (£8,625) is carried forward and averaged with future acquisitions (except any acquisitions not becoming part of the s.104 holding, because they are matched with recent disposals under the matching rules).

Example 2

Colin has the following transactions in the 25p ordinary shares of K plc, a quoted trading company.

				£
1.6.1990	purchased	1,000	shares at cost	525
1.9.2000	purchased	500	shares at cost	575
2.1.2003	purchased	2,500	shares at cost	3,500
10.10.2012	sold	3,000	shares, proceeds	36,000

The shares do not qualify for entrepreneurs' relief.

Calculate the chargeable gain for 2012/13 before annual exemption.

Suggested solution

General pool K plc		Number of shares	Qualifying expenditure £
1.6.1990	Purchase	1,000	525
1.9.2000	Purchase	500	575
2.1.2003	Purchase	2,500	3,500
	Total	4,000	4,600
10.10.2012	Disposal	3,000	3,450
11.10.2012	Balance remaining in pool	1,000	1,150

Colin CGT computation 2012/13

		£
10.10.2012	Proceeds of sale of 3,000 shares	36,000
	Allowable cost	3,450
	Chargeable gain before annual exemption	32,550

Share matching rules - incorporated entities

4. The following rules apply in deciding which shares out of a holding of particular type of share in a given company were sold:

1) Against any shares acquired on the same day as the disposal;

2) Against a pool of any shares acquired in the previous 9 days, on a first in first out (FIFO) basis;

3) Against the pool of shares acquired on or after 1 April 1982 (the s104 pool or the 'indexed pool');

4) Against the pool of shares acquired between 6 April 1965 and 31 March 1982 ('the 1982 holding');

5) Against any shares acquired before 6 April 1965, unpooled, on a last in first out (LIFO) basis.

Pooling rules - incorporated entities

The following are the main provisions which apply to working out the cost and the indexation allowance on cost for part-disposals from holdings of shares or securities of the same class by an incorporated entity.

a) Shares or securities acquired on or after the 1st April 1982 form 'the **section 104 holding**' for a company.

This is not the same definition as the section 104 holding for individuals, which since 2008 extends back to shares acquired from 6 April 1965 (though any shares held at 31 March 1982 count in the section 104 holding at their 1982 value, if greater than their original cost).

The section 104 shareholding pool of a company is indexed for inflation continuously, indexation allowance being added before every 'operative event' (either when its cost increases or when some shares leave the pool). To prevent rounding error the indexation factor calculated at each step is specifically <u>not</u> rounded to 3 decimal places like all other CGT indexation calculations, but is left as an unrounded fraction.

Shares or securities acquired from 1965 to 31 March 1982 by a corporate taxpayer are called 'the 1982 holding'. This is treated for chargeable gains calculations as a single asset, separate from the single asset that is the section 104 holding.

Disposals or part-disposals from the 1982 holding qualify for indexation allowance, calculated once the disposal is made (exactly as for non-share assets of companies). The indexation calculated applies only to the proportion of the pool disposed of at that time, and to the apportioned cost, not to the whole 1982 holding.

b) The re-basing rules apply to shares and securities held at the 31st March 1982. The rebased cost of the 1982 holding for company tax computations in FY2011 or FY2012 is the market value at March 1982 of all remaining shares in the 1982 holding at 1 April 1985, less any shares from that holding which were matched against part disposals since April 1982.

c) After checking for the same-day and nine-day prior purchases, share disposals by a company are matched first to the Section 104 Holding, until it is exhausted, and then to the 1982 Holding.

Example – share transactions and matching – incorporated taxpayer

V Ltd had the following transactions in the quoted shares of Z plc, a quoted trading company.

31.1.1983	Bought	8,000	shares costing	£15,600
31.5.1998	Bought	12,000	shares costing	£36,000
28.5.2012	Sold	15,000	shares for	£176,000

Compute the chargeable gain, assuming the value of the retail prices index for May 2012 was 244.5 (estimated).

Suggested solution

The first step is to construct the section 104 holding. In documenting a company's section 104 holding, 3 columns are required for the pooled cost records: an 'indexed cost' column is required as well as original (historic) 'cost'. Indexation must be calculated in the ' indexed cost' column between each pair of successive 'operative events'. An operative event means not only a chargeable disposal of any shares from the s. 104 holding, but also any addition of more shares to it, except an addition involving no actual or deemed cost to the shareholder (i.e. a bonus issue).

Section 104 holding	Number of shares	Cost £	Indexed pool £
31.1.1983 Pool starts	8,000	15,600	15,600
IA to 31.5.98 (operative event):			15,275
$\frac{163.5-82.61}{82.61}$ x 15,600 (do not round)			
31.5.1998 Purchase	12,000	36,000	36,000
IA to 28.5.12 (next operative event):			66,875
$\frac{244.5-163.5}{163.5}$ x 66,875			33,130
Total in pool at 28.5.12	20,000	51,600	100,005
28.5.2012 Disposal (15/20)	(15,000)	(38,700)	(75,004)
	5,000	12,900	25,001

V Ltd CG computation

	£
Sales proceeds (15,000 shares)	176,000
Allowable deductions:	
Cost (from s.104 pool working)	(38,700)
Un-indexed gain	137,300
Indexation from s. 104 pool working (75,004 − 38,700)	(36,304)
Chargeable gain added to TTP	100,996

Notes:

i)   The remaining balance in the pool will be held until the next 'operative event'.

ii)   Indexation should be shown separately, in case a loss on disposal is incurred. In the case of a loss the indexation allowance is restricted so as not to create or increase a loss on disposal. Thus if the shares in this example were disposed of for £50,000, the indexation allowance deduction would be restricted to £11,300 (equal to the unindexed gain, or the sale proceeds less the apportioned unindexed cost). A capital loss can only be allowed when the shareholding is sold for less than unindexed cost.

Bonus issues of similar shares

5. When a company makes a bonus or scrip issue of shares of the same class, then the cost (or market value at 31.3.1982) of the total holding is unchanged, but its number is increased, and hence the average cost per share is reduced. For an individual taxpayer the number of shares additionally received is simply added to the total holding so that the average cost per share will be less on future disposals.

For corporate taxpayers, the number of shares in the first column of the s.104 indexed pool is increased by the bonus issue but there is no change to the value of the columns for cost and indexed cost. Indexation allowance need not be computed on a bonus issue, as there is no change to cost, and no shares are leaving the pool. A bonus issue is not an 'operative event' in the legislation.

Example

T Ltd makes a bonus issue of 1 for 5 in respect of its ordinary shares on 1st August 2004. Alex had acquired 500 ordinary shares in T Ltd on 1st May 2002 at a cost of £1,250. In June 2012 Alex sells 250 of the shares for £650. The shares do not qualify for entrepreneurs' relief.

Compute the chargeable gain.

Suggested solution

Cost of shares

		£
1.5.2002 cost of	500 ordinary shares	1,250
1.8.2004 cost of	100 bonus shares	–
	600	1,250

The deemed date of acquisition of the bonus shares is the date of the original purchases.

CGT computation 2012/13	£
Proceeds of sale June 2012	650
Cost of 250 shares sold as at 1 May 2002:	
$\frac{250}{600} \times 1,250$	521

Chargeable gain subject to CGT (before annual exemption) | 129 |

Notes

i)   It is not legally correct to work out a share pool CGT computation on the basis of the proceeds and the pool cost per individual share. The whole share pool is a single asset for CGT. In this example, all shares in the pool before the sale made up a single asset, of which 250/600 was sold. The holding separated and sold is by tax law allocated a straight proportion of the pool cost, in this case £521..

ii) The value of the 350 shares carried forward is £1,250 – 521 i.e. £729.

Example

AB Ltd makes a bonus issue of 1 for 10 on the 30th June 2007. John had acquired 10,000 ordinary shares in AB Ltd in April 2000 at a cost of £15,000. John sells 2,000 shares in May 2012 for £8,000. The shares do not qualify for entrepreneurs' relief.

Compute the chargeable gain.

Solution: John CGT computation 2012/13

	£
Proceeds of sale – 2,000 shares	8,000
Apportioned cost on part-disposal (see pool working):	
$\dfrac{2000}{11000} \times 15,000 =$	(2,727)
Chargeable gain subject to capital gains tax (before annual exemption)	5,273

Notes

i) Section 104 holding of AB Ltd shares:

	Number	Cost £
April 2000 cost	10,000	15,000
June 2007 bonus	1,000	Nil
Pool at May 2012	11,000	15,000

ii) The pool cost carried forward for the remaining 9,000 shares is (£15,000 – £2,727) = £12,273.

Bonus issues of shares or debentures of a different class

6. A bonus issue of shares of a different class, or debentures, gives rise to two distinct classes of holdings, and the original cost of the shares must be apportioned between the two new holdings. The method of apportionment is as follows:

a) Quoted investments. Apportionment by reference to the market value of the new holding on the first day a price is quoted on the stock exchange.

b) Unquoted investments. The part-disposal formula is applied as and when a disposal occurs.

Example

T plc, a quoted company, made a bonus issue on the 31st August 2012 of 1 new £1 ordinary share for every 5 held, and 1 new £1 preference share for every 2 shares held. First day dealing prices on 1st September were 160p for the ordinary, and par for the preference shares. Andrew acquired T plc shares from his father's estate on 1st July 2004: 1,000 ordinary shares in T plc at that date had a probate value of £1,500.

Compute the apportioned costs for Andrew's holdings of T plc shares.

372

Solution

Calculation of apportioned cost   £

After bonus issue of 1 for 5. 1,200 ordinary shares held at cost of 1,500
This cost is partly allocated to the preference shares for future CGT costing:

	Market value 1.9.2012 £	Apportioned cost £
1,200 ordinary shares @ 160p	1,920	1,190 see below
500 preference shares @ 100p	500	310 see below
	2,420	1,500

Ordinary shares cost c/f : $\frac{1,920}{2,420} \times 1,500$ i.e.   £1,190

Preference shares cost c/f : $\frac{500}{2,420} \times 1,500$ i.e.   £310

The ordinary and preference shares cannot be in the same share pool for CGT, as they are different classes of share. However any further shares of either type that are acquired by Andrew will be added to the appropriate pool and the new cost will be averaged on a later disposal using the section 104 holding pooled cost method.

Rights issues of the same class of share

7. Where a company makes a rights issue of the same class of shares as existing ones and they are taken up, then for CGT purposes the following rules apply.

a)   The consideration paid for the shares by way of the rights issue is deemed to take place at the time when the cost of the rights becomes due.

b)   For corporate taxpayers, the rights shares are allocated to the 1982 holding and the section 104 holding in proportion to the shares already in that holding. Each pool cost is increased accordingly.

If some of the rights shares are issued in proportion to shares held since before 1965 these rights shares and the rights cost must be separately allocated to the pre-1965 holding. For individuals the rights shares and cost will either increase the section 104 holding or increase the pre-1965 holding. There is no separate 1982 holding share pool for individuals since April 2008 (following the removal of indexation allowance for individuals).

c)   For corporate taxpayers, indexation allowance calculated on a disposal from the 1982 holding, when dealing with cost added to the 1982 holding by a post- March 1982 rights issue, only counts the time since that rights issue.

Example

Jack acquired 1,000 ordinary shares in T plc for £1,300 on the 1st October 2002. T plc makes a rights issue on the 7th February 2004 of 1 new ordinary share for every 2 held, at a price of 125p per share. Jack sells 750 shares for £10,000 on the 25th October 2012.

Compute the chargeable gain.

Solution: CGT computation 2012/13

s.104 holding pool at October 2012	**Number of shares**	**Cost £**
1.10.2002 First acquisition	1,000	1,300
7.2.2004 Rights issue	500	625
Pool value @ 25th October 2012	1,500	1,925
25.10.2012 Disposal 750 shares	(750)	
$\dfrac{750}{1,500} \times 1,925$		(963)
Balance of pool c/f	750	962

Jack, CGT computation 2012/13	**£**
750 T plc shares Proceeds of sale -	10,000
Cost – from pool working	(963)
Chargeable gain subject to CGT before annual exemption	9,037

Note

The rights issue cost of 1 for 2 is 500 new shares at £1.25 per share i.e. £625.

Rights issues of a different class

8. Where the shareholder is offered shares of a different class, or securities, by way of a rights issue, then the same rules apply as for a bonus issue of shares of a different class, noted above. The different apportionment treatment for quoted and unquoted shares also applies to this type of rights issue. For indexation purposes the additional consideration becomes a separate asset as for rights issues in general.

Takeover bids

9. When a company succeeds in a bid for the shares of another company, one of the following disposal situations will arise for shareholders in the target company.

a)   The consideration is satisfied entirely by cash. In this case any shareholder who accepts the takeover offer has made a chargeable disposal of all their shares. CGT computations will be done on that basis, allocating proceeds pro rata between different CGT share pools or holdings, if more than one class of share is received on the takeover.

b) The consideration is satisfied in shares, ie a share for share exchange. In this case an accepting shareholder is deemed to have acquired the new shares at the cost of the original shareholding(s) now given in exchange for the new (for cost read 1982 value, if rebasing applies). In this case no disposal arises for CGT.

c) The consideration is partly in cash and partly in shares, or it consists of two or more different shares or securities issued in exchange for the target shares. In both these cases, it is necessary to use the market value of the separate components of the takeover consideration, in order to apportion the original cost. If part of the consideration is cash, that part of the transaction is a part-disposal of the previous holding by the shareholder.

Example

Arthur owns 10,000 ordinary shares in P Ltd which he acquired for £15,000 on 27th June 2003. On the 30th May 2012 Z plc makes a bid for P Ltd on the following terms:

For every 2 shares in P Ltd: 80p in cash, 1 ordinary £1 share in Z plc. The market value of Z plc shares when first quoted after the takeover is 375p.

Compute the apportioned CGT base cost of the Z plc shares received by Arthur, and the chargeable in 2012/13.

Solution	Market value	Apportioned cost (4:18.75)
Working:	£	£
Cash (10,000/2) x 80p	4,000	2,637
Ordinary shares (10,000/2) × 375p	18,750	12,363
	22,750	15,000

Arthur – T plc shares CGT computation 2012/13	
Disposal cash receipt	4,000
Less apportioned cost of part-disposal for cash	(2,637)
Chargeable gain (before annual exemption)	1,363

CGT base cost of 5,000 Z plc shares carried forward (from working) = £12,363.

Arthur then sells all his 5,000 ordinary shares in Z plc for £100,000, on the 1st December 2012.

Compute the chargeable gain before annual exemption.

Solution: Arthur – Z plc shares CGT computation 2012/13 £

Proceeds of sale 5,000 shares in Z plc	100,000
Less cost of acquisition (as above)	(12, 363)
Chargeable gain	
(before annual exemption)	87,637

Small capital distributions Section 122 TCGA 1992

10. Where a person receives cash by way of a capital distribution, e.g. on a takeover bid, in the course of a liquidation, or by the sale of rights, then there is normally a part-disposal for capital gains tax purposes.

However, if the cash received is small relative to the value of the total shareholding at the time, and does not exceed the CGT allowable base cost, then the cash received may be deducted from the acquisition cost. 'Small' here is defined as the higher of £3,000 or 5% of the value of the shares immediately after the capital distribution.

Example

Terry acquired 5,000 ordinary shares in A Ltd at a cost of £3,750 on 8 February 2008. On the 12th June 2012 the company made a rights issue of 1 for 10 at a price of 25p. Terry sold his rights for 60p each on the 1st August 2012, when the market value of the 5,000 ordinary shares was £7,000.

Compute the allowed cost carried forward for Terry's A Ltd shares and any CGT liability for 2012/13, if he makes a claim for small capital distribution treatment.

Solution: Terry CGT computation 2012/13

£

Proceeds of sale of rights 500 × 60p	300

As this is less than 5% of the market value of the shares of £7,000,
the cost of acquisition can be reduced instead of computing a gain on a part-disposal:

Cost of 5,000 ordinary shares	3,750
Less sale of rights August 2012 - proceeds	(300)
Allowed cost carried forward	3,450

Note

i)   As there is no part-disposal there is no CGT liability for 2012/13.

ii)   5% of MV of £7,000 = £350.

Example

Alex holds 100,000 ordinary shares in Beta plc, which he bought in September 2008 for £50,000. In May 2012 there was a rights offer of 1 for 10 which Alex did not take up. Instead he sold his rights for £20,000. The ex-rights price of the whole shareholding on the first day the shares went ex-rights was £120,000.

Compute Alex's chargeable gain for 2012/13.

Solution: Alex CGT computation 2012/13	£
Proceeds of sale of rights	20,000
Allowable cost (use part-disposal formula)	
$50,000 \times \dfrac{20,000}{20,000 + 120,000}$	(7,143)
Chargeable gain subject to capital gains tax before annual exemption	12,857

Note

5% × ex rights price £120,000 = £6,000, which is less than the proceeds of sale from the rights, therefore this gain cannot be deducted from the cost of the original acquisition under section 122. Instead it must be treated as a capital sum derived from the holding, using the part-disposals statutory formula to find the relevant allowable cost.

Student self-testing questions

1. Peter acquired the following shares in Hirst plc.

Date of acquisition	No. of shares	Cost
9/11/90	17,000	£25,000
4/8/05	7,000	£19,400
15/7/09	6,000	£19,000

He sold 24,000 shares on the 20th July 2012 for £80,000. The shares are not business assets for the purposes of entrepreneurs' relief. Calculate the chargeable gain arising.

Suggested solution

S.104 holding	Number of shares	Cost £
9/11/90 Acquisition	17,000	25,000
4/8/05 Acquisition	7,000	19,400
15/7/09 Acquisition	6,000	19,000
Total	30,000	63,400
20/7/12 sales (x 24/30)	(24,000)	(50,720)
Balance to carry forward	6,000	12,680

Peter CGT computation 2012/2013 £

Sale proceeds	80,000
Cost	(50,720)
Chargeable gain subject to capital gains tax before annual exemption	**29,280**

2. Paul had the following transactions in Super Ltd, in which he holds the position of Finance Director.

1.10.95	Bought 20,000 shares (10%) holding for £30,000
11.9.03	Bought 4,000 shares for £10,000
1.2.04	Took up rights issue 1 for 2 at £2.75 per share
14.10.12	Sold 10,000 shares for £40,000

Note: The shares meet the qualifying conditions for entrepreneurs' relief.

Compute the gain arising in October 2012 and the capital gains tax payable, assuming Paul has no other gains during the year and a taxable income of £75,000.

Solution:

S.104 holding	Number	Cost £
1.10.95 purchase	20,000	30,000
11.9.03 purchase	4,000	10,000
Pool at 1.2.04	24,000	40,000
Rights issues 1.2.04	12,000	33,000
	36,000	73,000
14.10.12 sale	(10,000)	(20,278)
C/F	26,000	52,722

Paul CGT computation 2012/2013	£
Sale proceeds	40,000
Cost	(20,278)
Chargeable gain	19,722
Annual exemption	(10,600)
Chargeable gain subject to CGT (qualifying for ER)	9,122
CGT payable @ entrepreneurs' relief rate (10%)	912

3. Tony has the following transactions in the 10p ordinary shares of W plc, a quoted trading company.

30.04.2002	purchased	1,500	shares cost	£2,475
20.5.2003	sold	500	shares for	£1,000
25.10.2009	purchased	500	shares cost	£1,000
30.3.2013	sold	1,200	shares proceeds	£10,000

Compute the chargeable gain for 2012/13.

Solution: Tony CG computation 2012/13.

Section 104 holding :Pool working		Number of shares	Qualifying expenditure £
i) 30.4.2002	Purchase	1,500	2,475
20.5.2003	Sale (1/3)	(500)	(825)
25.10.2009	Purchase	500	1,000
		1,500	2,650
30.3.2013 Sale (4/5)		(1,200)	(2,120)
s 104 holding Pool carried forward		300	530

CG computation :

Sale proceeds	10,000
Allowable cost:	
Section 104 holding	(2,120)
Chargeable gain before annual exemption	**7,880**

Note: If Tony had been an incorporated taxpayer, the CG computation would have involved also calculating indexation allowance within the share pool, and claiming it in the gain computation.

Questions without answers

1. Frank acquired 10,000 ordinary shares in Trent plc on 12th May 2002 for £1,500. On 15th December 2003, T plc made a rights issue of 1 for 5 at a price of 130p. Frank took up the rights and then sold half of his total holding on 10th May 2012, for £16,000.

Compute the CGT liability of Frank for 2012/13, if he had no other capital transactions and his taxable income is £65,000, with no Gift Aid or personal pension payments. The shares do not qualify for entrepreneurs' relief.

2. Trevor has the following transactions in the 10p ordinary shares of Baker plc, a quoted company. Trevor has taxable income of £38,000 for 2012/13.

4.5.02	purchased	5,300	@	100p	£5,300
16.5.02	purchased	1,000	@	104p	£1,040
30.4.03	purchased	3,000	@	125p	£3,750
5.9.10	purchased	2,000	@	150p	£3,000
31.3.13	sold	9,000	@	300p	£27,000

Compute CGT liability for 2012/13. The shares do not qualify for entrepreneurs' relief.

32 CGT special reliefs and CGs groups

Introduction

1.   This chapter discusses various important CGT reliefs. Most of them are given specifically to businesses or to chargeable assets of a business, but a few (mainly EIS reinvestment relief) have not been limited to gains on business assets. The first relief discussed, rollover on replacement of assets, is applicable to both companies and individuals. The next few reliefs only apply for individuals. At the end of the chapter further special rules and reliefs that apply to companies, especially in capital gains groups (CG groups) as defined by TCGA, are outlined but without giving detailed examples as this is a very specialised area of taxation and only covered by advanced texts.

2.   The rationale for most CGT reliefs is either fairness or convenience (or both).   Some of them are designed to reward entrepreneurship or to assist succession planning in family businesses. Holdover relief in respect of a gift of business assets is covered in Chapter 33.

3.   The earliest CGT business asset reliefs generally deferred a gain to a later time, while preserving its value. These can be grouped as 'deferral reliefs'. Some of these reliefs were automatic; some had to be claimed (and so were optional).

The significance of deferral business reliefs available for individuals has been changed by the introduction of entrepreneurs' relief. ER offers the certainty of a low tax rate, but requires tax to be paid upfront, with no deferral of potential liability to a future date. To get the certainty of the benefit of ER, a taxpayer must forgo any option to defer the gain to a later date. On the other hand, claiming a deferral relief, such as gift or incorporation relief, runs the genuine risk that CGT rates may change before the gain becomes chargeable.

4.   Corporate taxpayers do not have the option of the personal CGT reliefs designed for individuals, though they can get the rollover relief on replacement of assets. However one big change to company chargeable gains taxation was the introduction in 2004 of the 'substantial shareholdings exemption', discussed at section 9. This removed a form of double taxation that used to apply when companies sold shares in subsidiaries or associates.

5.   In this chapter the following topics will be examined:

a)   Rollover and holdover relief on replacement of business assets (available to individuals and companies, including groups of companies).

b)   Entrepreneurs' relief for individuals;

c)   Incorporation relief on transfer of the whole assets of an unincorporated business to a company;

d)   Capital Gains groups for companies (outline only).

e)   The Substantial Shareholdings Exemption (SSE) for companies.

f)   Assets transferred to or from trading stock.

Rollover relief on replacement of business assets

6. The rollover relief provisions allow a taxpayer to 'roll over' any gain, or part of a gain, arising on the disposal of a qualifying business asset, by reinvesting the proceeds in a replacement qualifying asset.

Further rules are as follows:

a)   A business asset is one used for the purposes of a trade and falling within the following classes as listed in the Act:

- land and buildings;

- fixed plant and machinery;

- satellites, space stations, space craft;

- ships, aircraft and hovercraft;

- goodwill * ;

- EU agricultural quotas *.

* Since 2002, the last two items, being intangible assets, are not chargeable assets for corporate taxpayers, and so cannot support a replacement asset deferral claim for a company. They remain qualifying assets for individuals.

It is not necessary that the asset disposed of and the asset(s) specified in the claim as the replacement(s) are in the same class of qualifying assets.

b)   If the new asset is not a 'depreciating asset', (see below) the gain is deferred indefinitely, which is technically a full rollover. The gain is deducted from the CGT cost of the replcemtn asset.

If it is a depreciating asset the gain is technically only 'held over,' for a maximum of ten years. The gain is not deducted from the cost of the new asset but is attached to the asset and held 'in suspense' until certain future events, but in any case for a maximum of ten years.

Replacement asset holdover relief is commonly called 'temporary rollover relief' to distinguish it from other business holdover reliefs, eg on gifts.

c)   The asset disposed of ('the old asset') must have been used for a trade throughout the period of ownership, measured only from 31 March 1982 if owned before then. Use for a trade includes, in the case of an individual, the use of personal assets (such as a building) by the taxpayer's personal company.

d)   The replacement asset acquired ('the new asset') must be brought into immediate use in the taxpayer's trade. Where a 'new asset' is not, on acquisition, immediately taken into use for the purposes of a trade, it will nevertheless qualify for relief provided:

  i)   the owner proposes to incur capital expenditure for the purpose of enhancing its value;

ii)   any work arising from such capital expenditure begins as soon as possible after acquisition, and is completed within a reasonable time;

iii) on completion of the work the asset is taken into use for the purpose of the trade and for no other purpose; and

iv)   the asset is not let or used for any non-trading purpose in the period between acquisition and the time it is taken into use for the purposes of the trade.

e)   The new asset must be acquired within 12 months before the date of disposal, or three years after. HMRC has power to extend these limits.

f)   Where a trader closes one trade and re-invests in business assets to be used in a new trade, relief is available providing the interval between the two trades is not greater than three years.

g)   Only partial relief is available where the whole of the proceeds of sale are not used in the replacement. In these circumstances, any proceeds not reinvested are matched exclusively against the gain. Therefore the gain immediately charged to tax is the lower of:

i)   the proceeds not reinvested , and

ii)   the chargeable gain (in which case the claim has not been effective).

By concession HMRC regard proceeds net of disposal costs for this purpose.

h)   Where the proceeds from the disposal of an asset are used as capital expenditure to enhance the value of existing assets, that can be treated as acquisition of a new asset , provided:

i)   the other assets are used only for the purposes of the trade, or

ii)   on completion of the work on which the expenditure was incurred, the assets are immediately taken into use and used only for the purposes of the trade.

Example – rollover relief for an individual

Peter purchased the goodwill of a retail business in 1989 for £15,000 and sold it on 1st December 2012 for £40,000. On 31st December 2012 Peter purchased the goodwill of a new business for £60,000.

Compute the chargeable gain.

Solution: Computation 2012/13	£
Proceeds of sale	40,000
Less cost	(15,000)
Chargeable gain eligible for rollover	25,000
Cost of new business	60,000
Less rolled over gain on old business	(25,000)
Deemed cost	35,000

Notes:

i)   The base cost on any subsequent disposal of the new business asset is £35,000.

ii)   There is no charge to CGT on the first disposal as all of the proceeds have been re-invested.

Example

Karen purchased a freehold factory for her business use in 1992 for £75,000. This was sold for £250,000 on 31st May 2012, and a new factory acquired for £230,000.

Compute the chargeable gain.

Solution: Computation 2012/13

	£	£
Proceeds of sale		250,000
Less cost		(75,000)
Chargeable gain		175,000
Less rollover relief:		
Gain	175,000	
Less amount of consideration not invested	(20,000)	(155,000)
Gain chargeable immediately		20,000

Notes

i)   The base cost for subsequent disposals would be £230,000 – £155,000 i.e. £75,000.

ii)   The rolled over gain is restricted by any part of the consideration not reinvested, i.e. (250,000 – 230,000) = 20,000.

Replacement with a depreciating asset

7. Where the old asset is replaced with a new depreciating asset, the gain is not deducted from the cost of the asset, i.e. the replacement asset, but is 'held over' until the earliest of the following occurs:

a)   disposal of the depreciating asset (e.g. sale, gift or scrappage), or

b)   the depreciating asset ceases to be used in a trade, or

c)   the expiry of 10 years from the date of the replacement.

A depreciating asset is one which will be a wasting asset for CGT within 10 years from the date of acquisition, i.e. a total of 60 years at the date of acquisition.

This effectively covers all assets on the approved rollover list except

i) land and buildings held on freehold or long-leasehold;

ii) exceptionally long-life fixed plant (such as certain fixtures in buildings);

iii) goodwill (for individual tax payers only).

Where a gain on a disposal is initially held over against a depreciating asset , and a suitable non-depreciating asset is bought later, before the held-over gain on the depreciating asset crystallises, it is possible to 'roll over' the held-over gain a second time, into a non-depreciating replacement.

Example – depreciating asset

John sold his freehold shop property used for trade purposes for £120,000 on 1st August 2009. The property was bought for £50,000 on 1st May 2001. In December 2009 John acquired fixed plant for £130,000 which he used immediately for trade purposes until he ceased trading altogether on 31st March 2013 when the plant was scrapped. He had no other gains in the year 2012/2013.

Compute the chargeable gain when the plant was scrapped.

Solution

John's CGT computation 2009/10

	£
1.8.2009 Proceeds of sale of property	120,000
1.5.2001 Cost of acquisition	(50,000)
Chargeable gain	70,000
Less amount held over	(70,000)
Assessable gain	Nil

John's CGT computation 2012/13

	£
Held over gain crystallising	70,000
Less annual exemption	(10,600)
Gain subject to CGT	59,400
CGT at 10%	5,940

Notes

i) As the business ceased to trade the held over gain has crystallised. Entrepreneurs' relief is assumed as the trade has ceased altogether.

ii) No further gain arises on the scrapping of the plant, as any proceeds of sale would be < cost. No allowable capital loss can arise on plant if the net cost is already relieved by way of capital allowances (see Chapter 13).

iii) The held over gain is not deducted from the cost of the replacement depreciating asset.

Entrepreneurs' relief (ER) for individuals and trustees

8. As explained in Chapter 26 (introduction), ER was introduced from 2008 to appease taxpayers who were disadvantaged by business asset taper relief being abolished. However it does not cover quite all disposals where BATR was

available. In particular it does not cover gains on single business assets that are sold or gifted without a disposal of the related trade (within a maximum of 12 months).

ER is not automatic and must be claimed. It is available in respect of gains made by individuals on the disposal of:

a)   all or part of a trading business which the individual carries on alone or in partnership;

b)   individual assets of the individual's or partnership's trading business, following the cessation of the business (the relief is available for one year after cessation);

c)   shares in (and securities of) the individual's 'personal' trading company (or holding company of a trading group). The relief is given on gains on disposals of shares in (and securities of) a trading company (or the holding company of a trading group) provided that throughout a one-year qualifying period before the disposal, the individual making the disposal:

   i)   is an officer or employee of the company, or of a company in the same group of companies; and

   ii)   owns at least 5 per cent of the ordinary share capital of the company, and that holding enables the individual to exercise at least 5 per cent of the voting rights in that company.

d)   assets owned by the individual and used rent-free by his / her 'personal' trading company (or group), or trading partnership.

e)   The rules for ER extend to assets held by trustees and personal representatives.

It is worth noting that a gain on any property used for furnished holiday lettings of the minimum period of twelve months qualifies for ER. Compared with a potential CGT liability at 28% this is a substantial incentive to landlords to run a FHL business rather than just an ordinary letting business.

In contrast to unincorporated business disposals (generally no ER unless there is a disposal of the whole business), in the case of a shareholding there can be series of disposals, and each of these can qualify for ER, so long as the owner continues to meet the ER requirement of a 'personal trading company' – which requires some employment with the company and at least 5% control.

The lifetime limit for all ER gains per individual is now £10 million. (This is not really a 'lifetime' limit, as ER gains did not exist before 6 April 2008.)

ER gains realised before 23 June 2010 were taxed in a different way: the gain itself, rather than the tax rate, was reduced. Any gains allocated to the cumulative lifetime limit before that date are the gross ER gains (before reduction) and not the reduced chargeable amount.

As ER gains are taxable at only 10%, it is necessary to have rules for allocating capital losses and the annual exemption to ER and non-ER gains if the taxpayer has both. The rule is that the annual exemption and any capital losses of the same year are set first against non-ER gains, if any, before setting them against ER gains. Capital losses brought forward are also set first against non-ER gains of a tax year, which is to the taxpayer's advantage (but any balance of brought forward losses will be set against ER gains).

Transfer of a business to a company Section 162

9. The transfer of a business to a company is a disposal of the assets of the business and can therefore give rise to a chargeable gain or loss.

A form of rollover relief exists where an individual transfers the whole of his or her business to a company in exchange for shares, wholly or partly. In effect the held over gain is deducted from the costs of the shares acquired. The gain to which this section relates is that arising on the transfer of chargeable business assets, and the amount deferred is equal to:

$$\text{The net gain} \times \frac{\text{Value of shares received}}{\text{Total value of consideration, i.e. shares and loans}}$$

All assets of the business must be transferred although cash balances and other non-business assets may be retained as a general rule.

The taxpayer can elect for the rollover relief *not* to apply, which may be advantageous in terms of his entrepreneurs relief entitlement

Example

Andrea transfers her business to Trent Ltd on 6th April 2012 in exchange for 100,000 ordinary shares of £1 each fully paid, having a value of par, and £25,000 by way of loans. Chargeable gains on the transfer of business assets to Trent Ltd amounted to £75,000. Andrea had been in business since 1990.

Compute the chargeable gain.

Solution: Calculation of rolled over gain 2012/13

	£
$75,000 \times \dfrac{100,000}{100,000 + 25,000} =$	60,000
Chargeable gain	75,000
Less amount rolled over	(60,000)
Gain subject to CGT	15,000
Deemed cost of shares carried forward	**£**
Value of shares	100,000
Less rolled over gain	(60,000)
Net cost	40,000

Capital Gains Groups

10 If a company's transactions involve other members of the same CGs group, special rules apply. The main rules and reliefs are outlined below but this is by no means a full coverage of the effect of CGs groups. This section explains how a CGs group is defined.

a) A CGs group comprises a principal company and all of its 75% subsidiaries.

b) A 75% subsidiary means a company whose ordinary share capital is owned by the other company, either directly or indirectly, to the extent of at least 75%. Ordinary share capital comprises all shares other than fixed interest preference shares.

c) A company is not a member of a given CGs group unless the principal member of the group has itself directly or indirectly more than 50% interest in the other company's profits and assets.

d) A CGs group differs in some cases from a group loss relief relationship. Because capital assets can be passed around within a CGs group without tax implications, no company can be in two different CGs groups at the same time. The principal company of a CGs group defines how the 75% ownership boundary is drawn, for all the other companies in that group.

For example, if A plc owns 75% of B Ltd and B Ltd owns 75% of C Ltd, then there is a > 50% assets relationship between A and C, as A's ownership interest in C is 56.25% (75% x 75%).

So A, B and C are in the same CGs group (assuming no one company owns > 75% of A plc, which would alter the position).

However, if C Ltd owns 80% of D Ltd, A's ownership interest in D Ltd is only 80% x 56.25% , which is 45%. So D Ltd cannot be included in A plc's CGs group.

In this example, A, B and C will form the A plc CGs group, with A plc defined as the principal company.

D Ltd is not in the A plc CGs group, (through D Ltd could in theory be the principal company of a different CGs group, consisting of itself and its 75% subsidiaries).

D Ltd cannot be in a CGs group with C Ltd either, even though there is 80% ownership link between them. This is because C Ltd cannot be principal company of its own group, if it already belongs to a group in which A plc is the principal company.

Effect of CGs groups on the tax treatment of transactions

11. It can be seen from above that the definition of a group for corporate capital gains is different from that for group loss reliefs. (See Chapter 24.) CG groups also have effects on the deemed proceeds, chargeable person involved or chargeable occasions arising from a capital asset transaction.

(a) For rollover relief on replacement of assets, the trades of all companies in the CGs group are deemed by law to be a single trade. Thus the gain on an asset disposal by one group Member Company can be reinvested in asset acquired by another group member company,

(b)   When a group company disposes of a chargeable asset to another company in the CGs group, then the asset disposal takes place for tax purposes at no-gain-no-loss. This treatment is automatic for companies in the same CGs group.

The no gain no loss treatment is achieved by deeming the consideration for the transfer (regardless of any actual payment) to be equal to all allowable deductions available to the previous owning company for CG purposes. Those deductions include indexation allowance up to the month of transfer. This deemed consideration becomes the allowable cost of the asset for the next company in the CGs group. to own the asset.

When the asset is ultimately disposed of outside the group, the gain on normal principles forms part of the taxable profits of the disposing company – unless it elects to transfer the disposal to another company.

(c)   Due to recent reforms, two group companies in a CGs group can now elect that a chargeable asset disposal legally made by one of them is to be treated for cooperation tax purposes as if it was made by the other company. This can be done whether the disposal gave rise to a chargeable gain or an allowable loss.

Until recently, for a company to set arising gains against its own losses brought forward, it actually had to have made the loss itself. The situation was simplified so that it was no longer necessary to keep all chargeable assets of a group in the ownership of one company in order for the group to use capital losses efficiently. A past capital loss can never be transfer between companies in a CGs group, but must stay in the company treated as having made the loss-making disposal.

The election to transfer a capital asset disposal, and hence a current year capital gain or loss arising, to another CGs group company must be made within two years after the end of the accounting period in which the actual disposal is made.

a)   From 1st April 2000, CG group companies are able to transfer assets to one another on a no gain/no loss basis in a wider range of circumstances than before. In particular, it is possible to make such transfers between:

   i)   two UK resident companies with a common non-resident parent company;

   ii)   a UK resident company and a non-resident company within the same world-wide group, where the latter company carries on a UK trade through a branch or agency.

Members of a consortium are not eligible for treatment as a group for the purposes of this section, nor are close investment holding companies, unless the transfer is between close investment holding companies.

Example

Zodiac Ltd and its 75% subsidiary company Burnham Ltd had the following results for the year ended 31st March 2013.

	Z Ltd	B Ltd
Trading profits	125,000	80,000
Chargeable gains (loss)	(75,000)	100,000

Zodiac Ltd and Burnham Ltd elect that the capital loss arising from the disposal of an asset by Zodiac Ltd be treated as a disposal by Burnham Ltd.

Show the effects of the election.

Solution: Corporation tax computations AP 31.3.2013

	Z Ltd	B Ltd
Trading profits	125,000	80,000
Chargeable gains		
(100,000 – 75,000)		25,000
	125,000	105,000
Corporation tax @ 20%	25,000	21,000

Notes

i) It is not necessary for Z Ltd to transfer the asset, giving rise to the loss of £75,000, to B Ltd under section 171.

ii) The election has to be made within two years of the end of the AP in which the assets disposed of outside the group i.e. by 31.3.15.

iii) The election can be made in respect of part of an asset.

iv) Without the transfer B Ltd would be taxed on the full £180,000 of its profits chargeable to corporation tax at the marginal rate. (2 companies 300,000÷2 = 150,000)

v) Group cash savings (305,000 – 230,000) @ 20% = £15,000.

Miscellaneous points

12. a) When an asset is disposed of by a group company to a company outside the group, then any net capital allowances granted to any member of the group relating to the asset are taken into consideration in computing any gain or loss.

b) If a company to which an asset has been transferred, ceases to be a member of a group within six years of the date of the transfer the position is as follows.

    i) At the date of the acquisition of the asset by the company now leaving the group, it is deemed to have sold and reacquired the asset at its market value.

ii) There will therefore be a chargeable gain or loss on the difference between the market value at the time of the past intra-group transfer, and the original cost to the group of the asset. This gain is charged on the group (usually on its principal company) in the accounting period when the company leaves the group.

This provision does not apply if a company ceases to be a member of a group by being wound up.

c) Where a company is a dual resident member of a group of companies detailed provisions exist which are designed to prevent:

i) the transfer of assets at a no gain/no loss value where the dual resident company would be exempt from CGT

ii) the granting of rollover relief for the replacement of business assets where the replacement assets are acquired by a dual resident company.

d) 'Pre-acquisition' Capital losses brought into a group, when a company joins with its own brought-forward capital losses from past transactions, up are not available to set against all future group gains even if the necessary election is made to transfer disposals. In effect such capital losses are only available for unrestricted set-off against gains on:

i) assets held by the company at the date that it joined the group or

ii) assets acquired by that company from outside the new group, and used in a trade carried on by that company before joining the group.

Substantial shareholdings exemption for companies

13. Since 2004, disposals by companies of 'substantial shareholdings' in other companies are exempt from UK corporation tax on chargeable gains, provided that certain conditions are met.

i) The relief is available for disposals by a trading company or a member of a trading group (the 'investing' company).

ii) It applies to gains on the disposal of a 'substantial shareholding' in another trading company, or holding company of a trading group (the 'investee' company).

iii) A substantial shareholding means at least a 10% interest.

iv) The substantial shareholding must have been held for a continuous period of at least 12 months in the two years immediately before the disposal.

In order to hold a substantial interest, the investing company needs to be beneficially entitled to at least 10% of the investee company's:

i) ordinary share capital; and

ii) profits available for distribution to equity holders; and

iii) assets available for distribution to equity holders in the event of a winding-up.

In determining whether a holding amounts to a substantial shareholding, shares held by other group members are aggregated over the world-wide group.

Trading stock

14. Trading stock is not a CGT chargeable asset – it is sold to generate taxable trading income.

Where an asset is appropriated from capital account to trading stock, there is a deemed disposal at the date of the appropriation if a gain or loss would have arisen from a sale of the asset at its market value. An election can be made to have the capital gain (or loss) deducted (or added) from the accounting value of the asset, so that the ultimate profit is all taxed as trading income.

If an asset is appropriated from trading stock to capital for any purpose, it is deemed to be acquired for CGT purposes at the disposal value taken into account in computing the taxable profit.

Example

Keith purchased an asset in October 1986 for £20,000 which he held as an investment until 31st July 2012 when it was transferred to trading stocks. Market value at 31st July was £45,000. It was sold as trading stock in December 2012 for £60,000.

Show the effects of the above both with and without an election

Solution

Without election. CGT computation 2012/13

	£	£
July 2012 market value		45,000
Less cost of acquisition		(20,000)
Chargeable gain subject to CGT		25,000
Trade profits		
Sale of inventory (trading stock)		60,000
Less cost		(45,000)
Taxable profit		15,000

With election. CGT computation 2012/13

	£	£
Trade profits		
Sale of inventory (trading stock)		60,000
Market value on appropriation	45,000	
Less gain (as above)	25,000	(20,000)
Taxable trade profits		40,000

Notes

i)   The asset must be of a kind sold in the ordinary course of trade.

ii)   The appropriation must be made with a view to resale at a profit.

iii)   An election is only available by a person taxable with trade profits.

Student self-testing questions

1. A sole trader bought a freehold factory in October 1998 and sold it for £140,000 on 18 May 2012 giving a gain of £35,900. He bought a replacement factory on 6 June 2012 for £120,000.

Requirement: Assuming a claim for rollover relief was made what is the base cost of the new factory.

Suggested solution

		£
Total gain		35,900
Amount not reinvested	(140,000 - 120,000)	(20,000)
Gain eligible for roll-over		15,900
Cost of new factory		120,000
Rolled over gain		(15,900)
Base cost of new factory		104,100
Gain chargeable immediately		20,000

2. Linda is a sole trader who bought a qualifying business asset for £341,250 on 5/11/1991 and sold it for £982,800 on 31/12/2012. A replacement business asset was acquired on 1/11/2012 at a cost of £1,092,000. This asset was sold on 3/9/2016 for £1,829,100. A rollover claim was made on the first sale only. Assume existing rules apply in 2016.

Requirement: Calculate the capital gain on the sale of the second asset.

Suggested solution

31/12/12 disposal

	£	£
Sale proceeds		982,800
Cost		(341,250)
Gain rolled over		641,550
3/9/16 disposal		
Sale proceeds		1,829,100
Cost (1/11/12)	1,092,000	
Rollover relief	(641,550)	(450,450)
Gain subject to CGT		1,378,650

3. Hadley Limited purchased a factory in November 1989 for £250,000. Not needing all the space, the company let out 15% of it. In April 2012 the company sold the factory for £600,000 and bought another in the same month for £700,000. Assume an indexation factor of 1.058 from November 1989 to April 2012.

Requirement: Calculate:

(a) **The chargeable gain or allowable loss, if any, arising on the disposal in April 2012**

(b) **The allowable expenditure (base cost) of the new factory.**

Suggested solution

(a)   Split the old factory & the new factory into qualifying and non-qualifying parts and compute the gains on them separately:

	Qualifying	Non qualifying
	£	£
Disposal proceeds (85%/15%)	510,000	90,000
Less cost	(212,500)	(37,500)
Unindexed gain	297,500	52,500
Indexation allowance		
212,500 and 37,500 x 1.058	(224,825)	(39,675)
Indexed gain	72,675	12,825

The gain of £12,825 will be taxed immediately as it does not qualify for rollover relief.

b)   The base cost of the new factory is reduced by the amount of the gain rolled over. It is therefore:

	£
Purchase cost	700,000
Less gain rolled over	(72,675)
	627,325

4. Harold bought a freehold shop for use in his business in June 2010 for £150,000. He sold it for £175,000 on 1st August 2012. On 8th July 2012 Harold bought some fixed plant and machinery to use in his business costing £178,000. He then sells the plant and machinery for £192,000 on 20th November 2014.

Show Harold's CGT position.

Suggested solution

	£
Gain deferred	
Proceeds of shop	175,000
Less cost	(150,000)
Gain	25,000

The gain is deferred in relation to the plant and machinery.

Sale of plant and machinery	£
Proceeds	192,000
Less cost	(178,000)
Gain	14,000
Total gain chargeable on sale	
(gain on plant and machinery plus deferred gain)	
£25,000 + £14,000 subject to CGT	39,000

Questions without answers

1. Tony purchased a grocery business on 1st June 1988 which he is considering selling in December 2012 for an estimated price of £400,000. The sale price is allocated between the business assets as follows:

	Consideration £
Freehold premises	275,000
Flat above premises (occupied by Tony since acquisition as his only residence)	40,000
Goodwill	50,000
Inventory (trading stock)	20,000
Shop fixtures	15,000
	400,000

The cost of the business at 1 June 1988 was £150,000 comprising the following:

	£
Freehold premises	60,000
Flat above premises	30,000
Goodwill	40,000
Inventory (trading stock)	15,000
Shop fixtures	5,000

Calculate the CGT liability which would arise should Tony sell the business and retire. He has no other chargeable gains arising in 2012-2013, and has taxable income of £45,000.

2. Chandra Khan disposed of the following assets during 2012/13:

a)   On 15 June 2012 Chandra sold 10,000 £1 ordinary shares (a 30% shareholding) in Universal Ltd, an unquoted trading company, to her daughter for £75,000. The market value of the shares on this date was £110,000. The shareholding was purchased on 10 July 1997 for £38,000. Chandra and her daughter have elected to hold over the gain as a gift of a business asset.

b)   On 8 November 2012 Chandra sold a freehold factory for £146,000. The factory was purchased on 3 January 1997 for £72,000. 75% of the factory has been used in a manufacturing business run by Chandra as a sole trader. However, the remaining 25% of the factory has never been used for business purposes. Chandra has claimed to rollover the gain on the factory against the replacement cost of a new freehold factory that was purchased on 10 November 2012 for £156,000. The new factory is used 100% for business purposes by Chandra.

c)   On 8 March 2013 Chandra incorporated a wholesale business that she has run as a sole trader since 1 May 2003. The market value of the business on 8 March 2013 was £250,000. All of the business assets were transferred to a new limited company, with the consideration consisting of 200,000 £1 ordinary shares valued at £200,000 and £50,000 in cash. The only chargeable asset of the business was goodwill, and this was valued at £100,000 on 8 March 2013. The goodwill has a nil cost.

Calculate the capital gains arising from Chandra's disposals during 2012/13. You should ignore the annual exemption. (ACCA updated)

3. Astute Ltd sold a factory on 15 February 2013 for £420,000. The factory was purchased on 24 October 1997 for £164,000, and was extended at a cost of £37,000 during March 1999. During May 2000 the roof of the factory was replaced at a cost of £24,000 following a fire. Astute Ltd incurred legal fees of £3,600 in connection with the purchase of the factory, and legal fees of £6,200 in connection with the disposal.

Astute Ltd is considering the following alternative ways of reinvesting the proceeds from the sale of its factory:

(1)   A freehold warehouse can be purchased for £440,000.

(2)   A freehold office building can be purchased for £375,000.

(3)   A leasehold factory on a 40-year lease can be acquired for a premium of £450,000.

The reinvestment will take place during May 2013. All of the above buildings have been, or will be, used for business purposes.

The following estimates for indexation factors are available:

October 1997 to February 2013	0·504 (estimated)
March 1999 to February 2013	0·462 (estimated)
May 2000 to February 2013	0·405 (estimated)

Required:

(a)   State the conditions that must be met in order that rollover relief can be claimed. You are not expected to list the categories of asset that qualify for rollover relief. **(3 marks)**

(b)   Before taking account of any available rollover relief, calculate
      Astute Ltd's chargeable gain in respect of the disposal of the
      factory.   (5 marks)

(c)   Advise Astute Ltd of the rollover relief that will be available in
      respect of EACH of the three alternative re-investments. Your
      answer should include details of the base cost of the replacement
      asset for each alternative.   (7 marks)

                                                            (15 marks)

                                                      (ACCA updated)

33 Gifts and CGT gift holdover relief

Introduction

1. This chapter is concerned with CGT treatment of gifts of chargeable assets. It begins with a list of exempt gifts and then examines the optional 'holdover' relief which can be claimed only on gifts of business assets.

Holdover relief can be considered here as any gain that normally arises on the gift of a business asset being deducted from the deemed acquisition cost of the person receiving the gift. Thus the person making the gift has potentially avoided a charge to capital gains tax. In the case of gifts of business assets then the relief can be valuable and provide succession for a family business or when a business asset is disposed of in a 'not at arm's length' transaction.

If the donee dies still owning the asset, then as there is no CGT on death a held-over gain is effectively never taxed.

Gift relief is technically called a 'holdover' and not a full 'rollover' deferral relief, because there is a circumstance in which the held-over gain can become chargeable in isolation, without the donee disposing of the asset. (See section 5). However in most cases it operates as a rollover relief and the gain is taxed only when the asset is disposed of by the donee. The tax is imposed by increasing the gain to the next owner (or reducing the allowable loss) when he or she disposes of the asset. If no chargeable disposal is made by the donee (eg the donee dies still owning it,), the relief can become permanent isnetad of deferral. This can also happened if CGT law is reformed in other ways. For example, when rebasing occurred in 1988, in effect the held-over gains on gifts made before 1982 fell out of charge.

2. A gift of a chargeable asset amounts to a disposal for capital gains tax purposes. Any disposal by bargain not at arm's length (eg a sale at undervalue to a favoured friend) is deemed to be made for consideration equal to market value.

Exemptions

3. The following gifts do not give rise to any chargeable gain or loss.

a) A gift to a charity or other approved institution such as the National Gallery, or the British Museum. Such a transfer is deemed to take place on a no gain or loss basis.

b) Gifts of works of art, manuscripts, historic buildings, scenic land etc., if the conditions required for inheritance tax exemption are satisfied.

c) A gift of a chattel with a market value of less than £6,000. See Chapter 30.

d) A gift of an exempt asset such as a private motor car, or the principal private residence of the taxpayer, unless otherwise taxable.

Gifts of business assets – Section 165

4.   The following are the main provisions relating to gifts of business assets.

a)   Gift holdover relief is available to an individual who makes a transfer at less than market price of:

  i)   business assets used for the purposes of a trade, profession or vocation carried on by:

  1. the transferor, or

  2. his or her personal company

  3. a member of a trading group, of which the holding company is his or her personal company.

  ii)   Shares or securities of any trading company, or of the holding company of a trading company where:

  1. the shares are neither quoted on a stock exchange nor dealt in on the AIM, or,

  2. the trading company or holding company is the transferor's personal company.

  iii) agricultural property qualifying for the 100% IHT relief.

b)   A personal company is one in which the individual is entitled to exercise 5% or more of the voting rights.

c)   The relief must be claimed jointly by the transferee and the transferor, within four years of the date of transfer.

d)   The relief is only available in respect of a business asset.

e)   Holdover relief is not available:

  i)   if the donee is non-resident, or is exempt from CGT by reason of a double tax treaty;

  ii)   if the recipient is a company controlled by non-residents who are connected with the donor.

f)   The held-over gain (in isolation) becomes chargeable on the donee, if the donee emigrates permanently from the UK within six tax years of a gift being made on which holdover relief was claimed. If this happens the held-over gain 'crystallises' as a gain realised by the new owner of the asset at the date of permanently ceasing UK residence and ordinary residence. If the donee becomes non-resident after more than six tax years, there is currently no crystallisation of the held over gain.

Example of gift holdover relief

Beryl purchased the goodwill and freehold property of a retail business for £90,000 in 1990, which she gave to her son in May 2012 when it was worth £200,000.

Compute the chargeable gain that can be held over.

Solution: Computation 2012/13

	£
Disposal at market price	200,000
Less Cost	(90,000)
Chargeable gain held over by gift relief	110,000

Acquisition by Beryl's son – base cost for future tax planning £

Market value of assets received by gift	200,000
Less held-over gain	(110,000)
Adjusted base cost on a future disposal	90,000

Example

William purchased freehold business premises in September 1988 for £40,000, and gave the asset to his son Ricky in May 2000 when it was worth £120,000. An election for gift holdover relief was made and accepted.

On 2nd June 2012 Ricky sold the premises for £200,000. Ricky had been running his own business from the premises for five years at the date of the sale.

Compute the chargeable gain to Ricky for 2012/13, and any earlier chargeable gain to William, on the business premises.

Solution: CGT 2000/2001

	£
Value of premises	120,000
Cost of acquisition	(40,000)
Held over gain	80,000
Chargeable gain to William	NIL

CGT 2012/13

Proceeds of sale	200,000
Base cost (120,000 – 80,000)	(40,000)
Chargeable gain to Ricky, subject to CGT at 10%	160,000

Note

i) The gain in 2012/13 is chargeable at 10% as the asset qualifies for entrepreneurs' relief for Ricky.

ii) The annual exemption of £10,600 will also be available, unless Ricky has other net gains in the year not qualifying for ER, which would take the annual exemption in priority to the ER gain.

Gift of shares in personal company

5. If the transfer by an individual is of shares in his or her personal company then the held over gain is restricted, where there are any non-business assets in the company. The gain is restricted where either:

a)   at any time within 12 months of disposal not less than 25% of the company's voting rights were exercisable by the transferor, or

b)   the company is his or her personal company at any time within that period.

$$\text{Chargeable gain} \times \frac{\text{Chargeable business assets of the company at date of disposal}}{\text{Chargeable assets of the company at date of disposal}}$$

$$= \frac{\text{CBA}}{\text{CA}}$$

Example

Terry acquired all the shares of X Ltd, a trading company, for £9,000 in March 1994, and transferred them by way of a gift to Phil in May 2012 when they were worth £140,000. At the date of the gift the company's assets were valued thus:

	£
Freehold land and buildings	30,000
Goodwill	30,000
Plant and machinery – all items > £6,000	25,000
Investment in quoted company	60,000
Inventory (stock), receivables (debtors) and cash	18,750

Solution: Computation 2012/13	£
Proceeds of sale of shares	140,000
Less cost of acquisition	(9,000)
Chargeable gain	131,000
Held over gain: $\frac{85}{145}$ x 131,000 (see working)	(76,793)
Chargeable gain	54,207

Working	**Chargeable business assets** (open market value at date of disposal)	**Chargeable assets**
	£	£
Freehold land	30,000	30,000
Goodwill	30,000	30,000
Investment	–	60,000
Plant and machinery	25,000	25,000
	85,000	145,000

400

Notes

i)   The deemed cost to Phil is £(140,000 – 76,793) i.e. £63,207

ii)   Chargeable business assets are any assets on the disposal of which a gain would be a chargeable gain, and excludes, therefore, motor cars and items of moveable plant purchased and sold for £6,000 or less. Other plant and machinery are chargeable business assets if tangible assets (chattels) worth over £6,000 per time.

iii)   Inventory (stock), receivables (debtors) and cash are exempt from capital gains tax, thus these are not chargeable business assets.

iv)   A business asset for gift relief purposes is an asset used for the purpose of trade.

v)   Goodwill counted in the business's or company's net asset value is a chargeable business asset for an individual therefore any amount paid for the business / the shares that exceeds the separable value of tangible assets can be deemed to relate to goodwill which is a chargeable business asset.

vi)   The investment held by the company is not a chargeable business asset.

Gifts of non-business assets, works of art etc.

6. Holdover relief is also available on gifts, where both the transferor and the transferee are individuals or trusts for:

i)   gifts which are immediately chargeable transfers for IHT purposes i.e. gifts to relevant property trusts (see Part V).

ii)   gifts which are either exempt or conditionally exempt for IHT purposes e.g. gifts to political parties or gifts of heritage property, but not PETs.

Payment of tax by instalments

7. a) Capital gains tax on gifts not eligible for full holdover relief may be paid by ten equal annual instalments where an election is made. This only applies to the following assets:

   i)   Land or any interest in land.

   ii)   Shares or securities in a company which immediately before the disposal gave control to the person making the disposal.

   iii)   Shares or securities of a company (not falling in (ii)) and not quoted on a recognised stock exchange nor dealt in on the USM/AIM.

b)   Where the gift is to a connected person, tax and accrued interest become payable where the donee subsequently disposes of the gift for a valuable consideration.

c)   The first instalment is due on the normal due date. Instalments are not interest free unless the gifted property is agricultural land qualifying for IHT agricultural property relief.

Student self-testing questions

1. Karen purchased a business in 1990 which she gave to Mark in May 1999 when the market value was £125,000. Both Karen and Mark elected to hold over the computed gain. Mark sold the business in May 2012 for £180,000. The cost in May 1990 was £40,000. The business qualifies for entrepreneurs' relief.

Show the CGT computations.

Solution

Karen CGT Computation 1999/2000	£
Deemed proceeds of sale (May 1999)	125,000
Cost (May 1990)	(40,000)
Gain held over	85,000

Mark CGT Computation 2012/13	£
Proceeds of sale (May 2012)	180,000
Deemed base cost (125,000 − 85,000)	(40,000)
Chargeable gain before annual exemption	140,000
Eligible for entrepreneurs' rate (10%)	

Notes:

i) No CGT is payable by Karen upon the gift of the asset to Mark.

2. On 5th December 2012 Michael sold to his son Simon a freehold shop valued at £250,000 for £75,000, and claimed gift relief. Michael had originally purchased the shop from which he has run his business in July 2001 for £45,000. Simon continued to run a business from the shop premises but decided to sell the shop in May 2014 for £230,000.

Compute any chargeable gains arising. Assume the rules of CGT in 2012/13 continue to apply in May 2014.

Suggested solution

Michael's CGT position 2012/13	£
Proceeds	250,000
Less cost	(45,000)
Gain	205,000
Less gain deferred by gift relief claim	
£205,000 − (£75,000-£45,000)	(175,000)
Gain left in charge subject to ER, annual exemption	30,000

Simon's CGT position 2014/15	£
Proceeds	230,000
Less cost £250,000 − £175,000 gift holdover	(75,000)
Gain subject to CGT (ER is likely)	155,000

Notes:

i) In this case for Michael the excess of consideration received over the original cost (£30,000) becomes a gain immediately chargeable to CGT.

ii) Michael's disposal of the shop will only qualify for entrepreneurs' relief if he closed or disposed of his own business at the same time as he disposed of the shop to Simon.

iii) Simon is deemed to have purchased the shop for £75,000. ER will apply to Simon's gain if he disposes of his own business along with the shop, but not if he merely relocates;

iv) Simon meets the ER qualifying condition of having owned and run his business for more than twelve months before disposal.

Question without answer

1. Frank purchased a controlling interest in Nominal Ltd, a trading company, for £100,000 in 1991 which he gave to his son on 1st April 2004 when he was 48 years of age. The market value of the interest at the date of the gift was £500,000. A joint claim under Section 165 TCGA 1992 was made. Frank's son sells the shareholding for £650,000 in June 2012.

There were no non-business, chargeable assets.

Compute the chargeable gains arising in 2012/13.

2. Jack Chan, aged 45, has been in business as a sole trader since 1 May 2001. On 28 February 2013 he transferred the business to his daughter Jill, at which time the following assets were sold to her:

(1) Goodwill with a market value of £60,000. The goodwill has been built up since 1 May 2001, and has a nil cost. Jill paid Jack £50,000 for the goodwill.

(2) A freehold office building with a market value of £130,000. The office building was purchased on 1 July 2003 for £110,000, and has always been used by Jack for business purposes. Jill paid Jack £105,000 for the office building.

(3) A freehold warehouse with a market value of £140,000. The warehouse was purchased on 1 September 2003 for £95,000, and has never been used by Jack for business purposes. Jill paid Jack £135,000 for the warehouse.

(4) A motor car with a market value of £25,000. The motor car was purchased on 1 November 2005 for £23,500, and has always been used by Jack for business purposes. Jill paid Jack £20,000 for the motor car.

Where possible, Jack and Jill have elected to hold over any gains arising.

Jack has unused capital losses of £6,400 brought forward from 2011-12.

Required: Calculate Jack's Capital gains tax liability for 2012–13, and advise him by when this should be paid. **(15 marks)**

(ACCA updated)

End of section questions and answers

1. David Plaine resigned as a full-time working director of Plaine Sailing Ltd, an unquoted personal company, on 1st July 2012, to become non-executive chairman and president of the company. He had joined the company on 1st July 1997, acquiring 30% of the ordinary shares at a cost of £180,000.

On 1st July 2012 he sold his entire interest for £800,000.

The following is a summary of the balance sheet of Plaine Sailing Ltd as at 30th June 2012 at market values:

	£
Freehold land and buildings	800,000
Goodwill	500,000
Plant and machinery (all items > £6,000)	300,000
Inventory (stocks) and work in progress	300,183
Trade receivables (debtors)	210,146
Cash in hand	32,000
Trade payables (creditors)	100,184
Bank overdraft	164,239

Compute the chargeable gain for 2012/13 after any claim for relief Plaine could make.

Plant and machinery was sold at a loss.

Solution: David Plaine CGT computation 2012/13

	£
1st July 2012 Sale proceeds	800,000
Less cost	(180,000)
Gain subject to CGT	620,000
Annual exemption	(10,600)
Chargeable gain	609,400
CGT @ 10%	60,940

End of section questions without answers

1. Earth Ltd sold the following shareholdings during the year ended 31 March 2013:

(a) On 20 November 2012 Earth Ltd sold 25,000 £1 ordinary shares in Venus plc for £115,000. Earth Ltd had originally purchased 40,000 shares in Venus plc on 19 June 1987 for £34,000. On 11 October 2002 Venus plc made a 1 for 4 bonus issue.

(b) On 22 January 2013 Earth Ltd sold 30,000 £1 ordinary shares in Saturn plc for £52,500. Earth Ltd purchased 30,000 shares in Saturn plc on 9 February 2001 for £97,500. On 3 January 2004 Saturn plc made a 1 for 2 rights issue. Earth Ltd took up its allocation under the rights issue in full, paying £1·50 for each new share issued.

(c) On 28 March 2013 Earth Ltd sold its entire holding of £1 ordinary shares in Jupiter plc for £55,000. Earth Ltd had originally purchased 10,000 shares in Mercury plc on 5 May 1995 for £14,000. The indexed value of the 1985 pool on 28 March 2013 was £18,900.

On 7 March 2010 Mercury plc was taken over by Jupiter plc. Earth Ltd received two £1 ordinary shares and one £1 preference share in Jupiter plc for each £1 ordinary share held in Mercury plc. Immediately after the takeover each £1 ordinary share in Jupiter plc was quoted at £2.50 and each £1 preference share was quoted at £1.25.

The following estimates for retail price indices (RPIs) are available:

November 2012	248.0 (estimated)
January 2013	249.0 (estimated)

Required: Calculate the chargeable gain or capital loss arising from each of Earth Ltd's disposals during the year ended 31 March 2013.

Each of the three sections of this question carries 5 marks (15 marks)

(ACCA updated)

2. Claudius had the following transactions.

(1) Sold 2,250 quoted ordinary shares of Nero plc for £23,150 in March 2013. Before making the sale he owned 6,750 shares, of which 4,500 were purchased in December 1988 for £4,599 and 2,250 were acquired in August 1992 on the occasion of the company's rights issue of 1 for 2 at 160p per share.

(2) Sold 2,550 quoted shares of Livia plc for £12,375 on 10 June 2012. His previous transactions in those shares had been as follows.

April 1988	Purchased	1,500	cost	£3,093
August 1990	Purchased	900	cost	£2,700
May 1992	Bonus issue	1 for 2		

(3) Sold 13,500 units of the Tiberius Unit Trust for £11,480 on 15 June 2012, which had cost £3,450 upon their original offer to the public in June 1987.

(4) Gave his brother 12,000 quoted shares in Augustus plc out of his holding of 30,000 shares in March 2013. He had originally purchased 22,500 shares in

January 1989 at a cost of £49,500 and received a scrip issue of 1 for 3 June 1991. At the date of the gift the shares were quoted at 150p each.

Claudius's taxable income for 2012/13 is £55,000.

Requirement:

Calculate Claudius' liability to capital gains tax in respect of the year ended 5 April 2013. None of the transactions qualify for entrepreneurs' relief. **(14 marks)**

Part V

Inheritance tax

34   General principles

Introduction

1. In this chapter the basic features of inheritance tax are outlined under the following headings:

> Basic IHT rates and the nil rate band
> Transfer of value – definition
> Chargeable transfers
> Potentially exempt transfers (PETs)
> Taper relief on PETs becoming chargeable and on CLTs taxed on death
> Gifts with reservation
> General scope of IHT
> Excluded property
> Location of assets
> General exemptions and reliefs
> Business and agricultural property relief
> Growing timber
> Quick succession relief
> Sales within one or four years of death
> Liabilities and expenses
> Intestacy
> Post death variations
> Administration and payment
> Trusts and IHT (outline only)
> IHT rates and nil rate bands

Chapter 35 goes on to consider inheritance tax computational examples. It should be noted that inheritance tax is a complex area and these chapters aim to provide only a basic introduction to the key concepts and principles. There are many more detailed aspects which are not covered here. The main consolidated legislation is to be found in the Inheritance Tax Act 1984 (IHTA 1984).

Note: Inheritance tax paid by trustees is beyond the scope of this basic introduction. However IHT aspects of trusts are covered below so far as relevant to the IHT affairs of individuals, namely:

a) IHT implications for the individual of making a gift to a trust after 22 March 2006;

b) IHT implications for an individual of being the income beneficiary ('life tenant') under either a pre-2006 'interest in possession' (IIP) trust, a post-2006 'immediate post-death interest' (IPDI) trust, or a 'disabled person's trust';

c) IHT implications for an individual of being a reversionary beneficiary under a trust (this has basically no IHT implications for the individual beneficiary, unless a gift with reservation is involved).

Basic IHT rates and the nil rate band

2. Since 6 April 2012 there are three rates of IHT for individuals on death: 0% and 40%, and with a reduced 36% rate where 10% or more of the deceased person's net estate is left to charity; and two rates on chargeable transfers during lifetime: 0% and 20%.

The 'gifts to charity' death rate reduction to 36% is a new provision in Finance Act 2012. Apart from that, IHT rates have not changed since 1988. However, the cumulative amount of transfers charged to IHT at nil rate (the 'nil rate band') has been regularly increased, and remains the subject of frequent political debate.

For the tax year 2012/13 the nil rate band is £325,000. This is unchanged from 2011/12.

The total amount which is liable to IHT on death consists of:

i) all chargeable transfers in the seven years before death (including 'potentially exempt transfers' brought into charge upon death), plus

ii) all the chargeable estate at death, plus

iii) any property given away before death, but which was subject to a 'reservation' in favour of the donor, or the donor's spouse, during any time within seven years of the donor's death.

The significance of the nil rate band is that whenever IHT falls to be computed on a transfer of value, the present nil rate band is applied to the cumulative chargeable transfers by the individual in the past seven years, in date order, to determine how much nil rate band (if any) remains to cover the next chargeable transfer (including transfers on death).

The tax due on a death transfer may be reduced by Quick Succession Relief to the extent that IHT was paid on the same property on another person's death within the past 3 years (see section 16).

IHT that is due on lifetime gifts because of the death of the donor within seven years may be reduced by taper relief if more than 3 years have elapsed between the relevant gift and the death (see section 7 below for rates, and and Chapter 35 section 3 onwards for worked examples). Only the final tax liability (if any), not the chargeable value of the original lifetime transfer (which also affects the tax rate on later transfers) is reduced by taper relief.

Transfer of value - definition

3. A transfer of value occurs where an individual's estate (ie property of any kind) is reduced in value as a result of a gift or disposition. The amount of the reduction in the donor's estate value is the 'transfer of value' for IHT purposes. This may not always be the same value by which the donee's estate is increased by the gift. For example, a gift of one third of a 60% shareholding in a private company to a person who had no prior holding in the company reduces the donor's estate by the difference between a 60% and a 40% shareholding, whereas it increases the donee's estate by the market value of a 20% holding in isolation.

In the case of transfers on a death, the whole estate is a transfer of value and the value transferred is the value of the individual's whole estate immediately prior to the death.

It should be noted that investments in ISAs and PEPs, which are outside the scope of income tax and capital gains tax during life, are included in the death estate for IHT.

Chargeable transfers

4. A chargeable transfer is any transfer of value which is not an exempt transfer. A potentially exempt transfer (PET) is treated as an exempt transfer until the date on which it becomes a chargeable transfer.

Immediately chargeable transfers that do not exceed the nil rate band and thus theoretically bear IHT at the nil rate, are not the same as exempt transfers. Exempt transfers (or exempt parts of larger transfers)are ignored when comparing the cumulative total of previous chargeable transfers with the current IHT nil rate band to find whether a liability at 20% or 40% arises on the latest transfer.

Since 1986, most lifetime gifts by individuals qualify as Potentially Exempt Transfers (PETs) – see paragraph 5 for more detail on these. PETs incur no immediate liability to IHT, but are retrospectively taxed as chargeable lifetime transfers if the donor dies within seven years.

In March 2006, the rules about IHT and Trusts were substantially reformed. Since 22 March 2006, the main type of lifetime transfer which is not a PET – and is thus an immediately chargeable transfer - is a transfer of value by an individual to a Relevant Property Trust.

The following are exempt transfers both in life and on death:
   i)   gifts or legacies to charities or political parties
   ii) gifts or legacies to a UK-domiciled spouse or civil partner.

The chargeable value of transfers in life or on death may be reduced by business and agricultural property reliefs (see section 14).

Potentially exempt transfers (PETs)

5. A potentially exempt transfer is a lifetime transfer of value made by an individual:

i)   to another individual, or

ii) to a discretionary trust primarily for the benefit of a disabled person (as defined).

Although a PET is a transfer of value, no inheritance tax is due when the transfer is made.

A PET is assumed to be an exempt transfer during the whole seven years following the transfer or, if earlier, until immediately before the transferor's death.

A PET made more than seven years before death becomes a wholly exempt transfer on the seventh anniversary of the PET.

If the transferor dies within seven years, the PET becomes a chargeable lifetime transfer.

When a PET becomes chargeable on the death of the donor, it is very common for there to be no actual IHT liability on the PET itself, because the PET (being earlier in date) will rank before later transfers in taking the benefit of the donor's available nil rate band.

However the inclusion of earlier 'failed PETs' in the cumulative lifetime transfers reduces the nil rate band available to the death estate and thus causes a higher tax liability on death.

In the less common situation where actual IHT (at a positive rate) becomes payable on a PET that 'fails' (ie becomes chargeable on death within 7 years), the IHT liability on that PET falls by default on the PET recipient.

If the recipient cannot be traced, or the gift was declared net of IHT when made, then the tax authorities will require the IHT on the PET to be met from the estate of the donor.

If IHT on a PET is paid out of the donor's estate, it is necessary to 'gross up' the value of the PET to find the IHT due on it. See the tables at the end of this chapter for the IHT grossing-up fractions applied on lifetime and death transfers made net of IHT in order to find the gross value before IHT.

6. Other chargeable transfers made by an individual during life ('inter vivos') are not PETs. They are known as Chargeable Lifetime Transfers (CLTs). CLTs include in particular:

i)   a transfer by an individual to a relevant property trust – from 22 March 2006 this term covers all trusts created by lifetime transfers, except qualifying disabled persons' trusts.

ii)   a transfer by an individual to a company.

IHT liability arises on a CLT at the time the transfer is made, at 50% of the death rates. If the donor dies within seven years of a chargeable lifetime transfer then the transfer is charged additional IHT to bring the tax up to the death rates, but a) the nil rate band that applies to the further liability calculation is the one applying at date of death, and not at the time the transfer was made; and b) any further IHT is subject to IHT taper relief where the interval between the CLT and the death is three years or more.

IHT Taper relief on PETs becoming chargeable, and on CLTs taxed further on death

7. Any inheritance tax payable upon death in respect of chargeable transfers made within seven years of the death of the donor (including PETs that have become chargeable) is reduced by reference to the following table:

Years between date of transfer and date of death	% of normal tax charged	% of normal tax deducted
0 – 3	100	–
3 – 4	80	20
4 – 5	60	40
5 – 6	40	60
6 – 7	20	80

Gifts with reservation

8. Where an individual makes a transfer of value, but still retains some interest in the property, then on his or her death the property is treated as part of the estate. He or she is deemed to be beneficially entitled to the whole property and it is taxed together with the rest of the estate.

Examples of gifts with a reservation are:

i)   a gift of a house where the donor or their spouse /CP remains in residence – unless a 'full market rent' is paid;

ii)   a gift to a trust where the donor or their spouse / CP is a beneficiary (even a remote beneficiary).

9. Property is subject to a reservation if:

i)   possession and enjoyment of the property is not bona fide assumed by the donee at or before the beginning of the 'relevant period', or

ii)   at any time in the 'relevant period' the property is not enjoyed to the entire exclusion, or virtually so, of the donor and of any benefits to him or her by contract or otherwise.

The relevant period is the period ending on the date of the donor's death and beginning seven years before then, or the date of the gift, if later.

General scope of IHT

10. If the individual making the transfer of value is domiciled in the UK, IHT applies to all his or her property wherever it is situated. This applies even if the person is non-resident in the UK for income tax and capital gains tax..

Where the transferor is domiciled outside the UK, then only property actually situated in the UK is chargeable to IHT. This would include shares in companies whose registered office/share register is located in the UK, but not shares in an offshore company, even if that company owned property in the UK.

For IHT purposes there are special rules by which an individual who has strong or recent UK residence connections is deemed to be domiciled in the UK for IHT purposes, even if legally domiciled elsewhere.

i)   a deemed UK domicile is acquired for IHT purposes once a person has been resident (for income tax purposes) in the UK for 17 of the last 20 tax years. Legal domicile is then irrelevant.

ii)   when someone formerly domiciled in the UK changes their legal domicile (eg by permanent emigration), their deemed domicile for IHT purposes remains the UK for another 3 tax years after the year of change of legal domicile.

Excluded property

11. The following types of property are not liable to IHT on a lifetime transfer, and do not form part of an individual's estate on death:

a)   property situated outside the UK where the owner is also domiciled (and deemed domiciled) outside the UK.

b)   reversionary interests in a settlement, except those acquired for money or money's worth or those where either the settlor or his or her spouse/CP is beneficially entitled to the reversion.

c)   any income entitlement/life interest in a Relevant Property Trust created on or after 22 March 2006.

d)   any life interest in a settlement made by a non-UK domiciled person and comprising only non-UK property.

e)   property of individuals killed on active service.

Location of assets

12. To qualify as excluded property owned by a non-UK domicile, the assets must be situated outside the UK. The location of assets is determined in accordance with the general principles of property and land law as follows:

Land	– Land, including leasehold property is situated where the land is physically located.
Tangible moveable property	– Assets such as furniture and paintings are situated where they are located.
	Coins and bank notes are situated where they are at the time of the transfer.
Shares/securities	– These are situated where the company share register is kept.
Bearer shares	– These are situated where the certificate of title is kept.
Debts	– These are located where the debtor resides.
Business assets	– Assets of a business are located where the place of business is situated.
	An interest in a partnership is located at where the head office is found.
Goodwill	– This is located where the business is carried on.
Trademark	– This is situated where it is registered.

General exemptions and reliefs

13. The following are the main exemptions and reliefs available in respect of lifetime and death transfers.

	LT	DT
a) Transfers between husband and wife or registered civil partners (No limit, except where the donee is not domiciled in the UK, in which case the exempt amount is limited to £55,000 over seven years).	✓	✓
b) Transfers each year up to £3,000 (the annual exemption).	✓	
c) Small gifts to any one person not exceeding £250.	✓	
d) Transfers by way of normal expenditure out of taxed income.	✓	
e) Gifts in consideration of marriage £5,000 max: donor is parent to one of the parties to the marriage £2,500 max: donor is grandparent/great grandparent £1,000 max: donor is in any other relationship.	✓	
f) Gifts to charities £ no limit: whenever made.	✓	✓
g) Gifts to political parties £ no limit: whenever made.	✓	✓
h) Gifts for national purposes or for public benefit.	✓	✓
i) Gifts made during lifetime for family maintenance including the education of children.	✓	

LT = Lifetime transfers (both original CLTs, and PETs chargeable on later death)

DT = Death transfers

From 9th October 2007 a surviving spouse or civil partner's IHT representatives on death may claim the unused proportion of a previously deceased spouse's or civil partner's nil rate band. Effectively this means that the nil rate band is to some extent now transferable between spouses and civil partners from the first to the second death.

The new system works as follows: the executors/personal representatives handling the IHT affairs of anyone dying after a legal spouse or civil partner can claim in the death IHT computation as much of a second nil rate band (measured at the time of the second death) as was unused in IHT computations applying on the death of the first spouse/CP.

The main purpose of this reform was to negate the need for complicated trust structures allowing spouses /civil partners to ensure that one nil rate band was not 'wasted' on the first death if (as is common) the bulk of the first to die's property was left to the survivor - an exempt transfer for IHT, but potentially pushing the widow or widower's estate up to a level where higher IHT would be payable on the second death.

For people who have had more than one predeceasing spouse or CP before their own death, all the available unused nil rate bands from all those other people's death estates may be combined, but the absolute maximum enhanced nil rate band available on the second death is double the normal nil rate band for an individual (measured at the date of the second death).

Extra unused NRB from a predeceasing partner is only available if the marriage/partnership still existed at the time of the first death. So it does not apply if the partners dissolved the partnership or divorced before the first death.

In general, for all IHT purposes, 'married' means legally married, and all spouse /civil partner treatments for IHT continue until the marriage or partnership is legally ended by divorce or dissolution, regardless of the parties' living arrangements.

Business and agricultural property reliefs

14. These important reliefs are available in respect of both transfers during lifetime (both PETs and immediately chargeable transfers) and on death. They are given effect to by a reduction in the value transferred.

a)   Relief for business property.

Percentage reductions available are as follows:

i)   Transfers of a business or partnership interest   100%

ii)   Transfers of business assets   50%

iii)   Transfers of shares in unquoted companies including USM, AIM   100%

iv)   Transfers of a controlling interest in a quoted company   50%

b)   Relief for agricultural property

Percentage reductions available are as follows:

i)   Where the transferor has the right to vacant possession or could obtain it within 12 months after a transfer   100%

ii)   Where the transferor does not have the right to vacant possession or cannot obtain it within 12 months of the transfer.   50%

Growing timber

15. Where land in the UK, not subject to agricultural or business relief, includes growing timber then the value of the timber may be excluded from a person's estate at death. IHT becomes payable on the later sale or lifetime transfer of the timber on the value at the date of the disposal.

Quick succession relief

16. This is available in respect of property transferred on the death of a person which has borne inheritance tax within the preceding five years. The relief is given by way of a percentage reduction of the original tax paid as follows:

		Reduction
Death within	1 year	100%
Death within	2 years	80%
Death within	3 years	60%
Death within	4 years	40%
Death within	5 years	20%

Sale within 1 or 4 years of death

17. Where shares are sold at arm's length within one year of death, or land is sold within four years of death, and the proceeds of sale are less than the probate value (value for IHT purposes) at the date of death, then relief may be claimed for any reduction in the price achieved below the amount treated as originally liable to IHT, and a refund of IHT paid on the difference in value may be obtained.

Liabilities and expenses

18. In general, liabilities are taken into account in computing the value of an estate for IHT purposes insofar as they have been incurred for a consideration in money's worth or imposed by law. Liabilities forming a charge on any property, such as a mortgage on a house, are deducted from the value of that property.

Intestacy

19. Where a person dies without making a will then there are rules of intestacy which prescribe the manner in which an estate must be distributed.

Post-death variations

20. The beneficiaries under a will or intestacy can vary the terms of the Will or the standard intestacy rules regarding who gets what, so long as all of them are of full legal capacity (so minor beneficiaries cannot have their shares of the estate altered or reduced in this way).

The legal document doing this is known as a 'Post-Death Deed of Variation' and to be effective for IHT it must satisfy the following conditions.

a) The instrument in writing must be made by the persons or any of the persons who benefit or would benefit under the dispositions of the property comprised in the deceased's estate immediately before his or her death.

b) The instrument must be made within two years after the death.

c) The instrument must clearly indicate the dispositions that are the subject of it, and vary their destination as laid down by the deceased's will or under the law relating to intestate estates, or otherwise.

d) A notice of election to vary the Will for IHT and CGT purposes must be given within six months of the date of the instrument, unless the Board sees fit to accept a late election.

e) Variation will automatically apply without election if the instrument itself states that it is to have that effect.

Any liability to IHT on death will be calculated on the basis of the revised estate distribution resulting from the Deed of Variation.

Deeds of Variation have no effect for income tax until the estate is distributed under the revised terms of the Deed. Therefore income (eg rents) may accrue during an estate administration period and be taxed on the previous estate beneficiary as income, even if they have given away the capital entitlement in a Deed of variation. A Deed of Variation is not an IHT transfer of value or a CGT chargeable disposal by any person entering into it who gives away property or inheritance rights to others by means of it.

Administration and payment

21. a) The HMRC offices which deal with IHT are known as the Capital Taxes Offices.

b)   Reporting lifetime transfers to the Capital Taxes Office is carried out as follows.

   i)   In the case of a chargeable lifetime transfer, the transferor must report it, unless some other person such as the donee liable for the tax has already done so. The account must be delivered within 12 months of the transfer or, if later, three months from the date on which he or she first becomes liable for the tax.

   ii) In the case of a PET it is the transferee's duty to report the transfer and pay any tax within 12 months after the end of the month in which death occurs. The Executors or Personal representatives are also responsible for listing the recipients of PETs that have become chargeable, and chargeable lifetime transfers that are liable to further tax on death, on the IHT return.

c)   Appeals against an IHT assessment are to the combined Tax Tribunal system.

d)   For transfers on death, probate or letters of administration are not given until an IHT account (provisional, if necessary) has been rendered and any IHT due paid (subject to the provisions for paying by instalments).

e)   Where the estate is 'excepted' (small in value), then there is no duty to make an IHT return on death. This applies where:

   i)   the gross value of the property at death + relevant life time-transfers $\leq$ the basic Nil rate band, and the deceased died domiciled in the UK; or

   ii) The aggregate gross value of the estate + relevant lifetime transfers $\leq$ £1.0m, and the aggregate value less any deductible liabilities and less transfers to spouse and charity) $\leq$ the basic nil rate band, and the deceased died domiciled in the UK; or

   iii) The deceased was never domiciled in the UK and the value of all UK estate $\leq$ £100,000.

f)   Payments of IHT may be made by instalments for these transfers on death:

   i)   land and buildings (freehold and leasehold wherever situated);

   ii) a controlling interest in a company, quoted or unquoted;

   iii) unquoted shares and securities where the value transferred exceeds £20,000 and the shares represent at least 10% of the nominal share capital;

   iv) the net value of a business, profession or vocation;

   v)   timber where the proceeds of sale basis of valuation is not used.

g)   Instalments are payable by 10 equal yearly amounts. Interest on IHT due on land other than land used for business or agricultural purposes is calculated on the whole amount outstanding and added to each instalment.

IHT due on other property payable by instalments only incurs interest when an instalment is in arrears.

The payment of tax by instalments is available on lifetime transfers of the appropriate property where the IHT is paid by the donee.

h)   IHT is due for payment as follows:

i)   On a transfer on death – six months after the end of the month in which the death takes place.

ii)   On a lifetime transfer:

made from 6th April to 30th September – the following April 30th

made from 1st October to 5th April – six months after end of month of transfer.

i)   IHT is paid on income that has accrued to the deceased at the date of death but was received after that date and is therefore subject to income tax on the post-death owner of the asset producing the income. Relief for this element of double taxation is given to the beneficiaries by an adjustment to their personal income tax liability on the income.

IHT and Trusts – outline

22. A trust is an arrangement whereby legal ownership of an asset or cash is vested in one or more persons (the trustee(s)) but all the benefit or income from the assets is passed on to other named person(s) (known as the trust beneficiaries). There are many choices available to the creator (known as the settlor) of a property trust or settlement. The terms on which the trust property is to be managed and held must all be set out in the Trust Deed: the settlor cannot vary them later as he or she relinquishes control of the assets when the trust is created. The Trust deed may be part of a Will if the trust is created on a death. The income benefit and capital benefit in a trust can be awarded differently. The destination of the various benefits can be laid down in ways which trustees cannot alter, or the trustees can be given discretion as to the final allocation of income and/or capital among various possible classes of beneficiary.

The trustees may also have power to accumulate income and add it to capital rather than paying it out to income beneficiaries as income.

The IHT regime for trusts was substantially changed on Budget Day 2006 from the regime which had broadly existed since 1974. Prior to 22 March 2006, all trusts were classified into three types for IHT, of which two were taxable persons in their own right (via the trustees as a body), while the third (the interest-in-possession trust) was treated as transparent with the current life tenant being treated as the owner of the underlying trusts property for all IHT purposes.

From 22 March 2006 there are still three types of trust for IHT, but an interest in possession trust created (or added to) during life time of the settlor will be a 'relevant property trust' which is taxed in the same way as a fully discretionary trust.

The only exception is a disabled person's trust as defined, which retains the IHT treatment of a pre-2006 interest in possession trust, even if legally a discretionary trust (ie the disabled person has no legal right to demand payment of income from the trustees). The disabled beneficiary is treated as owning the underlying property for IHT. and all gifts into the trust are treated as PETs to that person.

Relevant Property Trusts (which now covers discretionary trusts (except for disabled person), post-2006 lifetime IIP trusts, and any pre-2006 'Accumulation and Maintenance' Trusts which were not converted into IIP trusts under transitional provisions by 6 April 2008) are separate IHT taxpayers and the trustees must keep their own IHT cumulative transfer records. IHT arises on capital transfers of value out of an RPT, and also at ten-year intervals on property within an RPT. The details of IHT for RPT trustees are not considered further here.

Inheritance tax rates and nil rate bands - individuals

Death rates

	Cumulative Chargeable transfers (gross)	IHT rate %	Grossing up rate on a net transfer
6.4.12 – 5.4.13 and all prior tax years since 1986/7	Up to top of Nil Rate Band	Nil	Nil
	Above nil rate band	40%	2/3 (40/60)
6.4.12 – 5.4.13	Where 10% or more of the deceased person's net estate is left to charity	36%	

Lifetime rates

	Chargeable transfers (gross)	IHT %	IHT on transfer (net)
6.4.12 – 5.4.13 and all prior tax years since 1986/7	Up to top of Nil Rate Band	Nil	Nil
	Above nil rate band	20%	1/4 (20/80)

Nil Rate bands:

	£
2012/13	325,000
2011/12	325,000

35   Basic rules of computation

Introduction

1. In this chapter the basic rules of IHT computation are examined under the following headings:

> Grossing up procedures
>
> Taper relief and lifetime gifts
>
> Chargeable lifetime transfers
>
> Chargeable lifetime transfers – death within seven years
>
> Potentially exempt transfers within seven years of death
>
> Death with no chargeable transfers within seven years of death
>
> Transfers of value made within seven years of death and earlier transfers.
>
> Transfers of business assets

Grossing up procedures

2. Where a lifetime transfer is made and IHT is to be paid by the donor, e.g. on a transfer to a Relevant Property Trust, then it is necessary to 'gross up the net transfer' as IHT is payable on the gross amount. The donor can specify that any gift, including a PET, is to be a transfer net of IHT. If no such direction is made then a transfer bears its own IHT (ie the donee pays the IHT), and no grossing up is required.

Grossing up is also necessary, at death rates, where a death estate is divided in such a way that legacies of set amounts are chargeable to IHT but the residue (the balance of the estate) is left to one or more exempt beneficiaries i.e. a charity, surviving spouse or civil partner.

Example

Amy makes a net chargeable lifetime transfer to a RPT of £340,000 on 15th May 2012. Amy has never been married, and has not made any previous lifetime chargeable transfers or PETs.

Compute the amount of the gross transfer.

Solution

	£
15.5.2012 Net gift	340,000
Add IHT paid by donor: $\dfrac{20}{80} \times (340{,}000 - 325{,}000) =$	3,750
Gross transfer	343,750
Check Gross transfer	343,750
IHT $(343{,}750 - 325{,}000) \times 20\%$	(3,750)
Net transfer	340,000

The IHT of £3,750 is payable by Amy.

Taper relief and lifetime gifts

3. The inheritance tax payable in respect of transfers of value made within seven years of the death of an individual is reduced by reference to the following table.

Years between date of transfer and date of death	% of normal tax charged	% of normal tax relieved
0 – 3	100	–
3 – 4	80	20
4 – 5	60	40
5 – 6	40	60
6 – 7	20	80

4. For potentially exempt transfers no chargeable transfer arises unless death occurs within seven years of the date of the transfer. When this happens, IHT is calculated on the now non-exempt (ie chargeable) transfer using death rates and nil rate band amount at the date of death, but using the value of the chargeable transfer at the date it was made ie the date of the PET. The IHT on a 'failed PET' is payable by the donee, unless the transfer was stated to be a transfer net of any IHT becoming due in future, in which case grossing-up applies and the death estate bears the tax.

Other chargeable transfers (non-PETs) are taxed at half of the death rate at the time of making the transfer. If death occurs more than seven years after the date of the transfer then the position is as follows.

i)   The chargeable transfer is ignored in computing the IHT payable on the value of the estate.

ii)   There is no additional tax payable by the donee.

iii)   IHT already paid when the transfer was made is not recoverable.

Taper relief does not affect the amount of inheritance tax payable on an estate by the executors.

The computational principles of taper relief on CLTs within 7 years before death are illustrated in paragraphs 5 and 6.

Chargeable lifetime transfers (non-PETs)

5. These transfers are chargeable at half the death rate at the time of the transfer, and where necessary must be grossed up.

Example

Mike makes a transfer of £400,000 to a relevant property trust on 1st December 2012 agreeing to pay any IHT. All exemptions had been used and Mike had made no previous transfers.

Compute any IHT payable.

Solution

		£
1.12.12 Gift to relevant property trust		400,000
IHT on net gift of £400,000		
$(400,000 - 325,000) \times \frac{1}{4}$		18,750
Gross transfer		418,750
IHT payable by Mike at lifetime rate		18,750
Check $(418,750 - 325,000)$ at 20% =		18,750

Chargeable lifetime transfers (non-PETs) – death within seven years

6. When the transferor dies within seven years of making a chargeable transfer then the gift is retaxed at the death rates, net of any taper relief. Any IHT payable when the gift was first made is then deducted in arriving at any additional tax due by the donee.

The value of the transfer is taken at the date of the gift but any additional tax arising on the death of the donor can be calculated by reference to the lower of:

i)   the market value at date of donor's death, or

ii)   the proceeds of an earlier sale.

Example

Noel dies on 11th June 2012 leaving an estate valued at £100,000 to non-exempt beneficiaries. On 1st June 2009 he made a gift of £350,000 gross to a relevant property trust, inheritance tax of £7,600 being paid by the trustees on the lifetime transfer. Noel had never been married.

Calculate the IHT due in respect of Noel's estate and any additional tax payable on his death relating to the chargeable lifetime transfer.

Solution	£
11.6.2012 Value Noel's estate	100,000
Add: Gross chargeable transfers within previous 7 years	350,000
	450,000
IHT payable FA 2012 death rate	
325,000 – Nil	–
125,000 @ 40%	50,000
450,000	50,000
Less notional tax at death rates on transfers of £350,000 within last 7 years.	
325,000 – Nil	–
25,000 @ 40% revised IHT liability on lifetime CLT	(10,000)
350,000	
IHT payable by executors out of death estate (40% x 100,000)	40,000

Additional tax payable on lifetime gift:	£
1.6.09 Gross transfer	350,000
11.6.12 IHT (as above) due on this at death rates	10,000
Less taper relief:	
(3-4 years) 20% × 10,000	(2,000)
IHT liability after taper relief (borne by original donee, ie trust)	8,000
Less paid by trustees on original gift by X	(7,600)
Additional tax due by trustees on X's death	400

Notes

i)   If the additional tax payable is a 'negative amount', none is recoverable by the RPT.

ii)   There can be no refund of the IHT paid on the original gift into trust.

iii) Tax on the death estate is borne as the highest slice of the total assets, i.e. after allocating the nil rate band first to chargeable transfers within seven years of death.

iv)   Where the cumulative chargeable lifetime transfers exceed the nil rate band on death, and there are no exempt legacies, then the estate IHT is the value of the estate at the 40% death rate. In this example £100,000 @ 40% = £40,000.

v)   The lifetime gift IHT originally paid by the trustees on the gift by Mike is (350,000 − 312,000) @20% = 7,600. (£312,000 was the nil rate band for 2008/09).

vi)   The nil rate band for 2012/13 is £325,000.

Potentially exempt transfer within seven years of death

7. There is no inheritance tax payable when the transfer is made, since a potentially exempt transfer is assumed exempt until proved otherwise by death of the donor within seven years. Upon death within seven years of the transfer, the PET is taxable at the death rate, subject to taper relief if the interval is more than 3 years. In addition the PET (now a CLT) is added to the value of the estate to determine the rates of tax payable on the death transfer.

As with all lifetime transfers brought into charge, the estate is treated as the last transfer, and the cumulative transfers in the previous seven years as earlier transfers, to be allocated against the nil rate band on death, in date order.

8. For the purposes of calculating the tax payable by the donee (but not the estate), the market value at the date of death or the proceeds of an earlier sale by the donee may be used to compute the IHT on the lifetime gift, if this is lower than the value of the PET at the date of the transfer.

Example

Arthur dies on 10th October 2012 leaving to his daughter a net estate valued at £250,000. On 1st of December 2010 Arthur had made a gift to his son with a value of £400,000 after having used all relevant lifetime gift exemptions. Arthur had made no previous transfers of value, and had divorced his wife many years ago.

Calculate the IHT payable.

Solution

	£
10.10.2012 Value of Arthur's estate at death	250,000
Add cumulative transfers in previous 7 years	400,000
	650,000

IHT thereon (650,000 – 325,000) × 40%
(2012/13 Death Rates) — 130,000

Less notional tax on chargeable lifetime transfers within previous 7 years
- failed PETs of £400,000:

		£	£
NRB	325,000 @ 0%	–	
balance	75,000 @ 40%	30,000	
	400,000	30,000	(30,000)

IHT payable out of death estate by executors:
(borne by Arthur's daughter) — 100,000

	£
Tax payable by Arthur's son	
1.12.2010 Value of gift	400,000
IHT thereon as above	30,000
Less taper relief: (0–3 years) 0% × 30,000	–
IHT payable	30,000

Further example – fall-in-value relief

Using the data in the previous example, compute the IHT payable, if the PET to Arthur's son was a gift of an asset that was only worth £350,000 at the date of Arthur's death.

Solution

	£
10.10.2012 Value of Arthur's estate	250,000
Add cumulative transfers in previous 7 years	400,000
	650,000
IHT payable on estate	130,000 (as above)

IHT payable by Arthur's son on Arthur's death:

	£
1.12.10 Value of gift	400,000
Less fall in value relief (£400,000 - £350,000)	(50,000)
10.10.2012 Value of gift retrospectively	350,000
IHT on £350,000	
(350,000 – 325,000) × 40%	10,000
Less taper relief NIL (less than 3 years)	–
IHT payable by Arthur's son	10,000

Notes

i)   The value of the original gift is included in calculations of IHT on the death estate. In other words, it is still 'cumulated' at the original value.

ii) The fall-in-value relief only affects the amount of any tax or additional tax due when a PET becomes a CLT on death, or a CLT becomes liable at death rates, (less taper relief if any.

iii) Additional tax due on earlier lifetime transfers because of a death is in principle a cost borne by the donee. If it is borne by the donor's estate (which could only be by specific direction of the donor) then the tax on the gift (at grossed-up rate) is an additional transfer of value under the will.

iv) In practice, the donee or the donor of a lifetime gift can often without difficulty, and at fairly modest cost, insure the donor's life for the next 7 years, to cover the cost of an extra IHT liability arising within 7 years of a lifetime gift. This is done using a single-premium seven-year term insurance policy, the proceeds of which can be used by the donee to pay the estimated maximum IHT. If the donor does not die within 7 years no insurance money is repayable to the donee but there is no IHT to pay either. (If the donor pays the insurance premium and writes the proceeds of the policy in trust for the donee, this is not itself a chargeable transfer of value.)

Death after no chargeable transfers or PETs within seven years

9. On the death of a person who has not made chargeable transfers within the previous seven years, the death rates and nil rate band are simply applied to the value of the death estate, subject to any exemptions and reliefs.

Example

Tony died on 14 June 2012, leaving a chargeable estate of £485,000. He had made no lifetime transfers, and was divorced from his previous spouse before she died. Compute the IHT payable.

Solution: Tony deceased IHT computation 14.6.2012

Total value of estate:		485,000
Tax payable:		
325,000 @ 0%		–
160,000 @ 40%		64,000
485,000		64,000

Notes

Estate rate of IHT = $\dfrac{64,000}{485,000} \times 100 = 13.19\%$

The estate rate is relevant where there is any IHT payable by instalments e.g. UK land, or by different persons. It is also relevant where Double Tax Relief is claimed for overseas IHT.

Transfers of value made within seven years of death and earlier

10. Transfers of value made more than seven years before the date of death are not accumulated to arrive at the IHT rate at the date of death. However, where a chargeable lifetime transfer was made within the seven years before the date of death, then in determining any additional IHT payable on death by the recipient, any chargeable transfers made in the seven years before the date of that transfer must be considered.

Example

Kate made a gross chargeable transfer (after exemptions) to a discretionary trust for her adult children of £350,000 on 1st February 2004. On 1st November 2008 Kate gave her son £75,000 after annual exemptions. Kate dies on 30th August 2012, leaving an estate of £500,000 to her 3 adult children.

Calculate the IHT payable on the estate of K and on the failed PET of £75,000.

Solution   **£**

30.8.2012 Value of Kate's estate	500,000
Add transfers of value made within previous 7 years	
1.11.08 Gift to son – gross chargeable transfer	75,000
	575,000

IHT payable: (2012/13 rates)

325,000 Nil		–
250,000 @ 40%		100,000
575,000		100,000

Less notional tax on transfers within previous 7 years £75,000

Nil rate band covers this in full so the tax is   Nil

IHT payable by executors out of death estate (borne by heirs)   100,000

Tax payable by Kate's son on failed PET

		Gross (FA 2012 death rates)	IHT
1.2.04	Gross transfer to discretionary trust (350,000 – 325,000 @ 40%)	350,000	10,000
1.11.08	Gift to son	75,000	30,000
		425,000	40,000

IHT nil rate band	325,000	–			
Death rates	100,000 @ 40%	40,000			
				425,000	40,000

Deduct transfers made more than 7 years
prior to date of death   350,000   10,000

	75,000 30,000
less taper relief	
3–4 years 20% × 30,000	(6,000)
IHT payable on failed PET	24,000

Notes

i) The IHT payable at the death rate on the failed PET is calculated by reference to the value of **all** chargeable transfers in the seven years before the date of the gift.

ii) The tax in this case actually due on the failed PET of £24,000 is not the same as the amount deducted in computing the IHT payable on the estate by the executors.

iii)   The taper relief for a chargeable lifetime transfer made between three and four years before death is 20% (see Chapter 35 section 7).

Business Property Relief

11. Relief is available for transfers of value during life (inter vivos) or on the death of an individual, of relevant business property.

The relief is given by way of a percentage reduction from the valuation of the property.

This section begins with a summary of the relief available, followed by a definition of relevant business property and the associated rules. Worked examples then show the computations to be made.

Summary of relief

12.

a) Property consisting of a business or interest in a business such as a   100% partnership or sole trader. A business includes total assets including goodwill, less liabilities.

b) Shares or securities in unquoted companies including USM/AIM.   100%

c) Shares or securities of a quoted company which gave the transferor   50% control of the company immediately before the transfer.

d) Business assets such as land and buildings, plant and machinery   50% owned by the transferor as a sole trader, partner, or as a controlling director, and used in that business.

e) Business assets such as land and buildings, plant and machinery   50% used by the transferor in a business which was settled property in which he or she had an interest in possession.

Relevant business property

13. In addition to the details shown in the summary above, the following should be noted.

a)   To qualify for relief, the property must have been owned by the transferor for at least two years immediately prior to the transfer. Where property replaces other property and the two years criteria cannot be met then relief is still available, provided aggregate ownership is greater than two years out of the previous five.

b)   Assets not used wholly or mainly for the purposes of the business within the two year period noted in (a) above are excepted assets (e.g. investments or surplus cash) and relief is not available for those items.

c)   Relief is not available for a transfer of business property which is used wholly or mainly for the following purposes:

    i)   Dealing in stocks, shares or securities. (Stock market makers and discount houses are, however, eligible for relief.)

    ii)   Dealing in land or buildings.

    iii)   Making or holding investments.

d)   The expression business includes a profession or vocation but does not include a business carried on otherwise than for gain.

e)   Shares in a holding company qualify if the subsidiaries themselves qualify for relief.

f)   The original property (or if sold, its replacement) must be owned by the transferee throughout the period beginning with the chargeable transfer and ending on the transferor's death to retain the full benefit of the relief.

g)   Where the original property is disposed of before the transferor's death and the proceeds are used to purchase replacement property full relief is available if:

    i) the whole of the proceeds are used to purchase a replacement

    ii) both sale and purchase take place within three years of each other.

h)   If only part of the original property (or its replacement) is in the transferee's possession on the death of the transferor, then only that part will be eligible for relief.

i)   Relief reduces the value of the transfer before any available exemptions are given.

Where any of the relief is clawed back the additional tax payable by the transferee is calculated on the transfer before BPR. However, the net transfer i.e. after BPR included in the transferor's cumulative total remains unchanged.

Excepted assets for BPR

14. The BPR will be restricted on a transfer of shares if the company holds 'excepted assets' on its balance sheet. An 'excepted asset' is an asset that is not used for business purposes throughout the two years immediately preceding a transfer, or is not required for future use in the business. The amount of the transfer qualifying for BPR, is the value of the shares gifted multiplied by the fraction below:

$$\text{Qualifying transfer} = \text{Gift} \times \left(\frac{\text{Total assets - excepted assets}}{\text{Total assets}} \right)$$

If the company has no excepted assets, all of the value of the shares will qualify for BPR. If non-trading assets make up more than 50% of total assets, the IR may seek to deny BPR completely on the grounds that the company is not trading.

PETS and business property relief

15. If the property eligible for business property relief is transferred by a PET, it follows that tax will only be payable on the death of the transferor within seven years of the date of the transfer. BPR which has been assumed at the time of a lifetime gift (PET) to reduce the chargeable value of the PET may be lost as a result of events after the PET. BPR is not available when a PET becomes chargeable (ie on the donor's death within 7 years) unless either:

a) the property (or its identifiable replacement) is still held by the donee as relevant business property at the donor's death, or

b) the donee has died before the donor.

This rule can cause an unwelcome IHT exposure for the donee of business property. The risk of the donor's death should be covered by term life insurance if the donee does not intend to retain the gift as his or her own relevant business property for 7 years.

Example

A who had made no previous transfers gave his controlling interest in Z Ltd, a private company, to his son on April 12th 2009. The interest was valued at £440,000. A's controlling interest was acquired for £50,000 in 1993. A died on the 10th August 2012 leaving an estate of £380,000. A's son has retained the controlling interest in Z Ltd.

Compute the IHT arising on A's death.

Solution

	£	£
10.8.2012 Value of A's estate		380,000
Add transfers made within previous 7 years		
12.4.09 gift to son	440,000	
Less business property relief 100% × 440,000	440,000	—
		380,000
IHT payable on this at FA 2012 rates:		
325,000 @ Nil	—	
55,000 @ 40%	22,000	22,000
380,000		22,000
Less notional IHT on gift to son of	440,000	Nil
IHT payable by executors		22,000
IHT payable on PET		Nil

Notes

i) No IHT was payable in April 2009 as the transfer of value was then a PET.

ii) Business property relief at 100% applies to the gift, so there is no IHT payable by A's son on A's death of his father, as he has retained the gifted business as relevant business property. However the PET is no longer exempt but has become chargeable and BPR needs to be claimed in the IHT retrun submitted on the death.

iii) The original cost of A's controlling interest is irrelevant to the IHT position, though it is relevant to A's CGT in the tax year when he gave it away. (See part 4 of this book, CGT business reliefs.)

Student self-testing questions

1. Z dies on 22nd October 2012 leaving a net estate of £250,000. During his lifetime he had made the following transfers of value, after using all available exemptions.

1st December 2006 Gift to his daughter of £130,000.

20th June 2009   Gift to an accumulation and maintenance trust of £240,000.

Compute the IHT payable on the death of Z.

Solution		£	£
22.10.2012 Z's estate			250,000
Add transfers of value made in previous 7 years			
1.12.06 Gift to daughter		130,000	
20.6.09 Gift to trust		240,000	370,000
			620,000
IHT payable (FA 2012 rates):			
325,000		—	
295,000 @ 40%		118,000	
620,000		118,000	118,000
Less notional tax on lifetime transfers of £370,000			
(370,000 − 325,000) × 40% =			18,000
IHT payable by executors			100,000
IHT payable by donees:			
1.12.06 gift to daughter within nil rate band		130,000	nil
20.6.09 Gift to accumulation and maintenance trust			240,000
Add gifts in previous 7 years			
Gift to Z's daughter (1.12.06)			130,000
			370,000
IHT payable:			
(370,000 − 325,000) × 40%			18,000
Less notional IHT on gift to Z's daughter of £130,000			—
			18,000
Less taper relief: (3-4 years) 20% × 18,000			(3,600)
Tax payable by trustees			14,400

Cumulative transfers	Gross £	Tax £
1.12.2006 Gift to daughter	130,000	
IHT payable @ FA 2012 death rates	–	–
	130,000	–
20.6.09 Gift to accumulation trust	240,000	18,000
	370,000	18,000
Taper relief		(3,600)
Less transfers made more than 7 years prior to 22.10.2012		Nil
	370,000	14,400

Notes

i) Both of the transfers during Z's lifetime are PETs.

ii) The tax due in respect of each gift is computed separately beginning first with the one furthest from the date of death, within the seven years period.

iii) IHT payable on the second gift is calculated after deducting any notional tax on the previous gift to Z's daughter which in this case is nil.

iv) Taper relief 20.6.09 –22.10.12 is three to four years.

2. B dies on 7th April 2012 leaving the following estate:

	£
20% interest in Q Ltd, an unquoted private company	125,000
Freehold land used by Q Ltd	35,000
Shares in Z plc, a quoted company (< 1% holding)	15,000
Other property (net)	312,500

Three years before his death B had transferred a 15% interest in the shares in Q Ltd to his son. B has made no other transfers but has used all his annual exemptions. B's son has retained his interest in Q Ltd which at the date of the gift was valued at £40,000, and on B's death was worth £280,000.

Calculate the IHT arising on B's death.

Solution

	£	£
7.4.2012 value of B's estate:		
20% interest in Q Ltd	125,000	
Less business property relief 100% × 125,000	(125,000)	–
Freehold land used by Q Ltd		35,000
Shares in Z plc		15,000
Other property		312,500
		362,500

Add transfer within previous 7 years		
Gift of shares in Q Ltd	40,000	
Business property relief 100% × 40,000	(40,000)	–
		362,500
IHT thereon FA 2012 rates:		
325,000 per table 2012/13	Nil	
37,500 @ 40%	15,000	
362,500		15,000
Less notional IT on gift within last 7 years		–
IT payable by executors		15,000

Notes

i) There is no inheritance tax payable in respect of the gift as it was below the threshold level of £325,000 for 2012/13.

ii) The BPR rate of 100% applies to the shares in Q Ltd and the gift to B's son.

iii) No relief is available for the freehold land used by Q Ltd as B did not have a controlling interest.

iv) The PET is valued at the date of the transfer and not the date of B's death for estate purposes. Where the death value is lower than the transfer value, that value is used to compute any IHT on the transfer at death borne by the donee.

3. Jamie, a generous uncle, makes a PET of £200,000 by a cash gift to his nephew Tom in October 2011, and suddenly dies one year later, in October 2012.

Due to previous chargeable transfers by Jamie (earlier PETs which have become chargeable on Jamie's death) only £50,000 of Jamie's nil rate band is available to cover Tom's PET. The IHT rate applicable to the rest of Tom's PET is 40% (death rates apply to lifetime transfers taxed on death).

Calculate the IHT payable on the 'failed' PET to Tom as a result of Jamie's death, if:

a) Tom pays the IHT on the failed PET

b) Jamie's estate pays the IHT on the failed PET.

Solution

a) If Tom pays the IHT on the 'failed' £200,000 PET (the normal/default situation) then Tom would pay IHT of (0% x £50,000 + 40% x £150,000), i.e. £60,000.

This obligation and the tax liability would be notified to him by the Executors of Jamie's estate.

b) If the PET to Tom was stated by Jamie at the time it was made to be 'made net of IHT', or if for some other reason Jamie's estate ends up paying the IHT on the failed PET (eg Tom is now insolvent), then the value to be taxed at 40% must be **grossed up** for the tax liability taken on by Jamie.

Thus the gross transfer becomes (retrospectively)

Value taxed at nil IHT	£50,000
Value taxed at 40% (£200,000 gifted - £50,000 nil rate band) x 100/60 =	£250,000
Gross transfer value, total	£300,000
tax due on this gross value (40% of £250,000)	= £100,000

This £100,000 is payable by Jamie's estate and the grossed up amount of £300,000 is recorded in the record of chargeable PETs reported by Jamie's Executors as the gross value of the lifetime gift made to Tom.

Part VI

Value added tax

36   General principles

Introduction

1. Value added tax is a tax on the supply of goods and services made by a registered taxable person, in the course of business, within the UK. Prior to 2008 the UK's VAT rates had been constant for many years. In response to the financial crisis of 2008, the Government announced a temporary reduction in VAT standard rate in November 2008, cutting it by 2.5% from 17.5% to 15% for a period of 13 months. From 1ˢᵗ January 2010 the standard VAT rate reverted to 17.5%.

Following the change of Government in May 2010, it was announced that the UK's standard rate of VAT would be 20% from 4 January 2011.

Unlike the 2008 VAT rate change, the 2011 change is not 'temporary', so may be assumed a long-term policy. Other EU countries have also recently raised their standard rates of VAT, in response to well-publicised public spending deficits.

This chapter begins with a summary of the headings under which the basic rules of VAT will be described.

Summary of topic headings

2.
Legislative background	Voluntary registration
VAT rates	Voluntary de-registration
Classification of goods and services	Group registration
Zero-rated goods and services	Companies organised into divisions
Reduced rate goods and services	Accounts and records
Exempt goods and services	Administration
Land and buildings	Late registration
Taxable persons	Default surcharge
Business splitting	Errors on VAT returns
Registration limits	Tax avoidance schemes

Legislative background

3. Value added tax was introduced in the UK with effect from 1st April 1973, superseding purchase tax and selective employment tax. The main provisions of VAT law are now contained in the Value Added Tax Act 1994, as amended by subsequent Finance Acts and expanded by Regulations. Many UK VAT law changes since 1973 have implemented VAT Directives issued by the European Union. Governments of all Member States are obliged to implement these Directives, as a condition of membership, with the aim of maintaining a common VAT system in the EU Fiscal Area.

The general principles of VAT are thus common to the whole EU fiscal area. VAT is levied on goods and services on a common basis of charge, but domestic VAT rates may be varied, within limits, by individual Member-states. The maximum rate of VAT that is currently allowed under EU law is 25% and the minimum reduced or lower rate that is allowed for social reasons is 5%.

The UK's zero-rate of VAT, which still applies to certain goods and services, is a historical anomaly dating from before the UK's accession to the European Community in 1973. In terms of VAT law any transaction that is zero-rated for VAT is still a 'taxable supply' and fully part of the VAT reporting system.

Also, any reference in the VAT Acts to 'zero-rated goods and services' covers reduced-rate goods and services as well, even if not separately specified.

In VAT law, all supplies are taxable supplies unless they are either exempt supplies or supplies outside the scope of VAT. Supplies outside the scope of VAT include employment services performed in return for a wage or salary, supplies within a VAT group (see section 16), and any supply by a non-taxable person. Exempt supplies are defined in Schedule 9 of the VAT Act (see section 8 below).

VAT rates and the VAT fraction

4. VAT has to be charged on the taxable supply of goods and services within the UK by a taxable person. VAT is charged at the following rates:

Standard rate	20.0%
Reduced rate	5.0%
Zero rate	0.0%

In the UK, consumer protection law requires that prices quoted directly to consumers by VAT-registered traders, such as retailers, are stated inclusive of VAT. The invoice or retail receipt should however identify the amount of VAT separately.

UK traders who sell to both consumers and businesses, or only to businesses, may quote prices net of VAT and add the VAT later on the invoice.

Since the current standard rate is 20%, it follows that the VAT element of a price stated inclusive of VAT is $^{20}/_{120}$ or $^1/_6$. This is known as 'the VAT fraction', and can be applied to any VAT-inclusive price for a standard-rated supply to find the VAT amount contained within it.

When the standard rate was 17.5% before January 2011, the VAT fraction was $^{17.5}/_{117.5}$ or $^7/_{47}$. While standard rate of VAT was temporarily 15%, the VAT fraction was $^{15}/_{115}$ or $^3/_{23}$.

The VAT fraction for reduced-rate goods and services liable to VAT at 5% is $^5/_{105}$ or $^1/_{21}$.

Classification of goods and services

5. A taxable supply is a supply of goods or services made in the UK in the course of business by a VAT-registered trader, other than an exempt supply.

For VAT rating purposes, goods and services are classified into four groups as listed below, but as noted above the zero-rated and reduced-rate group are for legal definition purposes treated as one single group.

Standard-rated supplies   All goods and services not specifically listed as zero-rated, reduced- rated or exempt

Zero-rated supplies   Goods and services which are subject to a zero rate of VAT, e.g. printed matter, public transport (section 6).

Reduced rate supplies   Goods and services which are subject to the reduced (currently 5%) rate of VAT (see section 7). These are mainly items which were formerly standard-rated but for social or welfare reasons have been reduced to the lowest possible rate that can now be imposed.

Exempt supplies   Goods and services which are not subject to VAT, e.g. healthcare, education, banking and insurance (see section 8).

Definitions of zero-rated, reduced rate and exempt supplies are set out in the VAT Act, and summarised below.

Standard-rated supplies are not defined in the VAT Act but this is the default classification of any goods or service supplied for a consideration in the course of business, if none of the other specified descriptions applies.

Since the UK's accession to the European Community in 1973, it is not possible to introduce new categories of zero-rated supply, but the previous ones continue until amended. For example, the Conservative government in the 1990s removed the VAT zero-rating of domestic fuel and power (ie home electricity and gas bills). When Labour came to power in 1997, despite a manifesto promise to reverse this VAT increase, they could not reduce the rate on domestic fuel and power to less than 5% (which it still is).

Zero-rated (ZR) goods and services

6. Particulars of the goods and services which are zero-rated are contained in Schedule 8 to the VAT Act 1994 and there are sixteen groups each containing separate listed items, as follows.

Group 1: Food. Most food for human consumption is ZR, unless supplied as a restaurant meal or catering service, when it is standard-rated (SR). Cold takeaway food sold for consumption off the promises is ZR, but hot takeaway food is SR. Cold food and beverage products not sold in the course of a catering service are in principle ZR but there is a long list of exceptions to this rule, meaning that certain foodstuffs and drinks are SR.

The policy rationale given for excluding certain foods and beverages from zero-rating is that such items are 'non-essential' or 'luxuries'. Examples of items not eligible for zero-rating include ice cream, sweets and chocolate, potato crisps, alcoholic drinks, fruit juices and chocolate-covered biscuits (but chocolate-covered cakes are ZR). Pet foods are also SR, but general animal feeding stuffs are ZR.

Group 2: Sewerage services and water. The supply of water and sewerage to domestic customers is ZR, but not distilled and mineral water. The supply of water and sewerage services to industry is SR.

Group 3: Books and printed matter. The supply of books and magazines, newspapers, music, maps and charts is ZR. Diaries and printed stationery (ie printed items intended to be written in or on by the purchaser) are SR. E-books supplied electronically to be printed out by the customer are SR services not ZR goods, as are online journals or newspapers supplied for consideration, unless a printed version of the publication is also included in the supply.

Group 4: Talking books for the blind and handicapped, and wireless sets for the blind. ZR items include magnetic tapes, tape recorders and accessories, if supplied to approved agencies such as the Royal National Institute for the Blind and similar charities.

The supply of information other than photographs to newspapers or to the public by news agencies is ZR.

Group 5: Construction of buildings. The position under this heading may be summarised as follows.

Zero-rated

i)   Construction of new domestic buildings.

ii) Approved alterations to domestic listed buildings.

Standard-rated

i)   Construction of new non-domestic buildings.

ii) Repair, maintenance or alteration of existing buildings.

iii) Civil engineering services or new work.

iv) Civil engineering services or repair, maintenance or alteration of existing buildings.

v) Demolition of domestic and non-domestic buildings.

vi) The construction of a building for own use in business.

Group 6: Protected buildings.

Group 7: International services.

Group 8: Transport. Zero-rating applies to the supply of passenger transport both inland and international, international freight transport, and the supply, repair and maintenance of certain ships and aircraft. Standard-rating applies to taxis (if the provider is VAT-registered), transport in cars or aeroplanes carrying fewer than six people,   hire cars, car parking and luggage storage.

Group 9: Caravans and house-boats. Caravans are ZR if they exceed 7 metres in length or 2.3 metres in width, the maximum size permitted for use on public roads. Smaller towable caravans are SR, as is the supply of caravan holiday accommodation. House-boats if suitable for permanent habitation are ZR.

Group 10: Gold. The supply of gold coins which are legal tender is taxable at the standard rate. The supply of gold held in the UK, by a central bank to another central bank or a member of the London Gold Market, and reciprocal transactions, are ZR.

Group 11: Bank notes. The issue of bank notes payable to bearer is zero-rated.

Group 12: Drugs, medicines, aids for the handicapped etc. The following supplies are ZR: goods dispensed by a registered pharmacist on prescription, medical and surgical appliances, electrical and mechanical appliances for a handicapped person. Other drugs and medicines sold or dispensed without prescription are SR.

Group 13: Imports, exports etc. The transfer of goods from the UK, without a legal sale taking place, by a person carrying on a business both inside and outside the EU, to the non-EU located business is also ZR. This would cover, for example, the transfer of parts to be assembled into products from a UK VAT-registered company to its non-EU branch.

Group 14: Tax-free shops. This covers any shop situated in an airport, port or Channel Tunnel terminal approved by HMRC for the purposes of this Group, and also sales of limited amounts of goods by the providers of air or sea transport or Channel tunnel shuttle trains to passengers who have purchased transport services from them.

Group 15: Charities etc. Zero-rating applies to the supply by a charity established primarily for the relief of distress or the benefit or protection of animals, of goods donated for sale, any exports, medical or scientific equipment used solely in medical research, and appliances for the handicapped. The supply by a charity shop of goods purchased for resale is standard-rated - there is no general exemption for charity shops (though a small charity shop may be able to keep total taxable turnover below the registration limit).

Group 16: Clothing and footwear. Children's clothing and footwear are ZR. Protective boots and helmets are SR when supplied to a person for use by his or her employees. Supplies of protective boots and helmets to any other person for industrial use remain zero-rated. Also zero-rated are motor cycle helmets. Other clothing is SR.

Reduced rate goods and services

7. Particulars of goods and services which are reduced-rated supplies are contained in the Schedule 7A to the VAT Act 1994, and there are 11 groups.

Group 1: Fuel and power supplied for domestic and charity use.

Group 2: Installation of energy-saving materials.

Group 3: Grant-funded installations of heating or security equipment.

Group 4: Women's sanitary products

Group 5: Children's car seats and car seat bases

Group 6: Certain residential conversions

Group 7: Certain residential renovations and alterations

Group 8: Contraceptive products (unless exempt from VAT ie NHS or private healthcare)

Group 9: Welfare advice supplied by charities/ state-regulated private welfare institutions

Group 10: Installation of mobility aids for the elderly

Group 11: Smoking cessation products.

Reduced-rate supplies can in general be characterised as those on which a previously higher applicable rate of VAT has been reduced, as a deliberate policy, for social or welfare reasons.

Exempt goods and services

8. Particulars of goods and services which are exempt supplies are contained in Schedule 9 to the VAT Act 1994 and there are 15 groups, classified as follows.

Group 1: Land. See section 9 below for more details.

Group 2: Insurance. All forms of insurance are exempted and this includes insurance broking and agency services.

Group 3: Postal services. The conveyance of postal packets other than telegrams, by the Royal Mail was exempted up to 31 January 2011. Postal services rendered by persons other than the post office were taxable. However as part of EU policy to reduce distortion of competition between state and private providers, the UK Royal Mail lost its exemption in respect of parcel services and certain other postal services, and from 31 January 2011 these are SR.

Group 4: Betting, gaming and lotteries. Examples of exempt services under this group are bookmakers, charges for bingo and profits from casino games. Admission charges to any premises where betting or the playing of games of chance takes place are however taxable at SR, as are takings from gaming or entertainment machines.

Group 5: Finance. In general, banking services relating to the borrowing or lending, receipt and transfer of money are exempt. Specific services offered by banks such as executorship and trustee work, portfolio management etc. are taxable at SR, as are the commissions from stockbroking, and management fees of unit trusts.

Group 6: Education. Non-profit educational services provided by schools, colleges, universities and youth clubs are exempt, as are the supply of goods and services to those establishments. However, services provided by organisations selling training or education with a view to profit, such as correspondence courses, are taxable at standard rate. Where training or education is SR, printed learning materials are SR if supplied exclusively for the training course, but are ZR if they are also available to buy alone, without buying the training course.

Group 7: Health and welfare. The supply of goods and services by registered healthcare providers such as doctors, dentists, opticians, occupational therapists etc. is exempted. Goods supplied under a prescription by a pharmacist are ZR.

Group 8: Burial and cremation. The services of undertakers in connection with a funeral or cremation are exempt, and within limits this includes charges for the supply of a coffin, shroud etc. but not flowers.

Group 9: Trade unions and professional bodies. VAT exemption is given for membership fees and other mutual services, and related goods supplied by a trade union and most non-profit-making professional, learned or representational bodies.

Group 10: Sports competitions. The grant of a right to enter a competition in sport or physical recreation, where the consideration for the grant consists in money which is to be used wholly for the provision of prizes, is exempt.

Group 11: Works of art etc. The disposal of works of art in circumstances where there is no liability to inheritance tax or capital gains tax (broadly, sale to public collections for the public benefit) is exempt.

Group 12: Fund raising activities by charities.

Group 13: Cultural services etc.

Group 14: Supplies of goods where input tax cannot be recovered.

Group 15: Investment gold.

Land and buildings

9. The VAT treatment of supplies of land and buildings is complex. This is a very brief summary:

Always Exempt

i)   The sale of used domestic buildings;

ii)   Leases of used domestic buildings;

iii)   Leases of new domestic buildings where the lease is less than 21 years;

iv)   The sale of building land for domestic building.

Always Zero-rated

i)   Sales of new domestic buildings, provided the seller is the person constructing the building;

ii)   Leases of new domestic buildings where the lease is capable of exceeding 21 years.

Always Standard-rated

i)   Sales of new non-domestic buildings;

ii)   Sales of building land for non-domestic building;

iii) The grant of any interest, right or licence consisting of a right to take game or fish;

iv)   The provision in an hotel, inn, boarding house or similar establishment of sleeping accommodation or of accommodation in rooms which are provided in conjunction with sleeping accommodation or for the purpose of a supply of catering;

v)   The provision of holiday accommodation in a house, flat, caravan, house-boat or tent;

vi)   The provision of seasonal pitches for caravans, and the grant of facilities at caravan parks to persons for whom such pitches are provided;

vii) The provision of pitches for tents or of camping facilities;

viii) The grant of facilities for parking a vehicle;

ix)   The grant of any right to fell and remove standing timber;

x)   The grant of facilities for housing, or storage of, an aircraft or for mooring or storage of, a ship, boat or other vessel;

xi)   The grant of any right to occupy a box, seat or other accommodation at a sports ground, theatre, concert hall or other place of entertainment;

xii) The grant of facilities for playing any sport or participating in any physical recreation.

Either exempt or SR, depending on whether the supplier has elected to waive the exemption.

i) Sales of used non-domestic buildings;

ii) Leases of used non-domestic buildings

Where stamp duty land tax is payable on the sale or lease of land or buildings, the consideration liable to VAT is the sale price plus the stamp duty land tax.

Taxable persons

10. A taxable person is any person who is, or should be, registered for VAT. Person includes an individual, partnership, company, club, society or trust. Any person may register for VAT who is carrying on a business that involves making taxable supplies for a consideration. The business in question need not be a profit-making or profit-seeking business. VAT registration is compulsory once turnover of taxable supplies exceeds a set level (See section 13).

Business splitting

11. If the same person carries on two businesses then both businesses have to be registered under the same registration and have to be considered as one when applying the VAT registration limits. HMRC is alert to the possibility that to keep turnover under the VAT registration threshold, two members of a family, or two individuals, sometimes operate two apparently independent businesses from the same premises, or one business is run by a partnership alongside a connected business operated by one of the partners as a sole trader. HMRC has indicated that the following factors will be taken into consideration in deciding whether or not a genuine independent business exists for VAT registration purposes.

i)   Appropriate premises and equipment for each business should be provided by the person carrying on the business.

ii)   Day-to-day records identifying each business should be kept and where appropriate separate annual accounts.

iii)   Purchase and sales invoices for each business should be in the name of the person carrying on the trade who should be legally responsible for all trading activities.

iv)   A separate bank account should be opened for each business.

v)   All payroll payments should be paid by the person carrying on the business.

vi)   Each business should be treated as an independent business for income tax purposes.

Formerly, HMRC could not require separate businesses to register as a single trader for VAT purposes unless it could show that the main reason (or one of the main reasons) for keeping those businesses separate was to avoid a liability to be VAT-registered.

This limitation has been removed, and 'connected businesses which have avoided liability for VAT by artificially separating will be liable to be treated as one, whatever the purported reason for the separation'. For example, HMRC can direct that a series of limited companies running a pub, launderette or other retail outlet for only one month a year each, in order to keep the turnover of each company below the registration threshold, will be treated as one business.

Artificial separation of business activities

12. According to HMRC it is impracticable to give a complete list of all the circumstances in which a separation will be artificial, as each case will depend on its own facts. However, HMRC 'would at least make further enquiries' where:

a)   Separate entities supply registered and unregistered customers.

b)   The same equipment and/or premises are used by different entities on a regular basis – this may be particularly relevant where an ice cream van (for example) is used by traders in rotation.

c)   A supply, which is usually a single supply, is split into separate parts – for example, a bed-and breakfast establishment where the bedroom is said to be supplied by the husband and the breakfast by the wife.

d)   Where the separated parts retain the appearance of a single business: the example given being that of pub catering where 'in most cases the customer will consider the food and the drinks as bought from the pub and not from two independent businesses'. However, franchised 'shops within shops' will usually be accepted as truly independent businesses.

e)   One person has a controlling influence in two or more businesses which make the same type of supply at separate locations.

Registration limits

13.   VAT registration is compulsory once a business's turnover of taxable supplies exceeds a threshold set out in the legislation, which is usually increased each year on 1 April (occasionally on 1 May). The latest thresholds are as follows:

UK taxable supplies	Past turnover 1 year	Past turnover Unless turnover for next year will not exceed:	Future turnover 30 days
	£	£	£
From 1.4.2012	77,000	75,000	77,000
From 1.4.2011	73,000	71,000	73,000

Notes

i)   Turnover of taxable supplies includes all zero and positive-rated supplies.

ii)   Registration is mandatory in the following circumstances:

a)   At the end of any month, if the value of the taxable supplies in the past year has exceeded the table limits.

b)   At any time, if there are reasonable grounds for believing that the value of the taxable supplies in the next 30 days will exceed the future turnover figure.

iii)   For ii) a) notification to HMRC must be made within 30 days of the end of the relevant month. Registration is effective from the end of the month following the relevant month, or such earlier date as may be mutually agreed. The relevant month is the month at the end of which historic 12-month turnover exceeds the threshold, so that a liability to register arises.

iv)   For ii) b) notification must be made before the end of the 30 day period. Registration is effective from the beginning of the 30 day period.

Voluntary registration

14. Where a person who is not required by law to be registered satisfies HMRC that he or she:

i)   makes taxable supplies; or

ii)   is carrying on a business and intends to make such supplies in the course or furtherance of that business;

445

then, if the person so requests, he or she can be voluntarily registered, with effect from the day on which the request is made or such earlier date as may be mutually agreed.

Voluntary de-registration

15. A registered person may apply for de-registration if in the next year his or her taxable turnover excluding VAT is not expected to exceed £75,000 (£71,000 until 31 March 2012).

De-registration in principles requires the trader to account for output VAT on a self-supply of all inventory and fixed assets, on which input VAT was previously recovered, which are still on hand at deregistration. However, if the amount of VAT involved in the self-supply charge on deregistration is less than £2,000, the liability is ignored, being deemed 'de minimis' (too small to matter).

Group registration

16. Under Section 43 VATA 1994, as amended, two or more companies or limited liability partnerships (collectively referred to as corporate bodies) may register as a single taxable person, known as a VAT Group, if

i)   each body has a permanent establishment in the UK;

ii)   they are under common control, for example one or more company is a subsidiary of a common parent company, or both/ all of them are controlled by a business partnership, or by an individual.

A restriction applies where the turnover of a prospective VAT group is over £10 million per year and the group is partly owned or managed by a third party (e.g. a joint owner owning 50% of the parent company but not itself in the VAT group. This entity can only register as a group for VAT if:

i)   no more than 50 per cent of benefits generated by the business go to third parties;

ii)   under GAAP the whole VAT group uses consolidated accounting ;

iii)   no third party consolidates the VAT group into its accounts.

The effects of a group registration are as follows.

i)   The VAT administration is handled by one group company, known as the representative member, and only one VAT return is required for all transactions by the group. All group companies use the same VAT number.

ii)   Intra-group supplies are outside the scope of (ie not subject to) VAT.

iii)   All members of the group are jointly and severally liable for the VAT due from the representative member.

iv)   Turnover limits for registration, deregistration, special schemes and partial exemption (see Chapter 37 for these two) are based on the group figures.

Companies organised into divisions – Divisional registration

17. A company carrying on UK business in several divisions may register its divisions separately as unincorporated traders, as follows.

i) All divisions of the company must be registered separately. It is not possible to exclude certain divisions from registration e.g. where they fall below the registration limits.

ii) A separate VAT return is made by each division.

iii) However, the separate divisions are not separately taxed persons and the company remains liable for the whole VAT.

iv) Inter-divisional transfers are not subject to VAT.

v) Each division should be an independent unit with its own accounting and administration, carrying on business activities in separate locations.

vi) Input tax attributable to exempt supplies (exempt input tax) by the corporate body as a whole must be less than the limits referred to in Chapter 37 (Section 17).

Divisional registration is subject to the approval of HMRC.

Accounts and records

18. There have been recent changes to the book-keeping arrangements required for VAT purposes. From 1 April 2011 almost all VAT returns must be submitted online and VAT payments made online. Paper records may still be kept supporting input VAT, though electronic records are equally acceptable.

a) Any taxable supply of goods or services must be supported by a 'tax invoice', the details of which are described in Chapter 37 section 9.

b) At regular intervals, usually quarterly, a VAT return must be completed showing the amounts of output and input tax for the period, and the net amount payable to or receivable from HMRC. The period covered by a VAT return is known as a tax period and each return must be submitted not later than one month after the end of that tax period.

c) Adequate records and accounts of all transactions involving VAT must be maintained to support both the amount of output tax chargeable, and the claims for deductible input tax. To support input tax claims the primary requirement is keep valid tax invoices received from suppliers. These records are checked on control visits by HMRC officers.

d) Books and records, including electronic records, must be kept for a period of six years. Business records include the following:

Orders and delivery notes

Relevant business correspondence

Purchase and sales books

Cash books and other account books

Purchase invoices and copy sales invoices

    Records of daily takings e.g. till rolls

    Annual accounts – balance sheet and profit and loss accounts

    Import and export documents

    Bank statements and paying-in-slips

    Any credit/debit notes issued or received.

e)   There are some optional special schemes for retailers to simplify record keeping for VAT purposes and these are covered in Chapter 37.

Administration

19. HM Revenue and Customs is the government department responsible for the administration and collection of VAT (except Import VAT, which is collected by the UK Border Agency).

Dispute and appeals procedure

In the event of a dispute between a taxable person and the VAT office, there is first an optional internal review procedure in which a Revenue Officer who has not been involved in the case before is asked to review the complaint and respond within 45 days. If this review supports the decision of the original Revenue Officer, or if there is no internal review, the taxpayer can appeal within 30 days to the Tax Chamber of the First-Tier Tribunal (this handles disputes on both direct and indirect taxes and took over all cases from the former UK VAT Tribunals on 1 April 2009). Appeals to the First-tier Tribunal might cover matters such as:

a)   Registration or cancellation of registration.

b)   Assessment of tax.

c)   Amount of tax chargeable.

d)   Amount of input tax deductible.

e)   Bad debt claims.

f)   Group registration matters.

g)   Matters concerned with the value or categorisation of supplies.

On questions of law a further appeal can be made to the Upper Tribunal (Tax and Chancery Chamber) from which further appeal lies to the Court of Appeal (Inner House in Scotland).

As VAT is European Law, questions of the interpretation of EU Directives or Regulations, and of whether domestic VAT legislation or HMRC practice is compatible with EU law, can be referred by the judge directly from any UK Court or Tribunal to the European Court of Justice, for a definitive ruling on the relevant point of European Law. The UK courts are obliged to follow the ECJ's rulings in applying VAT law to cases before them and if anything in the UK VAT legislation is found incompatible with the EU VAT Directives then the UK Government are obliged to change the law. In deciding UK VAT cases the UK courts also take account of similar decisions on VAT matters from the courts and VAT tribunals of other EU Member States.

Late registration penalty

20. a)   Failure to notify HMRC at the proper time that a business should be registered for VAT purposes may incur a tax-based penalty, subject to a minimum of £50.

Number of months late for registration	% of VAT due
0 – 9	5%
10 – 18	10%
19 –	15%

The amount of VAT due is the sum of VAT due (calculated retrospectively) from the date the registration should have been made.

The penalty is not due if the trader can satisfy HMRC that there was a reasonable excuse for the failure.

The following does not amount to reasonable excuse:

i)   insufficiency of funds to pay the tax

ii)   reliance on a third party to pay the tax

iii)   ignorance of the law relating to registration.

b)   HMRC has indicated that the following guidelines show circumstances where there might be a reasonable excuse for late registration.

i)   **Compassionate circumstances** where an individual is totally responsible for running a small business and he or she, or a member of the immediate family, was seriously ill or recovering from such illness at the time notification was required.

ii)   **Transfer of a business as a going concern** where such a business is taken over with little or no break in the trading activities and returns have been submitted and tax paid on time under the registration number of the previous owner.

iii)   **Doubt about liabilities of supplies** where there is written evidence of an enquiry to HMRC about the liability of supplies and liability has remained in doubt.

iv)   **Uncertainty about employment status** where there are genuine doubts as to whether a person is employed or self-employed or where correspondence with HMRC can be produced about these doubts.

v)   **Effective date of registration earlier than required** where a person has requested registration from an earlier date than was legally required in the mistaken belief that he or she had to do so to recover input tax on stocks and assets for the business. This excuse could only apply if there was no reason to believe that taxable turnover would exceed the registration threshold from the required date.

The default surcharge – Section 59 VATA 1994

21. The default surcharge regime has been in place for many years but its details have changed with the 2011 change to online VAT reporting. Online VAT returns and electronic VAT payments are now required for all traders with a VAT-exclusive turnover exceeding £100,000, and all newly registered traders, since April 2011.

The long-established due date for both payments and returns, which was one calendar month after the end of the return period, is extended by seven days for all online returns and payments. The one-month deadline still applies to traders who are not yet filing and paying online.

The rules about VAT default surcharge work as follows:

a) A person is in VAT default if a return is not submitted on time, or if a payment is made late.

b) A trader can be in default for one return period without incurring a monetary penalty. However, the first time the taxpayer is in default, HMRC serve a surcharge liability notice. The surcharge liability notice once issued remains in force for a period of 12 months, during which time there must be no further default.

c) While the notice is in force, a default surcharge liability arises for any period in which there is another default. In addition, each time there is a default in an existing notice period (surcharge period), the current surcharge period is extended for a further 12 months.

d) The penalty is based on the amount of VAT due and unpaid at the time when the default occurred. The percentage penalty goes up the more defaults there are in the same surcharge period. The surcharge period continues until there have been twelve months with no default.

e) The rates of surcharge are:

	% of VAT
1st default	2%
2nd default	5%
3rd default	10%
4th and subsequent	15%

f) Surcharge assessments at rates below 10% will not be issued if the calculated penalty is £400 or less.

g) Once the rate reaches 10% (third default), an assessment will be issued for £30 minimum, or the calculated surcharge if greater.

h) The above surcharge regime take effect more slowly for businesses with an annual turnover of less than £150,000. On the first default (late return or late tax payment) by such a trader, HMRC will send a letter offering help and support. If the business, having either received or declined the help and support service, is late with another VAT return or tax payment in the next twelve months, a surcharge liability notice will then be issued, and a normal surcharge period will then commence.

i) **Reasonable excuses:** A person is not liable to a surcharge if he or she satisfies the Commissioners that in the case of a default:

   i) the return, or as the case may be the tax, was despatched at such time and in such manner that it was reasonable to expect that it would be received within the appropriate time limit, or

   ii) there is a reasonable excuse for the return or the tax not having been despatched.

   The following are not reasonable excuses (section 71 VAT Act):

   i) Insufficiency of funds to pay any tax;

   ii) Where reliance is placed on any other person to perform any task, the fact of that reliance or the fact of any other dilatoriness or inaccuracy on the part of the person relied upon.

After April 2011 it would seem that the 'despatched on time' argument, dating from when VAT returns were all submitted by post, can now apply only to traders who do not have to submit online. However it is conceivable that an IT problem might arise such that a trader could prove that an online return or payment was correctly sent, despite failing to reach HMRC on time.

Errors on VAT returns

22. a) The Error Correction rules cover how taxpayers should report and correct any errors discovered on past VAT returns. The rules are behaviour-based, and designed to reward and not penalise registered traders who co-operate with HMRC and try their best to operate VAT correctly. The regime distinguishes between 'non-careless errors' (which the tax authorities accept can occur in any business) and 'careless' or 'deliberate' errors. In all cases the trader must keep a record of all errors discovered on VAT returns already submitted and the action taken. These records may be reviewed on a VAT control visit at any time.

b) If the taxpayer discovers an error, and it was not a deliberate error, it may be adjusted directly on the VAT return for the period of discovery, provided the net amount of VAT involved is less than the de minimis limit. (The figure in question is the net of all previous errors discovered by the taxpayer in the same VAT return period.)

c) The de minimis limit is the greater of (i) £10,000 or (ii) 1% of turnover for the current return period, subject to a maximum in all cases of £50,000.

d)   In summary, the current rules for the reporting of errors are as follows:

Non-deliberate errors within the de minimis limit	Separate notification is not compulsory. The taxpayer can enter the relevant corrections to the input and/ or output VAT figures on the next submitted return.
	If the registered person prefers to make formal disclosure, they can also notify on form 652 or by letter, explaining all the circumstances of the error and noting that they have corrected it on the VAT return. No interest is charged on de minimis underpayments corrected by the registered trader on a later return. Errors may be corrected using this method for up to four years after they arose.
Non-deliberate errors amounting to more than the de minimis limit	HMRC must be notified by letter or using VAT Form 652, explaining the circumstances of the error.
	HMRC will issue an assessment for the VAT due. Interest may be charged from the date when any net underpaid VAT was originally due until the date of payment. Interest represents commercial restitution and not a penalty. Therefore HMRC may agree not to charge interest if there has been no monetary loss to the Crown – for example supplies made were incorrectly zero-rated but the customer could have reclaimed the input VAT immediately if they had been correctly standard-rated.
	No penalty will be charged provided that HMRC accepts that the circumstances of the error do not indicate carelessness.
Deliberate errors of any size	HMRC must be notified either by letter or on form VAT 652. Interest is likely to be charged. For possible penalties see b) below.
Errors discovered by HMRC and not the registered trader	HMRC will issue an assessment which will include interest and a behaviour based penalty depending on the level of co-operation and care shown by the trader.
Default interest	VAT interest and penalties are not an expense of trade for income tax purposes.

e) If previous errors have not been disclosed and are discovered by HMRC, then a VAT Misdeclaration Penalty (MP) may be imposed. Its purpose is not to imply dishonesty but simply to encourage full VAT compliance in future.

The standard penalty is triggered if the under-declaration of VAT uncovered equals or exceeds either

(i)   30% of the correct amount of VAT payable, or

(ii)   the greater of £1 million and 5% of the true amount of VAT payable.

The MP is generally 15% of the under-declaration but in some circumstances another 'penalty base' can be used.

f) A MP will not normally be imposed:

   i)   during the period from the end of a reporting period to the due date for furnishing the VAT return for the following reporting period;

   ii) when a VAT return is misdeclared but this has been corrected by a compensating misdeclaration in respect of the same transaction for the following accounting period, with no overall loss of VAT.

g) If the trader's conduct in misdeclaring VAT involves dishonesty, a civil evasion penalty of up to 100% of VAT under-declared can be imposed. Where circumstances warrant it, criminal proceedings may also be brought.

Tax avoidance schemes - VAT

23. Businesses making taxable supplies ≥ £600,000 must disclose their use of specific VAT avoidance schemes, which HMRC publishes in a statutory list. This must be done within 30 days of the date when the first return affected by the scheme becomes due. Failure to disclose incurs a penalty of 15% of tax avoided. Businesses with taxable supplies > £10m must disclose the use of any schemes that have 'the hallmarks of avoidance'.

Student self-testing question with answer

A Ltd owns a quarry. It extracts stone from this quarry and sells the stone to B Ltd for £10,000 plus VAT. B Ltd converts all the stone into paving slabs and sells these slabs to C Ltd for £18,000 plus VAT. C Ltd owns and runs a garden centre, where the slabs are sold to the general public for a total of £32,000 plus VAT.

Requirement:

Show how VAT is charged and collected at each stage of the process. (Assume that VAT is to be accounted for at 20% throughout).

Suggested answer

	Cost price before VAT	Input tax	Selling price before VAT	Output tax	Paid to HMRC
	£	£	£	£	£
A Ltd	-	-	10,000	2,000	2,000
B Ltd	10,000	2,000	18,000	3,600	1,600
C Ltd	18,000	3,600	32,000	6,400	2,800
					6,400

37   The VAT system in more detail

Introduction

1.   This chapter covers further features of the VAT system under the following main topic headings:

The VAT return	Imports – removal from warehouse
Zero rated and exempt supplies	Exports
Taxable supply of goods and services	Goods for personal use
Taxable persons	Bad debts
The supply of goods and services	Transfer of business
Place of supply	Sale of business assets
Tax point	Business assets – capital allowances
Tax invoice/credit notes	VAT on capital goods – partly exempt businesses
Value of goods and services	Rents
Mixed supplies/composite supplies	Changes in tax rates
Input tax – deductions	Cash/annual accounting schemes
Input tax – no deduction	Flat rate scheme – small firms
Fuel for private motoring	Special retail schemes
Partial exemption	Miscellaneous

The VAT return

2. A taxable person is required to charge VAT on taxable supplies to customers, which is called output tax. He or she is also able to claim credit for the tax paid on business purchases, expenses, and assets, and this is known as input tax.

At the end of a VAT accounting period, usually a month or three months, the trader has to submit a VAT return to HMRC. This must show the total taxable supplies made and the VAT charged (output tax), together with the VAT on all purchase and expense invoices received (input tax), but excluding any input VAT that is blocked from recovery (see section 15). If the tax charged exceeds the amount paid then the balance is payable to HMRC. Where the output tax is less than the input tax then a repayment can be claimed.

Example

	£	£
Total taxable turnover (SR) for the quarter	100,000	
Output tax @ 20%		20,000
Total taxable inputs (SR) for the quarter	80,000	
Input tax @ 20%		16,000
Balance of VAT payable to HMRC		4,000

Zero-rated and exempt supplies

3. Goods or services which fall within the zero-rated or exempt categories do not include any VAT at all in the total invoiced price, and for this reason are often thought by students to be similar. However, there are very important differences between zero rated and exempt supplies.

a)   Zero-rated goods or services are taxable outputs, but liable at a nil rate of output tax. It follows that any input tax incurred in providing those outputs can be reclaimed by the supplier, and will be reclaimable in full, since there is no output tax collected from customers to give a normal means of recovering the supplier's input VAT.

b)   Supplies of exempt goods and services are made outside the VAT system and therefore, in principle, any input tax incurred in making such supplies cannot be reclaimed by the trader. Irrecoverable input VAT is an allowable business cost for income or corporation tax (unless the related cost is disallowable for direct tax purposes, eg entertaining).

c)   A business which makes only exempt supplies, such as an insurance company, cannot register for VAT.

d)   However, small amounts of input tax relating to exempt supplies may be reclaimable, if the exempt trader also makes taxable supplies. For the implications of a trader being 'partially exempt' (making both taxable and exempt supplies) see section 17 below.

Taxable supply of goods and services

4. VAT is chargeable on any supply made in the UK, or imported, where the supply is taxable under VAT law. The supply must be of non-exempt goods and services made for consideration by a taxable person in the course of business.

Taxable persons

5. A taxable person is any person who has registered for VAT, and this is required if the total value of his or her taxable supplies for any one year are greater than £77,000. All business activities must be aggregated in order to determine whether or not a person should register. Registration can be for an individual, partnership or limited company. The total of taxable business supplies (excluding related VAT) is called taxable turnover.

The supply of goods and services

6. The supply of goods can include any of the following:
a)   sale by ordinary commercial transaction;
b)   sale by auction or through agents;
c)   sale under a credit sale agreement or by hire purchase;
d)   goods supplied for further processing;

e)   goods supplied for personal use.

The supply of services covers any which are provided for money or money's worth, and includes the hire, lease or rental of any goods. Services which are ancillary to the supply of goods, such as postage and packing and delivery, are normally treated as services and not as part of the goods sold, if they are shown separately on the sales invoice.

Place of supply

7. In principle only goods and services supplied in the UK are chargeable to UK VAT so that the determination of the place of supply is important.

Goods

If the goods to be supplied are physically located in the UK then they are within the scope of UK VAT even where they may be subsequently exported. Goods that are located wholly outside the EU fiscal area and remain so are not subject to UK VAT at any time during the course of their supply. They are outside the scope of VAT, even if a UK trader enters into business transactions involving these goods. This could arise, for example, where a shipping company arranges for a consignment of goods to be sold and transferred from one country to another, but they never enter the EU Fiscal Area.

For VAT purposes the UK includes the Isle of Man, but not the Channel Isles.

For VAT treatment of imports and exports of goods to/from the UK, see sections 18 to 20.

Services

For VAT purposes, the place where a service is treated as being supplied is the only place where it is liable to VAT (if any). A particular service can have only one place of supply.

Prior to 1 January 2010 the EU VAT rules about the place of supply of services were complex with many detailed exceptions, not explored here. However the basic rule was that (subject to the exceptions mentioned), services were supplied in the place 'where the supplier belongs'.

Belonging in this sense means where the supplier has its principal place of business or its main business establishment. So if the supplier's principal place of business was in the UK, and it was registered for UK VAT, then in general all its services would be liable to UK VAT.

Where both the supplier and the customer are in the UK then generally there is no problem about deeming the place of supply of services as this will (on basic principles) be the UK.

The problems of competing places of supply arise when the customer is not in the UK and the supplier is, or vice versa. The rules are different depending on whether the customer is a business customer or a non-business customer.

If the customer belongs outside the UK, and provides evidence to the UK supplier that it is in genuine business in its own country, then the supply of services is treated from 1 January 2010 as taking place where the customer belongs, not where the supplier belongs. For UK VAT purposes, the supply of services to business customers outside the UK is outside the scope of UK VAT and so no UK VAT should be charged on it. (Note that the supplies do not count as exempt or zero-rated supplies – 'outside the scope' means they are not taxable supplies at all.)

However, if the customer belongs in another EU state, and the UK supplier also has its own VAT registration in that other state (which is possible; a trader can register for VAT in any number of different EU states where it does business). In this case having determined the place of supply, the supplier should charge VAT at the rate applying in that other state and include it on the VAT return in the other State.

If the business customer belongs in another EU member state but the UK supplier has no VAT registration in that other EU state, and therefore has treated the supply as outside the scope of VAT, the Customer must account for output VAT itself in its own state, using the reverse charge procedure (see section 19).

If the customer is not in business, the UK supplier should charge VAT at the UK rate on the services and issue a UK VAT invoice.

Time of supply – tax point

8. The tax point determines the period in which a supply falls, therefore when the supply should be included on the next VAT return and what rate of VAT applies if there is a change in rate. As with place of supply, the tax point rules differ depending on whether a supply is one of goods or of services.

For goods the basic tax point is the date when the goods are delivered or made available, and for services the basic tax point is the date of performance. However, there are two key exceptions.

a)   If an invoice is issued within 14 days after the time when goods are delivered or made available, then the date of the invoice becomes the tax point. This practice is widely followed and enables the VAT return to be completed from invoice records. A longer period than 14 days between delivery and invoice may be agreed with HMRC if the business has a regular invoice billing cycle eg on the last day of the month,

b)   If payment of consideration for the supply is made in advance of the date when goods are delivered or made available, then it is the earliest of the invoice, delivery or payment date which determines the tax point.

The same rules apply for deciding the period in which taxable inputs of goods arise. The most common tax point is the invoice date. If credit is taken on business purchases, relief for input tax may well be obtained in an earlier VAT quarter than the time when the supplier is paid.

Tax invoice

9. A tax invoice is a sales invoice issued by a registered person in respect of any goods or services supplied by him or her to another taxable person. The invoice must contain:

a)   supplier's name, address and VAT registration number

b)   customer's name and address

c)   type of supply i.e. whether a sale, sale by HP, hire or rental

d)   description of goods or services supplied together with the amount payable for each excluding VAT; items chargeable at different VAT rates must be shown separately, and the exact number of items of each type must be stated.

e)   total amount payable without VAT

f)   particulars of any cash discounts offered

g)   total amount of VAT .

A less detailed invoice, omitting the customer's name and address, may be used where individual supplies by a retailer amount to less than £250, including VAT.

Credit notes

10. Regulations require all registered traders to show the related VAT on credit or debit notes, whenever a price adjustment alters the amount of VAT due on a previous invoice.

Value of goods and services

11. The general rule is that the value on which VAT is chargeable is the amount of money (excluding VAT) which a customer has to pay for the goods or services supplied. This is known in VAT law as the consideration. The following should be noted.

a)   Price discounts (eg for customer loyalty) must be deducted from the invoiced amount to determine the VAT value.

b)   Prompt payment discounts, if offered, should be assumed to be going to be taken in full when computing the VAT on the sale price. If the prompt payment discount is not taken (i.e. the customer takes a longer credit period than the discount terms require), the difference paid by the customer is not subject to VAT.

c)   If a supply is not made for money consideration then the open market value of the supply, less any VAT included in that value, should be taken as the value of the supply, and VAT computed on it. This would apply for example on a part-exchange transaction.

d)   The cost of the goods to the supplier may be used to determine the value of a taxable supply. This would apply to goods appropriated from trading stock for personal use, and to the trader's own built plant and machinery, on which input VAT is accounted for under the 'self-supply' rules.

Mixed supplies

12. A mixed supply occurs where a single inclusive price is charged for a number of separate supplies of goods and services. Where all the supplies are taxable at the same rate then the normal rules of VAT can be easily applied to compute the VAT element. However, where different rates apply then an apportionment must be made which is 'fair and justifiable'. (See Card Protection Plan V CIR. 2001 STC)

Example

B makes a mixed supply of goods at a VAT-inclusive price of £160. The product costs show zero rated goods costing £30 and standard rated goods costing £50 (exclusive of VAT).

Solution

Computation of VAT

Proportion of total cost at SR $\dfrac{50 + \text{VAT}}{(50 + \text{VAT}) + 30}$ = 60/90

VAT inclusive price of standard-rated goods $60/90 \times £160$ = £106.67

VAT included = £106.67 × 20/120 = £17.78

Sale value of zero-rated supply = (160 − 106.67) = £53.33.

Analysis of total price as apportioned

	£
Value of standard-rated supply (107 − 17.83)	88.89
VAT on standard-rated supply 20% × 88.89	17.78
Zero-rated supply	53.33
Price of mixed supply	160.00

Other methods of apportionment e.g. based on market values, can be used. Apportionment must not be made where the supply is a composite supply (see next section). Examples of a mixed supply are:

Annual subscription to the AA (C & E v AA QB 1974 STC 192)

Fees for correspondence courses (Rapid Results College Ltd 1973 VAT TR 197)

(Books are zero rated. Tuition is standard rated).

Composite supply

13. This occurs where goods and services supplied together make up a single indivisible supply, and apportionment must not be made for VAT rating purposes as the components cannot be viewed as separable. The VAT treatment of a composite supply depends on the judgment as to what is the principal supply, with the other parts of a different type being classed as ancillary. If the composite supply, as a whole package, does not clearly qualify for exemption or zero-rating then it must be standard-rated. Examples of supplies that have been held in decided cases to be composite supplies include:

Services of a launderette (supplies of water, heat, use of machinery)	Mander Laundries Ltd 1973 VAT TR 136
A course in dress design (material and guidance notes)	Betty Foster (Fashion Sewing) 1976 VAT TR 229

Input tax – Deduction

14. Input tax is the VAT suffered on business purchases and expenses, including imported goods, goods removed from an import warehouse, and capital expenditure.

To be deductible, the input tax must be in respect of goods and services for the purposes of the business, and not of a class where the tax is specifically not recoverable.

Input tax can be reclaimed providing that it is attributable to the making of:

i) standard- or zero-rated supplies (which term includes reduced rate supplies);

ii) supplies made in the course of business which are outside the scope of UK VAT, but would have been subject to standard or zero rate if made in the UK (eg the supplies of services deemed supplied outside the UK under the rules in section 11 above)

iii) supplies of warehoused goods.

Input tax incurred in respect of any other activity not covered by (i) to (iii) above is not reclaimable.

Input tax on business overheads or research and development expenditure can be claimed as input tax provided that the overheads or R&D are attributable to the three activities noted above. If the overhead or R&D expenditure is partially attributable to exempt supplies or to activities outside the three categories above, then only the part of the input tax that can be attributed to the three listed activities is reclaimable.

Input tax incurred in relation to making exempt supplies may however be recoverable where after calculating the total amount for a period, it is found to fall under a specified de minimis level. (See partial exemption, section 17.)

Input tax – Blocked deduction

15. Input tax charged in respect of the following is non-deductible.

a) The purchase of private motor cars, except:

i)   Cars purchased for use exclusively for business purposes, and not being capable of additional private use by the trader.

ii)   Cars used solely for business such as taxis, self-drive hire cars.

iii) New cars purchased for resale by a car dealer.

VAT on the purchase of commercial vehicles such as vans is deductible.

b)   To mirror the rule that input VAT on purchased cars is usually blocked, only 50% of the input VAT incurred on leasing any private car(s) is deductible on a fully taxable trader's VAT retrun. The VAT-exclusive rental, plus 50% of the VAT incurred, is therefore charged in the accounts as an allowable expense for direct tax purposes. This rule does not apply to very short hires of cars, eg for a few days.

c)   Motor accessories. When a motor car is purchased, VAT on the accessories provided at first registration is not reclaimable, even if invoiced separately. VAT on accessories purchased and fitted later is deductible, provided that the car is still in business use.

d)   Business entertainment expenses. Input tax on this kind of expenditure is only allowable where it is incurred for staff entertainment for the purpose of the business, eg provision of meals and seasonal staff entertainment. In principle, VAT cannot be reclaimed on the entertainment of customers, suppliers or prospective customers/members of the public.

e)   However, in 2010 in the case of Danfoss/AstraZeneca (C-371/07), the European Court of Justice held that VAT on the cost of 'basic' meals provided to overseas business contacts to facilitate sales meetings should be recoverable, as it had a clear business purpose. HMRC then issued guidance that VAT recovery would now be allowed for such entertainment costs (the guidance notes suggested this only covered 'necessary' meals and transport). This change was confirmed by Finance Act 2011, but the relaxation only applies to non-UK customers, and only where the entertaining is reasonable, and has a clear business purpose.

Fuel purchased by a business and used by staff or proprietor for private motoring – the scale charge

16. Input tax on all road fuel purchased by a VAT registered trader which is then applied for business and private use is reclaimable, so long as the business is making taxable supplies to which the fuel purchases can be attributed. However, if exempt supplies are made, part of the input tax on fuel may not be recoverable.

If there is any onward supply of fuel to proprietors or employees for private motoring (ie they do not fully reimburse the business for the cost of any fuel used for private mileage), a flat rate 'fuel scale charge ' must be accounted for per car /employee. This charges VAT on an assumed or notional amount of fuel that is deemed to be supplied onwards for private use to the employee(s) or the business proprietor(s) out of the VAT registered business's fuel purchases. Output tax is charged on this notional supply, and must be paid by the business, by reference to the fuel scale charge rates.

Like car income tax benefit in kind charges, VAT scale charges are based on the CO_2 emissions of the car. A separate output VAT scale charge must be entered on each VAT return for every car that had use of business fuel for private motoring.

VAT fuel rates 2012/13

CO_2 band	VAT fuel scale charge, 3 month period £	VAT on 3 month charge 20% £
120 or below	166	27.67
125	250	41.67
130	266	44.33
135	283	47.17
140	300	50.00
145	316	52.67
150	333	55.50
155	350	58.33
160	366	61.00
165	383	63.83
170	400	66.67
175	416	69.33
180	433	72.17
185	450	75.00
190	467	77.83
195	483	80.50
200	500	83.33
205	517	86.17
210	533	88.83
215	550	91.67
220	567	94.50
225 or above	583	97.17

For monthly or annual VAT return periods, pro-rate the above charges accordingly.

Partial exemption

17. A trader who makes supplies of taxable goods and/or services, and also makes supplies of exempt goods and/or services, is referred to as a partially exempt trader. The special rules about input VAT recovery by partially exempt traders are outlined below. (Note that the term 'exempt input tax' is used in the VAT legislation to refer to input tax attributed to the making of exempt supplies rather than taxable supplies.)

i) Where a business makes exempt supplies of financial or land-related services, and these are not incurred in the course of carrying on a business in the financial sector, then all exempt input tax can be recovered provided it has been incurred in relation to any of the following supplies:

    a) the granting of any lease or tenancy of land, or any licence to occupy land (provided that the exempt input tax related to all such supplies made by the business is less than £1,000 per tax year, and that the business does not incur any exempt input tax other than that related to those supplies listed in this paragraph)

    b) any deposit of money

    c) any services of arranging insurance

    d) any services of arranging mortgages

    e) any services of arranging hire-purchase, credit sale or conditional sale transactions

    f) the assignment of any debt in respect of a supply of goods or services by the assignor.

If the exempt input tax is incurred in relation to supplies other than those listed above, then the tax must be taken into consideration in determining the 'de minimis limit'.

ii) A business can be treated as fully taxable (ie can recover all its input VAT) providing its exempt input tax is not more than £625 per month on average. This de minimis test applies for the business's VAT year but is provisionally applied to each return separately with adjustment at the end of the year if necessary.

In addition businesses must also satisfy the additional condition that the exempt input tax disregarded must be no more than 50% of total input VAT.

The legislation was recently amended to set out two alternative tests which may be easier for businesses to apply, depending on how they prefer to work out their partial exemption position. However the original test above still achieves exactly the same result. The two alternative tests are:

    a) If total input tax is no more than £625 per month on average, and the value of exempt supplies is no more than 50% of the value of all supplies; or

b) If total input tax, less input tax directly attributable to taxable supplies, is no more than £625 per month on average, and the value of exempt supplies is no more than 50% of the value of all supplies.

iii) Exempt input tax must be considered where financial businesses are carried on, such as a bank, building society, money lender, credit card company etc.

iv) The standard method of calculation to be used to apportion input VAT between taxable and exempt supplies, where the business is making partially exempt and partially taxable supplies in the period, is as follows.

a) Identify the input tax that is directly attributable to taxable supplies

b) Identify the input tax that is directly attributable to exempt supplies.

c) The balance of input tax is input tax that is not attributable to any particular supplies (non-attributable input tax)

d) Calculate the percentage, rounded up to the next whole number, of such non-attributable input tax which is equal to:

$$\frac{\text{Value of taxable supplies (excl. VAT)}}{\text{Value of taxable supplies (excl. VAT)} + \text{Value of exempt supplies}}$$

e) Add the percentage obtained at (d) to the input tax already attributed to taxable supplies at (a). This input tax can all be treated as relating to taxable supplies.

f) Add the remainder of the non–attributable input tax [(c) less (d)] to the exempt input tax already attributed to exempt supplies, at (b)

g) If the total of exempt input tax at (f) is below the de minimis limit of £625 per month AND 50% of all input tax, then it can be reclaimed. If it exceeds the de minimis limit, it is irrecoverable.

vi) The standard method is the default method provided by the VAT Act but it is not mandatory: a trader can apply to use any other special method more suited to its business, provided advance agreement is obtained from HMRC. Commonly used special methods to allocate input tax between taxable and exempt supplies include methods based on staff numbers, floorspace occupied, relative purchases (whereas the standard method uses sales) or transaction counts. Any VAT partial exemption method approved by HMRC has to be 'fair and reasonable'.

vii) For convenience, it is possible for an established business to use last year's overall partial exemption fraction as an estimated apportionment method for the first three quarters of its next VAT year, and only carry out a detailed annual calculation in the final VAT quarter of that year.

Example – Partial exemption calculation

A Ltd had the following transactions in the quarter to 31st December 2012:

	£
Supplies made:	
Standard-rated supplies (excluding VAT)	150,000
Zero-rated supplies	50,000
Exempt supplies	100,000

Input tax has been paid on input costs attributable to the following outputs and activities:

	£
Standard-rated supplies	12,000
Zero-rated supplies	–
Exempt supplies	17,000
General overheads	4,000

The general overhead input tax cannot be directly attributed to any of the listed supplies.

Compute the VAT payable for the quarter to 31st December 2012.

Solution: A Ltd VAT return: quarter to 31st December 2012

		£	£
Output tax 150,000 @ 20%			30,000
Input tax:	Attributable to SR supplies	12,000	
	Attributable to ZR supplies	–	
	Overheads (see note (i))	2,680	(14,680)
VAT due			15,320

Notes

i) VAT attributable to overheads:

$$\frac{150,000(SR) + 50,000(ZR)}{150,000(SR) + 50,000(ZR) + 100,000(EX)} \times 4,000 = 67\% \times 4,000 = 2,680$$

ii) 67% (rounded up from 66.7%) of the non-attributable input tax on overheads can be apportioned to taxable supplies and recovered along with the input tax attributed to taxable supplies. The other 33% of the VAT on overheads, added to the £17,000 of input tax directly attributed to making exempt supplies, clearly exceeds the de minimis levels for exempt input tax, so the rest of the input VAT is irrecoverable.

iii) An annual computation is not required to decide the final position in this case because the exempt input tax in this one quarter exceeds even the annual de minimis level, which is £7,500 (12 x £625).

Imports

18. VAT on Imports of goods

There are many special rules about import of goods to the UK, especially from outside the EU Fiscal Area. This is an outline of the basic VAT rules only.

VAT is charged at the appropriate rate (zero, reduced or standard) on goods imported into the UK (including business acquisitions both from within the EU and from outside the EU). Private individuals also have to pay VAT on personal imports of goods into the UK (subject to certain personal exemptions). VAT collection on imports is operated by the UK Border Agency.

Payment of VAT on imported goods is due at the time of importation, or removal from a bonded customs warehouse, unless deferment arrangements have been made. A registered trader approved by HMRC may defer payment of tax on goods imported in the course of business during a calendar month until the 15th of the following month (or the next working day after the 15th if that day is a holiday). The VAT is normally collected by a direct debit mandate which forms part of the application for deferment.

VAT on imported goods can be reclaimed by UK traders as normal input tax, subject to the normal rules. (This does not apply to imports in a private capacity, even if the importer also has a business VAT registration). The claim for the VAT as input tax must be made in the return for the accounting period during which the importation or removal from the relevant warehouse occurred.

Warehoused goods

When goods are warehoused for customs and excise purposes, payment of import VAT is usually suspended. VAT becomes payable when the goods are removed from the warehouse for use in the UK.

19. Imports of services – Reverse charge procedure

Where services are received from other EU countries outside the UK by UK businesses, and do not have any VAT applied in the state of the supplier or in the UK by the supplier, this means the supplier has classed the place of supply of the services as the UK, and not being VAT-registered in the UK they have treated the service as outside the scope of VAT on their own home-country VAT return

In this situation, the UK-registered trader (who is the customer) must operate the **reverse charge** procedure. This means he/she/it must account for both UK output VAT on the imported services (as though self-supplied) and also UK input VAT of the same amount, which it has in effect 'charged itself' and now seeks to recover. Both figures (input VAT and output VAT) will be the same figure, and appear on the same VAT return - unless partial exemption restricts input tax recovery.

So long as the UK purchasing business is making fully taxable supplies, there is no net VAT cost from operating the reverse charge on imports, as the same amount is added to input VAT and output VAT in the same period. This puts it in the same cash position as if it had used a UK supplier for the services – i.e. it pays VAT on the services, but the input VAT is all recovered against its own taxable supplies. However, if the UK trader is partially exempt, and the service purchased related wholly or partly to its exempt supplies, then some input VAT will be irrecoverable. The same amount of UK VAT would have been irrecoverable if the services had been purchased in the UK, and normal UK VAT had been paid.

One purpose of the reverse charge procedure is to remove the unfair pricing advantage that non- UK businesses would enjoy over UK sellers, when selling their services to partially-exempt UK businesses.

This example also shows how the reverse charge (which works the same way across the EU fiscal area) prevents a loss of tax to the UK Government, by ensuring that VAT recoverable in the UK, on imported services treated as supplied in the UK, has been paid in the UK.

Exports from the UK

20. Exports of goods to an overseas customer outside the EU Fiscal area are zero-rated. Where goods are sent to a final exporter in the UK then they will not be zero-rated by the UK supplier, as there is a supply in the UK being made; but they can be if there is delivery to a port or a central clearance depot for shipment.

Exports (technically called Intra-Community Supplies) to business customers in the EU are also zero-rated, but the business customer has to pay VAT in their own country.

Supplies of goods to non-business customers in the EU are liable to UK VAT and

Goods for personal use

21. Where goods which belong to a business are put to private use outside the business, then a taxable supply is being made and output tax is chargeable. Thus if trading stock is withdrawn from the business for private use, or an employee uses a business asset for private purposes, in principle a taxable supply occurs.

VAT is chargeable on the cost to the business (for income tax purposes it is the market value in the case of trading stock withdrawn from a business by a sole trader) of the supply, and the tax point is the time when the goods are made available for non-business use.

The special rules for the private use of fuel for motor cars were covered at section 16 above.

Bad debts

22. VAT Relief is available for bad debts incurred by a taxable person, and a claim can be made for a refund of the appropriate output tax previously reported and paid (in effect as if it were new input tax suffered). The conditions for a claim are that the goods or services were supplied for a monetary consideration, and VAT on the supply was charged and paid; and one of the following applies:

a) the customer has become insolvent. This means an official determination of inability to pay debts such as bankruptcy, or the winding up of a company.

b) the trader has obtained a certificate from the 'administrator' or 'administrative receiver' of a company stating that in his or her opinion if the company went into liquidation its assets would be insufficient to pay secured and preferential creditors.

c) any other debt which is more than six months old which has been reasonably written off in the trader's accounts can be claimed as a bad debt for VAT purposes. The six-month period runs from the date the payment was due under normal trade terms, not the time of supply.

d) In theory a business that has made a claim for input tax on a supply on which the supplier has claimed bad debt relief, should repay the VAT reclaimed to HMRC. In order to assist this, a business claiming bad debt relief is asked to state the VAT number of the customer on the claim, if it was a VAT registered trader. However if the customer is already insolvent, HMRC may not be able to enforce the repayment in practice.

Bad debts – Claim

23. The amount of the claim will usually be readily ascertainable by reference to the actual debt outstanding. However, where there are payments on account (not allocated by the debtor to any particular supply) then these are allocated to the earliest supplies in the account after adjusting for any mutual supplies ie contra items.

Example

R Ltd is registered for VAT. One of its customers, X Ltd, went into liquidation on 31st July 2012.

The sales ledger account for the last two months to 31st July 2012 was as follows:

R Ltd sales ledger receivable account for Customer X Ltd

		£			£
1.5.12	Balance b/f	12,000	30.6.12	Cheque May a/c paid	12,000
25.5.12	1. Goods (inc. VAT)	36,000	23.7.12	Cheque payment on a/c	10,000
15.6.12	2. Goods (zero rated)	9,000	31.7.12	Balance c/f	50,000
20.7.12	3. Goods (inc. VAT)	15,000			
		72,000			72,000
31.7.12	Balance b/d	50,000			

Compute the bad debt relief available to R Ltd.

Solution

Amount due from X Ltd at 31st July 2012 £50,000

		Gross	VAT
		£	£
Invoice	No. 3	15,000	2,500
	No. 2	9,000	–
	No. 1 (part)	26,000	4,333
		50,000	6,833

Notes

i) VAT on Invoice No.1 $36,000 \times {}^{20}/_{120} = 6,000$

Proportion $\dfrac{26,000}{36,000} \times 6,000 \quad = 4,333$

ii) VAT recoverable is £6,833.

iii) Assuming VAT at 20% standard rate.

Transfer of a business as a going concern

24. a) The sale of the assets of a business as a going concern is not a supply of goods or services and is outside the scope of VAT, provided that:

> i) the assets are to be used by the purchaser in carrying on the same kind of business, whether as part of an existing business or not.

> ii) in a case where the seller is a taxable person, the purchaser if not already registered must register for VAT immediately.

b) A sale of part of a business may be treated as a sale of a going concern, provided that the part sold is capable of separate operation.

c) The purchaser cannot claim any input tax in respect of the purchase of the business, even where this has been incorrectly charged to him or her.

d) The provisions do not apply where the business is a different one after the transfer to that carried on by the seller.

e) The transfer of a sole trader's business to a limited company, or into partnership with one or more other persons falls within these transfer provisions, and is therefore outside the scope of VAT.

f) Where the business is transferred as a going concern, it is possible for the VAT Registration number of the vendor to be transferred to the purchaser, subject to certain conditions, and the approval of HMRC.

g) Where a business carried on by a taxable person is transferred to another person who is not registered at the time of the transfer, the new owner must register for VAT immediately if the treatment as outside the scope of VAT is claimed on the business sale.

A business sale that does not meet the above conditions (for instance, the purchaser is not going to register for VAT) is standard-rated in respect of the price paid for all goods (assets or Stock) transferred by sale, except those that are exempt, eg second hand cars or buildings.

Sale of business assets

25. The sale of assets used by a person in the course of business, e.g. plant and machinery, is subject to VAT as a taxable supply. This also applies where a VAT-registered person ceases to trade or deregisters for VAT (even if the assets are not immediately sold).

VAT is not chargeable on the disposal of a motor car second-hand unless input VAT was reclaimed on the purchase of the car. The circumstances when this can be done are limited to businesses where there is no possibility of private use of the car.

Other assets sold by a registered trader which have been used in the business (eg computers) are generally subject to standard rate VAT on the price charged when sold.

Business assets – cost for Capital Allowances

26. In general there is no difference between the treatment of capital goods and other inputs for VAT purposes and in most cases the input tax will be recovered and hence does not qualify as part of the cost for capital allowances. However, where a trader's supplies are exempt, or partially exempt, or the trader is not VAT registered, then they may not be able to recover all or part of the input tax on the capital goods. In such cases the VAT not reclaimable can be added to the cost of the asset for capital allowance purposes.

For motor cars the VAT is not recoverable input tax and is therefore added to the cost of the asset for capital allowance purposes.

VAT on capital goods – Partly exempt businesses

27. Input tax recovered by a trader on certain high-value capital assets when first acquired may have to be refunded to HMRC if there is a change in the business use to which they are applied eg from use in making taxable supplies to use in making exempt supplies.

The assets to which these rules apply are:

a)   computers and computer equipment worth over £50,000, if their use changes within five years of acquisition.

b)   land and buildings worth over £250,000, if their use changes within ten years of acquisition.

Rents

28. As noted in Chapter 36 section 9, landlords can elect to charge VAT on rents from non-domestic buildings. The election must be made on a building by building basis, and once made will apply to all future transactions in the property, i.e. lettings or sales by the landlord. Businesses which are fully taxable will not be greatly affected by this change but those which are exempt or partially exempt may be affected, such as Group 2 Insurance and Group 5 Finance.

Changes in the tax rates

29. When a change in the standard rate of VAT occurs, the following rules apply.

a)   Output tax is calculated under the normal rules i.e. by reference to the tax point - unless the special change of rate provisions are applied

b)   Under these provisions, where the rate goes up, the tax at the old rate can be charged on goods removed or services performed before the date of change, even though a tax invoice would normally have been issued after the date of change.

c)   Where a supply of services takes place which crosses the threshold date of change in rate, then the supply can be apportioned by reference to normal costing or pricing procedures. Tax at the old rate may be charged on services performed before the date of the change if the supplier apportions the total bill. However the supplier may choose not to do an apportionment.

d)   It is generally the supplier's decision how to apply the tax point rules at a change in rate. The amount of input tax paid by the purchaser following a change in rate is obtained from the supplier's invoice, and only the amount actually charged can be reclaimed. For less detailed tax invoices which do not show the VAT separately, the amount of input tax can be computed at the rate appropriate at the stated tax point of the whole invoice.

Cash accounting scheme

30. The cash accounting scheme is optional for all businesses with a taxable supplies turnover of less than £1,350,000. It achieves a cash flow benefit for businesses whose customers take longer credit periods than the business takes against its own trade creditors. The main features of the scheme are;

a)   VAT on inputs and outputs is included in the VAT return for the period when cash was received or paid to settle the invoice, rather than on the basis of the invoice date (or earlier tax point rule).

b)   Applications for the scheme, once approved, remain in force for two years.

c)   The problem of obtaining relief for VAT on bad debts does not arise since output Vat is not paid over until after the customers have paid. However, the business will not be able to reclaim input VAT until it has actually paid the relevant business cost.

Annual accounting scheme

31. This scheme is available to traders who have been VAT-registered for at least one year, and whose annual turnover is less than £1,350,000. The main features of the scheme are:

a)   Businesses choosing the annual accounting make only one VAT return a year instead of the usual four. It is submitted two months after the VAT year-end

b)   They make nine equal payments on account by direct debit during the year, which are each set as 10% of the total VAT paid for the previous year. A tenth, balancing, payment is made with the annual return to make up the correct amount of VAT actually due for the year.

c)   Businesses already using the scheme will be able to continue until their turnover reaches £1,600,000.

Flat rate scheme – small firms only

32.   The flat-rate VAT scheme is available by application, and suits very small businesses. The scheme is available to traders whose annual taxable turnover, including reduced and zero-rated supplies, does not exceed £150,000 in the year of entry to the scheme.

i)   Under the flat-rate scheme, traders avoid having to account internally for input VAT on all their purchases and output VAT on their supplies. Instead they calculate the net VAT liability as a flat rate percentage of their total turnover, including standard-rate, reduced-rate, zero-rate and also exempt supplies.

ii)   Traders using the flat-rate scheme issue invoices to their customers showing normal VAT details i.e. at the standard, reduced or zero rates, or that the sale is VAT-exempt. The flat rate percentage is merely used to simplify the calculation of the net VAT payable on the trader's own VAT return. The flat-rate scheme does not affect the customers, who receive normal VAT invoices to support their own VAT reclaims (if registered).

iii) Once operating a flat-rate scheme the trader merely applies the standard quoted percentage to all business turnover, including exempt supplies, to arrive at the 'net amount of VAT' due for the period. The flat rate percentage reflects a notional average for the net output tax due after offsetting input tax on expenses (the amount actually incurred will not be relevant) and is the only calculation needed to operate the scheme. Actual input tax suffered is not reported on the trader's VAT return.

iv)   The flat rate percentage applied to turnover depends on the trade classification set by HMRC. These vary between 2% for food, tobacco, and newsagent retailers to 13% for computer and IT service providers.

v)   The rates for the flat rate scheme allow for low value capital expenditure purchases. However, input VAT on VAT-inclusive capital expenditure over £2,000 can be recovered outside the flat rate scheme. Such separate treatment does not cover cars, since input VAT recovery on these is generally excluded. Where VAT recovery on larger capital purchases has been dealt with separately outside the flat rate scheme, output tax on their later disposal (or deemed disposal, in the case of de-registration) is also dealt with separately.

vi) For businesses using the VAT flat rate scheme , business accounts will be prepared using gross receipts less flat rate VAT percentage for turnover, and expenses will include irrecoverable input VAT. Limited companies are required by law to show their turnover net of VAT.

Special retail schemes

33. a)   There are five standard retail schemes:

> Point of sale scheme
>
> Apportionment scheme (2 schemes)
>
> Direct calculation scheme (2 schemes)

Details may be found at http://www.hmrc.gov.uk/vat/schemes/index.htm

b)   No trader will be allowed to use any retail scheme if it is reasonably practicable for them to account for VAT in the usual way.

c)   Retail schemes can only be used for retail sales. If a trader makes some retail sales and others to VAT-registered traders than the usual VAT procedures must be applied to the latter.

d)   Turnover limits of £1m and £130m restrict availability of the retail schemes. Details may be found on the HMRC website.

Miscellaneous

34. i)   **Pre-registration expenditure.** Input tax on pre-registration business expenditure can be included in the first VAT return after registration. In the case of input tax on goods (as distinct from services) the goods must either be still retained at the date of first registration, or have been converted into other goods still retained. For services, the expenditure must have been incurred (tax point of the invoice) within the six months prior to the date of first registration.

ii) **Business gifts**. In general traders are not required to account for VAT as a taxable supply on the value of small business gifts such as diaries and calendars. The limit on such goods is £50 per item. The treatment of a series of business gifts in any 12 month period to the same person is aligned with that of a single gift. Where the limit is exceeded, output tax is due on the value of all the gifts made up to that point.

473

Student self-testing question with answer

Octavius Limited is a fully taxable trader and does not operate the flat rate or cash accounting VAT scheme. You are provided with the following information relating to Octavius Limited for the quarter ended 31 August 2012:

The VAT-exclusive accounts show the following

	£	£
Sales		165,000
Sales returns		(11,000)
		154,000
Purchases	96,000	
Purchases returns	(3,000)	
	93,000	
Bad debts written off	15,000	
Other expenses	24,000	
		(132,000)
Profit		22,000

The sales, purchases and 'other expenses' are all standard-rated for VAT.

All input VAT is reclaimable.

The sales and purchases returns are all evidenced by credit notes issued and received.

The bad debts were written off in August 2012. Payment for the original sales was due by 16 April 2012.

A sales invoice for £3,000, excluding VAT, had been omitted in error from the VAT return for the quarter to 28 February 2012.

Included in the expense figure is the cost of both business and private petrol for Managing Director's car, which had CO_2 emissions of 210g/km.

Requirement

(a) Complete the VAT account for the three month period ended 31 August 2012, showing how much VAT is payable to HM Revenue and Customs. **(7 marks)**

(b) When is the tax shown by (a) above payable? **(1 mark)**

(c) State the course of action is open to a taxpayer who disagrees with a decision by HMRC on the application of VAT. **(1 mark)**

(d) What are the consequences of any action taken by the taxpayer in (c) above?

(ACCA updated)

Suggested solution

(a)

	£
Output tax :	
On Sales (165,000 x 20%)	33,000
On Car fuel scale charge (see table Chapter 37 section 16)	88
Less refunded on sales returns (11,000 x 20%)	(2,200)
Adjust output tax error on February VAT return (3,000 x 20%)	600
	31,488

	£	
Input tax:		
On purchases and expenses (96,000+24,000) x 20%	24,000	
Less refunded on purchase returns (3,000 x 20%)	(600)	
		(23,400)
Net VAT due to HMRC for quarter		8,088

Note: The bad debts are not yet eligible for relief, as payment was due less than six months ago.

(b) The VAT is payable within one month of the end of the quarter, i.e. by 30 September 2012.

(c) A taxpayer who disagrees with a decision by HMRC on the application of VAT may apply within 30 days to the local VAT office asking them to re-consider their decision.

(d) After re-considering their decision HMRC will either:

Confirm their original decision. The taxpayer then has 21 days to submit an appeal to the first-tier tax tribunal; or

Revise their original decision. The taxpayer then has 30 days to submit an appeal to the first-tier tax tribunal.

Questions without answers

1. You are provided with the following information relating to Portia Limited, a consultancy company, for the quarter ended 30 November 2012:

	£
Fees (standard-rated and exclusive of tax)	60,000
Rent received from sub-letting part of the company's offices	6,000
Car purchase (exclusive of VAT)	18,000
Overheads (standard-rated and exclusive of VAT)	9,000
Input VAT attributable to taxable supplies	2,000

Notes

The car was purchased on 1 September 2012 and had CO_2 emissions of 190g/km. Petrol for both private and business motoring was charged through the business and not refunded.

Bad debts of £550 (exclusive of VAT @ 20%) were written off during November 2012; the date payment was due for the services was February 2012.

Portia has not made an election to waive VAT exemption for the office rental income.

Requirement:

Calculate the VAT payable for the quarter ended 30 November 2012 and state when this will be payable to HMRC. **(9 marks)**

(ACCA updated)

2. Antrobus Limited had the following transactions in the quarter to 30 June 2012:

Sales:	£
Standard-rated supplies (excluding VAT)	150,000
Zero-rated supplies	50,000
Exempt supplies	100,000

Input tax on expenses had been paid as follows:

Standard-related supplies	12,000
Zero-related supplies	5,000
Exempt supplies	9,000
General overheads	4,000

The general overhead input tax cannot be directly attributed to any of the listed supplies.

Requirement: (a) Calculate the VAT payable by Antrobus Limited for the quarter **(5 marks)**

(b) State the records and accounts which must be kept for VAT purposes and state for how long they must be retained by the trader.

(6 marks)

Total: 11 marks

(ACCA updated)

Part VII

Tax Planning

38 Elements of tax planning

Introduction

1. This chapter is concerned with some of the basic principles of tax planning which can be applied where a taxpayer has a choice of alternative courses of action. The chapter starts by defining tax planning and outlining some of the objectives involved in this process. Some basic tax planning caveats are then considered followed by a tax planning summary table. The focus of the chapter is on the difference between income tax for the self employed and corporation tax for a small incorporated entity. This area of taxation has generated considerable interest over recent years, and as you will have seen from the sections on both income tax and corporation tax is subject to change on an annual basis.

What is tax planning?

2. Given a set of circumstances or a situation where a decision is to be made which involves the incidence of taxation, then tax planning is concerned with achieving the best result with respect to that decision from the taxation perspective. The 'best result' is usually taken to mean achieving the least amount of tax payable consistent with any cash flow advantages which are also often important.

There is no set body of knowledge called tax planning as it usually requires the application of threads of tax law and practice from across the whole spectrum of taxation and law. An exercise in tax planning therefore involves the following.

a)   Identification of the specific problem to be considered.

b)   Identification of the relevant parts of the tax statutes which have relevance to the problem.

c)   Application of the tax rules identified to the problem.

d)   Evaluation of the various options available in order to minimise the incidence of taxation.

e)   Identification and examination of any other factors of a legal, commercial or financial nature which should be taken into consideration.

Objectives of tax planning

3. Tax planning objectives for individuals may be summarised as follows.

a)   To reduce taxable income and/or chargeable gains falling to be assessed.

b)   To lower the rate of tax which is applicable to taxable income or chargeable gains.

c)   To defer the date on which tax becomes payable, thereby gaining a cash flow/interest advantage.

For companies in general, similar objectives can be applied. However, for family companies with shareholder directors/employees, tax planning for the individual must inevitably be considered together with that for the family company. This arises because in many cases most of the income of the family director/employee shareholder is in fact derived from family company sources, in the form of remuneration, benefits in kind and dividends.

Tax planning caveats

4. The following points should be borne in mind when undertaking any tax planning exercise.

a)   Tax planning, sometimes called tax avoidance, should not be confused with tax evasion. The latter, which is unlawful and may lead to criminal prosecution, is associated with fraudulent or dishonest plans to avoid taxation.

b)   Commercial factors should not be ignored just for the sake of a business tax planning exercise. For example, there is no point in investing in additional capital expenditure to obtain capital allowances if the capital project itself shows negative returns on investment.

c)   Future financial security should not be put at risk. The making of substantial lifetime gifts to mitigate IHT on the death of the donor should be balanced against the possible shortfall in annual income which might result.

d)   Possible changes in the law in the future may render current tax planning exercises less advantageous.

e)   Tax plans should be flexible to accommodate, if possible, changes in circumstances. There is no permanent long-term relationship between capital and income which will meet all the requirements of all taxpayers.

f)   Packaged "tax avoidance schemes" offered by any organised promoter must be disclosed to HMRC as soon as the first offer of the scheme is made to the public. HMRC maintain a register of such schemes. Taxpayers utilising any such registered scheme must disclose this fact and the scheme number in the self-assessment tax return. Advising individuals how to re-arrange their personal or business affairs with tax benefits, such as the examples below, do not count as "tax avoidance schemes" under this heading, so long as the steps involved have a main purpose and commercial effect beyond just the tax saving.

Tax planning summary

5. Individuals

I Income tax

	Employees	Self-employed	Directors
1. Claim expenses of employment	✓	–	✓
2. Claim capital allowances for privately owned asset/Authorised mileage rates	✓	✓	✓
3. Company pension scheme: consider AVC	✓		✓
4. No company pension scheme: maximise contributions up to 100% of net relevant earnings, but subject to annual maximum of £50,000.	✓	✓	✓
5. Inter-spouse transfer of assets to use PAs, lower rate tax bands, and MCAA where available	✓	✓	✓
6. Car fuel benefit/payment business mileage	✓	–	✓
7. Phase capital expenditure to save Class 4 NIC income tax	–	✓	–
8. Employ staff with earnings below NI thresholds	–	✓	–
9. Consider ISA – tax-free	✓	✓	✓
10. Consider Enterprise Investment scheme	✓	✓	✓
11. Consider Venture Capital Trust	✓	✓	✓

II Capital gains tax

	Employees	Self-employed	Directors
1. Consider entrepreneurs' relief on business or share disposals	-	✓	✓
2. Inter-spouse transfer of assets to minimise CGT	✓	✓	✓
3. Phase chargeable asset disposals between tax years to use Annual Exemption , and the lower CGT rate band	✓	✓	✓
4. On a takeover, consider cash/shares split and available reliefs to minimise or defer CGT	✓	✓	✓

III Inheritance tax

			Employees	Self-employed	Directors
1. Maximise use of general exemptions –		£250	✓	✓	✓
		£3,000	✓	✓	✓
	Normal expenditure –	for marriage	✓	✓	✓
		inter-spouse	✓	✓	✓
		charitable bequests	✓	✓	✓

2. Consider lifetime gifts/PETS – personal assets	✓	✓	✓
business assets	–	✓	–
3. Deeds of Variation to change distribution of a death estate to save IHT / maximise use of nil rate band	✓	✓	✓

IV VAT

1. Consider voluntary registration to claim input tax	–	✓	–
2. Phase capital expenditure to benefit cash flow from input tax recovery	–	✓	–
3. Consider payment for private fuel rather than scale charge	–	✓	–
4. Monitor turnover level as it approaches compulsory registration point	–	✓	–
5. Consider Flat Rate, Annual Accounting and/ or Cash Accounting scheme – small firms		✓	

6. Companies

1. Extended account period: 18 months, or 2 periods of 6 and then 12 months?

2. Phasing capital expenditure to maximise Annual Investment Allowance.

3. Consider whether additional payments to shareholder directors should be made as directors' remuneration or dividends – there is a NI saving for the latter.

4. Consider dividend payments in place of normal salary.

5. Maximise pension contributions made through the company as employer.

7. Sole trader vs incorporation

This area of taxation has received a considerable amount of interest due to the number of changes that have been made in relation to the small business corporation tax rules. This section provides an example of a small business and the choice of whether to incorporate or not. It should be noted that there are many factors to consider depending on the circumstances and this section provides simply a basic comparison, based on material previously studied in the income tax and corporation tax sections.

Example

Peter is a self employed electrical engineer and makes profits of £80,000 each year. He pays £8,000 net per year into an HMRC-approved personal pension scheme. He is considering whether he should incorporate his business and pay himself a minimal salary with the balance in dividends, or continue as a sole trader.

A possible approach: Compare net disposable income (2012/13 tax rates)

Sole trader:

			£	£
Profits				80,000
Total income				80,000
PA				(8,105)
Taxable income (all non-savings)				71,895
Tax liability:	BR £34,370	@ 20%	6,874	
(pens. conts. relief) extend	BR £10,000	@ 20%	2,000	
	HR £27,525	@ 40%	11,010	
	71,895			
Total income tax				19,884
NIC:				
Class 2	2.65 p/w (paid 6-monthly)		137	
Class 4	42,475 – 7,605 @ 9%		3,138	
Excess Class 4	80,000 - 42,475 @ 2%		750	
Total national insurance contributions				4,025
Total income tax and NIC				23,909

Disposable income – sole trader	£
Profits	80,000
Less pension contributions (net cost paid)	(8,000)
less IT and NIC	(23,909)
Disposable income	**48,091**

Incorporation:

Profit before proprietor's pay (company)	80,000
Salary (cost to company)	(8,105)
employer Class 1 secondary NI	
(cost to company)	
8,105-7,485 @ 13.8%	(85)
Pension cont'n (cost to company) (Assumed)	(10,000)
Company's taxable profit	61,810
CT @ 20%	(12,362)
After-tax profit for distribution – say distributes £49,410.	49448

Director income:

Salary				8,105
Dividend grossed for tax purposes				
(£49,410 x 100/90)				54,900
Total income				63,005
PA (against non-savings income)				(8,105)
Taxable income (all dividends)				54,900
Tax liability:	BR £34,370	@ 10%	3,437	
	HR £20,530	@ 32.5%	6,672	

Total income tax	10,109
Less tax credit on dividends 10% x £54,900	(5,490)
Net income tax payable by Peter	4,619
Add Employee's class 1 NIC on salary – annual earnings period for director	
8,105-7,605 @ 12%	60
Net employee income tax and primary NIC	4,679

Net disposable income - Director

Salary	8,105
Dividends (net)	49,410
less IT and NIC paid	(4,679)
less pension contributions paid personally	Nil
Disposable income	52,836

Total application of £80k profits:

	Incorporation £	Sole trader £
HMRC: Company tax and NI (12,362 +85)	12,447	0
HMRC: Peter's personal tax and NI	4,679	23,909
Transfer from HMRC to pension fund to top up net pension contributions received of £8,000	n/a	(2,000)
Total profits taken by HMRC	17,126	21,909
Pension savings - total cash received by pension fund of some kind (in sole trade, £8k from Peter and £2k from HMRC; under incorporation, all £10k from the company)	10,000	10,000
Peter's net disposable income	52,836	48,091
Retained earnings left in company	38	
Total pre-tax earnings	80,000	80,000
Less HMRC's 'take' (net tax and NIC)	(17,126)	(21,909)
Total value retained by Peter	62,874	58,091

Notes

i) This example produces a saving of £4,783 (21,909 – 17,126) in total taxation for the incorporation model when compared with a sole trader.

ii) This example assumes that under incorporation, Peter will make use of a non-contributory occupational director's pension scheme, with all contributions paid by the company, to save NIC.

The tax comparison above includes the £2,000 "basic rate tax refund" benefit that is paid by HMRC into Peter's personal pension under the sole trader route; this notional refund has been set against his personal tax bill, even though it is not legally done in that way under current tax legislation.

iii) The difference in disposable income is marked. There is a very clear NI cost saving from incorporation because of the very low salary paid (£159 of NIC costs, compared with £4,025 as a sole trader). The 2012/13 NIC threshold for employer's NIC is here assumed at £7,485; approximated from 52 x £144.

iv) There is also an income tax saving by the dividend route. The £49,410 dividend received would be grossed up at the 10% rate and accounted for in Peter's self assessment return as £54,900 of income.

On dividends, Peter's headline top rate of income tax is 32.5%. But because of the dividend tax credit and the imputation system, he actually incurs a top tax rate of only 25% and only on the top £18,447 of net dividends (£4,619 tax payable on £18,447 received).

The rest of his net dividend (£30,933) is effectively received tax-free, as the company's corporation tax covers Peter's own basic rate liability on £30,933 of dividends (£34,370 after 10/9 gross-up).

To the £4,619 of net tax paid by Peter on net dividends must be added the company's CT payable on its pre-dividend profits, 20% of £61,810 (=20/80 x £49,448) = £12,362.

Total tax and NIC liability with incorporation is £4,783 less than for the sole trader.

The NIC and income tax savings from incorporation are slightly offset by the fact that the company gets tax relief on the pension contribution at only 20%, which therefore costs it £8,000 net, whereas Peter obtained 40% tax relief on this payment (costing him £6,000 net) when he made it personally as a sole trader. 20% of this income tax relief was given within his tax computation, by extending the basic rate band, and the other 20% by HMRC augmenting his pension contribution by £2,000, claimed by the pension provider.

v) There are many other factors to consider in choosing to incorporate a sole trade, especially in terms of personal preferences for the pension contribution, dividend and salary (or benefits) combination; and also the CGT implications of company ownership, if assets are to be held or profits retained long-term in the company. This example provides a useful basic comparison only if the choice is made not to place significant assets or retain earnings in the company.

8. Example 2 – dividend or salary: existing company

P is the 100% owner of Alpha Ltd, an unquoted trading company with a year end of 30th June 2012.

Trade profits of Alpha Ltd are £280,000 for the year ended 30th June 2012 after director's remuneration to P of £80,000. There were no dividend payments.

P would like to have available cash of about £25,000 by December 2012 and requests advice as to the tax costs of extracting this sum from the company.

Advise P.

Solution

Cash required of £25,000 – Dividend Route	£	Tax cost £
Net cash required	25,000	
Tax on a post-tax dividend of £25,000 for a HR income tax payer (see note (i)) 25,000 x 25/75	8,333	8,333
Dividend required (25,000 x 100/75)	33,333	
Grossed-up dividend liable to HR income tax 33,333 × 100/90	37,037	
HR Income tax @ 32.5% × 37,037	12,037	
Less Tax credit @ 10% × 37,037	(3,704) (8,333)	
Net tax cost		8,333

Cash of £25,000 – Salary Route

		£	Tax cost £
Net cash required		25,000	
tax and NI on net salary of £25,000 for a HR income tax payer			
(see note (ii)) 25,000 x 42/58		18,103	18,103
Gross salary required 25,000 x 100/58		43,103	
Marginal Income tax @ 40% × 43,103	17,241		
Marginal Class 1 NIC 2% × 43,103	862	(18,103)	18,103
Net Cash		25,000	
Employer's NIC 13.8% × 43,103	5,948		
Net Corporation Tax saving (note (iii)) (43,103 + 5,948) × 20%	(9,810)		(3,862)
Net tax cost of payment to both director & company, after company tax relief			14,241

Total profits used up in profit extraction:	£
Salary: Cash received by director	25,000
Tax and NIC received by HMRC	14,241
Total	39,241
Dividend: Cash received by director	25,000
Tax received by HMRC (no NIC)	8,333
Total	33,333

Notes

i)   Higher rate dividend income tax @ (32.5 – 10)% of the grossed-up dividend is equivalent to 25% total income tax on the net dividend in the higher rate band

(100 × (32.5-10)% is equivalent to (100 – 10) × 25%).

ii)   The total tax cost is £5,908 higher for the salary route than the dividend.

iii) Corporation Tax saved: extra Salary cost + Employer's NIC = £49,051 × 20% = 9,810.

9.   Example 3

Mr Smith has a chain of shoe shops and expects trading profits of £200,000 for the year to 5th April 2013. He is currently operating as a sole trader and is considering whether he should incorporate his business or not. He informs you that he currently contributes £16,000 (net) each year into an approved personal pension plan. He also advises you that if he were to incorporate his business he would require a director's salary of £60,000 per year gross and that he would like the company to pay his pension for him with a non contributory arrangement.

Required:

Compute the total income tax and national insurance as a sole trader and the total income tax, corporation tax and national insurance as an incorporated entity for the year to 5th April 2013.

Solution:

Sole trader				£
Profits				200,000
Total income				200,000
Personal Allowance			8,105	
Restricted (200,000 – 100,000) x 1/2			(50,000)	0
Taxable income (all non-savings)				200,000
Tax liability	BR 34,370	@ 20%	6,874	
	extend BR 20,000	@ 20%	4,000	
	HR 115,630	@ 40%	46,252	
	AR 30,000	@ 50%	15,000	
	£200,000			
Total income tax				72,126
NI				
Class 2	2.65 per week		137	
Class 4	42,475 - 7,605	@ 9%	3,138	
excess	200,000 - 42,475	@ 2%	3,151	6,426

Total income tax and NI			<u>**78,552**</u>

Incorporation

Profit (company)	200,000
Salary cost to company	(60,000)
Employer NI (60,000-7,485 @ 13.8%)	(7,247)
Pension contribution	<u>(20,000)</u>
Taxable profit of company	112,753
CT @ 20%	<u>(22,550)</u>
Profit after tax	<u>90,203</u>

Director's income:

Salary				<u>60,000</u>
Total income				60,000
Personal Allowance	(not restricted)			<u>(8,105)</u>
Taxable income (non-savings)				<u>51,895</u>
Tax liability	BR 34,370	@ 20%	6,874	
	<u>HR 17,525</u>	@ 40%	<u>7,010</u>	
	51,895			
Total income tax				13,884
Employee's NI 42,475-7,605 @ 12%				4,184
60,000-42,475 @ 2%				<u>351</u>
Total income tax and NI				<u>18,419</u>

Summary : Total tax costs compared	
Incorporation:	
Director's tax and NI	18,419
Company's tax and NI	
(22,550 + 7,247)	<u>29,797</u>
Total tax and NI	<u>**48,216**</u>
Sole trader:	
Total tax and NI	<u>**78,552**</u>

Notes:

i) In this example, the owner is not extracting all the profits from the company, therefore a tax saving has arisen and incorporation results in an effective total tax saving on profits earned for the year of £30,336 (£78,552 - £48,216).

ii) Mr Smith could extract additional funds out of the business either in the form of an increase in salary or by dividends (or a combination of the two) if he required, but this would impact upon the personal tax saved by operating through a company.

iii) Mr Smith could also consider increasing his pension provision if he wished.

iv)   It may be more efficient for Mr Smith to draw out a dividend payment instead of part of the salary of £60,000, as shown in example 2 above.

Question without answer

1. Mr Chapman, a single man, is about to start a business which will be engaged in the repair of domestic appliances. His starting date is 1 April 2012 and he will make up accounts to 31 March each year.

His business plan shows that he is likely to make a taxable profit in the first few years, before any salary for himself, of approximately £80,000 per annum.

He is uncertain whether he should set up the business as a sole trader or as a limited company and seeks your advice. He has advised you that, if the business is run as a company, he will require a gross salary of £45,000 per annum.

Mr Chapman has no other sources of taxable income.

Required:

Draft a report for Mr Chapman, indicating the important differences from a tax and NIC point of view, of the two alternative methods of running the business. Your answer should contain, as an appendix, computations showing the overall tax and NIC burden which will arise in each case. Assume 2012/13 tax rules and rates apply throughout.

(15 marks)

(CIMA updated)

39 Additional questions without answers

Exam–type Questions on Corporate Taxation and VAT

Question 1

MJL Ltd is a small manufacturing company and has prepared the following income statement (profit and loss account) for the 18 month period to 30 September 2013.

		£
Sales		481,045
Cost of Sales	(note 1)	(199,655)
Gross profit		281,390
Distribution costs	(note 2)	(13,124)
Administrative expenses	(note 3)	(154,800)
Operating profit		113,466
Profit on sale of car park land	(note 7)	45,800
Interest payable on business overdraft		(2,800)
Dividends from unconnected UK companies	(note 8)	18,000
Rent receivable on car park land	(note 7)	3,500
Profit before taxation		177,966

(1) Cost of Sales includes

- Depreciation of £7,800

- Cost of refurbishment of a machine which was purchased for £1,200 (second-hand) from a bankrupt competitor in July 2012, but which turned out to be completely unusable in MJL Ltd's trade until it had been adapted at a cost of £3,750

(2) Distribution costs include

- A car leasing payment of £3,467 incurred on a 3 year operating lease, taken out in January 2013, of a car emitting 175g CO_2/km

(3) Administrative expenses include:

- Depreciation of £4,000

- A Gift Aid charitable payment to Oxfam of £750 paid on 1 September 2013

- A closing provision of £10,750 for employer pension contributions to top up the staff retirement pension scheme, which had not yet been paid to the pension provider by 30 September 2013

- Legal fees related to sale of land in November 2012, £800

(4)   At 1 April 2012 MJL Ltd has unrelieved trading losses of £27,500 and a capital loss of £4,500 agreed and brought forward from prior periods.

(5)   MJL Ltd has a capital allowances general pool written down value brought forward of £28,467 at 1 April 2012.

(6) There were no fixed asset additions in the period other than the second hand machine bought in July 2012 (see Note 1) and no disposals of fixed assets other than the land sold in November 2012 (see Note 7).

(7) The profit on sale of land recognised in the accounts related to a car park area that the company had originally used for its own business but had ceased to need, so it was rented out to a public car park operator at £500 per month from 1 April 2012 to 31 October 2012.

This car park land was sold outright to the car park operator (the former tenant) in November 2012 for £65,000, realising a chargeable gain of £18,600 for corporation tax purposes.

(8) Dividends were received as follows:

May 2013	£13,500
August 2013	£ 4,500

Required:

(a) Compute the tax-adjusted trading profits of MJL Ltd, before capital allowances, for the 18 month period of account to 30 September 2013.

(9 marks)

(b) Compute maximum capital allowances claimable by MJL Ltd for the corporation tax accounting periods covered by this 18 month period of account. **(6 marks)**

(c) Compute MJL Ltd's taxable total profits for the relevant corporation tax accounting periods, assuming that maximum capital allowances and loss reliefs are claimed. **(7 marks)**

(d) Compute MJL Ltd's corporation tax liability for the relevant accounting periods, if it has three associated companies, assuming that the corporation tax rates for FY 2012 continue unchanged in FY 2013.

(8 marks)

(Total 30 marks)

Question 2

Cardigan Cars Limited has 3 activities: new cars, children's car seats and finance. The VAT records for the quarter to 30 September 2012 show the following information:

Activity	New cars	Children's car seats	Finance	Head office
	£	£	£	£
Sales turnover, net of any VAT	675,000	195,000	90,000	
Rate of VAT	20%	5%	Exempt	
VAT on divisional purchase and expense invoices	97,500	8,250	11,750	
VAT on general overhead expense invoices				5,000

On 30 September 2012 Cardigan Cars Limited wrote off a bad debt due from Idle Interiors Limited of £12,000 inclusive of VAT at the standard rate of 20%. The debt was in respect of one £5,000 invoice for a car dated 1 February 2012 and a second invoice of £7,000 for another car dated 2 July 2012.

(a) Required: Calculate the VAT payable or refundable for the quarter ended 30 September 2012. **(9 marks)**

Archway Garages, the first land and buildings used by Cardigan Cars Limited, were bought in January 1995 for a price of £390,000, with a further £2,500 of professional fees as expenses of the acquisition.

The land and buildings were sold in February 2001, when the company moved to new premises. The sales proceeds of the old Archway land and buildings in February 2001 were £575,000. The proceeds were used to buy the new land and buildings at Bath Buildings in February 2001 for £550,000 and to pay for a magazine advertisement costing £25,000.

The company claimed rollover relief for the replacement of business assets on the change of business premises.
In May 2012 the new land and buildings at Bath Buildings were sold for gross proceeds of £738,000, incurring selling commission of £3,000.

(b) Required: Calculate the Corporation Tax payable as a result of the disposal of the new land and buildings, assuming Cardigan Cars Limited pays Corporation Tax at the full rate.(Assume the RPI in May 2012 was 244.5 (estimated)). **(12 marks)**

(c) Evaluate the extent to which Value Added Tax (VAT) contributes to desirable characteristics of the UK tax system (such as certainty, equity, convenience, and efficiency). **(9 marks)**
(Total 30 marks)

Question 3

(a) Splash Ltd is a UK resident company that manufactures hot tubs. It prepares financial statements to 31 March each year.

On 1 April 2012 the tax written down values of Splash Ltd's plant and machinery were as follows:

	£
General pool	119,280
Single short-life asset (2 years old)	13,440

During the year to 31 March 2013, Splash Ltd made the following purchases and sales of plant, equipment and motor vehicles.

		Cost/ (proceeds)
		£
14 April 2012	Purchased energy-saving plant	64,500
15 April 2012	Sold a lorry	(14,160)
5 May 2012	Purchased new machinery	55,000
15 May 2012	Purchased Toyota car CO_2 140 g/km	10,800
12 June 2012	Sold the short-life asset	(5,520)
22 Sept 2012	Purchased Fiat car CO_2 180 g/km	23,760

The plant purchased in April 2012 was certified energy-saving plant.

The lorry sold on 15 April 2012 had originally cost £21,600.

Required (a):

Calculate the maximum plant and machinery capital allowances available to Splash Ltd for the year ended 31 March 2013.   (10 marks)

(b) Dixon Limited is a successful UK trading company selling office equipment.

Its directors are considering expansion overseas to carry on the same trade in a non-UK country where the managing director has good business contacts.

They propose to do this either by setting up either a branch operation (a non-UK branch of the existing company) or a wholly-owned subsidiary company (a separate company, incorporated and resident in the non-UK country).

They have tested the overseas market, and consider there is a good chance that the overseas operation would be profitable from the start. However there is also a possibility that it will incur losses in at least the first two years of operation.

The overseas country in question charges a direct tax of 10% on the profits of all businesses located there and has a double taxation treaty with the UK.

Note: For the purposes of this question you should assume the directors of Dixon Ltd do not intend to make an irrevocable election to exclude a foreign branch from UK Corporation Tax.

Required (b):

Advise Dixon Limited's directors, in connection with the choice between setting up the overseas operation as a branch or as a subsidiary:

(i) How UK tax is charged on the profits of an overseas branch of a UK company and how the UK tax position differs if the same net profits are made in a non-UK subsidiary company, which later pays a dividend to its UK parent company.   (4 marks)

(ii) Whether net trading losses of an overseas branch can be set against UK profits for tax purposes and how this situation differs if the overseas operation is a wholly-owned subsidiary company.   (3 marks)

(iii)   In what circumstances the UK tax authorities can seek to adjust the transfer prices charged for goods sold from a UK company to an

overseas subsidiary company and why they might choose to use this
power.   (3 marks)
                                                               (Total 20 marks)

Question 4

On 1 April 2012 the tax written down values of plant and machinery of Zebra
Limited were as follows:

	£
General pool	10,600
Special rate pool – Subaru car	16,400
Short-life asset	2,900

The following transactions took place during the year ended 31 March 2013:

		Cost/(Proceeds) £
1 May 2012	Sold office equipment	(12,800)
15 June 2012	Sold the short-life asset	(800)
8 July 2012	Purchased packaging equipment	19,200
14 July 2012	Sold the Subaru car CO_2 emissions 180g/km	(9,700)
26 August 2012	Purchased Renault car CO_2 emissions 145g/km	15,800
19 November 2012	Purchased Honda low emissions car CO_2 emissions 105g/km	19,700
15 December 2012	Purchased air cooling system features integral to a building	10,000

None of the assets disposed of were sold for more than their original cost.

**(a) Required: Calculate the maximum capital allowances available to
Zebra Limited for the year ended 31 March 2013.** (9 marks)

Avocado plc was formed on 1 October 2011 and on that date it bought 100% of
Banana Limited, 80% of Citrus Limited and 60% of Damson Ltd, which are all
subsidiaries of Avocado plc. The results for the relevant periods of account are:

	Avocado plc Year to 30 September 2013	Banana Ltd Year to 30 September 2013	Citrus Ltd Year to 30 September 2013	Damson Ltd Year to 30 September 2013
Trade profit (loss)	Loss (320,000)	1,200,000	250,000	325,000
Interest income	80,000	-	-	-
Loss on property rentals	Loss (12,000)	-	-	-
Capital loss	Loss	-	-	-

	(4,000)			
Gift Aid	(9,000)	-	-	-
donations				

Required:

(b) Demonstrate how the losses of Avocado plc can be relieved using the single company loss reliefs and clearly showing the amount of any unrelieved losses and Gift Aid donations at 30 September 2013. (6 marks)

(c) Advise the directors of Avocado plc how group loss relief may be beneficial to the Avocado plc group.   (5 marks)

(Total 20 marks)

Question 5

Shelby Limited acquired 15,000 shares in Tobacco Exploitation plc in January 1995 at a cost of £29,000. In October 2000 Tobacco Exploitation plc made a bonus issue of 1 new share for every 2 held. In May 2004 Shelby Ltd bought its share of a 1 for 4 rights issue at a price of £1.60 per Tobacco Exploitation plc share. In May 2012 Shelby Limited sold one third of its shareholding in Tobacco Exploitation plc for a price of £13,000.

(a) Required: Calculate the chargeable gain or allowable loss on disposal of Tobacco Exploitation plc shares in May 2012. (Assume the RPI in May 2012 was 244.5 (estimated))   (9 marks)

(b)   The managing director of Shelby Ltd also requires advice on the tax treatment of certain proposed payments that will be made by the company in the next accounting period.

These payments are:

i) A political donation to the UK Liberal Democratic Party of £5,000.

ii)   The cost of taking 10 key sales staff and directors to an important sales conference in Morocco   (cost per head, £2,000 including flights, hotel, conference fee and meals).

iii) A fine of £3,500 for exceeding the axle weight permitted for the company's delivery lorries.

(b) Required: Advise the managing director whether or not each of the proposed payments (i) to (iii) can be treated for tax purposes as a trading expense of the next corporation tax accounting period by Shelby Ltd.   Give reasons for all your answers, either from specific rules of tax law or from general principles of the UK tax system.   (6 marks)

(c) Required: Using examples from the UK tax system, evaluate the extent to which the government is attempting to affect taxpayers' behaviour with respect to cars.   (5 marks)

(Total 20 marks)

Exam–type Questions on Personal Taxation, excluding IHT

Question 6

Assad is aged 35, and was employed as a mechanic until April 2012. His last salary payment, received on 30 April 2012, was £2,000 gross, from which PAYE tax was deducted of £320. Assad then decided to become a self - employed taxi driver, commencing business on 1 May 2012.

For the first 3 months he leased a car (Car 1) for business use. He made no private journeys in Car 1, which had a CO_2 emissions rating of 180g/km. In return for the monthly lease charge of £600 the lease company met all the car 1 running expenses except insurance and fuel.

On 1 August 2012 Assad terminated the Car 1 lease, having purchased a new car (Car 2) for £20,000, which had a CO_2 emissions rating of 172g/km. From the time of purchase, Car 2 was used in the business, and also 20% privately by Assad.

Assad used his business mobile phone 40% for private purposes.

Assad has drawn up his first accounts to 30 April 2013, showing the following results for the twelve month period:

	£	£
Taxi fares collected		46,200
Tips received		4,100
		50,300
Expenses:		
Commissions paid to taxi booking company	2,850	
Car expenses (see analysis below)	6,900	
Taxi operating licence (12 months)	1,980	
Traffic Speeding fine (incurred while working)	80	
Mobile phone contract (£40 a month)	480	
Meals /drinks while working at night	750	
Depreciation of Car 2	6,000	
Training course in computing	250	
		(19,290)
Net trading profit		31,010

The analysis of the Car expenses account is as follows:

	Car 1 £	Car 2 £
Petrol	750	2,500
Leasing cost of car 1 (3 months)	1,800	
Running costs for car 2 (9 months)		
(servicing, car tax etc)		850
Car insurance – Car 1 (May to August)	250	
– Car 2 (September to April)		750
	2,800	4,100
Total		6,900

From 6 June 2012, Assad rented out a bedroom in his house for £300 per month. Assad has calculated that the fair share of house bills (heating, electricity, etc) relating to the let bedroom is £25 a month.

Assad also received dividend income of £6,300 in January 2013 (cash amount received).

Required:

(a) Calculate Assad's adjusted trading profit, after claiming any available capital allowances, for the period of account to 30 April 2013.

(11 marks)

(b) Write brief notes explaining to Assad your treatment of the following expenses as allowable/ disallowable against his business income in the tax-adjusted profits computation:

(i) Car 2 running expenses and depreciation

(ii) Speeding fine incurred

(iii) Car 1 leasing costs

(iv) Computer training course (6 marks)

(c) Calculate Assad's taxable income and income tax liability for the tax year 2012/13, and the amount of tax still due. (9 marks)

(d) Calculate Assad's Class 4 national insurance liability for 2012/13.

(2 marks)

(e) Either calculate the amount, or if preferred, describe how you would calculate it if you had the necessary information, that should be paid by Assad as the first payment on account of income tax and class 4 NIC due for the tax year 2013/14. (2 mark)

(Total 30 marks)

Question 7

Simon, aged 45, is employed as a Public Relations consultant by Bogota Ltd. For the year ended 5 April 2013, he has provided the following information:

1. His basic annual salary was £38,000.

2. He received a performance bonus of £2,934 on 31 October 2012. This related to the six months ended 30 September 2012. On 1 April 2013 he was notified that he was entitled to a bonus of £1,250 for the six months to 31 March 2013, and this was paid to him on 30 April 2013.

3. He had the use of a diesel-engined company car from Bogota Ltd from 6 May 2012 (date of first registration) until after 5 April 2013. The car's list price was £22,500 but the company negotiated a 15% discount from a dealer. All business and personal fuel was paid for by the company and

Simon uses the car privately every week. The car has a CO_2 emission rating of 158g/km. Simon did not have a company car for the first month of tax year 2012/13.

4.   Simon had a company mobile phone, on which he was allowed to make private calls. The phone cost the employer rent and charges of £360.

5.   He was reimbursed £275 by Bogota Ltd during the year for expenses incurred entertaining clients.

6.   Simon received an interest-free loan of £15,000 from Bogota Ltd on 6 June 2012, which he repaid on 6 December 2012.

7.   Simon paid £200 per month into the Bogota Ltd occupational pension scheme, by direct deduction from his salary. This pension scheme is not contracted out of the state second pension.

Simon had no other income in the year 2012/13, but he sold a painting in November 2012 for £18,000. He had purchased the painting in 1998 for £2,500. He had no personal capital losses brought forward at 6 April 2012.

Simon tells you in July 2013 that he plans to leave his employment and become a self- employed PR consultant. He plans to advertise his services widely, and has already identified potential new clients.

He also hopes to sell some of his self-employed services to Bogota Ltd after he leaves their full-time employment. His current manager is willing to offer him some short-term tasks on a "freelance" basis, working with teams he knows.

Required:

a) Calculate Simon's assessable employment income for 2012/13.

(12 marks)

b) Calculate Simon's Class 1 NIC liability, and his employer's total NIC liability, in respect of earnings and benefits in 2012/13.   (3 marks)

c) Calculate Simon's capital gains tax liability for 2012/13, and state when he must pay the capital gains tax.   (5 marks)

d) Advise Simon how he would be wise to carry out his self-employed activities, including any services provided for a fee to Bogota Ltd, if he wishes to resist any suggestion from the tax authority that he is still an employee of Bogota Ltd.   (7 marks)

e) Explain how it would alter Simon's UK tax position if occasional work that he does for Bogota Ltd after he leaves employment there were viewed as a return to employment, not as self-employment.   (3 marks)

(Total 30 marks)

Question 8

(a) Lydia Smith has an established trading business and also lets 2 properties. Her income and losses for the four years to 31 March 2013, and expected results for the year to 31 March 2014, are as follows:

Year ending	31/03/10	31/03/11	31/03/12	31/03/13	Expected 31/03/14
Trading profit	28,000	25,000	10,000	Loss (65,000)	43,000
Bank deposit interest, net cash received	240	320	400	NIL	NIL
Property letting:					
16 Park Row	-	Loss (4,000)	10,500	Loss (5,000)	NIL
12 Highfield Grove	-	7,600	Loss (3,000)	11,000	6,500

Lydia always claims relief for losses as early as possible.

Required: Calculate Lydia's taxable income for each of the four years to 31 March 2013, and the expected taxable income for the year to 31 March 2014, showing appropriate claims for loss relief.   (10 marks)

b)   Ron is a higher rate income taxpayer and has the following disposals of assets during 2012/13, which were his only transactions relevant to Capital Gains Tax:

i) Sold a fish and chip shop for £250,000 in October 2012, from which £12,500 selling commission was deducted. The fish and chip shop cost £160,000 in August 1997. Ron claims entrepreneurs' relief on the disposal.

ii) Sold part of a plot of land in February 2013 for £40,000. The whole piece of land had cost £25,000 in November 1997. The value of the part retained was £30,000 in February 2013.

iii) Sold a sculpture for £10,000 in March 2013. The sculpture cost £18,500 in January 1991, with an additional £1,500 of acquisition costs.

Required: Calculate Ron's Capital Gains Tax liability for 2012/13.

(10 marks)
(Total 20 marks)

Question 9

(a) Gareth commenced business as a landscape architect on 1 November 2011 and prepared his first accounts to 30 April 2013. He purchased office equipment assets costing £11,500 on 1 November 2011, on which he claimed an Annual Investment Allowance equal to the full cost of the assets.

His tax-adjusted trading profit for the period ended 30 April 2013, before deducting the above capital allowances claim, was £67,500.

Required:

(i) Calculate the trading profits assessable for income tax purposes on Gareth for the tax years 2011/12, 2012/13 and 2013/14. (7 marks)

(ii) State the amount of Gareth's overlap profits and show how you have calculated this figure. (2 marks)

(iii) Is there anything which Gareth could have done to avoid having overlap profits arising in his business? (2 marks)

(b) Mary-Anne is 77 years old and is registered blind. She has the following income in 2012/13:

State pension (no tax deducted at source)	£5,200
Private pension (before £650 tax deducted at source under PAYE)	£8,440
Income from dividends (amount received)	£2,160
Income from Cash ISAs (amount received)	£1,780
Interest income from bank deposit accounts (amount received)	£8,000

Required:

Calculate Mary-Anne's income tax liability for tax year 2012/13, showing how much tax is still payable or repayable after the end of that year.

(9 marks)

(Total 20 marks)

Question 10

(a) Sam Street commenced trading on 1 May 2012 and prepares business accounts to each 31 December thereafter.

In May 2012 she bought the following assets:

Plant and machinery	30,184
Office furniture	4,500
3 Computers (3 year maximum useful life)	2,300
Photocopier/printer	500
A car which she uses privately for 25% of its annual mileage (CO_2 emissions, 156 g/km)	15,000

In the year to 31 December 2013 the following fixed asset transactions took place:

Sold an item of machinery for £3,500 which had originally cost £2,600.

Bought a van costing £11,500 to use for business deliveries.

Sold the 3 computers when they were 18 months old in November 2013, for £150 in total.

Required: Calculate the capital allowances available to Sam for her first two periods of account, assuming that she always claims the maximum allowances and makes elections to get quicker relief wherever possible.

(12 marks)

(b) Roberta has been a sole trader since 1990. On 31 March 2013 she transferred her business to her daughter Jill, at which time the following assets were sold to Jill:

- A shop with a market value of £150,000. It had been purchased on 1 August 2004 for £80,000 and has always been used for Roberta's business. Jill paid Roberta £50,000 for the shop.

- A warehouse with a market value of £120,000. It had been purchased in 1995 for £45,000 and has never been used for business purposes by Roberta but rented out. Jill paid Roberta £40,000 for the warehouse.

Wherever possible, Roberta and Jill have elected to hold over the gift element of the capital gains arising to Roberta on these sales.

Required: Assuming that gift holdover claims are made where possible, calculate Roberta's capital gains, before annual exemption, for 2012/13. Ignore entrepreneur's relief. (8 marks)

(Total 20 marks)

Index

The index numbers refer to chapters or to chapter sections.

Tax rates 2012/13

Income tax

Starting rate 10%	Savings income £0 – £2,710 band	
Basic rate	Savings/Non savings 20%	Dividends 10%
Higher rate	Savings/Non savings 40%	Dividends 32.5%
Additional rate	Savings/Non savings 50%	Dividends 42.5%

Taxable income £	Band £	Rate %	Tax payable on band £
0 – 34,370	34,370	20	6,874
34,371 – 150,000	115,630	40	46,252
150,000 +		50	

Personal reliefs 2012/13

	£
Personal allowance	8,105
Abatement income level	100,000
Allowances: Aged 65–74	
Personal allowance	10,500
Abatement income level	25,400
Allowances: aged 75+	
Personal allowance	10,660
Married couple's allowance (65 before 6.4.2000) min £2,960*	7,705*
Abatement income level for both above – PA abates before MCA	25,400
Blind person's allowance	2,100

*Relief only at 10%

National Insurance 2012/13

Retirement pension – single person – based on adequate contributions from a 30 year working life £5,587.

Self employed

Class 2 contributions		£2.65 per week
Class 4 contributions	9.0% of profits between	7,605 – 42,475
	2.0% above	42,475

Class 1 Employed earners from 6th April 2012

£ per week earnings	Not contracted-out	Contracted-out COSR	COMP
Employee			
Earnings up to £146 a week – ET	Nil	Nil	Nil
Earnings between £146 and £817 a week	12.0%	10.6%	12.0
Earnings over £817 a week	2.0%	2.0%	2.0

Employer

Earnings up to £144 a week	Nil	Nil	Nil
Earnings between £144 and £817 a week	13.8%	10.4%	13.8%
Earnings over £817 a week	13.8%	13.8%	13.8%
Class 1A Benefits in Kind	13.8%	13.8%	13.8%

Corporation tax

	Years to 31st March	
	2013	**2012**
Financial year	**FY12**	**FY11**
Full rate	24%	26%
Small profits rate	20%	20%
Small profits rate fraction	1/100	3/200
Small profit levels:		
Lower relevant amount	£300,000	£300,000
Higher relevant amount	£1,500,000	£1,500,000

Small profits rate marginal relief formula: (U-A) x $^N/_A$ x (the fraction)

Employees' Car Benefit	**Employees' Car Fuel Benefit**
List price × CO_2 emission% 10% for a car with up to 99g/km CO_2 emissions, 11% for cars with 100g/km increasing by 1% for every 5g/km to a maximum of 35% 3% supplement for diesels	£20,200 × CO_2 emission % for the car (as determined at left)

Capital allowances

Plant and machinery

Annual investment allowance	100% on £25,000 of expenditure per 12 months

Enhanced capital allowances	FYA	100%
Low Emission Cars	FYA	100%

Writing down allowance (WDA)

General pool of plant and machinery and cars with CO_2 emissions of 160 g/km or less	18% per year

Special rate pool features integral to a building, long life assets and cars with CO_2 emissions of more than 160 g/km	8% per year

Capital gains tax

	Rate	Exempt Amount for year
Individuals	Gains qualifying for Entrepreneurs' Relief – 10%	10,600
	All other gains: 18% within income tax basic rate band 2012/13, otherwise 28%	

Lease premium

Capital element of a premium received on a lease of less than 50 years

$$P \times 2\% \times (n - 1)$$

where

P = premium
n = length of lease in years

The rest of the premium is income

Value added tax

Standard rate	20.0% (1/6 x gross)
Lower/ Reduced rate	5%
Zero rate	0%
Registration threshold (From 1 April 2012)	£77,000 taxable turnover in cumulative 12 month period
	£77,000 taxable turnover in next 30 days
Deregistration threshold (From 1 April 2012)	£75,000

Inheritance tax

IHT on transfers on death on or after 6th April 2012

Chargeable transfer bands £	Rate of IT %
0 – 325,000	Nil
325,001 +	40*

Lower death rate of 36% where 10% or more of the deceased person's net estate is left to charity.